The Law on the Use of Force

This book provides a comprehensive feminist analysis of the relationship between international law on the use of force (law on war) and legal constructions of gender. State justifications for the use of force on the territory of another state are also analysed. Topics covered within the book include an analysis of the collective security regime under the UN system and the developing powers of the Security Council, as well as a critical review of the five Security Council resolutions on women, peace and security. Throughout the text, state practise and institutional documentation are analysed alongside key instances of the use of force. Additionally, the author provides a review and analysis of the global war against terrorism, the Responsibility to Protect and the policies of the Obama administration.

Gina Heathcote is a Senior Teaching Fellow at the School of Oriental and African Studies where she lectures on Public International Law and the International Law on the Use of Force.

Routledge Research in International Law

Available:

International Law and the Third World
Reshaping Justice
Richard Falk, Balakrishnan Rajagopal and Jacqueline Stevens (eds.)

International Legal Theory
Essays and Engagements, 1966–2006
Nicholas Onuf

The Problem of Enforcement in International Law
Countermeasures, the Non-Injured State and the Idea of
    International Community
Elena Katselli Proukaki

International Economic Actors and Human Rights
Adam McBeth

The Law of Consular Access
A Documentary Guide
John Quigley, William J. Aceves and Adele Shank

State Accountability under International Law
Holding States Accountable for a Breach of Jus Cogens Norms
Lisa Yarwood

International Organisations and the Idea of Autonomy
Institutional Independence in the International Legal Order
Richard Collins and Nigel D. White (eds.)

Self-Determination in the Post-9/11 Era
Elizabeth Chadwick

Participants in the International Legal System
Multiple Perspectives on Non-State Actors in International Law
Jean d'Aspremont

Sovereignty and Jurisdiction in the Airspace and Outer Space
Legal Criteria for Spatial Delimitation
Gbenga Oduntan

International Law in a Multipolar World
Matthew Happold (ed.)

The Law on the Use of Force
A Feminist Analysis
Gina Heathcote

Forthcoming titles in this series include:

International Law, Regulation and Resistance
Critical Spaces
Zoe Pearson

The ICJ and the Development of International Law
The Lasting Impact of the Corfu Channel Case
Karine Bannelier, Théodore Christakis and Sarah Heathcote (eds.)

The Right to Self-determination Under International Law
"Selfistans", Secession, and the Great Powers' Rule
Milena Sterio

The Cuban Embargo under International Law
El Bloqueo
Nigel D. White

Threats of Force
International Law and Strategy
Francis Grimal

Asian Approaches to International Law and the Legacy of Colonialism and Imperialism
The Law of the Sea, Territorial Disputes and International Dispute Settlement
Jin-Hyun Paik, Seok-Woo Lee, Kevin Y L Tan (eds)

The Law on the Use of Force

of Force

A feminist analysis

Gina Heathcote

Routledge
Taylor & Francis Group

LONDON AND NEW YORK

First published 2012
by Routledge
2 Park Square, Milton Park, Abingdon, Oxon OX14 4RN

Simultaneously published in the USA and Canada
by Routledge
711 Third Avenue, New York, NY 10017

Routledge is an imprint of the Taylor & Francis Group, an informa business

© 2012 Gina Heathcote

British Library Cataloguing in Publication Data
A catalogue record for this book is available from the British Library

Library of Congress Cataloging-in-Publication Data
Heathcote, Gina.
    The law on the use of force : a feminist analysis / Gina Heathcote.
        p. cm.—(Routledge research in international law)
    ISBN 978–0–415–49287–4 (hardback)—ISBN 978–0–203–80261–8 (e-book)
    1. War (International law) 2. Intervention (International law)
    3. Feminist jurisprudence. I. Title.
    KZ6355.H43 2011
    341.6—dc22   2011013525

ISBN 978–0–415–49287–4 (hbk)
ISBN 978–0–203–80261–8(ebk)

Typeset in Garamond by Swales & Willis Ltd, Exeter, Devon

Contents

Preface

I am walking home with a friend and our children. We have just collected the children from a party. The babies recline, momentarily peaceful, in their buggies. My oldest child picks up a stick. My friend's child follows suit but selects a larger stick and waves it around.

I ask my child to put the stick down. My friend turns to me, rolls her eyes and smiles as she says 'boys will be boys'. My son places his stick on the ground while expressing his disapproval at my request. His friend throws his stick carelessly over his head. The stick hits one of the babies on the arm; the little one begins to cry. My friend's son experiences the full wrath of parental rage and is humiliated and castigated in front of his friend, my son. The baby is, fortunately, unharmed. I am left contemplating the mixed messages we give our children, especially boys.

I raise my children under the motto that no matter how bad, how upsetting, how dangerous, how humiliating or how threatening the act of another may seem their own violence is an inadequate means to solve a problem. I am proud of my three children who from a young age have, mostly, been able to use creative thinking or the presence of an authoritative power (parents, teachers) to resolve conflict with other children. I have no idea whether this makes them good boys. I hope it will help them become wonderful people.

Important to my reflections on and engagements with my children is my understanding of international law on the use of force. Like our household, the international law on the use of force rests on a simple prohibition against force.[1] Unlike our household, international law allows for authorised force when a 'threat to the peace, breach of the peace or an act of aggression' is deemed to have occurred.[2] Furthermore, international customary international law demonstrates that, in addition to authorised force, justifications for force – especially self-defence – are an integral

---

1 UN Charter, Article 2(4).
2 UN Charter, Articles 39–42; indeed to continue the analogy, if authorised force were permitted within my family this would entail the use of force by my partner or me to halt violations of the prohibition on violence. As a mother I find little merit in challenging children's violence with greater violence and have experienced the frustrating long term consequences of such an approach in families around me; for a discussion of parental rights to use force to control their children, see: Durrant, *A Generation Without Smacking: The Impact of Sweden's Ban on Physical Punishment* (Save the Children (UK), 2000).

component of the law on the use of force or *jus ad bellum*.[3] In this book, I present an analysis of the international law that permits the authorisation of force by the collective security structure and the arguments of states that seek to justify unilateral force. Some – many – would argue that the international law on the use of force has nothing to do with the private, everyday, domestic interactions I have with my children. Yet, much that I wish to question is contained in my friend's phrase, 'boys will be boys', a phrase uttered routinely by those around me in my domestic relationships. How will boys be boys unless we tell them? Why does 'boys being boys' usually entail the justification of violent, dangerous or aggressive play? How do these childish interactions shape men's – and women's – perceptions of normal behaviour later in life? In this book I challenge the law on the use of force as both sexed and gendered through the repetition within those laws of sexed and gendered understandings of justified violence. To challenge the law on the use of force, I use feminist understandings of the role of law in the production of sex and gender. I also develop two specific methods that emerge from these broader reflections on the impact of sexed and gendered constructions on personhood.

First, I use a domestic analogy: that is, an analogy between accounts of interpersonal violence and international justifications for violence to demonstrate the patriarchal underpinnings of the international laws on the use of force.[4] Second, I regard law as a narrative, one telling among many with multiple potential meanings rather than as a source of objective and neutral 'truth'. Consequently, in the process of looking at law's narrative I look at many non-legal narratives to understand the impact of law. This is something Davies refers to as 'Flat Law Theory'.[5] To introduce the use of both the domestic analogy and law as narrative approaches, I wish to draw on a further personal example.

I often commute via train into London. On my return journey, I arrive at the local train station in the evening and must make a 15-min walk in the dark. It is a pleasant walk that passes a large park, playing fields, tennis courts, a secondary school, a local pre-school and a row of houses (of which my house is at the end). It should be an enjoyable walk. I know my partner makes that walk with headphones on, largely unaware of any person who might be walking nearby. In contrast, I turn off any music I might be listening to, place my mobile phone on automatic dial with my finger near the call button and grasp my keys in the other hand. I note who is walking ahead of

---

3 See Bowett, *Self-defence in International Law* (Manchester: Manchester University Press, 1958). International law distinguishes *jus ad bellum* (the law on the use of force) from *jus in bello* (the international humanitarian law of armed conflict), for a discussion of the origins of the terms, see Kolb, 'Origin of the Twin Terms *Jus ad Bellum* and *Jus in Bello*', 320, *International Review of the Red Cross* (1997) 553.

4 That is, I look at Western criminal codes, particularly common law defences to homicide, as providing a model for international justifications for violence. While I acknowledge the distinctions between the two systems and the impact of other legal systems on the international, key to my argument is the influence Western national criminal defences has on Western scholars' understandings of international justifications for the use of force. One of the clearest examples of the use of Western common law justifications as a model for establishing the normative credibility of the international can be found in Franck, *Recourse to Force* (Cambridge: Cambridge University Press, 2002), chapter 10.

5 Davies, "Feminism and the Flat Law Theory" 16 *Feminist Legal Studies* (2008) 281.

me and at what speed. I listen for footsteps behind me. I double check the shadows in front of me. I am conscious of the gender, dress, and actions of any of my fellow walkers. I have never been attacked or approached while walking home at night but I am acutely aware that if I was attacked there would be some question as to why I was walking alone at night. Most of my girlfriends would not make this same walk late at night, yet we live in a relatively safe, affluent and friendly London suburb.[6] My point is that women live with the fear of potential violence and internalise a degree of responsibility for external threats (e.g. I shouldn't walk out after dark). The threat is always gendered, that is, of men attacking, raping, harming or harassing, and, quite possibly, is largely unrealistic; women face a much greater threat from the men they choose to live with or grow up among. Every time I take this walk, in the dark, I am forced to recognise the relationship between gender and violence. I believe the relationship between constructions of justified violence and gender begins with the choices that we make as we raise our children. As a society we generally accept that women live with the threat and fear of the potential violence of men.

As a legal scholar, I am well aware of the disparity between women's response to the threat and existence of violence and what law regards as provocation defences. Provocation defences justify or mitigate actions that are in response to low level but persistent fears or threats. Put simply, men who are provoked to kill their nagging wives find their behaviour will usually be mitigated by law.[7] Similarly, men who fear their partner's sexual agency away from them and kill their partner as a result, or her assumed lover, often find their behaviour mitigated by law.[8] I wonder why women walk every night in fear of an attack from an unknown man with little more than a can of pepper spray (or a key) to protect them while some men find it reasonable to attack and kill a woman they have loved. Why does law provide excuses and justifications for some behaviour and not promote the use of justified violence in others? I wonder about the role law plays in the social dialogues and norms that are co-opted into gendered realities. In fact, from a feminist perspective, much is written about the role of law in perpetuating and excusing (justifying) gender violence against women by men. I draw on this scholarship extensively throughout this book. However, my primary concern is not the gendering or sexing of justifications for individual violence but rather to ask whether this same biased structure flows onto Western constructions of justifications for violence at the international level.

I use feminist understandings of the limitations of national laws that prohibit and justify violence to interrogate international justifications for inter-state violence. This is the domestic analogy. I also use non-legal sources to challenge the self-appointed role of law at the apex of social and cultural discourse. By using non-legal dialogues, I demonstrate the particularity of legal accounts, highlighting law as a narrative rather than as a series of objective truths and in a horizontal rather than vertical

---

6 For a similar discussion, see Morgan, *The Demon Lover: The Roots of Terrorism* (Piaktus, 2001, 2nd edition) at 15.
7 For a discussion of disparities in gender justice for intimate partner killings, see www.jfw.org.uk (last accessed February 2011).
8 Ibid.

relationship with other normative structures.[9] In the example above, my personal narrative would be meaningless in a formal legal analysis, which is not interested in the cultural phenomenon of gender fear and violence but in the regulative impact of, for example, anti-stalking legislation. The focus on law often overlooks the role of gender in stalking or in other forms of sexual harassment or violence. To understand the role of gender in legal relationships, it is necessary to appreciate law's role as a social and cultural narrative. This is to see law as a narrative.[10]

In this book, I interrogate international law on force from a feminist perspective: focusing on the power of the Security Council to authorise the use of force and state justifications for the use of force on the territory of other states. My starting point is the question: how do justifications for individual violence and force – challenged by feminist scholarship as sexed and gendered – re-emerge in international justifications for the use of force? To answer this question, I take the law on the use of force and consider the narratives produced under the auspices of international law, exposing their sexed and gendered assumptions. My motivation is the justification that I make to my children when expressing my desire for an absence of force and violence in their lives.

9 For example, I compare personal narratives of those experiencing the impact of force with those using force (chapters two, three, five). I use the narratives of women in nationalist movements in chapter four and I draw on feminist scholarship outside of the legal academy to explore the narrowness of legal narratives. See chapter six for a discussion of the limitations of this approach.

10 See Thornton, 'Introduction' in *Romancing the Tomes: Popular Culture, Law and Feminism* (London: Cavendish, 2002); also see Buss, 'Keeping Its Promise: Use of Force and the New Man of International Law' in Bartholomew, *Empire's Law* (London: Pluto, 2006).

Acknowledgements

This book owes a tremendous debt to a range of colleagues, friends and family members. First, the many friends who offered after-school teas, sleepovers and days out for my children – each offer made with kindness and generous enthusiasm that nurtured and broadened my children's lives while I nurtured the text. For me, you are the armies that keep the world fed and in motion. Thank you Sheila, Berni, Louise, Ania, Lisa and Eliz, Jo, Erica, Liliana, Caroline, Hilary, Jennie, and special thanks to Pam – for more Thursdays than I imagined possible to give.

Thank you to Tyrell for extended engagement with this text: reading it in its very first inception as a proposal and (many years later) assisting with the editing of the final book text; not to mention listening to angst and frustrations on the path between the two processes. You are a wonderful support and I treasure our lifelong friendship.

Thank you to my family in Melbourne. It is a great privilege to have a family home that I never need grow out of and that now offers a second home to my children. Thank you to my family in London, for never minding the piles of documents (and washing) as well as the hours spent at the computer; you all make me who I am and I love each of you, Paul, Joe, Finn and Oliver.

Thank you to Christine, your intellectual influence on this project and your personal support for it has been invaluable and helped propel the project into something I am proud to have written. Thank you also to Judith Gardam and Gerry Simpson for your careful reading and response to my work. The time you both gave to my scholarship is a great complement to the text, and I am deeply indebted to you both for the time and patience with which you approached the task. Thank you to Anne Orford and Dianne Otto for always welcoming at the Melbourne Law School and for your support for my work; both of you have also provided a tremendous intellectual template that keeps me inspired in my writing and thinking. For coffees and conversations *par excellence*, thank you to Louise Arimatsu.

Lastly, thank you to my colleagues and students at the School of Law, School of Oriental and African Studies – you are an inspirational bunch to work with. Special mention must be made of the following colleagues: Lynn (for seeing something in my work worth supporting), Tri (for unquestioned and unfailing support), Fareda (for letting me see what I might achieve) and Nadje (you are a constant source of inspiration). My students are too many to mention but thank you for the many lessons you have all given me, I continue to learn as I teach and, of course, thank you Chenaara for scaring the life out of me the day before my first lecture at SOAS. Your influence on this book is more subtle yet just as important. The text remains up to date to February 2011.

All errors remain my own.

Abbreviations

AJIL	American Journal of International Law
BYIL	British Journal of International Law
CEDAW	Convention on the Elimination of Discrimination against Women
DRC	Democratic Republic of the Congo
ECOWAS	Economic Community of West African States
EJIL	European Journal of International Law
EULEX	European Union Rule of Law Mission in Kosovo
EWCA	England and Wales Court of Appeal
FAO	Food and Agriculture Organisation
FARDC	Congolese Armed Forces
GA	General Assembly
HCA	High Court of Australia
ICC	International Criminal Court
ICISS	International Commission on Intervention and State Sovereignty
ICJ	International Court of Justice
ICTY	International Criminal Tribunal for the Former Yugoslavia
ICTR	International Criminal Tribunal for Rwanda
ILC	International Law commission
ILM	International Legal Materials
ILR	International Law Reports
INTERFET	UN International Force in East Timor
JSMP	East Timor Judicial System Monitoring Programme
KFOR	Kosovo Force (NATO)
NATO	North Atlantic Treaty
MINUSTAH	United Nations Stabilisation Mission in Haiti
MMORPG	Massive Multiplayer Online Role Playing Game
NATO	North Atlantic Treaty Organisation
NGO	Non-Governmental organisation
NLDA	Netherlands Defence Academy
NPT	Non-Proliferation Treaty
PKK	Kurdish Democratic Party (Patriotic Union of Kurdistan)
Res	Resolution
ROK	Republic of Korea

SADR   Saharawi Arab Democratic Republic
SC   Security Council
TWAIL   Third World Approaches to International Law
UN   United Nations
UNTAET   UN Transitional Administration in East Timor
UNIFEM   United Nations Fund for Women
UNMS   Union Nacional de Mujeres Saharau
UNYB   United Nations Yearbook
UK   United Kingdom
US   United States
USSR   United Soviet Socialist Republic
WFP   World Food Programme
WHO   World Health Organisation

Force is as pitiless to the man who possesses it, or thinks he does, as it is to its victims; the second it crushes, the first it intoxicates. The truth is, nobody really possesses it. The human race is not divided up, in the Iliad, into conquered persons, slaves, suppliants, on the one hand, and conquerors and chiefs on the other. In this poem there is not a single man who does not at one time or another have to bow his neck to force.

Simone Weil, 'The Iliad, or the Poem of Force',
in Simone Weil *et al.*, *War and the Iliad*,
(New York Review Books, 2005, first published 1945) 11

[n]atality; the beginning inherent in birth can make itself felt in the world only because the newcomer possesses the capacity of beginning something anew, that is, of acting. In this sense of initiative, an element of action and therefore natality, is inherent in all human actions. Moreover, since action is the political activity par excellence, natality, and not morality, may be the central category of political [thought].

Hannah Arendt, *The Human Condition* (Chicago, 1998, 2nd Edition) 9

1 Feminist legal approaches and international law on the use of force

International rules on the use of force are contained in the UN Charter and customary international law. The central provision on the use of force contained in the UN Charter is Article 2(4) which prohibits the threat or use of force by states. The prohibition is supplemented by a collective security structure that envisages the pacific settlement of disputes by states and regional organisations, detailed in chapters VI and VIII of the Charter, and the use of non-forcible and forcible measures authorised by the Security Council, under chapter VII of the Charter.[1] The UN Charter also retains the right of states to use force in self-defence under Article 51. All these provisions function and develop in tandem with customary international law on the use of force.[2] This book uses feminist methods to assess customary international law and UN Charter provisions on the use of force.

Since the year 2000 the United Nations has initiated a host of reforms to protect women during conflict,[3] as well as inserting standard form paragraphs in many conflict specific resolutions alerting states and UN personnel to the existence of sexual violence during armed conflict[4] while instituting a policy of zero-tolerance for sexual misconduct by peacekeepers.[5] The UN Secretary-General has had a Special Advisor on Gender Issues and the Advancement of Women since 1997 and in 2010 the UN General Assembly created 'UN Women' an umbrella institution to co-ordinate the increasing number of gender-based initiatives and departments within the United Nations.[6]

---

1 Regional organizations may be authorized by the Security Council to undertake enforcement operations under Article 53 of the UN Charter.
2 *Case Concerning Military and Paramilitary Activities in and against Nicaragua* (Nicaragua v USA), ICJ Reports (27 June 1986) 14, at paragraph 172–176.
3 SC Res 1325 (30 October 2000), SC Res 1820 (19 June 2008), SC Res 1888 (30 September 2009), SC Res 1889 (5 October 2009), SC Res 1960 (16 December 2010).
4 For example, SC Res 1962 (20 December 2010) on the situation in the Ivory Coast in operative paragraph nine: '*calls upon* all parties to take appropriate measures to refrain from, prevent and protect civilians from all forms of sexual violence'.
5 For example, SC Res 1944 (14 October 2010) on the situation in Haiti in operative paragraph 15: 'Requests the Secretary-General to continue to take the necessary measures to ensure full compliance of all MINUSTAH personnel with the United Nations zero-tolerance policy on sexual exploitation and abuse, and to keep the Council informed, and urges troop- and police-contributing countries to ensure that acts involving their personnel are properly investigated and punished'.
6 See: www.unwomen.org (last accessed February 2011).

The 1990s focus on gender mainstreaming in international institutions has consequently developed into a plethora of projects across the UN, over a host of issues, to challenge gender-based violence and discrimination, including in situations of armed conflict.

Within the Security Council, initiatives include the following: gender training for UN forces and peacekeeping operations,[7] clear disciplinary procedures for UN personnel found to violate the Code of Practice on sexual behaviour of personnel, Gender Affairs Units in many post-conflict communities, the condemnation of systematic and widespread sexual violence during conflict, the call for sanctions against perpetrators of sexual exploitation and abuse and the call for increased participation of women in post-conflict re-construction and decision-making. Despite clear limitations within this aspect of the UN Security Council's work, notably the interchange of the word 'women' with 'gender', the failure to challenge the links between the construction of masculinity as a social norm that implicitly condones violence and the continuance of the 'war system' within this model, these developments, on paper, appear to demonstrate what can be regarded as feminist inspired developments within the institutional setting of the United Nations.

Even with these impressive developments, and while a host of academic journals, university departments and NGOs prepared to mark 'ten years of Security Council Resolution 1325 on women, peace and security,'[8] mid-2010 saw reports of systematic sexual violence in the village of Luvungi, in the Democratic Republic of Congo (DRC). The reports were a chilling reminder of the gap between words and action. The UN Assistant Secretary-General for Peacekeeping, Mr Atul Khare, reported to the Security Council that 242 cases of civilians requiring treatment for rape had been recorded in Luvungi by medical personnel with an additional 260 cases reported from neighbouring towns. The sexual violence was believed to be the consequence of attacks by armed rebels between 30 July 2010 and 2 August 2010. UN Peacekeepers stationed nearby were recorded as unaware of the violence, having withdrawn patrols of the villages prior to the attacks taking place. Ostensibly, under Security Council Resolutions 1820 and 1888, the Security Council had announced its readiness to act and 'to address widespread or systematic sexual violence'.[9] Not until a month after the attacks did UN peacekeepers in the region demonstrate a commitment to increased patrols and visibility. In October 2010, UN peacekeepers had arrested the commander of the Mai Mai Cheka rebel group involved in the attacks, and the UN Special Representative on Sexual Violence in Conflict urged the Security Council to support processes to ensure the end of impunity for perpetrators of sexual violence during armed conflict.[10] By February 2011, and despite a new Security Council resolution on women, peace and security in December 2010, no Security Council response to this specific series of systematic sexual attacks had taken place.

7 See: http://cdu.unlb.org/UNStrategy/Prevention.aspx (last accessed February 2011).
8 See: http://www.unifem.org/campaigns/1325plus10/ (last accessed February 2011).
9 SC Res 1820 (19th June 2008); SC Res 1888 (30 September 2009). Also see SC Res 1960 (16 December 2010).
10 SC/10055, 14 October 2010, Recent Arrests in Mass Rape Cases in Democratic Republic of the Congo.

There is a chilling dissonance between the rape of 500 people in a systematic attack by armed groups in a region patrolled by a UN force, authorised to use force to protect civilians, and ten years of Security Council resolutions inclusive of paragraphs stating:

> that sexual violence, when used or commissioned as a tactic of war in order to deliberately target civilians or as a part of a widespread or systematic attack against civilian populations, can significantly exacerbate situations of armed conflict and may impede the restoration of international peace and security, *affirms* in this regard that effective steps to prevent and respond to such acts of sexual violence can significantly contribute to the maintenance of international peace and security, and *expresses its readiness*, when considering situations on the agenda of the Council, to, where necessary, adopt appropriate steps to address widespread or systematic sexual violence.[emphasis added][11]

Both the failure of UN words and the magnitude of harm are haunting. Consequently, every reference to the 'feminist' success found in contemporary international institutions, including the UN Security Council, seems to mark the pain of every individual harmed during the ongoing conflict in the DRC. Can words change actions? Can words stop wars, stop violence, stop conflict or rape? These questions underlie the thinking behind this book.

In this book, I examine the words (laws) that attempt to regulate state-led violence that constitutes the international legal definition of armed conflict. The book uses feminist legal methods as a means to analyse the way that international law on the use of force is constructed and understood. The discussion of events in the DRC, above, refers to the violence perpetrated during armed conflict that is generally governed by the international humanitarian law of armed conflict. However, the shift towards recognising the use of sexual violence as a systematic and widespread 'weapon' during armed conflict moves the international legal system on the use of force, the *jus ad bellum*, towards recognising sexual violence as a justification for the use of increased force. In fact, the UN's response to the violence perpetrated in Luvungi and nearby villages was for increased UN military action, even if this was temporally dislocated from the acts themselves. Throughout this book, I argue that institutional and state justifications for the use of military force mirror the gendered model of interpersonal justifications for violence apparent in Western liberal democracies such as the United Kingdom, the United States, Canada and Australia. Consequently, force deployed to 'save women' does little to halt sexual violence and other forms of gender-based violence in armed conflict or to halt armed conflict.

I also explore the continuum of harm that women experience during armed conflict and argue that women's experiences of armed conflict provide strong justification for increased *restraint* in the use of force, including the use of force on humanitarian grounds.

The endemic sexual violence in the DRC is not the subject of this book, although I was mindful of the violence that continues to be perpetrated in the DRC and

11 SC Res 1820 (19 June 2008) operative paragraph 1.

elsewhere as I wrote the book. Those who cannot speak in the Security Council due to the conditions they live in, stand as a reminder that UN reform on women, peace and security has not stopped violence. To this end, a furtherance of feminist politics and debates that look at the ways international laws are constructed and justified is a programme of re-thinking the possibilities of laws, of words and of change: this is the approach of this book.

The book presents claims directed at feminist legal theories and at international law on the use of force. For feminist legal theories, I argue that a re-examination of the foundations of feminist approaches to international law is required. While feminist studies of international law contribute an important critique of the contemporary contours of international law,[12] there remains only limited analysis of the norms regulating force and the question of when force is justified. The book reveals that this absence is reflective of a larger silence from feminist legal theories on the relationship between law and violence. I argue that Arendt's model of natality as a political framework, which is a focus on creativity through a central focus on birth rather than mortality, is useful to feminist politics seeking to disrupt the law and violence relationship.[13] This larger claim emerges from recognition that the law and violence relationship is supplemented by social constructions of gender. In exposing the relationship between law, gender and violence, I advocate the necessity of restricting unilateral state justifications for the use of force and for limiting the authorisation of force by the Security Council because justifications for force and the authorisation of force are conceptually tarred by the use of military structures. Alternative means of peace enforcement are consequently devalued and under-utilised within the collective security regime. Feminist action within the security structure must develop a fundamental re-engagement with the very concept of security and potential solutions to security concerns so as to provide answers that do not revolve around the deployment of further force.

The arguments directed at international law recognise recent responses to curb the sexual violence and sexual exploitation and abuse of women during armed conflict.[14] However, I argue that, without recognition of the sexed and gendered bias of the international legal structure itself, recent collective security developments are unable to move beyond the force and counter-force paradigm that assumes that the use of force, when legal, can also be rational and controlled. Furthermore, viewing the use of force through the experiences and narratives of women illustrates how the use of force perpetuates and exacerbates insecurity in women's lives.

---

12 Charlesworth and Chinkin, *The Boundaries of International Law: A Feminist Analysis* (Manchester: Manchester University Press, 2000); also see: Engle, 'International Human Rights and Feminisms: When Discourses Keep Meeting' in Buss and Manji (eds), *International Law: Modern Feminist Approaches* (Oxford: Hart, 2005), at 47, which offers a critical review of Charlesworth and Chinkin's body of work.

13 Arendt, *The Human Condition* (Chicago, 1998, 2nd edition), at 9; also see Jantzen, *Foundations of Violence* (London: Routledge, 2004) where she writes, '... in the west's obsession with death and mortality, our natality has been largely ignored. Yet it is in birth, in natality, that newness enters the world; and it is in the fact of new life that every other form of freedom and creativity is grounded', at 6.

14 See Report of the Secretary-General to the Security Council, 25 September 2008, S/2008/622.

In this chapter, in section two I introduce the project through a discussion of feminist approaches to international law and of the methodology developed: specifically the terms 'sex' and 'gender', the use of the domestic analogy and the use of the law as narrative technique to explain how they are deployed throughout the text. Section three introduces the international law on the use of force, or *jus ad bellum*, highlighting the features of the law on the use of force that are interrogated in this work, and outlines the overall structure and conclusions of this book.

Feminist legal methods

While situating itself within feminist approaches to international law generally,[15] in this book I have consciously developed three interrelated feminist methods: the use of sex and gender as categories for the interrogation of law, the domestic analogy and the law as narrative technique.

Feminist approaches to international law do not, however, represent a uniform methodological approach. Different strands of feminist legal theories emerge within the international project, and it is from these broader feminist dialogues – found across feminist approaches to international law, feminist legal theories and feminist theories generally – that I have developed the unique approach of this book. In this sense, I am mindful in the text of tensions within and across feminist legal theories (and their international counterparts) while seeking to make productive use of developments drawn from dialogues across the range of feminist approaches.[16] Despite this, the work itself is situated as a form of *Western* feminist legal theory and is primarily influenced by mainstream, Western feminist debates. Furthermore, the argument can be described as a form of structural bias feminism due to the attention given to the underlying structures of international law and the contention that these are sexed and gendered.

The use of the domestic analogy, when developed within a law as narrative technique, presents itself as attentive to the limitations of Western feminist approaches and is mindful of the role of international law on the use of force as a narrative of empowerment within my own culture/s.[17] The book draws considerably on Western feminist legal knowledge rather than projecting its conclusions on to the realities, or assumed realities, of non-Western women's lives. Consequently, the conclusions are directed at Western theories and approaches to international law, including Western feminist approaches to international law. Feminist legal theories that propose

---

15 For an introduction to the contours of feminist legal theories see: Charlesworth, Chinkin and Wright, 'Feminist Approaches to International Law' 85 *American Journal of International Law* (1991) 631; Charlesworth and Chinkin, above note 12, at 38–52; Buss and Manji (eds), above note 12; Charlesworth, 'Feminist Methods in International Law' 93 *American Journal of International Law* (1999) 379.

16 For a discussion of the range of Western feminist legal approaches see the discussion of Lacey, 'Feminist Legal Theory and the Rights of Women' in Knop (ed), *Gender and Human Rights* (Oxford: Oxford University Press, 2004).

17 See, for example, the discussion of methodological choices in: Murphy, 'Feminism Here and Feminism There: Law, Theory and Choice', in Buss and Manji (eds), above note 12, at 81.

an essential female experience as the ethical platform for feminism[18] are rejected in the text, which seeks to respond to the criticisms of Western feminist legal theories as essentialist[19] through the development of a method directed at Western feminist accounts.

Strands of feminist approaches within international law include structural bias feminisms, third world feminisms, post-colonial feminisms and structural bias instrumentalism.[20] The book, while attentive to the work of third world feminisms,[21] post-colonial feminisms[22] and postmodern feminisms,[23] situates itself within structural bias feminist approaches. This is the label given to the approach developed by Charlesworth, Chinkin and Wright in 1991.[24] Structural bias feminism argues that international law has persistent structural flaws that are sexed and gendered. Charlesworth and Chinkin's book, *The Boundaries of International Law*, presents a comprehensive development of structural bias feminism as a method applied to the tenets of international law. Charlesworth and Chinkin argue that international law is 'intertwined with a gendered and sexed subjectivity and reinforces a system of male symbols'.[25] In relation to the law on the use of force, Charlesworth and Chinkin conclude, 'peace is not achieved until states take seriously their internal obligations to ensure freedom from violence at home, within the community or committed by state agents'.[26] I extend this contention to include the need to recognise the structural biases that permeate the production of lawful justifications for violence. Furthermore, I contend that the collective security system of authorising force produces, rather than reduces, gendered harms.

Structural bias feminism has not emerged without criticism; internally from feminist legal theorists and externally from international legal scholars. Internal feminist critiques centre on three broader tensions present in feminist legal theories: the ongoing engagement with the critique of essentialism,[27] the tension between theory and

---

18 For example, cultural feminist accounts see: Ruddick, *Maternal Thinking: Towards a Politics of Peace* (New York: Beacon, 1995).
19 For example, Kapur, *Erotic Justice: Law and the New Politics of Postcolonialism* (London: Routledge, 2005), chapter 4.
20 Engle, above note 12.
21 On Third World Feminist knowledge, see: Mohanty, Russo and Torres, *Third World Women and the Politics of Feminism* (New Delhi: Indiana, 1991); Narayan, *Dislocating Cultures: Identities, Traditions and Third World Feminism* (London: Routledge, 1997); Nnaemeka (ed) *Sisterhood: Feminisms and Power from Africa to the Diaspora* (Renton, NJ: Africa World Press, 1998).
22 Kapur above note 19; Spivak, Spivak, G., 'The Subaltern Speaks' in Nelson, C., and Grossburg, L. (eds), *Marxism and the Interpretation of Culture* (Champaign, IL: University of Illinois Press, 1988).
23 For example: Butler, *Precarious Life: Powers of Violence and Mourning* (London: Verso, 2004); Butler, Frames of War (London: Verso, 2010).
24 Above note 15.
25 Above note 12, at 22.
26 Above note 12, at 273.
27 See: Harris, 'Race and Essentialism in Feminist Legal Theories,' 42, *Stanford Law Review* (1990), 581 describing gender essentialism as: 'the notion that a unitary, "essential" women's experience can be isolated and described independently of race, class, sexual orientation, and other realities of experience', at 585.

practice, and the representation of women under feminism as victims rather than agents. Specific feminist critiques of structural bias approaches include Engle's claim that the focus on law's construction of the public and private spheres ignores economic factors,[28] as well as Halley's criticism of the blurring of the distinction between feminist academics and feminist activists.[29] External, non-feminist criticisms, centre on the underlying political project of feminist theory arguing that this is misrepresentative through its potentially partial perspective[30] or due to an incipient utopianism that is unrealisable in the international arena.[31] For example, Mullerson criticises the partial perspective of feminist legal approaches to international law, arguing 'looking everywhere for hidden agendas may be misleading and lead to conspiracy theories'.[32]

In constructing the methods of the project, I have used the internal criticisms of feminist legal approaches as a means to introduce tensions, or dialogues, that require navigation rather than circumvention. As a result, I reflect on the impact of essentialism debates, the theory/practice nexus and constructions of victim and agency in feminist activism and theory throughout the study. Engle specifically challenges structural bias feminism for its emphasis on the role of public/private spheres in a manner that over emphasizes culture as an organising factor in women's lives rather than, say, economics.[33] However, this criticism ignores the relationship between cultural, economic and legal knowledge. Analysis of the constitutive role law plays in culture, culture plays in law and how each then contributes to economic outcomes, including the capacity for women to make and participate in economic structures, from the personal to the public, is a theme developed throughout this book. The law as a narrative approach specifically allows for an enlarged understanding of the horizontal web of norms: social, legal, economic, cultural and political that contribute to dominant constructions of gender. Halley's criticism of the institutional impact of feminist legal theories is regarded as misrepresentative of the terms under which feminist approaches have been accommodated by UN structures. Drawing on the work of McRobbie[34] and Otto,[35] I analyse the terms and limitations of contemporary feminist activism within the Security Council and find the reassignment of feminist approaches within international institutions remains a misuse of feminist approaches as fundamental concepts, such as gender, are undefined and deployed in such a

---

28 Above note 10.
29 Halley, 'Rape in Berlin: Reconsidering the Criminalisation of Rape in the International Law of Armed Conflict' 9 *Melbourne Journal of International Law* (2008) 78.
30 Preston and Ahrens, 'United Nations Convention Documents in Light of Feminist Theory' 8 *Michigan Journal of Gender and Law* (2001) 1; Mullerson, *Ordering Anarchy: International Law and International Society* (New York: Springer, 2000), at 63–66.
31 Koskenniemi, 'Book Review of Dallmeyer, *Reconceiving Reality: Women and International Law*', 89, *AJIL* (1995) 227, at 230.
32 Mullerson, above note 30, at 64.
33 Engle, above note 12, at 47.
34 McRobbie, *The Aftermath of Feminism* (London: Sage, 2008).
35 Otto, 'The Security Council's Alliance of 'Gender Legitimacy': The Symbolic Capital of Resolution 1325' in Charlesworth and Coicaud (eds), *Faultlines of Legitimacy* (Cambridge: Cambridge University Press, 2010).

range of contexts that the nuances of feminist histories are lost in their institutional representation.

In response to the external criticisms, that feminism presents a partial perspective that is ultimately limited by its underlying idealism, it must be acknowledged that as a partial perspective feminist legal theories offer no more a partial account than the current status quo of law. In fact, through the incorporation of multiple women's voices and multiple feminist perspectives to develop strategies for the reform of law, feminist legal theories are significantly less partial or biased than contemporary conceptions of the international legal model largely confined to the parameters of legal liberalism developed in Western patriarchal histories. In response to the criticism that constructing feminist utopias is of limited practical value, I follow the methods elaborated by Lacey, that feminist movement between critique, utopia and reform constructs '[u]topias [that] cannot be reached: rather they provide horizons towards which we attempt to move'.[36] Finally, I work from the premise that Mullerson's claim that feminism suffers from a certain paranoia regarding discrimination against women itself suffers from a myopia about the experiences of women's everyday[37] and a myopia with respect to the nature and histories of Western jurisprudence.[38]

Sex and gender

Although feminist projects vary immensely, the unifying political and ethical assumption of all feminist legal theories and methods is that sex or gender, or both, is social discourses that are important to understanding and explaining legal structures and relationships.[39] I regard *sex as a reference to the bodily, or biological, distinction between female and male body types*. I consider *gender as the social and cultural consequences of sex difference*. In line with contemporary feminist approaches to international law,[40] sex difference is also understood as socially dependent, projecting a socially situated theory of the body on to conceptions of maleness and femaleness.[41]

---

36   Above note 16, at 46.
37   Valchová and Biason (eds), *Women in an Insecure World* (Geneva: Geneva Centre for the Democratic Control of Armed Force, 2005).
38   Barnett, *Sourcebook of Feminist Jurisprudence* (London: Cavendish, 1997).
39   See the discussion of Bartlett, 'Cracking Foundations as Feminist Method', 8 *American University Journal of Gender, Social Policy and the Law* (2000), 31, at 34. However, note Engle's argument that structural bias feminisms have not adequately addressed the 'feminist' question. I read Engle's work as inferring a failure to commit to an ethical project in structural bias feminist approaches, see: Engle, above note 12, at 47.
40   See the discussion in Charlesworth and Chinkin, above note 12, at 3–4.
41   Naffine and Owens (eds), *Sexing the Subject of Law* (London: LBC, 1997); others argue the distinction between sex and gender is unnecessary because: 'No universal biological essence of "sex" exists, but rather a complex system of potentials that are activated by various internal *and* external influences. I see no useful border separating "sex" and "gender" as conventionally used. I therefore use "gender" to cover masculine and feminine roles and bodies alike, in all their aspects, including the (biological and cultural) structures, dynamics, roles, and scripts associated with each gender group. I reserve the word "sex" for sexual behaviours (recognizing that there is no precise dividing line here either)'. Goldstein, *War and Gender* (Cambridge: Cambridge University Press, 2003), at 2. The analytical separa-

In applying these discursive distinctions to the law on the use of force, I regard sex as a category of assumptions projected onto legal subjects and accepted legal categories. In liberal legal structures, dominant cultural and social expectations about the 'normal' legal subject specifically project masculine characteristics on to an assumed pre-legal subject. The consequence is an almost invisible sexing of the legal subject within liberal discourse. Feminist sexing projects work to expose the assumed sex of the legal subject, identifying what is included with categories of 'normalness' and what is excluded. For example, the perception of the state as an entity defined through territorial integrity and political independence incorporates into international law an international legal subject that parallels the bounded male body of Western liberal thought.[42] Charlesworth has demonstrated how the state, as the primary international legal subject, is imbued with sexed assumptions that project a masculine version of legal subjectivity onto the international legal subject.[43]

The development, within this book, of a method that draws upon theories of the sexed subject reflects earlier feminist analysis of the role of liberal binaries or dualisms in Western legal discourse, including the mind/body split.[44] Feminist legal theories critique the priority given to the mind (rational, male actor) over the body (irrational, female object). Consequently, law is described as functioning to ignore the corporeality of subjects. In her seminal account of the sexing project, Naffine exposes how the body of the legal person/subject, although ostensibly absent, is endowed with masculine characteristics. The silence of law on bodies thus constructs both the normal (bounded, male) body and the abnormal (fluid, female) body. Bringing this knowledge to international law requires analysis of how the state, as the primary international legal subject is assumed to parallel the bounded male subject of liberal discourse, as well as mapping the areas where the analogy is not developed.[45] In this sense the domestic analogy is a useful tool for identifying the sex of the legal subject, as it does not assume the sex of the legal subject but seeks to expose where legal discourse incorporates sexed assumptions about subjects.

Despite contemporary erosions into traditional conceptions of sovereignty, states retain their status as the primary interpreters and enforcers of international law on the use of force.[46] The current international legal formation of the state not only remains

---

tion of sex and gender does not, in this project, assume an essential biological category of sex, rather I regard sex as a category assumed to be derived through biology but in fact constructed through language and social discourse; for a parallel approach, see Kinsella, 'Gendering Grotius', 34 (2), *Political Theory* (2006).

42 On the bounded male body of liberal discourse, see Naffine, 'The Body Bag' in Naffine and Owens (eds), *ibid*; on the application of this to the state as the primary subject of international law, see Charlesworth, 'The Sex of the State in International Law' in Naffine and Owens (eds), *ibid*.

43 *Ibid.*, at 255.

44 See Olsen, 'Feminism and Critical Legal Theory: An American Perspective', 18, *International Journal of the Sociology of Law* (1990), 191.

45 Charlesworth, in Naffine and Owens, above note 41; also see Gardam, 'An Alien's View of the Law of Armed Conflict' in Naffine and Owens (eds), above note 41, from 233.

46 See Koskenniemi, 'Iraq and the "Bush Doctrine" of Pre-emptive Self-Defence' Crimes of War Project, Expert Analysis (20 August 2002), available at http://www.crimesofwar.org/print/expert/bush-Koskenniemi-print.html (last accessed February 2011) reflecting on the impact of states as 'auto-interpreters' of international law.

central to international law, this book seeks to demonstrate how the subject status of the state as the primary legal subject relies on a perception of the state imbued with male characteristics to qualify as 'normal'. Recent shifts towards the identification of 'failed states' in the international system also function to reinforce the implicit rationality attributed to the good/Western/democratic state because of the entrenchment of a sexed dichotomy in the failed state discourse. Failed state discourse has been used by states to justify the use of force on the territory of another state, for example, targeted strikes against terrorist actors in Somalia.[47] The penetrability of 'failed states' can be paralleled with Naffine's identification of the female body in liberal discourse that is contrasted to the image of the closed male body.

This book demonstrates how the law on the use of force plays a crucial role in the construction and perpetuation of the sexed state of international legal discourse. The law on the use of force cements the sexed state into the international structure through the assumption that states can use force in a legal manner that is equated with rationality (under Article 51 of the UN Charter and the customary international law right of states to use force in self-defence). However, the international construction of the sexed state mimics Western state domestic legal paradigms that posit a legal subject, also sexed male, through the assumption of the capacity for the deployment of rational and proportionate force in response to an attack. The necessary implication is that violence falling outside the legal construction of assumed 'normalness' is feminized and racialised as the acts of an unruly 'Other'.

In contrast to feminist sexing projects, the use of gender as a category of analysis provides a descriptive account of the relationship between law and society. A gender approach exposes the role of law in the construction of gender norms, as well as highlighting the role of gender in the application and interpretation of law. The gender component of this project argues for the recognition of the tripartite relationship between law, violence and gender.[48] Yet as a distinctly feminist project, this book does not merely seek to expose the representation and reproduction of gendered discourse in law. In this book I argue that law, including the international law on the use of force, also reflects and projects a form of hegemonic masculinity that has a negative impact on women's lives, reduces the opportunities for women's widespread participation in the public sphere and perpetuates threats to women's security and sexual integrity. In this sense, the project is attentive to feminist scholarship beyond structural bias feminism, including the work of third world feminist theorists that emphasises the complicated role of culture and gender as discourses of power and inequalities.[49] The

47 For a critical analysis with the concept of failed states, see; Wilde, 'The Skewed Responsibility of the Failed State Concept' 9 *ILSA Journal of International and Comparative Law* (2002), 425. On the use of force in failed states, see: The National Security Strategy of the United States 6 (September 2002), available at <http://www.comw.org/qdr/fulltext/nss2002.pdf> (last accessed February 2011) at 10–11; Schmitt, 'Qaeda Leader Reported Killed in Somalia', *The New York Times* (2 May 2008); Rice, '"Many Dead" in U.S. Airstrikes on Somalia', *The Guardian* (9 January 2007); also see chapter six.
48 For elaboration, see: Peach, 'The Gendering of Violence in the Law' in Rycenga and Waller (eds), *Frontline Feminisms* (London: Routledge, 2001).
49 On Postcolonial Feminism, see: Kapur, above note 19.

enormous variation of gender representations across (and within) cultural and social forms is accounted for through three aspects of the project.

First, through analysis of the relationship between law, violence and gender rather than just law and gender, the work of Goldstein on war and gender is incorporated within a legal framework. Goldstein argues that, although gender perceptions and categories vary globally (as do perceptions of warfare), what is consistent about gender, cross-culturally, is its integral role in the construction of war narratives. Goldstein concludes:

> War, then, is a tremendously diverse enterprise, operating in many contexts with many purposes, rules, and meanings. Gender norms outside war show similar diversity. The puzzle . . . is why this diversity disappears when it comes to the *connection* of war with gender. That connection is more stable, across cultures and through time, than are either gender roles outside of war or the forms and frequency of war itself.[50]

The global consistency of the war and gender dynamic raises questions about power and inequalities present in gender relationships. For feminist legal theories, gender is more than a dominant social discourse. Gender also constructs a consistent hierarchical relationship between men and women that functions to reinforce men's power and women's oppression.[51] Goldstein's exposure of the gendered dynamic of war,[52] when developed as a feminist legal contention, indicates that attention needs to be paid to the relationship between, not just law and gender (as international feminist legal theorists do) or to law and war (as scholars writing on the international law on the use of force do), but to the production of integrated narratives of law, violence and gender. The international law on the use of force, as the manifestation of the law/violence relationship within the international sphere, is also a gendered discourse that both reflects dominant social discourse on gender normality and plays a role in constructing gender norms. As such, the war and gender relationship represents a unique starting point for engaging international law that, by definition, has resonance across communities.

Second, the variation of gender relations across social and community groups means that the impact of the gender within legal discourse will also be varied. Therefore, I interrogate the gender of violence in the law in terms of its reflection and contribution to the production of dominant Western gender stereotypes.[53] That is, the text assumes the prevalence of Western legal forms in the production and histories of international law. This is not to project the Western legal form as universal or even

---

50 Goldstein, above note 41, at 21 [*emphasis in original*].
51 MacKinnon, *Women's Lives under Men's Laws* (Harvard, MA: Harvard University Press, 2005).
52 Also see: Enloe, *The Morning After* (Berkeley, CA: University of California, 1993); Enloe, *Bananas, Beaches and Bases* (Victoria, BC, Canada: Pandora, 1989); Enloe, *Does Khaki Become You?* (Pandora, 1988); Enloe, *The Curious Feminist* (Berkeley, CA: University of California, 2004).
53 See Kapur, above note 19, chapter 4; also see Drakopoulou, 'The Ethic of Care, Female Subjectivity and Feminist Legal Scholarship', 8, *Feminist Legal Studies* (2000), 1999.

preferred. Instead this is to acknowledge that Western legal discourse continues to project itself onto the international as universal, despite the important contributions of non-Western states, non-Western legal structures and non-Western approaches to the construction of contemporary public international law.[54]

To disrupt the universalising tendencies of Western legal forms, I specifically direct the project at Western legal liberalism as a particularised cultural model. The conclusions drawn about the international law on the use of force are thus acknowledged as of particular relevance to Western state self-perceptions. These include the very basic understanding of violence that the law on the use of force has been constructed to respond to: that is, at the time of its drafting, the focus of the UN Charter was on prohibiting interstate conflict and while the international understanding of the nature of armed conflict has expanded during the Charter era,[55] the Charter template of an interaction between two equal states/legal subjects continues to influence the range of legal responses available. Challenging Western and first world perceptions with regard to the range of threats to international security requires a fundamental re-assessment of the role and possibilities of law. To move towards such possibilities, analysis of the limitations of Western approaches such as those revealed by feminist methods is necessary.

Third, the reconstructive and reformative aspects of the text use knowledge garnered outside Western cultural and legal narratives. The justification for this is an understanding of the roots of feminist knowledge in the lived realities of women's lives. Drawing on Gunning's model of 'world travelling', an understanding of 'seeing oneself in context', 'seeing oneself as the other sees' and 'seeing the other in her context' is developed.[56] By developing non-Western feminist accounts as tools for change, the project, on the one hand, argues against dominant social, cultural and political forms while, on the other hand, is attentive to the feminist demand for women's participation in the construction (and re-construction) of international law. This aspect is in opposition to contemporary feminist developments in international institutions that draw primarily on Western feminisms, particularly governance feminism that is currently prevalent in the United States.[57]

The integration of a culturally sensitive approach within the definition of gender is representative of the basic premise that gender is the site of culturally constructed knowledge about assumed biological sex differences. In sum, this project asserts

---

54 See Anghie, Chimni, Mickelson and Okafor (eds), *The Third World and the International Order* (the Hague: Nijhoff, 2003).
55 Important developments include Protocol Additional to the Geneva Conventions of 12 August 1949 and relating to the Protection of Victims of International Armed Conflicts (Protocol 1), adopted on 8 June 1977, Article 1(4); GA Resolution 1514, 14 December 1960 (*Declaration on the Granting of Independence to Colonial Countries and Peoples*); GA Resolution 2625, 24 October 1970; for a discussion see Lowe, Roberts, Walsh and Zaum (eds), *The United Nations Security Council and War: the Evolution of Thought and Practice since 1945* (Oxford: Oxford University Press, 2008), at 34 (in the Introduction by the editors).
56 Gunning, 'Arrogant Perceptions, World-traveling and Multicultural Feminism', 23 *Columbia Human Rights Law Review* (1991), 189.
57 See the discussion in Engle, '"Calling in the Troops" The Uneasy Relationship among Women's Rights, Human Rights and Humanitarian Intervention,' 20 *Harvard Human Rights Journal* (2007), 189.

the relevance of sex and gender to the construction of international law on the use of force and entwines these two core feminist legal methods. As a sexing project assumed universal categories, particularly those that construct the international legal subject, are exposed as regularly drawing on the opposition between feminine and masculine archetypes to construct legal subjectivity. This leads to the domestic analogy (discussed below). As a gender analysis the book also engages law's production and embroilment in the social construction of masculine and feminine forms that tend to limit women's participation in law, construct specific forms of male violence as justifiable, and limit the representation of violence against women as relevant to international peace and security. The perception of law as a narrative is integral to the gender component of the project.

The domestic analogy

The use of the domestic analogy functions as a conceptual rather than a descriptive method. That is, I compare the contours of the regulation of international violence with those in Western legal structures regulating violence to demonstrate a conceptual analogy. I highlight points of comparison in fundamental legal categories that attempt to restrain or justify violence. In contrast, a descriptive or prescriptive project would attempt to find empirical correlations and sameness. An example of a prescriptive use of the domestic analogy is found in Franck's *Recourse to Force*. Franck looks at necessity defences developed under Common Law systems to explain his theory of necessity as a legitimating factor for the use of force to halt humanitarian crisis.[58] A prescriptive analogy assumes the correlation of domestic legal categories with international legal categories and, therefore, explains international legal justifications for violence by drawing upon domestic legal justifications for violence.[59] In contrast, the conceptual analysis developed in this book does not assume the sameness of international and domestic legal structures instead, it seeks, to expose concepts developed in Western domestic legal orders that are assumed to exist in the international legal system.

The central example of this conceptual analogy is the use of the self-defence justification in international law. Rather than assume the relevance of the domestic–international self-defence analogy, I interrogate the usefulness of the analogy through the feminist critique of interpersonal self-defence.[60] I argue that sexed and gendered fault lines in international law become apparent through exposure of the conceptual analogy between interpersonal justifications for violence and international justifications for violence. The conclusion drawn from this is not that the analogy between the two forms of justifications should be strengthened or that feminist solutions to domestic legal issues should be superimposed on to the international. Instead the feminist appraisal of the international law on the use of force, viewed through the lens of the domestic analogy, promotes a re-examination of the appropriateness of contemporary legal rules on the use of force.

58 Franck, *Recourse to Force* (Cambridge: Cambridge University Press, 2002), chapter 10.
59 See further chapter five on humanitarian intervention.
60 See further chapter three on Article 51 self-defence.

While review of the international law on the use of force has been somewhat fashionable in the past decade,[61] the literature on force rarely considers feminist methods as a means to understand or reconstruct the law on the use of force.[62] The domestic analogy exposes the particularity of international law apparent at the intersection of Western and masculine narratives of law and power. The domestic analogy also illustrates how legal concepts developed within the *jus ad bellum* framework, including self-defence, self-determination, humanitarian intervention, implied authorisation and pre-emptive force, while assumed to be neutral legal forms, are often imbued with sexed assumptions about the nature and possibilities of law. Furthermore, the domestic analogy exposes the state, the primary international legal subject, as built on Western legal models of subjectivity that are sexed male. I consider whether the international legal subject can be un-sexed or whether answers lie in de-personification of the state.[63]

Law as narrative

I have described the conceptual, or analytical, focus of this book as the domestic analogy. In contrast, I perceive the use of a law as narrative technique as a descriptive technique. The division between, and the use of both, an analytical and descriptive method reflects feminist engagement with the relationship between theory and action. Lacey and Jackson describe feminist jurisprudence as an interpretative theory, appreciating the value of normative and empirical jurisprudence while developing the strengths of both to acknowledge the interlinking of theory and practice.[64] Lacey also describes this as a process of critique, utopia and reform,[65] arguing that a movement

---

61 See, for example, Sands, *Lawless World* (London: Penguin, 2006); Kennedy, *Of War and Law* (Princeton, NJ: Princeton, 2006); Smith, *The Utility of Force* (London: Penguin, 2006); Stahn, '"Jus in bello, Jus ad bellum – Jus post Bellum"?: Rethinking the Conception of the Law of Armed Force', 17 *European Journal of International Law* (2006), 921.

62 Notable exceptions include: Buss, 'Keeping Its Promise: Use of Force and the New Man of International Law' in Bartholomew, *Empire's Law* (London: Pluto, 2006); Buchanan and Johnson, 'The 'Unforgiven' Sources of International Law: Nation-Building, Violence and Gender in the West(ern)' in Buss and Manji (eds) above note 3, at 131; Otto, 'Integrating Questions of Gender into Discussion of 'the Use of Force' in the International Law Curriculum', 6(2) *Legal Education Review* (1995), 219; Charlesworth and Chinkin, above note 12, chapter eight; Orford, *Reading Humanitarian Interventions* (Cambridge: Cambridge University Press, 2003); Stark, 'What We Talk about When we Talk about War', 32, *Stanford Journal of International Law* (1996), 91; Charlesworth approaches the law on the use of force tangentially in her reflection on the role of international lawyers in international relations and politics, in 'Saddam Hussein: My Part in His Downfall', 23, *Wisconsin International Law Journal* (2005), 127.

63 See the discussion in chapter three; also see chapter six.

64 Lacey and Jackson, 'Introducing Feminist Legal Theories', in Penner, Schiff, *et al.* (eds), *Jurisprudence and Legal Theory* (London: Butterworths, 2002) at 801.

65 Note, however, the very different meaning of 'utopian' projects in international legal discourse (often associated with neo-liberal accounts) that does not translate into the feminist use of the term; compare the discussion of Koskenniemi, *From Apology to Utopia* (Cambridge: Cambridge University Press, 2005, re-issued) chapter one and Lacey's account of feminist method, Lacey, 'Feminist Theory and the Rights of Women' in Knop, *Gender and Human Rights* (Oxford: Oxford University Press, 2004), at 46.

between the theoretical enterprise, re-construction of law and practical reform of laws in a manner that shapes a continued exchange between empirical and conceptual claims is central to feminist jurisprudence.[66] Law as narrative is a reference to the possibility of law as one telling among many rather than presenting law as an objective and universal standard. In this sense feminist knowledge of the theory–practice loop is facilitated by a view of law as narrative and a perception of law as existing in a horizontal relationship with other forms of social knowledge including normative structures. Narrative approaches, in addition to continuing a tradition drawn from the consciousness raising aspect of late twentieth century feminism, have three functions.

First, a law as narrative approach allows the sanctity of the legal text to be challenged and potentially deposed from its place at the top of a hierarchy of social knowledge. This discloses the partiality of law, despite its pretensions to objectivity and neutrality, and allows for a clearer understanding of the role of theory in practice and practice in theory.

Second, a law as narrative approach enables critical theories to validate and unearth the stories and experiences of those outside mainstream dialogues.[67] This facilitates the shift away from essentialism in discourse and is heightened by my understanding of Western accounts of the law on the use of force as producing a narrative rather than producing objective truths. The use of law as a narrative disrupts the segregation of mainstream accounts from feminist accounts as both emerge as possible descriptions of the law and of the world. Orford's identification of the implicitly gendered narratives of the hero that underpin law on the use of force influences my approach, so that it becomes important to consider the capacity of Western states to narrate themselves into a hero–spectator role in the enforcement of law on the use of force.[68] The narrative element is, therefore, in part geared towards the exposure of the latent, powerful and gendered narratives that dominate contemporary Western legal accounts of force, especially Western state justifications for the use of force on the territory of other states. Throughout the book, I work to broaden the range of narratives used to explain and understand international law. For example, in chapter four, in discussion of self-determination as a potential justification for the use of force in decolonisation contexts, the use of non-legal accounts of self-determination affords a re-imagining of the role individual and social self-determination might play in future accounts of legal or 'external' self-determination.

Finally, the law as narrative approach is grounded in the understanding that theoretical accounts of international law often function as a closed set of narratives. One of the consequences of this, in Western legal theories, is the ongoing reiteration of a

---

66 For example of the relationship between conceptual and empirical accounts/theory and practice see: Charlesworth, Sahgal and Lockett, *Gender, Human Rights and International Law*, Centre LGS Conversation, transcript and sound recording available at: http://www.kent.ac.uk/clgs/news-and-events/Conversations/Conversations.htm (last accessed February 2011).

67 Williams, 'On Being the Object of Property' 14 *Signs* (1988), 5.

68 Orford, *Reading Humanitarian Interventions* (Cambridge: Cambridge University Press, 2003) at 180; see further chapter five.

tension between positive and natural law approaches and between political and legal understandings of, or between, formalism and instrumentalism under international law. Feminist approaches to international law propose alternative narratives at the descriptive and the analytical levels of legal theories that may have the potential to shift beyond what are often regarded as immovable dichotomies or the boundaries of legal theory.[69] Analysis of strategies to challenge these recurrent binaries, for example between legal positivism and natural law, formalism and instrumentalism, is integral to the discussion in chapter five on humanitarian intervention as a justification for the use of force. I argue that to shift beyond the recurring dilemmas presented by humanitarian interventions, feminist approaches require strategies that work towards a disruption of the binary ordering common to mainstream theories of international law.

A narrative approach allows recognition of multiple sources and interdisciplinary insights whilst interrupting the self-regulating exclusivity of standard legal accounts. A law as narrative approach is not, however, a random gathering of interdisciplinary insights on the chosen topic.[70] Law as narrative functions as a means of widening the potential of international law, so as to appreciate the role of international law in cultural accounts and the role of culture in the construction of laws.[71] Through the use of feminist narratives on peace, security, violence and war, I develop specific conclusions regarding the need for the increased participation of women in local, national, regional and international power structures/governance. This aspect of the project has a theoretical base and outcome, acknowledging the structural inequalities produced through women's low participation in security structures. This claim also leads to one of the key practical conclusions of the book: that women's increased participation is necessary for a system of international security that is attentive to the security needs of diverse actors, agents and survivors.

The law as narrative approach is also connected to the acceptance of law, gender and violence as integrated social forms. The acceptance of the law and violence relationship requires acceptance of law as a connected rather than an isolated normative structure.[72] In terms of outcomes the law as narrative approach emerges across the chapters of the book. In chapter two, for example, the study of Security Council power to authorise the use of force is built on a study of the narratives of women, and militaries, after the use of force in Korea in 1950,[73] thus developing multiple sources and interdisciplinary insight to explain and understand the limitations of the law on collective security. In chapter three, the international law on

---

69 On political-legal dichotomies, see Koskenniemi, 'The Place of Law in Collective Security' 17 *Michigan Journal of International Law* (1996), 255; on the natural law-positive law dichotomy see, Koskenniemni, '"The Lady Doth Protest" Kosovo and the Turn to Ethics in International Law,' 65, *Modern Law Review* (2002), 159.
70 I return to this point in chapter six.
71 Thornton, *Romancing the Tomes* (London: Routledge, 2002), in introduction.
72 See: Cover, 'Violence and the Word' 95 (8) *Yale Law Journal* (1986), 1901; also see Derrida, The Force of Law, 11, *Cardozo Law Review* (1990), 1687.
73 SC Res 80 (14 March 1950).

self-defence is interrogated for its specific meaning in Western communities as a narrative of spectatorship and heroics. This allows for recognition of law as composed of specific narratives within specific communities. In chapter four, on self-determination, legal narratives are contrasted with narratives from feminist actors engaged with three specific self-determination conflicts so that the range of narratives used to explain and understand international law are broadened. In chapter five, through the domestic analogy, an important alternative account of the structural deficits of humanitarian intervention is offered. That is, chapter five uses feminist narratives on intervention into interpersonal domestic violence to explore the conceptual limitations of forceful interventions into domestic state violence. Chapter six considers the contours of the global war against terrorism as using narrative devices that have produced a gendered narrative on the international plane analogous to Western provocation defences. Despite the official 'end' of the war on terror with the Obama administration taking power in the United States, the sexed and gendered legacies of the global war against terror remain embedded in both legal doctrine and practice, especially the increasing use of targeted strikes by combat drones. Through the identification of the use of a provocation type excuse by the United States the limitations of this contemporary justification for the use of force are evidenced.

The conclusion across these accounts is a call for the increased participation of women in legal structures as a means to develop alternative legal possibilities. In line with the domestic analogy built in response to the internal feminist critique of essentialism,[74] the call for increased participation of women at all stages of the production of legal narratives is not, however, built on a cultural feminist ideal of an inherently different 'female' voice existing.[75] To seek women's full participation in legal processes is to begin a re-working of legal configurations and expectations. The achievement of women's full participation moves past quotas towards acknowledgment of the failure of current legal arrangements to be inclusive of women at their foundation. My claim is not that women's experiences, and knowledge are naturally different to men's. However, women's experiences and knowledge are informed, globally, by social and cultural norms that result in women having different priorities and needs from those of men. Reflecting the cultural diversity of women's experiences and knowledge, as well as the socially constructed spheres of reference understood as female, demands a re-creation of fundamental legal categories and processes built on women's participation that extends beyond proportionate representation. I reflect on the possibilities and limitations of the feminist 'utopia' of active inclusion of women in the making of the world and in understandings of the potential of international law.[76] This is a foundational claim, not merely instrumental. As a foundational claim, the call for the increased participation of women is directed at the basic processes that are assumed necessary to build Western liberal democracies and the consequent legal structures.

---

74 See Drakopoulou, above note 53.
75 For an account of cultural feminism, the discussion in West, 'Jurisprudence and Gender', 55, *University of Chicago Law Review* (1988), at 35 and Ruddick, *Maternal Thinking: Towards a Politics of Peace* (New York: Beacon, 1995).
76 On the use of the term 'utopia' in feminist legal theories, see above note 65.

In contrast, an instrumental claim would limit itself to the equal representation of women and men in law-making institutions.

To conclude this section, three tools are deployed across the book: the discursive engagement with sex and gender as they emerge in legal documents, the conceptual deployment of the domestic analogy, and the reliance on an understanding of law as a narrative rather than functioning as a series of objective or universal truths. The limitations of these methods, including the overriding simplicity of a feminist ethics (limiting the sex–gender claims), the risk of reproduction rather than challenge to Western forms through the domestic analogy and the myriad potential answers exposed by a law as narrative account, are returned to in the final chapter. I conclude that these limitations ultimately curb the claims the text can make while remaining a legal project. To this end, I consider Arendt's model of natality, that is, the capacity within us all, as humans, for new ideas, rebirth and creative ownership.[77] I argue that Arendt's natality provokes a radical re-conceptualisation of feminist ethics and a challenge to the law and violence relationship. To arrive at this point, I first deploy the methods discussed here in an analysis of the contours of the international law on the use of force. I begin with Security Council powers to authorise force followed by state-led justifications for the use of force. The following section of this chapter introduces the components of the international law on the use of force analysed in the remainder of the book.

International law on the use of force

The history of international law is entwined with the regulation of state violence and force. Key instruments of international law are often key instruments on the use of force.[78] The centrality of force to international legal dialogues is a product of historical choices that position post-conflict events as crucial legal moments connected to the founding of a legal order.[79] While the law on the use of force has a history in customary international law that precedes and parallels the UN Charter, the Charter can be described as providing the central contemporary legal narrative on the law of the use of force.[80] The use of force is prohibited under Article 2(4) of the Charter, may be justified under Article 51 of the Charter, and may be authorised through the collective

---

77 Above note 13; also see chapter six.
78 See UN Charter, Preamble; Neff, *War and the Law of Nations* (Cambridge: Cambridge University Press, 2005).
79 On the role of violence in the founding of legal orders, see Cover, above note 72; also see Charlesworth, 'International Law: A Discipline of Crisis', 65 *Modern Law Review* (2002), 377.
80 For an alternative view, which places international customary law at the centre of international legal narratives on the use of force, Ackerman, *International Law and the Preemptive Use of Force Against Iraq*, CRS Report for Congress, Order Code RS21314 (11 April 2003), available online at www.au.af.mil/au/awc/awcgate/crs/rs21324.pdf (last accessed February 2011), also see: O'Connell, 'Customary International Law on the Use of Force: The UN Charter, Practice and Opinio Juris', Workshop Presentation at the University of Macerata, *International Customary Law on the Use of Force: A Methodological Approach* (11–12 June 2004), available online at www.addix.it/internatzionale/relazoni/connell.pdf (last accessed February 2011).

security system articulated in chapter VII of the Charter. It is the model of force as prohibited yet able to be justified or authorised that I subject to a feminist analysis. After examining the power of the Security Council to authorise force and the right of states to use force in self-defence, I turn to justifications outside the Charter paradigm and track the role of customary international law in the adaptation, refinement and application of this 'cornerstone' of international law.[81]

My focus is on the mainstream documentation that informs Western state and academic approaches to the law on the use of force. By placing Western narratives on the use of force at the centre of my analysis, I challenge the assumption of universality that is portrayed in the bulk of contemporary Western scholarship, yet also recognise the complicity of feminist approaches to international law in Western cultural histories.[82] While I draw on non-Western feminist thinking to enlarge and re-imagine the law on the use of force, reflection on the cultural narratives produced in a writer's own academic, political and social environment is a component of feminist approaches to international law. For Buchanan and Johnson, the exposure of international law's foundational narratives and their own complicity in contemporary expressions of international law is a vital aspect of feminist projects.[83] Embracing what has been described as the 'interpretative' element of feminist legal theories, Lacey argues: 'feminist legal theories do not merely seek to rationalize legal practices; nor, conversely, do they typically engage in entirely external critique and prescription'.[84] I acknowledge and discursively challenge Western approaches to the international law on the use of force from a position recognised as 'within' (debates, cultures, the mainstream) as well as from 'outside' (as feminist, through recognising the mainstream of international law as a narrative rather than a universal).[85]

The book primarily presents an analysis of the international law on the use of force, *jus ad bellum*. The international humanitarian law of armed conflict, *jus in bello*, is an important overlapping and parallel component of international law also concerned with the international legal regulation of violence. While *jus ad bellum* is the focus, that feminist scholarship challenges the distinction that international law constructs between the regulation of decisions to use or restrain from the use of force, *jus ad bellum*, and the methods and means of armed conflict, *jus in bello*, is important.[86] The conceptual distinction between the two regimes implies that the decisions of powerful state actors to use force (mind) are dislocated from the individual acts that occur within an armed conflict (through the bodies of the military). Further study of the relationship between *jus ad bellum* and *jus in bello*, from a feminist perspective, would form an important adjunct to the analysis provided and I initiate this in the analysis of

---

81 See Greenwood, 'The Invasion of Kuwait and the Rule of Law', 55, *Modern Law Review* (1992), 153 describing the law on the use of force as 'the cornerstone of the post-1945 international legal order'.
82 See Orford, *Reading Humanitarian Intervention* (Cambridge: Cambridge University Press, 2003), at 67.
83 Buchanan and Johnson, above note 62.
84 Lacey, above note 16.
85 Otto, 'A Sign of "Weakness"? Disrupting Gender Certainties in the Implementation of Security Council Resolution 1325,' 13, *Michigan Journal of Gender and Law* (2006), 113.
86 On the overlap of the two regimes, see Gardam, 'Proportionality and Force in International Law', 87, *AJIL* (1993) 391.

the legal consequences of the use of unmanned drones in chapter six. In this section I introduce the Charter components – prohibition, authorisation and justification – and identify the key literature and sources of their elaboration.[87]

The prohibition on the use of force

The central Charter provision regulating force is Article 2(4), the prohibition on the threat or use of force.[88] Analysis of Article 2(4) illustrates the foundational nexus between law, violence and gender. Article 2(4) states that:

> All Members shall refrain in their international relations from the threat or use of force against the territorial integrity or political independence of any state, or in any other manner inconsistent with the Purposes of the United Nations.

The Article 2(4) prohibition functions as a restraint on the use of arbitrary force by the primary international legal subjects, states.[89] Prior to the UN era, no effective legal restraint on unilateral state force existed and states were free to make independent assessments as to whether the use of force could function as a satisfactory measure of self-help.[90] The pre-Charter model may be described as having its pedigree in Western political and philosophical histories that invoke the notion of 'just' war to indicate the competence of states to use force as a rational and objective response in interstate relations.[91] Pre-Charter customary international law is also perceived as underpinning contemporary understanding of the parameters and limits of international law on the use of force.[92] It is through the entwining of Charter and customary law narratives that the prohibition on force contained in Article 2(4) can be identified as a sign with an absolute nature and as a boundary that must accommodate state justifications for the use of force.

Law and violence scholarship illustrates the extent that the regulation of violence is conceived of as the implicit rationale for the legal edifice. For example, Cover argues that, 'violence . . . provides the occasion and method for founding legal orders, it gives

---

87   Gray, *International Law and the Use of Force* (Oxford: Oxford University Press, 2008, 3rd edition) represents an excellent introduction and coverage of the key issues, any references to the 2004 (2nd) edition of Gray's work are indicated; also see O'Connell, *International Law and the Use of Force* (Sydney: Federation, 2005).

88   On Article 2(4), see: Franck, *Recourse to Force* (Cambridge: Cambridge University Press, 2002), chapter 1; Gray, *ibid* (2004, 2nd edition), chapter 1; Franck, 'Who Killed Article 2(4)?' 64 (4), *AJIL* (1970), 809.

89   On the role of states as the international legal subject, see: Craven, Statehood, 'Self-determination and Recognition', in Evans, *International Law* (Oxford: Oxford University Press, 2010).

90   However, during the era of the League of Nations, Article 12 of the Covenant did attempt to impose a 'cooling off' period to orchestrate a collective response to the use of force. This was ultimately regarded as an ineffective legal mechanism, see: O'Connell, above note 87, at 126–128 and at 131–134 (discussing the Kellogg-Briand Pact).

91   Neff, above note 78.

92   O'Connell, above note 87, at 11–13; also see *Case Concerning Military and Paramilitary Activities in and Against Nicaragua* (Nicaragua v USA), Merits (1986 ICJ), Reports 14.

laws (as the regulator of force and coercion) a reason for being and it provides a means through which law acts'.[93] Cover's work, and subsequent law and violence scholarship,[94] although directed at national legal structures, illustrate an important element of the international legal system. That is, Cover's tripartite description of law and violence can be applied to international law to understand the inherent role of violence within the structure of the international legal system. First, violence is understood as providing the founding motivation for the contemporary international legal system, as the events of World War II lead to the pursuit of an international structure that would halt future aggression by states.[95] Second, violence also gives the international legal system its rationale for continued existence, that is, the unjustified violence of states using force unilaterally is seen as requiring a collective enforcement mechanism now enshrined in Article 42 of the UN Charter. Third, the means through which law 'acts' is grounded in violence; that is, chapter VII authorises legal coercion in the form of Article 41 acts (measures short of force) and Article 42 (the use of force).[96] Cover's approach is helpful as a means of bring to our attention the crucial role of violence in law, in this case in international law, to the surface. The dichotomy between illegal force (the rationale for a legal system) and authorised force (the means through which law acts) can be seen to underpin the international system or to provide what Franck calls the 'solar plexus' of the international system.[97]

My contention is that the absolute yet porous quality of the prohibition configures an international legal subject that replicates Western legal subjects understood through legal liberalism as male and masculinised.[98] On the one hand, the meaning of Article 2(4) is clear: States are prohibited from using force against other states. The reference to territorial integrity and political independence in Article 2(4) aids identification of the values enshrined in the recognition of a state while the reference to the purposes of the United Nations endows the prohibition with central importance and prestige. Yet, on the other hand, just as the prohibition is confirmed by Western scholarship as static and resolvable through the text of the Charter, it is also presented as a malleable boundary through the development of international customary law. This malleability is revealed at multiple sites. Arguments for certain types of force, such as belligerent reprisals, frontier incidents or the rescue of nationals abroad,[99] depend upon a

---

93 Cover, 'Violence and the Word' in Minow *et al.* (eds), *Narrative, Violence and the Law* (1992), 213.

94 Cover, 'Violence and the Word' in Minow *et al.* (eds), *Narrative, Violence and the Law* (1992), 213.; also see, Sarat, *Law, Violence and the Possibility of Justice* (Princeton, NJ: Princeton Press, 2001); Sarat and Kearns (eds), *Law's Violence* (Ann Arbor, MI: Michigan University Press, 1995).

95 However, also see Derrida's understanding of the semantic violence inherent in the founding of a legal system, Derrida, 'Force of Law', 11, *Cardozo Law Review* (1990), 1687; other scholars have inferred the founding violence of the international legal system is colonialism, see, Berman, 'In the Wake of Empire', 14, *American University International Law Review* (1998–1999), 1515.

96 Cover describes all legal acts as coercive and thus as violence, I argue that this approach has equal purchase to international legal coercion/acts as to national structures; for a discussion of Article 41 and 42, see chapter two.

97 Franck, 'The Laws of Force and the Turn to Evidence' *American Society of International Law Annual Meeting*, Conference Paper (Thursday, 28 March 2006).

98 See Naffine, above note 41.

99 However, note these aspects of the use of force are generally outside the scope of this book.

reinforcement of the prohibition's static and absolute nature alongside a crafted argument for these types of coercive measures to sit below the threshold invoked by the phrase 'the threat or use of force'. For example, O'Connell argues that the use of force by Israel against Lebanon in 2006 would not have violated the Article 2(4) prohibition if the actions of the Israeli government had been limited to the rescue of the Israeli soldiers kidnapped by Hezbollah, as this would have been perceived as a proportionate countermeasure (rather than as illegal aggression) by the wider international community.[100] Other writers use the final phrase in the prohibition, 'any manner inconsistent with the purposes of the United Nations', to justify force that would otherwise be in violation of the Charter. For example, in his justification for the use of force as 'humanitarian intervention', Tesón writes:

> The United Nation's purpose of promoting and protecting human rights found in Article 1(3), and by reference in Article 2(4) as a qualifying clause to the prohibition of war, has a *necessary* primacy over the respect for state sovereignty. Force used in defense of fundamental human rights is therefore *not* a use of force inconsistent with the purposes of the United Nations.[101]

The conundrum Article 2(4) presents as supreme yet able to be circumvented requires engagement and dissection. In this study, the role of Article 2(4) is treated as embedding assumptions about the role of violence under international law, what is tolerated and normalised as well as what is outlawed and illegal. I argue that this is more than a linkage of legal forms with violence as contemporary understandings of law and of violence are also co-opted into social constructions of gender.

As such any study of Article 2(4) must also explore the prohibition's role within the international legal system generally. Regardless of a writer's – or a state's – perspective on the more controversial justifications for the use of force, including preemptive force, humanitarian interventions, and implied authorisations, the prohibition will play a fundamental role in illustrating the argument and will be deployed as a static, dependable element of the international legal order.[102] For example, Greenwood argues for the possibility of implied authorisation from the Security Council as constituting an appropriate explanation for the use of force in Serbia by NATO in 1999 and in anticipation of the use of force by the United States and United Kingdom in Iraq in 2003, but does so after he reiterates the permanence and relevance of Article 2(4).[103] This is also seen in O'Connell and Tesón's accounts, above. The UN system has, consequently, been perceived as under greatest threat when states appear

---

100 O'Connell, *Proportionality and Sustainable Peace in the Middle East*, Policy Brief No. 12 (Notre Dame, IN: Joan B. Kroc Institute for International Peace Studies, August 2006) available online at: http://kroc.nd.edu/polbrief/documents/polbrief12.pdf (last accessed February 2011).

101 Tesón, *Humanitarian Intervention: An Inquiry into Law and Morality* (New York: Transnational, 1997), at 173–174.

102 For a view which challenges the continued relevance of Article 2(4), see: Glennon, 'How International Rules Die,' 93, *Georgetown Law Journal* (2005), 939.

103 Greenwood, 'International Law and the Preemptive Use of Force', 4, *San Diego Journal of International Law* (2003), 7, at 10–11.

to ignore Article 2(4), the prohibition on force. For example, Franck's lament, during the Vietnam conflict in 1970, of 'Who Killed Article 2(4)?' argues that, '[t]he failure of the UN Charter's normative system is tantamount to the inability of any rule, such as that set out in Article 2(4), in itself to have much control over the behaviour of states'.[104] The failure to see key international legal developments manifest in other aspects of international relationships: trade, human rights, environmental, health or economic and social developments or minority rights and anti-discrimination laws maintains an emphasis on force while downplaying the increasingly complex relationships that exist across, between and throughout states.

Feminist theory adds to law and violence scholarship the further feature of gender. That is, if we understand law as intimately co-opted in violence – dividing that which is authorised from that which is regulated and outlawed – inserting understandings of gender in violence highlights a fourth category of violence in Cover's model: violence that is invisible or deemed unimportant by the legal system. Violence against women often falls into this category under international and national legal structures. As a form of violence often associated with the private sphere, violence against women is not within Cover's category of acts to be regulated or acts authorised by law. Instead violence against women is often characterised as cultural, traditional or not violence at all and thus outside of law's proper domain.

Violence against women can be defined as physical harm directed at women and often tolerated within a community because the survivor or target of the violence is female. For example, honour crimes are a widespread form of violence against women.[105] Other forms of violence against women include social or cultural restrictions on women's bodily integrity, particularly sexual integrity, such as that caused by harmful cultural practices. Violence against women also includes the physical confinement of women through social norms that dictate women as inferior and therefore belonging within the private sphere, especially when such confinement limits women's capacity to be educated, to be literate, to have access to adequate health care or to become self-sufficient through earning. Violence against women also includes the spectrum of sexual violence, exploitation and abuse directed at and inflicted on women: sexual harassment, sexual servitude/slavery, sexual assault, incest, etc. Violence against women may be legal or illegal, criminalised or tolerated; what is significant is that the harmful practice is defined by the biological sexual identity of the victim, that is she is female, rather than by the type of violence inflicted.[106] Domestic violence is a form of violence primarily directed at women within the private sphere by family members, particularly husbands or intimate partners.[107]

The deficiencies of the international legal structure are exposed by inserting an understanding of the gender of violence in each element of Cover's law and violence

---

104 Franck, above note 88.
105 Welchman and Hossain, *Honor: Crimes, Paradigms and Violence Against Women* (London: Zed, 2006).
106 For a legal definition, see: Declaration on the Elimination of Violence Against Women, GA Res 48/103, 20 December 1993; also see *Secretary-General In-depth Study of All Forms of Violence against Women*, 9 October 2006, A/61/122/Add.1.
107 See the discussion in chapter five.

model.[108] At the original point of law's violence – what Cover calls the founding of a legal system – gendered violence functions to exclude women's voices in the constitutive acts of the legal system. This happens (at least) twice under international law. Not only were women for the most part absent (or kept on the other side of the door, out of the public space) during the foundation of national legal structures (states), which then come to constitute international legal subjects, but women's exclusion also occurs at the founding of each pivotal instrument in the evolution of international law – from the Peace of Westphalia to the UN Charter and Nuremberg.[109] This physical exclusion from public agreement on founding documents functions as violence enacted against women by the patriarchal histories of the communities we live within. This is then underscored by a discursive violence that further excludes women from subjectivity in legal documents either (originally) as citizens in nation states or through the limited representation offered to them in the international sphere by the international legal subject of the state.[110] Derrida describes this as the force of law, positing legal categories as spaces of violent exclusions through the binaries and boundaries that rein in some law and subjects whilst (violently) excluding others.[111] Beyond this, we can describe an additional violence faced by women as the historical and discursive combine to perpetuate the marginalisation of women in the legal system. The understanding provided by searching out the gendering of violence in law underpins the argument of this book and informs conclusions drawn on discursive and participatory disadvantages to women embedded in the law of use of force.

The second site of violence identified by Cover, which incorporates the acts that provoke law's gaze and are deemed criminal or deviant, is indicative of the dependence of legal representations of violence on social constructions of gender. Under national legal structures, the refusal and reluctance of the law to categorise violence against women – in all its social manifestations – as illegal is historically evidenced and continues to inform categories of criminality and regulation.[112] Domestic violence, sexual harassment, crimes of honour, sexual violence and sex discrimination may have begun to appear in the legal landscape after three decades (and more) of feminist scholarship and activism, yet each remain ad hoc legal categories or underdeveloped categories of criminal behaviour. The aim of this book is to expose how this gendering of law and violence embedded in Western national systems is present in international laws, which identify and regulate the criminal or deviant acts (aggression) of states. Particular attention is paid to the failure of the international system

---

108 Hunter, 'Law's (Masculine) Violence', 17 (1), *Law and Critique* 27 (2006), 27.
109 See Knop, *Diversity and Self-determination in International Law* (Cambridge: Cambridge University Press, 2002); Otto, 'International Peace Activism: The Contributions Made by Women', 82, *Reform: A Journal of National and International Law Reform* (2003), 30; both of these authors demonstrate the influence of women's peace movements on international law in the first half of the twentieth century.
110 Charlesworth, 'The Sex of State in International Law' in Naffine and Owens, above note 41.
111 Above note 72.
112 Dobash and Dobash, 'Violent Men and Violent Contexts' in Dobash and Dobash (eds), *Rethinking Violence Against Women* (Sage, 1998), at 141–168; McColgan, 'General Defences' in Bibbings and Nicolson, *Feminist Perspectives on Criminal Law* (London: Cavendish, 2000).

to register violence against women during armed conflict or peacetime as a threat to international peace and security.

Finally, Cover's third site of violence – the enforcement of law – remains unresponsive to crimes and violence against women under national legal forms, with low arrest rates, gendered defences such as provocation and self-defence, low reportage and conviction rates often nullifying the recognition of gender-based violence within Western legal structures. The enforcement of international law is the focus of this book. The positioning of the use of force as the ultimate enforcement mechanism in the international system is a clear acknowledgement of the relationship between law and violence. The argument here demonstrates the additional relationship between each of these categories and sex or gender. I accordingly develop the contention that the invocation of a domestic analogy with national criminal justifications for violence incorporates a sexed narrative into international law. When women use violence, Western legal structures have appeared reluctant to accommodate this within legal perceptions of justifiable acts. The book argues that international justifications are construed in analogous terms. Feminist scholarship would not necessarily advocate the use of force to halt violence against women, instead the *conceptual* challenge mounted by an approach to law that seeks to expose the gender of violence in the law is important. The conceptual claim is underscored by the wealth of empirical and descriptive evidence of the impact of the use of force on the lives of women.

In addition to a conceptual gendering, the international law on the use of force has neglected the role of women at the level of participation. A consequence of this is that the conceptual exclusion of women appears 'normal' or 'natural'. When mainstream international legal narratives produce a gradual march from the Peace of Westphalia, through the Concert of Europe towards the Hague Peace Conferences, beyond the Kellogg–Briand Pact and the Covenant of the League of Nations to the proclamation of the United Nations' prohibition on the use of force, women are not absent. Women are, quite literally, on the other side of the door, invisible yet present in the proceedings, in the language of law and in acts that are to be regulated, authorised and outlawed. The gendering of violence in the law therefore begins in international law through women's physical exclusion from decision-making processes. Otto recognises this in two ways in her work. First, in a similar manner to Knop, she works to reinstall recognition of the presence of women, as advocates of peace, as stateswomen and diplomats, at the meetings that produce the great instruments of international law.[113] Second, Otto exposes the role of woman as 'other' to the legal subject that constitutes the texts and acts of the legal system. Thus Otto writes:

> While women were seldom produced explicitly by early legal texts, they were implicit in every representation of masculinity. . . . Many of the boundaries, concepts and metaphors that inform international legal thinking have also played a role in the legal reproduction of the dualisms of sex, such as the division between

---

113 Knop, above note 104; Otto, 'Lost in Translation' in Orford (ed), *International Law and Its Others* (Cambridge: Cambridge University Press, 2007).

public and private spheres and the idea of the sovereign nation state, which privilege masculine forms of power over those associated with the feminine. . . .[114]

Otto then applies this approach to specific legal documents, in this case the Hague Conventions on the laws of war or *jus in bello*:

The first international instruments that set out to regulate war illustrate the reproduction of sexed subjects in hierarchal relations. They were concerned almost exclusively with (male) combatants, despite the already long history of war-time sexual abuse of women.[115]

Otto's exposure of the complicity of the social construction of gender in international legal histories focuses on the international law of armed conflict/humanitarian laws and international human rights laws. The myth of military protection, which in reality circumvents women's 'dignity and autonomy',[116] as indicated by Otto, is also a narrative that underscores the law that governs *jus ad bellum*.

An understanding of the gendered continuum of violence becomes crucial to understanding the possibilities of exposing the 'gendering of violence in the law'.[117] The gendered continuum plays out both in regular legal histories of international law, which continually refer to national or domestic legal structures to explain and underpin the international legal edifice, and in doctrinal incursions into international law. Cockburn refers to the domestic analogy as 'a connection between the violence women experience in everyday life and the violence of war. Women talk about a 'continuum of violence'. The linking factor is 'gender'.[118] By exploring the 'gendered continuum of violence' cultural understandings of femininity and masculinity are exposed as relevant to international law on the use of force. Yet rather than seeking gender's removal or gender reversal my approach is to seek out, following Otto, gender's fluidity.[119] For Otto, this would require understanding women's participation (in peace and security processes) as making a 'transformative difference' that can be used to 'challenge the ideas that war and masculinity are intertwined and that women are the peacemakers'.[120] For Otto the key is to perceive a gender analysis as leading towards a '"multi-gendered" transformation rather than one that is gender-free'.[121]

---

114 Ibid. at 322.
115 *Ibid.*
116 Ibid. at 323.
117 Peach, 'The Gendering of Violence in the Law' in Waller and Rycenga, *Frontline Feminisms* (London: Routledge, 2001).
118 Cockburn, 'Feminist Antimilitarism', in *Women's Teach-In: Antimilitarism, Fundamentalisms/Secularism and Civil Liberties and Anti-Terrorism Legislation after 11 September 2001*, Occasional Paper 14 (Women Living Under Muslim Laws, November 2003).
119 Otto, 'A Sign of "Weakness"? Disrupting Gender Certainties in the Implementation of Security Council Resolution 1325,' 13 *Michigan Journal of Gender and Law* (2006) 113, at 170.
120 Ibid.
121 Ibid.

Article 2(4) is perceived as the normative lynchpin of the international order however the boundary between prohibited and justified force has a gendered history and functions as a sexed concept. When Article 2(4) is analysed as a lynchpin in the relationship between law, gender and violence the structural inequalities of international law are exposed. As a consequence feminist legal approaches must, on the one hand, challenge the limitations of Article 2(4) from a place 'within' the contemporary international law on the use of force. The re-structuring and development of the prohibition within Article 2(4) represents this type of necessary feminist project. On the other hand, as an approach to international law built on challenging the international legal structure from its foundations, feminist legal theory requires concurrent strategies that work to produce a re-conceptualisation and re-imagining of international law and its boundaries, including Article 2(4) and justifications for the use of force, outside of mainstream legal approaches.

I return to the prohibition in the concluding chapter and argue that the prohibition demands increased attention and legal expansion rather than continued attention to potential justifications for the use of force. This conclusion is drawn from the underlying contention that the use of force, as a form of military behaviour, has adverse consequences for women regardless of the justification or authorisation underlying or legitimating force. The articulation of justifications ignores the gendered impact of military behaviour. Instead, I argue, a renewed focus on the prohibition encourages peace building and preventative strategies.

Authorising force

Under chapter VII of the UN Charter, the power to authorise collective enforcement measures for the maintenance of international peace and security is granted to the Security Council. In the preceding chapter of the Charter, chapter VI, the Council is directed to recommend the pacific settlement of disputes through 'negotiation, enquiry, mediation, conciliation, arbitration, judicial settlement . . . or other peaceful means'.[122] In contrast to the mandatory cooling-off period in the Covenant of the League of Nations, chapter VI has been utilised through largely non-binding language by the Security Council with respect to the pacific settlement of disputes and engages a low threshold, applying chapter VI powers to events 'likely to endanger international peace and security' in Article 33 or 'any dispute, or any situation which might lead to international friction or give rise to a dispute' under Article 34. Chapter VII, in contrast, gives the Council binding powers under a higher threshold for the purposes of authorising the use of force. Under Article 39 the Council should respond to 'any threat to the peace, breach of the peace or act of aggression' to 'maintain or to restore international peace and security'.[123]

---

122 Chapter VI of the United Nations Charter, Article 33. This article is directed at the parties to a dispute who 'shall, first of all, seek a solution' (through the means listed in the text), Article 36 (1) permits the Security Council to take action/recommend procedures.
123 Chapter VII of the United Nations Charter, Article 39; however, note the Advisory Opinion of the ICJ in the *Legal Consequences for States of the Continued presence of South Africa in Namibia (South West Africa)*

The tension between soft and hard law developments in international law is of feminist interest.[124] Chapter VI, with its emphasis on alternative methods of dispute resolution and preventative action, is a form of soft law,[125] while chapter VII in conjunction with Article 25 of the Charter,[126] empowers the Security Council to authorise coercive measures, including force, and grants the Council the capacity to create binding, hard law directing the use of force.[127] Feminist scholarship interrogates legal categories that invoke a distinction between peace and coercion and argues that the dichotomy replicates a gendered hierarchy between socially constructed forms of feminine and masculine knowledge.[128] I consider the social and cultural narratives that link authorised force and masculinity, implicitly distancing women and non-forceful means of conflict resolution.

The primacy of gender in military behaviour, however, extends beyond the association of masculinity with the law authorising the use of force. Chapter VII, under Article 41, empowers the Security Council to authorise measures short of the use of force. Article 42 empowers the Security Council to authorise measures as may be necessary, including force. Article 41 has been developed by the Security Council primarily through economic sanctions, through contemporary targeted sanctions regimes and through the post-conflict justice regimes of the *ad hoc* tribunals for the former Yugoslavia and Rwanda. The Security Council has also extended its remit through the authorisation of peacekeeping forces.[129] The power of the Security Council to define threats, breaches of the peace and acts of aggression (Article 39), to authorise sanctions (Article 41), and to authorise the use of force (Article 42) forms the substantive focus of chapter two. A system focussed on the authorisation of collective force embeds assumptions about the capacity of states and militaries to use force in a proportionate manner and towards positive ends. The current system ignores the complicity of states and militaries in gendered violence, overlooking the manner in which women's security is threatened in peacetime and armed conflict, it also ignores the negative and lasting impact of conflict on women.[130]

The authorisation of force by the Security Council, even when it was rarely used during the Cold War, has been perceived as a settled and necessary aspect of the UN legal structure. State practices that seek to extend the range of justifications for unilateral state force tend to explain unilateral action with references to the corollary

---

notwithstanding Security Council 276 (1970) where the Court emphasised that the powers of the Security Council are derived from Article 25 of the Charter regardless of whether they are chapters VI or chapter VII resolutions.

124 Charlesworth and Chinkin, above note 12, at 279.

125 Ibid., at 65–67.

126 Article 25 states: 'The Members of the United Nations agree to accept and carry out the decisions of the Security Council in accordance with the present Charter'.

127 See Gray, above note 87, at 261–262, discussing the Security Council's capacity to mandate peacekeeping operations.

128 Otto, above note 109.

129 Higgins, 'A General Assessment of UN Peace-Keeping' in Cassese (ed), *United Nations Peace-Keeping* (1978), 1–14.

130 Cockburn and Zarkov (eds), *The Postwar Moment* (London: Lawrence and Wishart, 2002).

powers of the Security Council.[131] For example, the United States led its allies into Iraq in 2003 and, although often regarded as a rejection or 'bypass' of the Security Council enforcement system, the justification narratives deployed by the United States were tied expressly to prior Security Council resolutions, such as Resolution 1441, to establish the legality of the use of force in Iraq.[132] Subsequent explanations of the invasion rely on this sense of 'implied' authorisation in past Security Council resolutions.[133] In this sense, the capacity of the Security Council to authorise the use of force plays an important role in state justifications for the use of force. Despite the perception of Article 2(4) as a constraint on the use of force, a system that configures authorised force as possible and, consequently, as an effective method to resolve disputes, gives justifications for the use of force, voiced unilaterally by states, increased viability and range.

Chapter two analyses the power of the Security Council to define threats to the peace, breaches of the peace and acts of aggression (Article 39) and the power under Article 42 to authorise the use of force. I analyse the feminist ambivalence for contemporary developments with respect to the criminalisation of sexual violence in armed conflict and connect this to larger concerns about feminist expansion at the institutional level that are, at times, disconnected from the plurality of feminist discourse in the academy.[134] The primary argument in chapter two is that the lasting and negative impact of force as a gendered solution limits the usefulness of force as an enforcement mechanism, evidenced through analysis of Article 42. This approach challenges the paradigm of international law built on a conception of law in a permanent relationship with violence. The extreme nature of this claim is revisited in the final chapter regarding the use of force in the era of terrorism.

Justifications for the use of force

Chapters three, four and five of this book focus on the construction of justifications for the use of force by states. The Charter permits states to use force unilaterally, outside Security Council authorisation, as a form of self-defence in response to an armed attack. Article 51 states:

> Nothing in the present Charter shall impair the inherent right of individual or collective self-defence if an armed attack occurs against a Member of the United Nations, until the Security Council has taken measures necessary to maintain international peace and security. Measures taken by Members in the exercise of

131 See, for example: Greenwood, 'International Law and the NATO Intervention in Kosovo', 49 (4) *International and Comparative Law Quarterly* (2000), 926, at 927, 930.
132 US Secretary of State, Colin Powell, Address to UN Security Council (5 February 2003) available online at: http://www.whitehouse.gov/news/releases/2003/02/20030205-1.html (accessed February 2011); also see Security Council Res 1441 (8 November 2002).
133 Greenwood, above note 103.
134 Heathcote, 'Force, Feminism and the Security Council' SOAS School of Law Research Paper No. 06-2010, July 2010, available online at http://papers.ssrn.com/sol3/papers.cfm?abstract_id=1636887 (last accessed February 2011).

this right of self-defence shall be immediately reported to the Security Council and shall not in any way affect the authority and responsibility of the Security Council under the present Charter to take at any time such action as it deems necessary in order to maintain or restore international peace and security.

The existence of a right of states to act in self-defence is perceived as a customary international law right preserved in Article 51 of the Charter.[135] Past treaties, such as the Kellogg–Briand Pact, and state practice, notably the *Caroline* Incident of 1837,[136] are often invoked to explain the preservation of the right and the necessity of the continuance of a right of states to act in self-defence, as well as the contours of the right, in the UN era. The pedigree of Article 51 self-defence is often underscored by references to writers as far back as Augustine, St Thomas of Aquinas, Grotius, Vattel and Vitoria, to name a few.[137] Each of these authors then comes to play a role in the Western narrative on the use of force, establishing the timelessness of aggression between states and the capacity of international law to recognise some acts of force as justified. For example, Vattel is recorded as writing:

'[a] nation has the right to resist the injury another seeks to inflict upon it, and to use force . . . against the aggressor. It may even anticipate the other's design, being careful, however, not to act upon vague or doubtful suspicions, lest it should run the risk of becoming itself the aggressor'.[138]

One of the tasks of the book is to consider how justifications for force, such as that used in self-defence, gain credibility through international legal narratives that invoke certain criteria to underpin their normativity. Historical narratives play a role in grounding the continued resonance of the self-defence justification.[139] My interest is in how analogies with interpersonal self-defence play a role in international legal accounts to explain the existence of the right of states to use defensive force. This can be traced back at least as far as Grotius who finds that the right of states to act in self-defence is self-evident through analogy with the right of individuals to act in self-defence as, 'we shall hold to this principle, that by nature every one is the defender of his own rights; that is why hands were given us'.[140] Grotius's analogy and texts continue to be utilised in contemporary accounts that also seek to demonstrate the self-defence analogy with interpersonal self-defence. As a consequence, the perceived self-evidence of individuals to repel attacks on their bodily integrity is often granted by analogy to states to repel attacks on their territorial integrity.

In contrast to approaches that take for granted the self-evidence of an individual's right to act in self-defence (assuming the act meets tests of proportionately and

---

135 *Nicaragua* Case, above note 2, at paragraph 176, 191–195.
136 See Jennings, 'The Caroline and McLeod Cases,' 32, *AJIL* (1938).
137 O'Connell, above note 87, at 106–126.
138 De Vattel, *The Law of Nations*, Vol IV, at 3 (1758).
139 O'Connell, above note 87, chapter one; Detter, I., *The Law of War* (Cambridge: Cambridge University Press, 2000); Dinstein, *War, Aggression and Self-defence* (Cambridge: Cambridge University Press, 2001, 3rd edition), at 163–165; also see, Kinsella, 'Gendering Grotius,' 34 (2), *Political Theory* (2006), 161.
140 Grotius, *On Law of War and Peace*, Book I, chapter III (1814) at: http://www.constitution.org/gro/djbp.htm (last accessed February 2011), paragraph 1, 102.

necessity), feminist legal scholars have exposed the central role of legal self-defence in the perpetuation and construction of a masculine 'normal' subject in Western legal systems.[141] It is this feminist engagement with the particularity and exclusionary nature of the interpersonal justification of self-defence that I test against the international justification of self-defence. I argue that the sexed and gendered features of self-defence replicated in Article 51 are not limited to the Charter: the paradigm of a sexed state exercising rational force in a controlled and proportionate manner is enhanced by customary law justifications. This is in part through the features of self-defence (proportionality and necessity) that mirror interpersonal limits on self-defence and are extended under international law to other forms of justified force and is in part due to contemporary understandings of how force is able to protect a population or a state.[142]

Beyond the domestic analogy, I analyse Article 51 through reference to the defence of Kuwait in 1991. This has been described by Western commentators as a 'textbook case' of self-defence.[143] The Iraqi aggression was, mainstream narratives tell us, controlled and defended through the application of proportionate force.[144] That Article 51 defined self-defence is found to have occurred in a single event in the history of the UN Charter, despite state attempts to accommodate a range of other events within Article 51, calls that system into question. This is acknowledged by the increasing references to preemptive force and humanitarian interventions, yet enlarged models of justificatory force given voice in the West embed Article 51 in the narrative as central, useful and illustrative of a state's capacity to use force in a controlled way. I argue that, far from suggesting a shift away from the self-defence paradigm, twenty-first century narratives reinforce the relevance and persistence of Article 51 self-defence. By looking at conflicts often outside the Western gaze, particularly conflicts in Africa, a very different understanding of conflict is illuminated.[145] Although the text only peripherally engages non-Western understandings and strategies for challenging armed conflict, non-Western approaches provide evidence of the failure of the West to shift from a narrative of 'the hero's quest'[146] to the slow path to peace. The hero's walk is an excellent description of the predominant Western understanding of force as it identifies a Western hero that is male and that uses violence under international law without cultural or gender sensitivity.[147] The central concern of this text is with exposing the sexed and gendered nature of the international legal narratives on force. The cultural insensitivity of this narrative is thus a secondary, although no less important, theme.[148]

---

141 See, for example, Jacobs and Ogle, *Self-Defense and Battered Women Who Kill: A New Framework* (New York: Praeger, 2002); *R v. Lavalee*, [1990] 1, S.C.R.

142 Chinkin, 'The Legality of NATO's Action in the Former Yugoslavia (FRY) under International Law', 49 (4), *International and Comparative Law Quarterly* (2000), 910.

143 O'Connell, above note 87, at 2.

144 Greenwood, 'International Humanitarian Law', in Evans, *International Law* (2006), at 792–793.

145 See, for example, Mgbeoji, *Collective Insecurity* (Vancouver, BC: British Columbia Press, 2004).

146 Orford, above note 62, at 67.

147 Buchanan and Johnson, above note 62, at 157–158.

148 Note, however, Murphy's discussion of the accommodation of difference in feminist legal theories, Murphy, 'Feminism Here and Feminism There: Law, Theory and Choice', in Buss and Manji, above note 12.

In chapter three, I consider how the self-defence justification, contained in Article 51 of the UN Charter, functions alongside of the Article 2(4) prohibition on the use of force to replicate a model of behaviour drawn from interpersonal relations and projected onto states as international legal subjects. The following three chapters test this contention against contemporary developments with respect to the use of force to support self-determination struggles,[149] humanitarian intervention[150] and the use of preemptive force in the pursuit of terrorist actors.[151] Each of these chapters also provides arguments for the re-conceptualisation of international law on the use of force; either through a further extension of the domestic analogy (as in chapter five on humanitarian intervention) or through the elevation of alternative narratives (as in chapter four on self-determination). The analysis of the use of force against terrorist actors is presented in chapter six; however, this is developed alongside the recognition (in chapter three on self-defence) that contemporary narratives on preemptive force and the global war against terrorists function to disguise the sexed and gendered narratives in the international law on the use of force. In this sense, the arguments in response to the US use of force against terrorist actors remain important to demonstrate the reach of sex and gender in contemporary accounts of war and law but are not the primary contention.

The use of force in the era of global terrorism

Chapter six, the concluding chapter, reflects on the overall conclusions of this book and what they mean for future feminist approaches to international law and for the international law on the use of force. I argue that feminist approaches can play a central role in the re-conceptualisation of the international law on the use of force. Such re-conceptualisation pivots on strengthening the prohibition on violence and on force. Integral to this development is the insertion of feminist dialogues on natality, on women's participation and on the inclusion of alternative narratives. The argument does not project these as simple or even complete answers, rather as starting points for future feminist and mainstream dialogues that seek to disrupt the law–gender–violence paradigms that lead to women's oppression, insecurity and discrimination. Underlying this conclusion is the knowledge that feminist legal projects must work 'within' accepted legal paradigms/narratives as well as from a position 'outside' mainstream projections of law.

---

149 See General Assembly Resolution 1514; for discussion, see: Crawford, *The Creation of States in International Law* (Oxford: Oxford University Press, 2nd edition, 2006), at 135, Crawford lists four different situations where the relationship between self-determination and the use of force must be considered.

150 For a survey of issues and opinions, see: Holzgrefe and Keohane, *Humanitarian Intervention: Ethical, Legal and Political Dilemmas* (Cambridge: Cambridge University Press, 2003); International Commission on Intervention and State Sovereignty, *The Responsibility to Protect* (Ottawa, ON: International Development Research Centre, December 2001).

151 Byers, 'Terrorism, the Use of Force and International Law after 11 September', 14, *EJIL* (2003), 227; Taft and Buchwald, 'Preemption, Iraq, and International Law', 97, *AJIL* (2003), 557; Reisman and Armstrong, 'The Past and Future of the Claim of Preemptive Self-Defense', 100 (3) *AJIL* (2006), 525.

Of particular concern in chapter six, is the unanswered question of whether the use of force could, or should, be justified under a feminist approach. Although some feminist approaches have answered this in the affirmative, for example, in response to the widespread sexual violence in the former Yugoslavia during the 1990s, this remains an under-analysed aspect of feminist legal theories.[152] Returning to the domestic analogy, feminist advocacy within domestic legal structures have persistently argued for recognition of the use of fatal violence by survivors of intimate partner abuse as a legal justification. I do not argue that a parallel enlargement of justifications for state force would be a useful feminist development. This is because underlying the domestic feminist claim for recognition of battered women who kill is an acceptance that state strategies to halt domestic violence are inadequate. On the international plane, I argue, before justifications for the use of force can be analysed from a feminist perspective recognition needs to be given to the relationship between law, gender and violence. This is in contrast to contemporary developments in the collective security structure that have recently indicated the possibility of the use of force to challenge violations of women's rights, particularly Security Council resolutions 1820 and 1888 on women, peace and security and Security Council resolution 1807 on the possibility of the use of targeted sanctions against perpetrators of sexual violence in the Democratic Republic of the Congo.[153]

The justifications for the use of force analysed in the book are not the only justifications that states make when using military force on the territory of another state. Nor are state justifications always clearly articulated. Furthermore, state justifications are often argued in the alternative rather than presented as straightforward or as isolated reasons for the deployment of force. The pleadings of NATO states before the ICJ in the *Legality of the Use of Force* preliminary proceedings illustrate the range of perceptions different states take with regard to their justifications for using force even when acting in concert.[154] Some of the justifications that remain outside the focus of the book include the use of force with the consent (or invitation) of the state whose territory the force is deployed within,[155] armed reprisals,[156] countermeasures,[157] protecting nationals abroad[158] and intervention into civil wars.[159]

---

152 Above note, 57.
153 SC Res 1820, 18 June 2008, on women, peace and security in operative paragraph one '*expresses its readiness*, when considering situations on the agenda of the Council, to, where necessary, adopt appropriate steps to address widespread or systematic sexual violence'; SC Res 1807 (31 March 2008); see further chapter two for discussion of these resolutions.
154 *Legality of the Use of Force* (Provisional Measures), ICJ Reports 1999 compare the written submission of the Kingdom of Belgium (setting out a doctrine of humanitarian intervention) with that of the United States (listing a variety of justifications) for further discussion see Gray, above note 87 (3rd edition), at 45–46.
155 For an indication of the range of state claims in this area, see: Gray, above note 87 (3rd edition), chapter 3.
156 Dinstein, *War, Aggression and Self-defense* (Oxford: Oxford University Press, 2001, 3rd edition) at 194–195 describing armed reprisals as 'measures of counter-force, short of war, undertaken by one state against another in response to an earlier violation'.
157 See Franck, above note 58, chapter 8.
158 Ibid. chapter 6.
159 Above note 87 (3rd edition), chapter 3; ibid. chapters 4 and 5.

With respect to the international law on the use of force, I make some specific recommendations, for example, advocating a focus on strategies that reinforce the value and purpose of the prohibition on force rather than a focus on justifications for violence. I make such recommendations with caution and with awareness that legal reform will always be circumscribed by the sexed and gendered discourse that unconsciously informs the self-perceptions of humans across communities, states and cultures. I also consider the two-way impact of force; on states using force as well as on states that are the sites of conflict. I argue that until Western states fully engage with the destructive (sexed and gendered) consequences of military behaviour within our own communities we will remain blind to the failure of force as an enforcement mechanism.[160] In this sense, the larger purpose of the book is to advance Western self-reflection on the assumptions integral to our narratives of law, violence and gender and how we, as Western citizens, often come to international law projecting those assumptions as universals. By identifying the sexed and gendered contours of the international law on the use of force, a key particular masked as a universal is exposed, challenged and re-imagined.

160   Weil, 'The Iliad, or the Poem of Force', in Weil *et al.*, *War and the Iliad* (New York: New York Review Books, 2005, first published 1945).

2 Collective security

This chapter analyses the collective security regime administered by the UN Security Council under chapter VII of the UN Charter. The Security Council is empowered to identify threats to the peace, breaches of the peace and acts of aggression under Article 39, to mandate measures short of force under Article 41 and to authorise the use of force under Article 42 of the Charter. Chapter VII of the UN Charter also envisages a UN standing force under Article 43, and a military staff committee under Articles 44–47. While these articles have not been developed in the sense intended, Security Council and state practice has established, and entrenched, a working model of collective security across the UN era and significantly since 1990. Thorough analysis of this model, and the contingencies of state practice, is available elsewhere.[1] The purpose of the analysis in this book is to engage the Charter-derived rules on collective security and the practice of the Security Council with feminist arguments on the structural limitations of contemporary legal arrangements.

I argue that the strengthening of the collective security structure through Security Council practices entrenches the perceived relevance on military structures for nation states. The authorisation of force under Article 42 measures, and also the use of Article 41 to instigate sanctions, enhances unilateral state justifications for the use of force. This is demonstrated through the Security Council practice of widening the category of threats, under Article 39, and the extension of the subjects of sanctions, under Article 41. I argue that these practices have enhanced state claims for legitimate humanitarian interventions and the legality of targeted strikes against terrorist actors, as well as in the larger sense that military action can provide security within a community.

I also argue that the advent of collective security initiatives by the Security Council on women, peace and security, while addressing some aspects of women's rights or liberal feminist agendas, must be regarded as the initiation of a dialogue rather than a comprehensive feminist law reform. This is demonstrated through analysis of Security Council resolution 1807 which has seen individuals listed under the UN sanction regime for complicity in widespread and systematic sexual violence perpetrated in

---

1 Frowein and Krisch, 'Chapter VII' in Simma, *The Charter of the United Nations* (Oxford: Oxford University Press, 2002, 2nd edition); Lowe, Roberts, Welsh and Zaum, The *United Nations Security Council and War: The Evolution of Thought and Practice since 1945* (Oxford: Oxford University Press, 2008).

the Democratic Republic of Congo (DRC). The shift towards inclusion of sexual violence as a trigger for Security Council action is the beginning of feminist debates rather than the conclusion of feminist dialogues, on both the capacity of the Security Council to provide security for women and on the diversity of women's needs and experiences.

A feminist analysis of collective security challenges the perpetuation of force as the ultimate enforcement tool in the international legal structure. I argue that this allows the United Nations to avoid strengthening alternative methods for challenging the behaviour of states and ignores the impact of military behaviour on women within any community. In this chapter, section two is an analysis of the threshold for chapter VII action contained in Article 39 of the UN Charter. Section three is an analysis of Article 41, on measures short of force. Section four provides an analysis of Article 42 of the UN Charter, on authorised force through a focus on the sex industries in the Republic of Korea (ROK) that are adjacent to US bases. Section five concludes the chapter with an analysis of post-millennium institutional narratives on collective security and the role of peacekeeping operations as an alternative to force, contrasting these with feminist approaches.

Article 39

This section begins the analysis of the relationship between international law and force through an examination of the acts, identified in Article 39 of the UN Charter, that trigger chapter VII authorised force (Article 42) or measures short of force (Article 41). Article 39 grants the Security Council the power to determine the existence of threats to the peace, breaches of the peace and acts of aggression for the purpose of initiating chapter VII acts. Article 39 states:

> The Security Council shall determine the existence of any threat to the peace, breach of the peace, or act of aggression and shall make recommendations, or decide what measures shall be taken in accordance with Article 41 and 42 to maintain or restore international peace and security.

The security narrative produced through the application of Article 39 can be described as particularised in two ways. In the first, application of Article 39 is developed from jurisprudence that forms Western liberal philosophical accounts of law. Second, like Western liberalism, the narrative is particularised through the reliance on a historically male form of legal subjectivity. Both of these assumptions are linked to the model of law that utilises violence at the apex of enforcement and pivot around the state as the primary international legal subject whose sovereignty mirrors that of individuals within domestic systems. While the international legal structure is variously described as 'horizontal'[2] or consensus driven, the function of chapter VII is to shift the auto-enforcement powers of states to the collective regime. This shift from state

---

2 Cassese, *International Law* (Oxford: Oxford University Press, 2003), at 5.

enforcement powers to a collective security structure is an important component of the international legal structure asserting its legitimacy through the control of force (violence). Liberal constructions of citizenship – derived from the Western notion of the family headed by a patriarch – profoundly inform constructions of international sovereignty giving the international a platform of assumptions that sex the security structure.[3] Despite the changing understanding of sovereignty produced in response to internal state violations[4] and non-Western theoretical accounts of state power,[5] traditional conceptions of sovereignty continue to inform the construction of the law on the use of force. Traditional conceptions of sovereignty produce a model of security where states, as sovereign citizens in the international order, are produced as actors analogous to the Western, liberal (masculine) subject requiring analogous forms of policing.

Post-millennium discourse on the impact of transnational networks – for example, in the fields of finance, security, media and human rights – have played a role in providing legitimacy to the strengthening of state boundaries, powers and control rather than negating the role of the state. Although transnational threats and movements are regarded as undermining the state in significant ways, the response in the field of collective security has been a re-affirmation of the role of the state as a bulwark against the excesses of transitional and global networks.[6] The existence of states is a necessary pre-condition of the collective security regime, which shifts the site of legitimate violence to the collective enforcement body. Thus, Gardam finds 'the appropriate analogy from national law is . . . the rules regulating the use of collective force by representatives of the State, such as the police. With some notable exceptions, most jurisdictions place legal restraints on the amount of force that may be used by such individuals in their public capacity'.[7] However, in addition to the restraints on police powers, omissions in police action continue to define the risk of violence in the lives of many women. Within the international system, similar omissions of action apply and define threats to women's security as outside of international legal and political concern.

---

3 Note, I am writing here of the mainstream Western narrative on force, rather than an inherent quality of the law on the use of force. This reflects my concern with the situated subject and the need for Western feminists to reflect and analyse the status quo of their own culture; see the discussion of culture and gender in chapter one.

4 Evans, Sahnoun, *et al.*, *The Responsibility to Protect*, Report of the International Commission on Intervention and State Sovereignty (Ottawa, ON: International Development Research Centre, Canada, December 2001).

5 Anghie, 'Finding the Peripheries: Sovereignty and Colonialism in Nineteenth Century International Law', 40, *Harvard International Law Journal* (1999), 1.

6 Graham, *Cities under Siege: the New Military Urbanism*, Verso, 2010; however, this has affirmed the boundaries of powerful states while fragmenting the sovereignty of less powerful states, also see: Anghie, *Imperialism, Sovereignty and the Making of International Law* (Cambridge: Cambridge University Press, 2006).

7 Gardam, 'Legal Restraints on Military Enforcement Action', 17, *Michigan Journal of International Law* (1996) 285, at 306; Frowein and Krisch, above note 1, at 721 stating 'chapter VII confers upon the Security Council solely a police function'.

In this section, I argue that the widening of the category of threats by the Security Council under Article 39 has led to the expansion of unilateral state justifications for the use of force by states. This claim appears counter-intuitive as it would be expected that a strengthening of the range of situations that the Council is prepared to act should strengthen the collective security structure and diminish state arguments for self-help. Yet the articulation of new threats – to human security and notably in response to internal conflicts and humanitarian crises within a state – by the Security Council has underpinned state justifications for the use of force on similar grounds.

In 2008, the Security Council asserted its readiness to use any means necessary to challenge widespread and systematic sexual violence that impedes the restoration of international peace and security.[8] On the one hand, this represents recognition of the advocacy and activism of feminist scholars who, since the atrocious sexual violence in the Former Yugoslavia and before, have campaigned for recognition of the specific harm women experience during armed conflict.[9] On the other hand, and as I argue in this chapter, the use of force to combat a wider range of threats, including widespread and systematic sexual violence, overlooks feminist analysis that challenges military force as a perpetuation of gendered inequalities[10] and challenges the use of military force under international law as a structurally limited understanding of global governance.[11] As such, I argue there is a need to sever the law–force relationship to conceive of alternative means and methods for challenging widespread and systematic violence against men and women, including sexual violence. I argue that feminist approaches that seek to engage and understand peace, feminism anti-militarism and a politics of natality are best placed for the pursuit of new understandings.

Threats to the peace, breaches of the peace and acts of aggression

Unlike Article 2(4) that prohibits the threat of *force*, Article 39 invokes Security Council action in response to any threat to the *peace*. This is significant, as it suggests while only threats that are associated with armed force are prohibited, collective enforcement action may attempt to curb a much wider category of behaviour. The capacity to broaden the nature of threats has been a feature of Security Council action apparent in the history of Article 39's application. Throughout its history the Security Council has developed the understanding of the phrase 'threats to international peace and security' to include violence internal to a state. For example, the Security Council in Resolution 221 authorised the use of force to secure the embargo on oil tankers finding breaches of the embargo would constitute a threat to the peace. This was to

8 SC Res 1820 (18 June 2008); also see SC Res 1888 (30th September 2009) and SC Res 1960 (16 December 2010).

9 Stiglmayer (ed.), *Mass Rape: The War against Women in Bosnia–Herzegovina* (Lincoln, NE: University of Nebraska Press, 1994).

10 Enloe, *Maneuvers: The International Politics of Militarising Women's Lives* (Berkeley, CA: University of California Press, 2000); Cockburn, and Zarkov (eds), *The Postwar Moment: Militaries, Masculinities and International Peacekeeping* (London: Lawrence and Wishart, 2002); Al-Ali, and Pratt, *What Kind of Liberation? Women and the Occupation in Iraq* (Berkeley, CA: University of California Press, 2009).

11 Charlesworth, 'International Law: A Discipline of Crisis', 65 (3), *Modern Law Review* (2002), 377.

support the sanctions regime instigated to challenge Ian Smith's government's attempt to control Southern Rhodesia.[12] Despite the internal nature of the political upheaval in Southern Rhodesia, the Security Council described the situation as a threat to international peace and security. In Resolution 232, of 16 December 1966, the Council defined the situation in Southern Rhodesia as a continued threat to international peace and security.[13]

The Security Council had previously invoked chapter VII and identified a threat to international peace and security in 1948 in resolution 54[14] in response to Israeli hostilities in Palestine and in 1963 labelled South African apartheid as 'seriously disturbing' international peace and security in resolution 181.[15] While in 1960, under resolutions 157[16] and 161[17] on the Congo, the Security Council had linked the civil war in the Congo to threats to international peace and security. In 1960 the Council emphasised the internal nature of the conflict in Southern Rhodesia and permitted the deployment of UN military actors without a mandate to use force, rather as a peacekeeping operation.[18] Before the authorisation of force by the Security Council in 1966 in Southern Rhodesia, these resolutions stretched the notion of threats to incorporate threats internal to a state yet refrain from authorising force as a response. The identification of a threat to the peace and the authorisation of the use of force to enforce the trade embargo against Southern Rhodesia in 1966 were therefore in line with the emerging jurisprudence of the Security Council, even if unimagined by the drafters of the UN Charter.

This broad use of Article 39 was replicated in the 1990s when the Cold War deadlock on the Council ended and the collective security system was able to operate extensively.[19] Importantly, the conflicts that invoked the collective security system after 1990 were primarily of an internal character, often humanitarian rather than military crises and assumed to be within Article 39 powers rather than clearly articulated as coming under Article 39 in resolutions.[20] For example, in 1991, in Resolution 688, the Security Council expressed grave concerns over 'the massive flows of

---

12 SC Resolution 221 (9 April 1966).
13 SC Res 232 (16 December 1966) 'Determines that the present situation in southern Rhodesia constitutes a threat to international peace and security'.
14 SC Res 54 (15 July 1948).
15 SC Res 181 (7 August 1963).
16 SC Res 157 (17 September 1960).
17 SC Res 161 (21 February 1960).
18 See SC Res 143 (17 July 1960) authorising 'military assistance as may be necessary' but clarifying in the subsequent resolution, 146 (9 August 1960), 'that the United Nations Force in the Congo will not be a party to or, in any way, intervene in or be used to influence the outcome of any internal conflict' in Operative Paragraph 4; although this was adapted under SC Res 169 (24 November 1961) to include authorised force 'in consultation with the Government of the Republic of the Congo'.
19 *Repertoire of the Practice of the Security Council*, 1989–992, chapter XI.
20 See SC Res 929 (Rwanda, 22 June 1994), 841 (Haiti, 16 June 1994), SC Res 1125 (Central African Republic, 6 August 1997), in each case the threat was of a non-international nature and consisted of a humanitarian rather than military crisis. Security Council responses to Somalia and Liberia in Resolution 794 (3 December 1992) and Res 813 (26 March 1993) respectively, refer to a threat to peace and security in the region rather than an international threat.

refugees towards and across international frontiers and instigated measures to protect the Kurdish population in Iraq'.[21] Similarly in 1993, Security Council resolutions identified the failure of the Libyan government to renounce terrorism as a threat to international peace and security.[22] While in 1994, the humanitarian crisis and internal violence in Haiti, after the removal of the elected government by a military coup, led to the Security Council's identification of a threat to regional peace and security, so that 'acting under chapter VII' the Council established a 'multinational force' with the power to 'use all means necessary' although the 'unique' and 'exceptional circumstances' were emphasised by the Council.[23] Security Council actions in Albania and in the Central African Republic in 1997 were also instigated under chapter VII powers. In these two situations the unrest was internal, and in the case of Albania in response to financial crisis, yet described as constituting, in both cases, 'a threat to peace and security in the region'.[24]

In the post-2000 security environment a similar broadening of the range of threats the Security Council has been prepared to respond to under Article 39 has occurred. Security Council resolutions in response to terrorist acts have resulted in a significant broadening of the scope of Article 39; as individual and non-state actors have been recognised as constituting threats to international peace and security within the scope of Article 39. Prior to the terrorist acts in the United States in September 2001, the Security Council had acknowledged that 'the suppression of terrorism is essential for the maintenance of international peace and security'[25] and, by 1999, had specifically identified the Taliban failure to comply with earlier resolutions challenging terrorist actors as constituting a threat to international peace and security.[26] In 2001– before the 9/11 attacks – the Security Council determined the situation in Afghanistan constituted a threat to international peace and security, at that stage emphasising humanitarian concerns and identifying resolution 1363 as a chapter VII resolution.[27] After the 9/11 terrorist attacks against the United States, the Security Council adapted the type of authorisations it issued – instigating the 1373 sanctions regime against terrorist actors[28] and later the International Security Assistance force for Afghanistan[29] – but the identification of the type of Article 39 trigger remains fairly muted as identification of the 'situation in Afghanistan still constitut[ing] a threat to international peace and security'.[30]

---

21 SC Res 688 (5 April 1991); although the Security Council did not authorise any action in this resolution it was later relied on by the US, the UK and France to justify the establish the non-fly zones in parts of Northern and Southern Iraq, see the discussion in Dinstein, *War, Aggression and Self-defence* (Cambridge: Cambridge University Press, 2005, 4th edition), 297.
22 SC Res 883 (11 November 1993).
23 SC Res 933 (30 June 1994) and SC Res 940 (31 July 1994).
24 See SC Res 1114 (Albania, 19 June 1997); SC Res 1125 (Central African Republic, 6 August 1997).
25 See SC Res 1214 (1998); also see SC Res 748 (31 March 1992), condemning the failure of the Libyan government to renounce terrorist actors.
26 SC Res 1267 (15 October 1999).
27 SC Res 1363 (30 July 2001).
28 SC Res 1373 (28 September 2001).
29 SC Res 1386 (20 December 2001).
30 SC Res 1386 (20 December 2001).

Security Council resolutions identifying internal conflicts and humanitarian crises as a threat to international peace and security were also maintained, albeit selectively, between 2000 and 2010. For example, the Security Council authorised a chapter VII force in Haiti in 2004, identifying 'the existence of challenges to the political, social and economic stability of Haiti and determining that the situation in Haiti continued to constitute a threat to peace and security in the region'.[31] Threats were also identified in Liberia and dealt with under chapter VII powers. In a comprehensive chapter VII resolution in 2003 and after identifying a threat to peace and security in the region, the Council decided, amongst other things, 'that all states shall take the necessary measures to prevent the import into their territories of all round logs and timber products originating in Liberia'.[32] In 2008 the Council supplemented its forces in Liberia with increased personnel after identifying a continued threat to international peace and security.[33] The border violence in the sub-region containing the Sudan, Chad and the Central African Republic has also been described by the Council as constituting a threat to international peace and security. The Council began with the construction of a 'multidimensional presence' in eastern Chad and north-eastern Central African Republic[34] and subsequently authorised a chapter VII use of force.[35] Although this is a selective account of the Council's Article 39 determinations over this period, the increased activity of the Council across an increasing range of situations continues.

An example of the changing focus of the Security Council in its use of Article 39 threats is demonstrated by a review of the chapter VII resolution issued during the first six months of 2010. The Council began the eleventh year of the new millennium with a response to the catastrophic earthquake in Haiti, identifying the situation as 'dire circumstances in need of an urgent response'.[36] As a Security Council multinational force was already present in Haiti (MINUSTAH),[37] the Security Council supplemented MINUSTAH with increased personnel to deal with the consequences of the devastation caused by the earthquake. The Council also found the contravention of arms embargoes in Somalia and Eritrea as constituting a threat to international peace and security[38] and the pre-electoral violence in the Ivory Coast as a significant enough threat to international peace and security in the region to authorise a chapter VII use of force.[39] Over this same period the Council continued to identify the situation in the DRC as a threat to international peace and security,[40] although significant,

---

31 SC Res 1542 (30 April 2004).
32 SC Res 1521 (22 December 2003).
33 SC Res 1819 (18 June 2008), and SC Res 1836 (29 September 2008).
34 SC Res 1778 (25 September 2007).
35 Sc Res 1834 (2008), SC Res 1862 (14 January 2009).
36 SC Res 1908 (19 January 2010).
37 See SC Res 1529 (29 February 2004), SC Res 1542 (30 April 2004); the latter established the United Nations Stabilisation Mission in Haiti (MINUSTAH).
38 SC Res 1916 (19 March 2010).
39 SC Res 1911 (28 January 2010), SC Res 1927 (27 May 2010), SC Res 1933 (30 June 2010), SC Res 1951 (24 November 2010).
40 SC Res 1925 (28 May 2010).

widespread acts of sexual violence inflicted on large proportions of specific communities did not draw comment from the Security Council or action from UN military personnel in the region.[41] The range of issues the Security Council has incorporated in to the definition of threats to the peace across this period, even from a small cross-section of the actual resolutions issued, demonstrates the continued increase in the range of diverse situations (environmental, domestic unrest, arms transfer) the Council is incorporating with the understanding Article 39. However, the Security Council, while broadening the definition of threats, continues to remain selective in the situations on its agenda. For example, no response to the humanitarian disaster caused by floods in Pakistan in 2010 or, as noted above, to the sexual violence in the DRC was instigated in the Council nor did the escalation of violence in Indian Kashmir during 2010 draw recognition in terms of the threat posed.

Article 39 also uses the term 'breaches of the peace' as a threshold for Security Council action under chapter VII. The term 'breach of the peace' has rarely been utilised by the Security Council in its resolutions. Occasions when it has have been used include in response to North Korean force against South Korea in 1950, during the 1980s Iran–Iraq conflict, in response to the 1982 Argentinean invasion of the UK-occupied Falklands Islands and after the Iraq invasion of Kuwait in 1990.[42] These four instances stand in contrast to the actual uses of military force that could be said to have 'breached the peace' since the inception of the UN Charter.[43] For example, interstate conflicts in Armenia and Azerbaijan in 1993[44], in the Cameroon and Nigeria in 1994,[45] and in Ethiopia and Eritrea in 2000,[46] as well as the ongoing violence in Kashmir[47] have not led to Security Council identification of aggression or a breach of the peace, thus continuing the Cold War trend that saw the interests of powerful states dictate the range of violence that drew international attention. This was despite the cross-border nature of these conflicts.

---

41 See Report of the Secretary-General, S/2010/512 (8 October 2010).

42 SC Res 82 (7 July 1950) (Korea); SC Res 502 (3 April 1982) (Falkland Islands); SC Res 598 (20 July 1987) (Iraq–Iran).

43 For a detailed list see Franck, *Recourse to Force* (Cambridge: Cambridge University Press, 2003); for discussion see Gray, *The Use of Force and International Law* (Oxford: Oxford University Press, 2004, 2nd edition), at 204.

44 SC Res 822 (30 April 1993): 'Notes with alarm . . . the latest invasion of the Kelbadjar district of the Republic of Azerbaijan by local Armenian forces' while 'reaffirming also the inviolability of international borders and the inadmissibility of the use of force for the acquisition of territory'.

45 See *Case Concerning the Land and Maritime Boundary between Cameroon and Nigeria*, ICJ Reports (10 October 2002); in response to the Court's findings Nigeria withdraw its troops from the disputed region, the Bakassi Peninsula in 2006.

46 In SC Res 1297 (12 September 2000) and SC Res 1298 (17 September 2000) the Security Council identifies a threat to international peace and security in response to the hostilities between the two states, in subsequent resolutions the Council refrains from identifying any Article 39 breach other than referencing back to these two earlier resolutions, see, for example, SC Res 1312 (31 July 2000) establishing the UN Mission in Ethiopia and Eritrea.

47 See Bradnock, *Kashmir: Paths to Peace*, Chatham House Report (London: Royal Institute of International Affairs, 2010).

A breach of the peace may be regarded as less than an act of aggression yet more than a threat.[48] Considering the countless frontier incidents, belligerent reprisals, illegal occupations, armed conflicts, acts of political violence and political repression across the second half of the twentieth century (many of which have continued into the twenty first century) the development of this aspect of Article 39 by the Security Council appears limited. The absence of many conflicts from the list has, in part, to do with the consequences of finding an initiatory breach to trigger chapter VII powers, as well as the political nature of conflict and of the Council. The reluctance of the Security Council to identify breaches of the peace is connected to the implications of doing so, as either Article 41 or Article 42 action may be the next step. However, as a form of violence that is constituted as less than aggression, Article 39 breaches of the peace represent an area of undeveloped potential for the Security Council, where identification of a range of violent scenarios may be addressed without apportioning blame on a specific state. The linkage of Security Council identification of an act of aggression with the procedure for bringing investigations into crimes of aggression under the ICC statute further illustrates the usefulness of the Security Council utilising the breach of the peace classification in the future. While some authors argue the term 'breach of peace' is roughly equivalent to the term 'act of aggression' and thus both could render justifiable Article 51 self-defence,[49] this view rests on the reluctance of the Security Council to elaborate and develop understandings of what constitutes a breach of the peace and thus does not diminish the capacity for the Security Council to develop future practice in this area.[50]

The third element of Article 39 identifies acts of aggression as triggering chapter VII powers of the Security Council. The Security Council has, in the past, identified acts of aggression under Article 39 from three states: Israel, South Africa and Southern Rhodesia.[51] The scarcity of incidents is in part because identification of an act of aggression would initiate a state's right to individual and collective self-defence under Article 51 of the Charter. As many conflicts result in both parties to a conflict claiming self-defence, the Security Council has shown a reluctance to expressly grant the right of self- defence or to imply a right through the identification of an act of aggression.[52]

48 Although note the view of Dinstein: 'the Charter . . . does not provide any clear guidance in discriminating between the two expressions . . . it is of little consequence whether one stamp or the other is affixed to the measures taken' above note 21, at 288.

49 *Ibid.*, at 314.

50 For example, recent Security Council practice has been to explicitly state that the sanctions regime in place against Iran was not trigger for future authorised force; SC Res 1929 (9 June 2010) where the Security Council stresses 'that nothing in this resolution compels states to take measures or actions exceeding the scope of this resolution, including the use of force or the threat of the use of force'.

51 SC Res 573 (4 October 1985), 611 (25 April 1988) on Israel/ Tunisia, SC Res 387 (31 March 1976), 567 (20 June 1985), 571 (20 September 1985), 574 (7 October 1985) on South Africa/ Angola, 455 (23 November 1979) on Southern Rhodesia/ Zambia. Additionally, although commentators perceive the attacks in New York on 11 September 2001 as constituting an armed attack for the purposes of Article 51 self-defence, the Security Council, in Resolution 1368 defines the attacks as constituting a threat to international peace and security. The Resolution does, however, make reference to the right of states to use force in self-defence.

52 Also, note, when the Security Council has been bound through political stalemate the General Assembly has demonstrated a willingness to identify acts of aggression. For example, the General Assembly

The reluctance of the Security Council to identify acts of aggression, combined with the potential for political deadlocks amongst the permanent members of the Council, led the General Assembly to clarify the meaning of 'aggression' in 1975.[53] The General Assembly Definition of Aggression sets forth the type of acts that constitute unjustifiable aggression and has been accepted under the ICC statute as the appropriate definition of aggression for the purposes of prosecuting the crime of aggression. Article 3 of the General Assembly Definition includes invasion and attack by armed forces, military occupation, annexation of territory, blockade of ports or coastlines, bombardment or the use of any weapons against another state or its armed forces and the acts of armed bands, groups, irregulars and mercenaries which carry out acts of such gravity as to amount to the equivalent of any of the other components of the definition.[54] In Article 4, the General Assembly acknowledges this is not an exhaustive list. Despite being open-ended, the focus of Resolution 3314 is on military force and military behaviour.

The Definition of Aggression was accepted by state parties to the Statute for the International Criminal Court (ICC) in Kampala in 2010. State parties also accepted amendments to the Rome Statute that differentiated between Security Council identifications of acts of aggression and the crime of aggression. While Security Council identification of an act of aggression could trigger an investigation under the ICC this is to be separate to the finding of a crime of aggression which requires further evidence of the 'planning, preparation, initiation or execution by a person in a position of leadership of an act of aggression'.[55] The Security Council retains its power to identify acts of aggression and will continue to have the capacity to halt investigations into acts of aggression under Art 16 of the ICC Statute.[56] The final wording agreed at the 2010 ICC Review conference in Uganda reiterated the military and state centric view of aggression for the purposes of international criminal law and international law generally. Thus, incorporating a definition of aggression that defines aggression as state against state attacks and constituting a 'manifest violation of the Charter'.[57]

Although there has been limited identification of acts of aggression by the Security Council, the definition of aggression illustrates the state-centric, military under-

condemned the Israeli bombing of an Iraqi nuclear reactor in 1981 as an act of aggression in Resolution 36/27. The use of the term 'act of aggression' did draw criticism from some states that saw this as an impingement on Security Council powers and abstained from voting for the resolution. (1982 UNYB 425. GA Res 36/27 (109-2-34) 'condemns Israel for its premeditated and unprecedented act of aggression'). It should be noted that the resolution did recommend further Security Council action rather than attempting to replace Security Council action: in paragraph 5 the General Assembly 'Reiterates its request to the Security Council to institute effective enforcement action to prevent Israel from further endangering international peace and security'.
53   GA Res 3314, 14 December 1974.
54   *Military and Paramilitary Activities in and Against Nicaragua, Merits*, 1986 ICJ Reports 14, [henceforth *Nicaragua* case], paragraph 195.
55   Rome Statute of the International Criminal Court, Article 8bis.
56   Special Working Group on the Crime of Aggression, *Report of the Sixth Session*, 20 February, 2009, ICC-ASP/7/SWGCA/2; for discussion see, Weisbord, 'Prosecuting Aggression', 49, *Harvard International Law Journal* (2008) 162.
57   *Ibid.*, see Annex 1 of the Report.

standing of aggression under chapter VII and under ICC developments. In contrast, through its generous application of the notion of threats under Article 39 the Security Council has shifted away from its role as an arbiter of the external relationships between states and increasingly shown a willingness to interrogate the 'domestic' or internal acts of states. Humanitarian crises and civil conflicts have been brought to the attention of international institutions, as have arms sales and arms movement (Eritrea and Somalia), financial crises (Albania), natural disasters (Haiti), electoral processes (Ivory Coast) and the removal of a democratically elected government (Haiti), and have been defined as threats to international order under Article 39. In some cases, this has led to the authorisation of Articles 41 and Article 42 acts by the Security Council, that is, the use of measures short of force under Article 41 or the authorisation of force under Article 42. The internationalisation of crises internal to a state, however, has been selective and has developed in a way that does not impact significantly on the domestic structure of powerful states. Consequently, the limited definition of aggression, confined to interstate military force maintains state impunity for aggressive acts, particularly internal structural violence that targets civilian security through the negation of women's security. This has distinct consequences for the potential for violence against women to emerge on the international security agenda. Furthermore, the selective nature of interventions into internal disturbances/crises/conflict/unrest mimics the selective nature of interventions into domestic family violence within national legal structures, demonstrating how omissions to act, as well as choices to intervene, function to regulate both public and private spheres.[58]

In response to Article 39, and of concern to feminist approaches to international law, are questions of how the three categories of violence exclude aggressive state policies that dictate women's poverty, segregation, ill-health and death. Consequently, the destructive and fatal cost of Taliban policies for women in Afghanistan in the 1990s was not identified by either the Security Council or the General Assembly as aggression, as a threat to or a breach of the peace.[59] Although Security Council resolutions during the 1990s identified concerns over discrimination against women and girls in Afghanistan this limited recognition of the extent of Taliban practices – that were harmful and often deadly to women – teetered off as the sanctions regime, and later the use of force, against Afghanistan consolidated global responses to the 9/11 attacks. At no stage was the removal of women from public space, the denial of education and the denial of health services, the 'apartheid' system, that was overt and aggressive in Afghanistan, defined as an act of aggression or considered to be related to the subsequent threat to international peace and security posed by the Taliban harbouring of the terrorist organization, Al-Qaida.[60] Thus, legal scholarship emphasises the Taliban regime's complicity in terrorism, while the gross human rights abuses

58 See the discussion in Chapter five.
59 See, for example, SC Res 1363 (30 July 2001) and Perrin 'Women Banned from Kabul Hospitals', in Sassóli and Bouvier, *How Does Law Protect in War? Vol II Cases and Documents* (2nd edition, ICRC, 2006), at 2297.
60 See SC Res 1363 (30 July 2001); SC Res 1378 (14 November 2001).

directed at the population, particularly women, under the regime are downplayed as issues of discrimination or presented as historical.[61]

In contrast to the failure of the Security Council to connect the Taliban sexist apartheid with its complicity in terrorist attacks, in resolutions issued by the Security Council from 1976 through 1985, the acts of aggression that South Africa directed at neighbouring states were consistently linked with the racist apartheid regime within that state.[62] In early resolutions the link is implied. For example, in Resolution 387 (1976) the Council condemns South African attacks on Angola as acts of aggression and condemns the apartheid structure separately in a resolution that follows, stating, 'the policy of apartheid is a crime against conscience and dignity of mankind (sic) and seriously disturbs international peace and security'.[63] By 1985 the link is explicitly stated by the Council. The preamble to Resolution 577 states, 'these wanton acts of aggression by the minority racist regime in South Africa form a consistent and sustained pattern'.[64] Unlike the linkage of the South African history of apartheid and external aggression, the Taliban internal policy of aggression against women and the harbouring of terrorists have not been explicitly linked in legal instruments. However, the Afghan reality joins studies of pre-conflict indicators[65] and four decades of feminist scholarship that acknowledges the role violence against women, as an aggressive state policy, plays in undermining international peace and security.[66]

The domestic analogy

Feminist theory identifies the 'domestic' or private acts of a state as aligned with the private sphere of liberalism that is traditionally left unregulated by the legal structure. However, feminist legal theory also exposes the fallacy of this aspect of liberalism by highlighting the range of interferences that the liberal state has always conducted in the 'private' sphere.[67] The overt claim of international law, as governing the external relations between states, is challenged by the range of interferences by the international legal structure, through the actions of the Security Council, into the internal (domestic) activities of the state, and (more recently) through Article 41 measures

---

61   For example, Gray's account makes no mention of the Taliban's oppressive gender apartheid, despite the obvious legacy this will have on attempts to re-structure Afghan political and social infrastructure, see Gray, International Law and the use of Force (Cambridge: Cambridge University Press, 2008, 3rd edition), 341–342; Greenwood, 'International Law and the Preemptive Use of Force: Afghanistan, Al-Qaida and Iraq', 4, *San Diego International Law Journal* (2003), 7; Franck, above note 43; compare to the approach of Charlesworth and Chinkin, 'Sex, Gender and September 11', 96 (3), *AJIL* (2002), 600.

62   This is not to suggest the impact of racist state policy can be simply aligned with state orchestrated or tolerated gendered oppression, nor to ignore the complex inter-relationship and overlap of racialised and gendered violence.

63   SC Res 392 (19 June 1976).

64   SC Res 577 (6 December 1985).

65   Schmeidl, *Gender and Conflict Early Warning: A Framework for Action*, International Alert, June 2002.

66   Morgan, *The Demon Lover* (London: Piaktus, 2001, 2nd edition), chapter two; also see: also see Amis, *The Second Plane* (London: Jonathon Cape, 2008) connecting the masculine violence of the 9/11 terrorists with negation of female citizenship common to religious fundamentalism, at 19, 49.

67   Lacey, *Unspeakable Subjects* (Oxford: Hart, 1997), 73–78.

that target individuals. However, any gains achieved from bringing the 'private' or 'domestic' into the realm of international legal regulation are countered by the confines of the system that continues to marginalise actors that fail the test of statehood. Therefore, while the Security Council has given the appearance of broadening the scope of Article 39, at least with respect to threats, this application generally rests on the assumption that the threat must be to a state and to the continued capacity of the state under attack to exist.[68] The 'broadening' of Article 39, under this analysis, plays a role in perpetuating in international law the flaws of liberalism identified by Western feminist accounts, that is, the Security Council's approach to threats under Article 39 may remove some boundaries but maintains a boundary between public and private regulation that is sexed.

In a similar manner, the *In Larger Freedom* Report uses the concept of human security to enlarge the list of threats to international peace and security that falls within the purview of international law. The Report was constructed by the then Secretary-General, Kofi Annan, to address the success and implementation of the Millennium Development goals five years after their construction and to preface the Millennium Outcomes document that state parties were to vote on later in 2005.[69] The Report states that:

> The threats to peace and security in the twenty-first century include not just international war and conflict but civil violence, organized crime, terrorism and weapons of mass destruction. They also include poverty, deadly infectious disease and environmental degradation since these can have equally catastrophic consequences . . . .[70]

The *In Larger Freedom* Report develops the recommendations of the earlier report, *A More Secure World*, commissioned by the Secretary-General and constructed by a high-level panel of experts. *A More Secure World* describes a threat as 'any event or process that leads to large-scale death or lessening of life chances and undermines *States* as the basic unit of the international system'.[71] This appears to mimic and consolidate the proclivity of the Security Council to see threats to the peace as more than cross-border aggression. Yet this attempt to utilise the concept of human security within the collective security system ties potential threats to the existence of the state.

---

68 The establishment of no-fly zones to protect the Kurdish people in northern Iraq stands as isolated example, although the Security Council did not explicitly authorise the use of force, see McDonald, 'Self-determination and Kurdish Women', in Mojab, *Women of a Non-state Nation* (Costa Mesa, CA: Mazda, 2001).

69 See: http://www.un.org/millenniumgoals/ (last accessed February 2011); GA Resolution A/Res/60/1 2005 [henceforth the World Summit Outcome].

70 Report of the Secretary-General, *In Larger Freedom: Towards development, security and human rights for all*, 2 March 2005, A/59/2005 (henceforth *In Larger Freedom*], paragraph 78.

71 Report of the Secretary-General's High Level Panel on Threats, Challenges and Change, *A More Secure World: Our Shared Responsibility*, 2 December 2004, UN Doc A/59/565, at 12 [italics added] and page 15, which states, 'we all know all too well that the biggest security threats we face now, and in the decades ahead, go far beyond states waging aggressive war'.

Widespread violence against women, while able to fulfil the first aspect of this test, fails the second test because violence against women is not perceived as undermining the primacy of the state in the international system. Violence against women, both during and outside of officially recognised armed conflicts, tends to occur in private and is, consequently, cast as an offence against the individual rather than the group.[72] In fact, feminist texts challenging global violence against women specifically seek to re-imagine the state in international relations, often arguing the state may be a barrier to the eradication of violence against women.[73]

In addition, social, cultural and political norms combine to construct a large proportion of violence against women as occurring within the private domain and this is then represented in legal norms as 'normal'. These intertwined sets of norms may particularise in individual communities yet they have global consistency. This intersection of social norms and cultural norms with political and legal norms, consequently, creates a specifically gendered form of 'domestic', 'private' and 'cultural' harms that are invisible to political and legal regulation.[74] Feminist activism within domestic legal structures within the West has shifted towards preventative strategies that seek to arrest women's social and cultural vulnerability while also working to change legal cultures so that outcomes cease to be measured through sentencing levels. These types of strategies are regarded as tackling violence against women more effectively than strategies solely centred on legal remedies.[75] The nexus between individual women's experiences of insecurity and insecurity within and between states remains outside of the collective security regime's engagements with regard to the concept of threats. The consequence is violence against women remains tethered to the private sphere, despite the role the public sphere plays in producing the conditions for the toleration and perpetuation of gendered violence within a state, as well as across states.

For example, the UN Secretary-General's High Level Panel report, *A More Secure World*, when considering human security, identifies six major threats to international peace and security: economic and social threats (including poverty, infectious diseases and environmental degradation), inter-state conflict, internal conflict, nuclear, radiological, chemical and biological weapons, terrorism and transnational organised crime. Focus on just one aspect of these threats: poverty, illustrates how the understanding of threats developed by UN institutions, in assuming the state as the basic unit of international relations, ignores how these threats affect women in a different

---

72 See Valchová and Biason (eds), *Women in an Insecure World* (Geneva: DCAF, 2005).

73 Knop, 'Re/statements: Feminism and Sovereignty in International Law', 3 *Transnational Law and Contemporary Problems* (1993), 293, at 308, 316.

74 However, note the readiness of the international community to respond to transnational organized crime, UN Convention Against Transnational Organised Crime, GA Doc. 55/25, 15 November 2000 (entered into force 29 September 2003). For a UN wide strategy on challenging violence against women, see *Secretary-General In-depth Study of All Forms of Violence against Women*, 9 October, 2006, A/61/122/Add.1. The Report does not contain specific recommendations for the Security Council to act on.

75 Ursel, 'The Possibilities of Criminal Justice Intervention in Domestic Violence: A Canadian Case Study', 8(3), *Current Issues Criminal Justice* (1997), 263; see further the discussion of strategies to halt domestic family violence in Chapter five.

way from how they affect men. International data suggests, of the 100 million people who live in extreme poverty, the overwhelming percentage are women.[76] In *A More Secure World*, there is a failure to identify the nexus between sex and poverty, or what other UN Reports label the 'Feminisation of Poverty'.[77] The Report, within the discussion of poverty, twice makes specific reference to women, first, as at risk of maternal mortality when living in poverty,[78] and second, through a reference to gender equality in the list of 'ambitious but feasible' goals of the UN Millennium Declaration (later the Millennium Development Goals).[79]

The post-2000 Security Council agenda on women, peace and security, discussed below, further emphasises the limited identification of women as legal subjects under the collective security regime. While the initial Security Council resolution 1325,[80] in 2000, is wide ranging in its identification of the issues pertinent to peace and security – including the need to increase women's participation and education and for the eradication of violence against women in conflict zones – the subsequent two resolutions on women, peace and security focus on women as sexually vulnerable actors in armed conflict.[81] The fourth resolution is broader in scope;[82] however, there remains a failure to identify broader threats to international peace and security – such as those identified by the reports, *A More Secure World* and *In Larger Freedom* – as also containing a gendered perspective. For example, women's disproportionate vulnerability to poverty, experienced by women in all states due to gendered expectations with respect to women's role across social forms, are not considered in the resolutions on women, peace and security. The fifth resolution, issued in December 2010, returns the focus of the women, peace and security agenda to sexual violence.[83]

In missing the opportunity to see poverty as a gendered problem that disproportionately affects women, *A More Secure World* exposes the sexed assumptions the international security dialogues function within, which represent threats to international peace and security as gender neutral. By failing to incorporate recognition of women as the main victims of poverty, *A More Secure World* is unlikely to lead to tangible strategies for hearing the needs of those who face the extreme consequences of poverty: women. Furthermore, the consequential threats that women face during conflict can often be linked to their vulnerability as economic actors. The oblique references to maternal health and gender equality expose the limited normative perceptions of the collective security system, as there is a failure to see women as more than mothers or statistics. This approach is replicated in the later report from the Secretary-General, *In Larger Freedom*.[84]

76 Above note 71, at page 26 (quoting 100 million people living in extreme poverty); also see, UN Fourth World Conference on Women, *Beijing Platform for Action*, September 1995, paragraph 47.
77 *Ibid.* paragraph 48.
78 *A More Secure World*, above note 71.
79 Above note 71, at 28 (paragraph 57); the Report goes on to acknowledge in paragraph 59 'Little has been done to address the gender aspects of the Millennium Development Goals'.
80 SC Res 1325 (30 October 2000).
81 SC Res 1820 (18 June 2008) and SC Res 1888 (30 September 2009).
82 SC Res 1889 (5 October 2009).
83 SC Res 1960 (16 December 2010).
84 Above note 70.

Under this analysis, what is implicit in the past action of the Security Council is made explicit in the recent reports from the Secretary-General and the five Security Council resolutions on women, peace and security. That is, while the international system is able to accommodate a broad range of threats to international peace and security, and invoke chapter VII powers as a consequence, there continues to be a weighted assumption that the threat must be to a state. The incorporation of a division between legal subjects with standing to invoke the collective enforcement mechanisms and legal subjects without access to the Security Council chambers reflects a sexing of the international legal subject of the state. Women, by definition, exist outside *and* within the structure of the state. As a consequence women are 'theoretically' given access to the international security structures through the vehicle of the state, yet the poverty of actual representation of women in state institutions ultimately mitigates against this facilitating reforms that comprehensively challenge violence against women. As such, threats to women are not usually perceived as threats to the continued existence of the state.

After the conclusion of Kofi Annan's period as Secretary-General of the United Nations, the production of broad-ranging reports addressing the flaws of the collective security structure have emerged in the work of the General Assembly (rather than the Security Council) and little consensus has emerged, although the 2009 General Assembly debates on the 'Responsibility to Protect' demonstrated a concern of state parties to return to the issue of humanitarian intervention and the production of clearer norms and criteria for when such interventions might be acceptable under international law. The Responsibility to Protect, although accepted by member states in General Assembly Resolution 63/308 as requiring increased consideration, in debates in 2009 did little more than reiterate acceptance of paragraphs 138 and 139 of the World Summit Outcomes document.[85] The push for UN reform and a collective security structure responsive to emergent security concerns that seemed urgent at the outset of the millennium has refracted into detailed Security Council responses to specific, selective crises and conflicts rather than wide scale institutional or normative change.

Feminist analysis of international law has developed limited narratives on potential ways forward in response to the legal framing of collective security. On the one hand, social and empirical accounts of violence against women have argued for the recognition of the gendered continuum of violence; that is an understanding of the continuity of gendered understandings of justified violence across social, economic and political forms. This has influenced institutional activism and led to the five Security Council resolutions on women, peace and security: resolutions 1325, 1820, 1888, 1889 and 1960.[86] Of these resolutions, resolutions 1820 and 1888, indicate the possibility of widespread sexual violence in conflict as constituting a threat to international peace and security and thus as a possible trigger for future authorised force under Article 42. On the other hand, critical scholarship from feminist scholars has, however, indicated apprehension at the turn to international enforcement to regulate widespread sexual

85 Above note 69.
86 Above notes 80–83.

violence during conflict without thorough analysis of the sexed and gendered parameters international security mechanisms function within.[87] In terms of the domestic analogy, the turn to the Security Council to police violence against women, or under Security Council resolution 1820 sexual violence perpetrated by militaries, replicates the turn to national legal structures to police domestic violence and sexual violence that, as feminist scholarship documents, has been marred by institutional and structural limitations that parallel cultural gender inequalities.[88]

Three arguments are evidenced from this analysis. First, the broadening of threats in the contemporary collective security environment replicates a Western domestic model built on a distinction between public and private spheres to co-ordinate the regulation of legal subjects. Despite incursions into the private (or domestic) space of states, women are denied a voice or adequate participation within the private arena of states, particularly states that are recognised as threats to international peace and security. Second, even when women's security is paramount, for example, in situations of extreme poverty, the gender component of this threat is either erased through gender neutral language or frustrated through sexed and sexualised stereotypes that represent women as mothers or women as sexually vulnerable rather than as actors with capacity, rights or agency. Third, despite attempts, through recent collective security documents to contain responses to broader categories of threat within the collective security structure, state justifications for force have mirrored Security Council enlargement of the category of threat. The paradigm case is arguments for unilateral humanitarian interventions that emerge after the Security Council included humanitarian crises within the range of threats under Article 39 during the 1990s.

Finally, in two resolutions the Security Council has identified the impact that widespread and systematic sexual violence has on the restoration of international peace and security. This raises unanswered questions for feminist scholars and activists: if violence against women, women's poverty and sexual violence are to be recognised as threats to international, regional or local peace and security, how should the collective security regime, particularly the UN Security Council respond? I address this question in the following section and then expand on the conclusions drawn from this first through an analysis of the Security Council powers to authorise non-forceful acts under Article 41 and then in discussion of the Security Council's powers to authorise the use of force.

Article 41

In this section, I argue that the recent shift by the Security Council to challenge some sexual violence in armed conflict situations through the sanctions regime[89] requires contextualisation within a broader feminist analysis of the sanctions regime under Article 41. As such, after identifying the scope of measures instigated under

87 Otto, 'A Sign of "Weakness"? Disrupting Gender Certainties in the Implementation of Security Council Resolution 1325,' 13, *Michigan Journal of Gender and Law* (2006), 113.
88 Graycar and Morgan, *The Hidden Gender of the Law* (Sydney: Federation, 2002, 2nd edition).
89 See SC Res 1807 (31 March 2008).

Article 41, I interrogate the relationship between the sanctions regime and the use of force, through a specific focus on the sanctions regimes that have been utilised by states to develop justifications for the use of force: first, the implied authorisation argument developed in response to the sanctions regime in Iraq in the 1990s and second, the use of the language and methods of the targeted sanctions regime to justify the use of force against terrorist actors. This section also provides analysis of Security Council resolution 1807. This is the first Security Council resolution to make use of sanctions to combat violence against women and specifically target perpetrators of widespread sexual violence in armed conflict. The section concludes with reflections on the relationship between force and sanctions, between authorised and justified force and on the relationship between law, violence and gender.

The UN sanctions regime

Article 41 empowers the Security Council to authorise measures short of force. The text of Article 41 states that:

> The Security Council may decide what measures not involving the use of armed force are to be employed to give effect to its decisions, and it may call upon the Members of the United Nations to apply such measures. These may include complete or partial interruption of economic relations and of rail, sea, air, postal, telegraphic, radio, and other means of communication, and the severance of diplomatic relations.

Feminist analysis of Article 41 and its role in the collective security regime has not been extensive.[90] Feminist scholarship tends to focus on specific measures authorised under Article 41 and the consequences of such measures for women.[91] The two types of provisions the Security Council has developed under Article 41 are sanctions and transitional justice mechanisms, such as the *ad hoc* tribunals for Rwanda and the former Yugoslavia, as well as the Special Court for Sierra Leone. Feminist analysis of sanctions emerged after the decade long sanctions directed against the state of Iraq.[92] Feminist analyses of the ICTY and the ICTR have critiqued,[93] challenged,[94] praised[95]

---

90 For a starting point, see the discussion of Charlesworth and Chinkin, *The Boundaries of International Law* (Manchester: Manchester University Press, 2000), from 301.

91 See, for example, Buck, Gallant and Nossal, 'Sanctions as a Gendered Instrument of Statecraft', 24, *Review of International Studies* (1998), 69; Stark, 'UN Sanctions Against the Taliban', 95, *ASIL Proceedings* (2001), 24-25; Bahdi, 'Iraq, Sanctions and Security: A Critique,' 9, *Duke Journal of Gender Law and Policy* (2002), 237.

92 Orford, 'The Politics of Collective Security' 17 *Michigan Journal of International Law* (1996) 373, at 379–380.

93 Chinkin, 'Feminist Reflections on International Criminal Law' in Zimmerman (ed.), *International Criminal Law and the Current Development of Public International Law* (Berlin: Duncker and Humblot, 2002), 125.

94 Buss, 'The Curious Visibility of Wartime Rape: Gender and Ethnicity in International Criminal Law", 25, *Windsor Journal of Access to Justice* (2007), 3.

95 Bergoffen, 'Toward a Politic of the Vulnerable Body', 18 (1), *Hypatia* (2003), 116.

and influenced the role of these institutions in prosecuting sexual violence during conflict.[96] Feminist scholarship has less often assessed the role of the *ad hoc* tribunals in the development of contemporary norms on the use of force.[97]

Both sanctions and transitional justice mechanisms play a role in consolidating Article 42 authorised force as part of an apparently gender neutral and therefore responsive collective security regime. Sanctions are often structured as a precursor to the use of force (as was the case in Southern Rhodesia in 1966 when the use of force was authorised to implement the sanctions regime). As such, Article 41 functions to bolster the appearance of Article 42 force as a viable solution to the increased range of threats the Security Council has acknowledged as within the concern of the collective security structure. Furthermore, the reliance of states on the existence of Article 41 sanctions to strengthen unilateral justifications for force remains unexplored in the international security literature. Yet the nexus between Article 41 acts and unilateral force continues to emerge in contemporary state arguments for implied authorisation for past acts and in justifications for targeted strikes against terrorist actors, each of which I discuss below. With the shift towards the use of targeted sanctions as the rationale for future unilateral strikes, the potential use of sanctions to combat sexual violence in conflict, therefore, represents a site where feminist perspectives require articulation and reflection. The Security Council's use of Article 41 measures as post-conflict initiatives, for example, transitional justice mechanisms, have received extensive feminist debate although primarily as an element of contemporary international criminal law. Increased feminist analysis of the relationship between transitional justice measures and the use of force would be complimentary to the project developed in this book.[98]

From blunt instrument to smart sanctions

The Security Council first used Article 41 in 1966 when Security Council resolution 221 authorised the use of sanctions against Southern Rhodesia. However, it was the prolonged use of sanctions in Iraq during the 1990s that illustrated the ineffectiveness of broad-based economic sanctions and instigated international concern regarding the impact of sanctions on civilians.[99] By 1995, the Secretary-General had concluded that sanctions 'raise the ethical question of whether suffering inflicted on vulnerable groups in the target country is a legitimate means of exerting pressure on political leaders whose behaviour is unlikely to be affected . . .'.[100] The Secretary-General also noted the obstruction of humanitarian efforts caused by sanctions against the

---

96 Halley, 'Rape at Rome: Feminist Interventions in the Criminalization of Sex-Related Violence in Positive International Criminal Law', 30 *Michigan Journal of International Law* (2008), 1.
97 See Chinkin, 'Rape and Sexual Abuse of Women in International Law', 5, *EJIL* (1994), 326.
98 Gardam, 'War, Law, Terror, Nothing New for Women' 32 *Australian Feminist Law Journal* (2010) 61.
99 See, for example, Bhatia, Kawar and Shahin, *Unheard Voices: Iraqi Women on War and Sanctions* (CHANGE, 2001); Bossuyt, *Adverse Consequences of Economic Sanctions and the Enjoyment of Human Rights*, UN ECOSOC, E/CN.42/200/33 (2000).
100 Supplement to an Agenda for Peace (1995), paragraph 70.

Iraqi government, the spill-over effect on neighbouring economies, the potential to enhance a leader's credibility (as the United Nations appears as the cause of the greater suffering) and the long-term implications for the target economy as features of Article 41 sanctions.[101] The decade of sanctions against Iraq also highlighted the negative consequences of Article 41 measures in terms of nutrition, health and civil infrastructure for target populations.[102] Feminist scholarship has demonstrated how economic sanctions have specific consequences for civilian women.[103]

Consequently, the development of 'smart' and 'targeted' sanctions in the past decade has been, in part, a response to the criticisms of the severe consequences of the sanctions against Iraq in the 1990s.[104] Even before the instigation of the 'War on Terror' by the United States and its allies, the Security Council acknowledged the need for a sanctions regime that impacted less on civilian wellbeing.[105] Smart sanctions have developed as strategies that are directed at significant economic enterprises that fuel conflict, for example, the diamond trade in Sierra Leone.[106] Targeted sanctions compel states to take action against named individuals or groups. For example, Security Council Resolution 1267, of 15 October 1999, established the 'Al-Qaida and Taliban Sanctions Committee' that directs governments to freeze assets, apply travel embargoes and arms embargoes on (suspected) members of Al-Qaida or the Taliban.[107] This has resulted in a shift towards the Security Council preference for sanctions targeted at individuals, and their assets, rather than broad-based sanctions against states. This can be contrasted with the discussion of threats to individuals in the previous section. Under the analysis of Article 39, I argued that threats to individuals within a state must reach a threshold that also represents a threat to the stability of the state as a whole. Threats to women's security do not reach this threshold suggesting a reconfiguration of the state may be necessary to effectively halt violence against women. In contrast, under the sanctions regime, the Security Council has shown itself willing to direct Article 41 resolutions at individuals and effectively bypass the state. In recent Security Council resolutions on women, peace and security, the targeted

---

101 *Ibid.*

102 'Report of the Second Panel Established Pursuant to the Note by the Security Council of 30 January 1990 (S/1999/100), Concerning the Current Humanitarian Situation in Iraq', s/1999/346, annex (30 March 1999); also see FAO/WFP/WHO, 'Assessment of Food and Nutrition in Iraq (May/June 2000). However, also see the work of Cortright and Lopez which suggests the failure to find weapons of mass destruction in Iraq suggests the decade of sanctions against Saddam Hussein's regime was successful, see 'Containing Iraq: Sanctions Worked', 83 (4), *Foreign Affairs* (July/Aug 2004), 90–103 available at www.fourthfreedom.org (last accessed February 2011).

103 Buck, Gallant and Nossal, 'Sanctions as a Gendered Instrument of Statecraft', 24, *Review of International Studies* (1998), 69; Al-Ali, N, 'Women, Gender Relations, and Sanctions in Iraq' in Shams (ed.), *Iraq: Its History, People and Politics*. Amherst (2003).

104 Craven, 'Humanitarianism and the Quest for Smarter Sanctions', 13 (1), *EJIL* (2002), 43.

105 Gardam, 'Legal Restraints on Military Enforcement Action', 17, *Michigan Journal of International Law* (1996) 285; O'Connell, 'Debating the Law of Sanctions', 13, *EJIL* (2002), 63.

106 See SC Res 1306 (5 July 2000); however, I do not provide an analysis of smart sanctions.

107 SC Res 1267 (15 October 1999); see also SC Res 1333 (2000), 1390 (2002), 1455 (2003), 1526 (2004), 1617 (2005) and 1735 (2006) that develop the broader approach of Res 1267 to apply to named individuals.

sanctions regime has been identified as a method for challenging widespread and systematic sexual violence within a conflict or post-conflict situation.[108] A key concern in relation to the current approach of the Security Council is the permissive role given to the security services of powerful states in locating and identifying potential terrorists without the necessity of providing evidence or compliance with democratic norms on the rights of an accused. In response to criticisms of this aspect of the targeted sanctions regime, the Security Council amended the listing process and appointed an ombudsman to review listings, although the reforms were instigated alongside recognition that the targeted sanctions regime is 'preventative in nature and [is] not reliant upon criminal standards set out under national law'.[109] The inclusion of this statement identifies why Security Council resolutions on targeted sanctions is seen as policing that may not have to comply with human rights norms.

Targeted sanctions may also play a role in justifications for targeted strikes against terrorist actors, illustrating the continued nexus between Article 41 and the use of force. That is, targeted strikes as a form of justified military force and as a key tactic in the global war against terrorism, replicates developments under the authority of the Security Council in the construction of targeted sanctions under Article 41. However, when individuals are wrongly listed under Article 41 measures it may still be possible for those individuals to challenge the mis-labelling. This position is strengthened by the recent Security Council amendments to the listing process, after key judicial criticisms of the insufficient checks in the original listing process.[110] When the model is used to justify the use of force, as has been the policy of the United States since at least 2006, there is little scope for those killed to challenge any potential miscarriages of justice. Media reports from Somalia,[111] Syria,[112] Yemen,[113] Afghanistan[114] and Pakistan,[115] where this type of 'targeted' force has been used by the United States, also suggest that targeted strikes carry high risks to civilians.

It is not only the language of 'targeted' sanctions and 'targeted' strikes that is parallel, the reliance on security services evidence to establish who constitutes a terrorist for the purposes of either sanctions under Security Council resolution 1373 or

108 SC Res 1807 (31 March 2008); SC Res 1960 (16 December 2010) operative paragraph 7, states: '[The Security Council] reiterates its intention, when adopting or renewing targeted sanctions in situations of armed conflict, to consider including, where appropriate, designation criteria pertaining to acts of rape and other forms of sexual violence'.
109 SC Res 1904 (17 December 2009) in preamble.
110 *Kadi v Council of the European Union and the Commission of the European Communities*, Case T-315/01.
111 Clayton, 'US Strikes at al-Qaeda in Somalia', *The Times*, 9 January 2009.
112 Scott, Tyson and Knickmeyer, 'US Calls Raid a Warning to Syria' *The Washington Post*, 28 October 2008.
113 McGreal, C., 'US Plots Retaliatory Strikes in Yemen over Plane Bomber' *The Guardian*, UK, Wednesday 30th December 2009.
114 McGreal, C., 'US Tanks go into Afghanistan amid Warnings over Air Strikes Toll', *The Guardian*, UK, Friday 19 November 2010; also see: Jackson, A, 'Nowhere to Turn: the Failure to Protect Civilians in Afghanistan' *Joint Briefing Paper by 29 Aid Agencies in Afghanistan*, Oxfam, 19–20 November 2010, available online at: http://www.oxfam.org.uk/resources/policy/conflict_disasters/downloads/bp-nowhere-to-turn-afghanistan-191110-en.pdf (last accessed February 2011).
115 Sturke, '27 Dead in US Strikes says Pakistan', *The Guardian*, 31 October 2008.

unilateral military attacks circumvents the basic civil and political rights that are the cornerstone of democratic political structures. Moreover, the blurring of 'military' enforcement and policing (or law enforcement) is apparent in international discourse on targeted sanctions and targeted strikes. The Security Council, in asserting that targeted sanctions against terrorist actors as not regulated by national criminal law standards shifts the sanctions regime outside of the universal civil and political rights that apply within states. Yet as measures short of force (described by the Council as preventative in nature) the narrative also circumvents the application of human rights laws that have been developed under the international humanitarian law of armed conflict. The US post-millennium practice of targeted strikes against terrorist actors attempts a similar jurisdictional caveat. Targeted strikes are referred to by supporters of the US practice as measures short of force, in the sense that they do not occur within armed conflict and therefore the international humanitarian laws of armed conflict do not apply. Yet the strikes are also described as outside of domestic policing, with authority apparently derived from Security Council resolution 1373 on targeted sanctions. The Security Council's targeted sanctions regime is argued as offering implicit authorisation of the use of any measures to halt terrorist actors and the legal regime that governs this 'policing' is argued as outside of international law, yet neither are the unilateral strikes policing in the sense that they can be regulated by the limits on domestic policing behaviour.

Targeted sanctions, which are directed at individuals rather than states, appear to have also functioned to implicitly condone the use of military force against individuals that are perceived as a threat to international peace and security, at least in contemporary justifications elaborated by the United States. Consequently, Article 41 measures raise a host of conceptual questions. In terms of the law on the use of force, implied authority arguments and targeted strikes against terrorist actors illustrate the role states have used Article 41 sanctions, far from being a 'humane alternative to war',[116] as a means to add legitimacy to unilateral justifications for the use of force.

The sanctions against Iraq, and the failure of the Iraqi government to capitulate to the demands underlying the sanctions regime, also demonstrate the relationship between Article 41 and the use of force. Although often regarded as a failure of the collective security regime, the sanctions regime imposed on Iraq by the Security Council in the 1990s can be seen to have played an important role in the justifications made by the United States and its allies in 2003 for the use of force in Iraq. Early justifications attempt to avoid the claim that the use of force was illegal through a focus on the earlier Security Council resolutions which imposed sanctions and the weapons inspection regime, arguing that the consistent failure of the Iraqi state to comply with the demands in these earlier resolutions provided an implied authorisation for states to implement the resolutions. In 2010, this justification was articulated as built on a response to Iraq's material breach of Security Council resolution 687.[117]

116 Badhi, 'Iraq, Sanctions and Security: A Critique', 9, *Duke Journal of Gender Law and Policy* (2002), 237, at 237.
117 See the oral evidence of Lord Goldsmith to the Chilcot Inquiry, available online at: http://www.iraqinquiry.org.uk/transcripts/oralevidence-bydate/100127.aspx (last accessed February 2011).

Although the international law on state responsibility does not recognise a material breach of a Security Council resolution as creating an enforcement right or duty on other state parties, the development of the law on countermeasures and on *erga omnes* responsibilities within the International Law Commission's Articles on state responsibility and the potential for continued development of the law on the use of force through the notion of 'material breach' of or 'implied authorisation' derived from Security Council resolutions remains unexplored. While the Security Council has expressly sought to avoid this type of argument in response to Iran's failure to comply with sanctions imposed on is energy industry, states have utilised the language of a material breach of Security Council resolutions in a range of contexts.[118] The material breach argument by the United States and its allies demonstrates the nexus between the collective security structure and unilateral force. Rather than constructing a shift away from the use of unilateral force, the practice of the Security Council continues to create space for state justifications that appear to coalesce with or respond to past Security Council practice.

The final aspect of Security Council practice under Article 41 to be analysed is the post-millennium sanctions regime against Iran. The UN sanctions imposed on the state of Iran have been complemented by an ever increasing US sanctions regime that has been implemented to challenge Iran's non-compliance with inspections of the state's nuclear weapons capabilities.[119] Although the UN model falls short of imposing a comprehensive sanctions model on Iran, the United States has consistently pushed for the return of a comprehensive sanctions regime and has implemented this model domestically. During 2010, the US Senate approved the Comprehensive Iran Sanctions, Accountability and Divestment Act 2010, which attempts to restrict the Iranian energy sector, restrict trade with Iran, freeze bank accounts and bank activity and restrict trade with states that provide high technology to Iran. The European Union instigated a copy cat regime on 27 July 2010 and numerous other countries followed suit in this period (including Norway, Japan and Australia). This approach indicates that the 'lessons learnt' from the decade of Iraq sanctions may have been less about human rights and the suffering of civilians and more about the ends ultimately achieved, which for the United States and its allies has been regime change, occupation and economic change. Importantly the UN Security Council has consistently asserted that the sanctions against Iran constitute Article 41 measures and any further action (e.g. the use of force) would require a separate resolution from the Council.[120] The insertion of this clause in resolutions directing the collective sanctions against Iran are specifically used to avoid the implied authorisation and material breach arguments that the United States and its allies used as a justification for the use of force in Iraq in 2003.

---

118 For example, Lebanon argued that Israeli warplanes that entered its airspace in late 2010 constituted a material breach of Security Council resolution 1701 (11 August 2006).
119 SC Res 1929 (9 June 2010); also see SC Res 1696 (31 July 2006), 1737 (27 December 2006), 1747 (24 March 2007), 1803 (3 March 2008), 1835 (27 September 2008) and 1887 (24 September 2009).
120 See SC Res 1929 (9 June 2010) in operative paragraph 37 and in the preamble.

Sanctions against perpetrators of sexual violence in armed conflict

The study above illustrates the relationship between sanctions and force. Force, or the threat of force, may provide the justification for sanctions and force functions as a further enforcement tool, either to aid implementation of sanctions regimes (as in Rhodesia in 1969) or sanctions can be instrumentalised by states to strengthen unilateral justifications for the use of force, as has been the case with targeted strikes against suspected terrorist actors (by the United States), and through arguments for implied authorisation, as was argued in 2003 in Iraq. I have identified, above, the recognition by the Security Council in its resolutions on women, peace and security of the impact of widespread and systematic sexual violence on the restoration on international peace and security. In addition to finding widespread and systematic sexual violence as constituting a potential Article 39 type threat, the resolutions on women, peace and security envisage the use of Article 41 to challenge sexual violence during armed conflict.

Comprehensive sanctions aim to stop a breach of international law by a state. Targeted sanctions, directed at individuals, function as international law enforcement. The shift to targeted sanctions in the post-millennium security structure has resulted in sanctions against a range of actors. The models developed in response to conflict and unrest in the DRC and the Ivory Coast specifically incorporate perpetrators of widespread and systematic sexual violence as sanctions targets. Security Council resolution 1807 indicates, in Operative Paragraph 13 (e) that: 'Individuals operating in the Democratic Republic of the Congo and committing serious violations of international law involving the targeting of children or women in situations of armed conflict, including killing and maiming, sexual violence, abduction and forced displacement' fall within the categories of individuals subject to targeted sanctions. The Security Council in Resolution 1807[121] envisaged targeted sanctions as a potential means to challenge impunity with respect to sexual violence in the DRC and has resulted in the listing of three actors in the DRC on the grounds of their involvement in sexual abuse (amongst other offences).[122] This provision was further strengthened in October 2010 when leaders in the Congolese Armed Forces (FARDC), believed to be responsible for the sexual assaults in the Kivu province, were arrested.[123]

Feminist legal theories must open debates on the nature of law and violence and ask when force would, if ever, be justified from a feminist perspective, especially in light of recent institutional developments regarding sexual violence during armed conflict. If the Security Council continues to move towards the use of sanctions to challenge sexual violence in armed conflict and during humanitarian crises,[124] and in light of the analysis above, the possibility of widespread sexual violence emerging as a justification for force must be addressed by feminists advocating such a move.[125] I argue that the

---

121 SC Res 1807 (31 March 2008).
122 See http://ukun.fco.gov.uk/en/news/?view=News&id=286240682 (last accessed February 2011).
123 SC/1055: Recent Arrests in Mass Rape Cases in Democratic Republic of the Congo, 14 October 2005.
124 Also see Security Council 1820 (18 June 2008), operative paragraph 1.
125 For an early statement of the need for sanctions to address feminist issues, see 'UN Sanctions Taliban Abuse of Women' *Ms. Magazine*, 21 September 1999.

use of force is itself a limited solution that perpetuates and increases sexual violence and sexual exploitation and abuse in a manner that is specifically harmful to women. As a consequence, the use of force to halt violence against women, sexual violence or sexual exploitation and abuse is not a feminist use of force. It is from this perspective a feminist account of Article 41 sanctions must initiate debate and action.

In Security Council resolution 1807 on the DRC, the Security Council identified sexual violence as a potential reason for the listing of individuals by the Sanctions Committee. In 2010, three individuals operating in the DRC had been listed for, among other crimes, sexual assault and as 2010 drew to a close the trial of Joseph Bemba commenced at the ICC for crimes against humanity and war crimes that included command responsibility for the use of rape as a weapon.

However, studies show that sexual violence in armed conflict, as well as sexual exploitation and abuse, are near universal consequences of military behaviours. This is so with regard to military bases in states experiencing peace time, in conjunction with military bases run by a state's allies on its territories and is perpetrated by local, foreign, paramilitary and UN military personnel. The scale of sexual violence and sexual exploitation and abuse in the DRC has received considerable international media and institutional attention and has been identified with the acts of UN personnel, paramilitary groups operating in the territory and the DRC's own forces. The additional crimes of using child soldiers and child kidnapping are also known to be prolific in the DRC and may also include components of sexual violence and sexual abuse. Furthermore, specific studies identify the use of sexual violence as both an everyday act within military communities, for example, in situations of what has been described as survival sex, and as means of community repression where the use of sexual violence in a community is directed, widespread and co-ordinated. The combination of these factors have led to the Security Council specifically invoking the sanctions regime as a response to a relationship between abhorrent sexual violence and the insecurity in the DRC.

The enforcement of Article 41 in the context of the DRC raises the first issue of concern. Despite the listing and trials of a limited number of leaders in the DRC, the insecurity and instability caused by the sexual violence in the DRC remains. The policing of this by UN actors within the state of the DRC has consistently been limited to reactive rather than preventative measures.

The distinction between sexual abuse and exploitation – the regulation of which is directed at UN personnel – and sexual violence in armed conflict – the regulation of which is directed at non-state actors and military groups within the DRC is the second issue of concern.

The third concern is the role the DRC plays in the larger collective security discourse as an 'extreme' case, thus distancing 'everyday' military behaviour from gendered crimes, particularly sexual abuse, sexual exploitation, sexual assault and sexual violence. Recognition of the fundamental limitation of using military actors to challenge behaviour that is intrinsic in the structure of military institutions is required. At the same time recognition of the role unsuccessful attempts to challenge sexual violence in the DRC plays in the perpetuation of an image of sexual violence as extreme depravity occurring in unruly, unmanageable conflicts, rather than as a feature institutionally tolerated and accommodated by military structures generally.

The level of desperation and depravity associated with any single act of sexual violence is difficult to comprehend, when compounded and magnified in number and, as has occurred in the DRC, finding viable solutions stretches to the limit our capacity to know ourselves as human. A clear strategy is to highlight the worst of acts and demonise the perpetrators, as the sanctions regime under Security Council resolution 1807 does in its incorporation of sexual violence as a category for targeted sanctions listing. However, this has the unfortunate effect of normalising the un-challenged, un-prosecuted, unacknowledged sexual violence and the misogyny that is fundamental and a pivotal element of military identities globally.

Just as challenging sexual violence in Western communities has increasingly required a shift from the need for better enforcement of, or more, rules towards campaigns aimed at cultural and social awareness and education, it seems the policing of sexual violence in armed conflict through listing by targeted sanctions committees overlooks the widespread and entrenched gendered models that militaries function through. In this sense the United Nations has in place a range of measures to develop an end to the culture of impunity surrounding sexual violence and sexual exploitation and abuse during armed conflict but that overlook the relationship between gender and military behaviour.

These initiatives can be contrasted with the attempt to incorporate sexual violence offences within the targeted sanctions regime. If targeted sanctions facilitate US-targeted strikes against terrorist actors, then feminist activists and scholars seeking to make use of Article 41 measures must consider if sanctions to stop widespread and systematic sexual violence in armed conflict prove ineffective (which DRC in 2010 seems to indicate), why not use force instead? In the section on Article 42, I analyse Security Council authorised force and feminist arguments that negate the use of force as a potentially feminist friendly enforcement tool.

Article 42

The implicit condoning of the use of force, apparent in Article 41 measures, is explicit in Article 42 of the Charter. Article 42 states:

> Should the Security Council consider that measures provided for in Article 41 would be inadequate or have proved to be inadequate, it may take such action by air, sea, or land forces as may be necessary to maintain or restore international peace and security. Such action may include demonstrations, blockade, and other operations by air, sea, or land forces of Members of the United Nations.

This section analyses the Security Council power to authorise the use of military force under Article 42 of the UN Charter. The first authorisation of military force by the Security Council occurred in 1950.[126] In Resolution 82, the Council identified North

---

126 However, note the argument of Dinstein that Article 42 measures have never been instituted by the Security Council, see: Dinstein, *War, Aggression and Self-defence* (Cambridge: Cambridge University Press, 2005, 4th edition), at 296 and 307, describing the Security Council as using 'non-Article 42 enforcement measures'.

Korean armed attacks on South Korean territory as a breach of the peace.[127] In Resolution 83, the Council recommended that Member states 'furnish such assistance to the ROK as may be necessary to repel the armed attack and to restore international peace and security to the area'.[128] This authorisation of force was then expanded in Resolution 84, which placed the US command in Korea under the UN flag.[129] As the only authorised use of force during the Cold War, the force in Korea was an anomaly rather than an indication of a norm of Cold War security.[130] However, the use of military threats to control the actions of states was very much a part of Cold War security.[131]

The second set of Security Council resolutions authorising the use of force occurred in the early 1990s, after the Cold War stalemate had ended. The increased capacity of the permanent members of the Security Council to work in concert led, in 1990, to the authorisation of force against the Iraq state.[132] In response to Iraqi aggression against Kuwait, Security Council Resolution 678 permitted member states to use 'all means necessary' to secure the removal of Iraqi forces from Kuwaiti territory.[133] The use of force in Kuwait to expel the Iraqi military provides the pivot between the Cold War era, when Article 42 force was exceptional, and the post-Cold War environment, when the use of force has been authorised by the Security Council in multiple contexts and situations, including in 2010 in response to pre-electoral violence in the Côte d'Ivoire and in response to the January 2010 earthquake in Haiti.[134] One consequence of this increased activity, and the increased number and type of situations the Security Council has seen fit to authorise enforcement action for, has been a distancing from the formal structure of the Charter as resolutions authorising force have not always been made expressly under Article 42 powers or even with clear reference to a violation of Article 39.

The use of force has been authorised by the Security Council in Somalia (1992), Yugoslavia (1992 and in 1996), Rwanda (1994), the Great Lakes (1996),[135] Albania

---

127 SC Res 82 (25 July 1950), also see SC Res 83 (27 June 1950).

128 *Ibid.*

129 SC Res 84 (7 July 1950).

130 Note, SC Res 232 (16 December 1966) which authorized the UK to use force to secure compliance with sanctions against Southern Rhodesia.

131 See (on the use of gendered language during the Cold War) Cohen, 'Sex and Death in the Rational World of Defense Intellectuals' in Wyer (ed.), *Women, Science and Technology: A Reader* (London: Routledge, 2001).

132 Although China abstained from voting 'because it sought a peaceful solution and had difficulty accepting the resolution because the phrase "all means necessary" permitted the use of military action'; Gray 'From Unity to Polarization: International Law and the Use of Force Against Iraq', 13, *EJIL* (2002), 9.

133 Greenwood, 'New World Order or Old? The Invasion of the Kuwait and the Rule of Law,' 55 (2), *Modern Law Review* (1992), 153; Heathcote, 'Article 51 Self-defence as a Narrative: Spectators and Heroes in International Law', 12 (1), *Texas Wesleyan Law* Review (Fall 2005).

134 SC Res 1933 (30 June 2010) authorising the UNOCI forces to 'use all means necessary' as pre-electoral violence constitutes a threat to international peace and security in the region; SC Res 1908 (19 Jan 2010) deploying over 8000 military and 3700 police to Haiti.

135 SC Res 1080 (15 November 1996) although this force was not, in fact, deployed.

(1997), the Central African Republic (1997) and Sierra Leone (1997) and East Timor (1999).[136] The use of force by NATO in Serbia in 1999 was later endorsed under Security Council Resolution 1244, although the legality of the initial decision to use force remains controversial.[137] Since 2000, the Security Council has recognised the right of the United States to act in self-defence after the 11 September 2001 attacks on the Twin Towers in New York[138] and acknowledged the foreign military presence in Iraq in the months subsequent to the 2003 invasion.[139] The Security Council has also authorised the use of force in Liberia,[140] the Democratic Republic of the Congo[141] and the Côte d'Ivoire,[142] although in these three instances the actions were perceived as limited operations, the military nature of the operations indicates their status as chapter VII authorised force.[143] The propensity of the Security Council to author-ise force during the 1990s, and beyond, prefigures *A More Secure World* and *In Larger Freedom*,[144] highlighting how the collective security structure has consistently broad-ened the meaning of threats, while relying on force as the central form of legal coer-cion that may be taken in response to the threat articulated.

My study of Article 42 is constructed around the argument that military force func-tions to perpetuate and aggravate violence against women rather than offer a solution to women's security. My approach to Article 42 is somewhat unusual. I take the 1950 use of authorised force under the US command in Korea, and with UN authorisation, as the central dialogue. I am not, however, interested in debating the usual legal con-troversies. I will not discuss the legality of Security Council Resolutions 82 through 84, which authorise the use of force or discuss the adjacent political issues pertinent to any Cold War conflict. Rather, I wish to examine the consequences a foreign military presence has held for Korean women.

The use of military force and sex workers in Korea

While the UN mandate ceased in 1951,[145] US military bases remain as a legacy in the ROK. This has important, contemporary parallels with the use of force in Kosovo

---

136 Somalia: SC Res 794 (3rDecember 1992); Former Yugoslavian Republic: SC Res 752 (15 May 1992), 761 (29 June 1992), 781 (9 October 1992), 998 (16 June 1995), 1037 (15 January 1996); Rwanda: 929 (22 June 1994); Albania: 1101 (28 March 1997); Central African Republic: 1125 (6 August 1997); Sierra Leone 1132 (8 October 1997); East Timor: 1264 (15 September 1997).

137 SC Res 1244 (10 June 1999); see further chapter five.

138 SC Res 1368 (12 September 2001) and SC Res 1373 (28 September 2001); on the status of this force (i.e. as coming under Article 51 rather than Article 42) see: Greenwood, 'International Law and the Preemptive Use of Force: Afghanistan, Al-Qaida and Iraq', 4, *San Diego International Law Journal* (2003), 7, at 21.

139 SC Res 1511 (16 October 2003), paragraph 13; SC Res 1546 (8 June 2004).

140 SC Res 1497 (1 August 2003).

141 SC Res 1484 (30 May 2003).

142 SC Res 1464 (4 February 2003).

143 Gray, above note 61, at 257–260; in 2007 the Security Council authorised a military force, acting under Chapter VII, in the Darfur region of Sudan, SC Res 1769 (31 July 2007).

144 Above notes 70 and 71.

145 See SC Res 90 (31 January 1951).

(in 1999), which also saw (contentious) authorised force led to the establishment of a large foreign (US) military base.[146] At writing, US military personnel remain stationed in the ROK although this is no longer a UN force (they remain at the request of the government of the ROK).[147] The long-term consequences of that force must be included in future dialogues on force, so as to adequately address women's security. Furthermore, the ill-defined boundary between peacekeeping and the use of force, as well as the awareness of the embroilment of some peacekeeping personnel in crimes of sexual exploitation and sexual abuse,[148] identifies the necessity for historical and contemporary analysis of the complicity of legal narratives in the sexual violence of militaries. I will highlight, first, the sex industries that were shaped by the Korean War. Through this account social dialogues can be seen to challenge the role of militaries as protectors of communities, particularly women in post-conflict communities. Consequently, the merits of placing Security Council authorised force as the ultimate international sanction is open to question.

In Resolution 84, the Security Council authorised a 'coalition of the willing' to use 'all means necessary' to obstruct North Korean forces from passing the 38th parallel.[149] Around 35 000 US military personnel continue to be stationed in the ROK across 85 sites.[150] What is less well documented is the recruitment of over a million South Korean women to work in the state-sanctioned sex industries that have existed on the peripheries of the US bases since the authorised force in 1950.[151] Moon's study of sex workers, or kijich'on, in the ROK, *Sex Among Allies*, illustrates how the US and the ROK security policies regulated the sexuality and sex of soldiers while facilitating sex, sex industries and constructions of sexual identity with little regard for social consequences in civilian communities.[152]

The authorised use of force in Korea in the 1950s was controversial because the Security Council member representing the USSR was absent when the vote to authorise the action occurred. That force was authorised and that the force was of a military nature was not controversial. Indeed this is assumed to be the correct role for the Security Council. Consequently, the sexual demands of militaries on civilian communities are deemed part of the status quo of force and are assumed to be no more destructive than the sexual demands individual men make of individual women. For over one million women in the ROK, who have worked and who continue to work as kijich'on, this is not incidental of military behaviour.[153] Furthermore, the paradox between protector

146 Godec, 'Between Rhetoric and Reality: Exploring the Impact of Military Humanitarianism on Post-conflict Sexual Violence' No. 877 *International Review of the Red Cross*, 31 March 2010.
147 A similar situation continues in Iraq today, as US military forces remain at the 'request' of the Iraqi government.
148 Report of the Secretary-General, Comprehensive Report prepared pursuant to General Assembly Resolution 59/296 on sexual exploitation and sexual abuse, UN Doc. A/60/862 (24 May 2006).
149 Above note 129.
150 For an update, see: www.globalsecurity.org/military/agency/dod/usfk.htm (accessed February 2011).
151 Moon, *Sex Among Allies: Military Prostitution in US–Korea Relations* (New York: Columbia University Press, 1997).
152 *Ibid.* chapter three.
153 *Ibid.* in prologue.

and aggressor enacted in individual relations between kijich'on women and US military customers highlights the illusionary and inadequate 'security' supplied by military forces. The hostilities over more than 60 years between North and South Korea must be judged alongside the complicated relationship between US military behaviour and South Korean life. 'All of the women I interviewed', writes Moon:

> . . . stated that their greatest need for ROK government protection (after the Korean war) was not from Northern Korea threats but the exploitation and abuse of club/owners/pimps, local Korean police and VD clinic officials, and the power of the US army bases. In other words, they needed protection from a Korean law enforcement system that inadequately provided for their legal, economic, political and human rights and a Korean government too cowardly and self-interested to protect them against violence and abuse by US soldiers.[154]

Moon's study of the experiences of kijich'on women can be connected to the experiences of women who globally, in peace and war, experience greater threats from interpersonal relationships than any other source.[155] Many of the women Moon spoke with experienced violence at the hands of US servicemen or their 'pimps', many lived in abhorrent conditions and all lived with social exclusion, as did their children. Moon's findings are replicated in studies of other US military bases in Asia,[156] in studies of US homeland bases where domestic violence levels are three times higher than civilian rates,[157] and in communities globally where, 'the risk of violence and violation within the household is one thing women, irrespective of their social position, creed, colour or culture, share in common'.[158]

Three points can be drawn from Moon's study of the kijich'on women's experiences. First, studying the 'campfollowers' or kijich'on women illustrates the distortion of public and private space in women's lives. For women in the camptowns adjacent to US bases, the division between 'work' and 'family' was and is not always clear. Moon describes the social hierarchies that construct both the kijich'on woman's home and work environments, with women married to US servicemen at the top of the social hierarchy followed by women who had a 'cohabitation contract' (*kyeyak tonggo*).[159] A cohabitation contract involves the setting up of house by a sex worker and a serviceman for an agreed period (dependent on the tour of duty and training schedule of the man). The woman performs the role of the 'wife' while he pays her club debt and provides for her financially.[160] Moon records, 'all the women I met in

154 Ibid. at 26.
155 Kelly, 'Wars Against Women', in Jacobs, Jacobson and Marchbank (eds), *States of Conflict* (London: Zed, 2001).
156 Sturdevant and Stolzfus (eds), *Let the Good Times Role: Prostitution and the US Military in Asia* (New York: New Press, 1992).
157 Special Edition on Intimate Partner Violence and the Military, 9, *Violence Against Women* (2003), 1039 [various authors].
158 MacKinnon, *Are Women Human? And Other International Dialogues* (Harvard, MA: Harvard University Press, 2006), at 31.
159 Above note 151, at 26.
160 Above note 151, at 26.

camptowns either actively dreamed or had dreamed of leaving prostitution and leading so called normal lives, marrying a GI'.[161]

The paradox of sex industries serving US foreign military bases lies in the offer of potential security that occurs at both the personal and public level. Yet the threat to women's personal security is also constructed through both spheres. Ostensibly the presence of the United States in the ROK serves to protect the community from Northern Korean aggression. Likewise, women who dream of marrying US military personnel perceive some escape from the dangers of camptown prostitution through the sexual contract of marriage. At the same time, the continued US presence in South Korea may be the persistent obstacle to unification or cessation of hostilities between the two Koreas and, at a personal level, the presence of US military bases provides the greatest individual threats to individual women working in the adjacent sex industries.[162] This information must be framed in terms of sex workers' rights, and, through acknowledgement of every woman's right to health and the freedom to live and work free from the threat or infliction of violence. Yet international legal narratives on these issues remain conceptually dislocated from the law on the use of force. When the Security Council does 'see' the sex in military behaviour this has been through narratives of deviance (suggesting soldiers having sex with local women is unusual) or through stories of female sexual vulnerability (and therefore in need of protection both from and via military institutions).

The second issue to note is that this discussion focuses on one group of women in Korea and cannot illustrate how the presence of US forces in Korea has affected all Korean women and, likewise, questions concerning men's safety and the construction of masculinity, sit outside the immediate discussion. However, the discussion does have broader relevance as discourse around 'good' and 'bad' women develops directly from identification of kijich'on women as acting outside social norms of female behaviour. This serves to reinforce conservative gender roles in the lives of non-kijich'on women in the ROK. Enloe has demonstrated how similar social discourse emerges in US (homeland) military communities and on other foreign military bases, including those in Bosnia in the 1990s and at present in Kosovo.[163] Social discourse in the ROK from the latter half of the twentieth century indicates a division between 'bad' women, who worked as prostitutes around military bases, and 'good' women, who conformed to traditional Korean stereotypes of femininity.[164] These discourses influence the company women keep, women's access to public spaces and the types of clothes women are expected to wear, as well as their access to sex.[165] While these may seem like benign social discourses, of interest but perhaps not of great importance to international law, for feminist jurisprudence the production of gendered cultural norms within a community and, globally, play a direct role in the

---

161 Above note 151, at 26.
162 Above note 151, at 26.
163 Enloe, *Maneuvers: the International Politics of Militarising Women's Lives* (Berkeley, CA: University of California, 2000).
164 Above note 151, at 39.
165 Enloe, 'It Takes Two' in Sturdevant and Stolzfus (eds), above note 156.

perpetuation of violence against women. Historical and contemporary studies demonstrate that the role gender norms play in limiting women's full access to political, health and labour rights.

Finally, the impact of US military bases on adjacent communities is not merely a historical issue. In addition to the development of sex industries around bases, current research highlights the role of foreign military bases in fuelling human trafficking industries. In Kosovo, the growth of a local sex industry, and the emergence of Pristina as a transit and receiving point for the trafficking of women, parallels the arrival of the US$36.6 million US military base and the UN forces, KFOR.[166] While the exact relationship between the two industries (trafficking and the military) is at times obfuscated, the arrival of the UN peacekeepers and the US military is definitely a contributory factor. While reports suggest international clientele represent only 20 per cent of sex industry business in Pristina, it should be acknowledged this is assessed in terms of client numbers rather than client expenditure.[167] Additionally, evidence of individual peacekeepers direct involvement in trafficking has emerged as a grim reminder of the relationship between militaries and sex.[168] Institutional recognition of this knowledge has been exponential since the advent of the new millennium. However, institutional responses have hinged around highly gendered images of women and men that do not necessarily generate positive cultural dialogues.[169] This is because attempts to challenge sexual exploitation and abuse by peacekeepers have not been extended to Article 42 actors, have not been in the context of the 'normalness' of military actors having sex and have failed to challenge stereotypes of female sexual vulnerability.

In the legal histories of Western liberal democracies, the distinction between the protected and protector is aligned with images of femininity and masculinity. Law's role is assumed to be protective, a role that is often sexed male in Western cultures, while those offered the law's protection are feminised (rather than merely gendered these are perceived as natural and universal categories). The consequence is a sexing of legal categories and legal actors, which has continuing consequences for the acts and rights of individuals, although these sexed normative claims are not, in themselves, addressed to any particular man or woman.

To conclude, that local women are co-opted into supplying sexual services for foreign militaries during conflicts, including Security Council authorised force, is a fact that requires inclusion in the international legal narrative on the use of force,

---

166 Amnesty International USA, *So What Does it Mean That We Have Rights? Protecting the Human Rights of Women and Girls Trafficked for Forced Prostitution in Kosovo*, available at Amnesty USA Website: www. amnestyusa.org/news (last accessed February 2011); UNMIK, *Combating Human Trafficking in Kosovo, Strategy and Commitment* (May 2004) available online at: http://unpan1.un.org/intradoc/groups/public/documents/untc/unpan019190.pdf (last accessed February 2011); on state responsibility for the actions of peacekeepers and UN actors in Kosovo, see Krieger, 'A Credibility Gap: The Behrami and Saramati Decision of the ECHR', 13, *Journal of International Peacekeeping* (2009), 159.

167 Amnesty International Report, Ibid.

168 Ibid.

169 Otto, 'Making Sense of Zero Tolerance Policies in Peacekeeping Sexual Economies' in Munro and Stychin (eds), *Sexuality and the Law: Feminist Engagements* (London: Routledge, 2007), 259–282.

specifically in discussions of the possibilities of Article 42 measures. This is because military prostitution often involves conditions akin to trafficking, as the women are often in situations of debt-bonds, suffer violence at the hands of their 'clients' and are often restricted or controlled in their access to the provision of basic services, including medical treatment, food and shelter.[170] Workers are underpaid, or not paid at all; suffer social exclusion and risk pregnancy as well as illegal abortions and sexually transmitted diseases. As Sturdveyant and Stolzfus demonstrate that the experiences of Korean women are replicated in the communities adjacent to US military bases in the Philippines and in Japan.[171]

In October 2003, the Security Council acting within its chapter VII powers authorised 'a multinational force under unified command to take all necessary measures to contribute to the maintenance of security and stability in Iraq'.[172] While questions may be raised about the legality of foreign military forces in Iraq prior to this time, after Resolution 1511 there is clear Security Council authorisation under chapter VII for the foreign military presence. At this stage, who the foreign militaries in Iraq are having sex with, and under what conditions, can be only speculated upon; although narratives that have emerged in the Western media surrounding Western sexual violence in Iraq after the 2003 invasion have been disturbing.[173] Unfortunately, it is clear from the *In Larger Freedom* report that this aspect of military behaviour will have little, if any, impact on future Security Council decisions to authorise the use of force. The *In Larger Freedom* Report, *More Secure World* Report and the *2005 World Summit Outcome* Document do not address this issue. Since these reports were issued the Security Council has endorsed four new resolutions on women, peace and security but the two different strategies – the reform of Security Council practice and gender initiatives within the Council – remains conceptually and practically separate.

In contrast to the argument presented here, that identifies an ongoing and structural association between sexual violence, exploitation and abuse and military actors, institutional developments continue to perceive sexual violence in armed conflict as the acts of non-state and non-UN actors, so while recognising the danger of the 'post conflict moment' for women a recent Secretary-General Report finds:

> . . . owing to the increased civilian-combatant interface of current conflicts, the targeted use of sexual violence is increasingly becoming a potent weapon of war and a destabilising factor in conflict and post-conflict societies.[174]

170 See, for example, the narratives of kijich'on women in Sturdevant and Stolzfus (eds), above note 156.
171 See, for example, the narratives of kijich'on women in Sturdevant and Stolzfus (eds), above note 156.
172 Security Council Res 1511 (16 October 2003).
173 See Women's International League for Peace and Freedom, the Peacewomen Project 1325 Security Council Monitor Resolution Watch (29 June 2007) online at http://www.peacewomen.org/un/sc/1325-Monitor/RW/theme_PK_Ops.htm (last accessed February 2011).
174 Report of Secretary-General on women, peace and security, 25 September 2008, S/2008/622, paragraph 5.

The Report ignores the role of UN forces in sexual violence, sexual exploitation and abuse and locates the trivialisation of responses as the consequences of local police, military and judicial tardiness. This contributes to a general impression of sexual violence and abuse during conflict as happening outside the mainstream of international collective initiatives. At the same time Security Council resolutions have shifted to include routine prohibition on sexual relations when constructing peacekeeping mandates that do little to challenge the sexual and domestic cultures of militaries, due to non-mandatory language and the responsibility for action to be left to the individual troop-contributing states.[175]

Alternative narratives

This chapter has analysed the central components of the collective security regime under chapter VII of the UN Charter. In analysing Articles 39, 41 and 42, I have considered the relationship between the collective security structure and unilateral justifications for the use of force to demonstrate how women's security has rarely gained from the UN structure. Recent initiatives on women, peace and security, studied alongside the history of the Council's work, are demonstrated as circumvented by the structure and model of collective security that defines threats through the entity of the state and that defines security through the provision of military security. Neither states nor militaries are gender free, and feminist scholarship demonstrates how both states and militaries contribute to the daily insecurity many women experience globally.

Orford argues that mainstream international law commentators should regard feminist dialogues on difference as a starting point for re-defining security to be inclusive of difference, including women's difference.[176] To redefine security and, therefore, to redefine the meaning of Article 39:

> [m]ainstream international lawyers should recognise that there is something to be learnt from feminist scholars . . . the emphasis which feminist theorists place on difference, far from being anarchical or nihilistic, lays new ground for negotiating interconnections and alliances among differently situated individuals. [177]

Feminist theory provides in-depth understanding of its own partiality, and cultural limitations, which could be developed to create a model for the re-definition and re-imagining of security norms.[178] However, at present, despite the broad understanding of what constitutes a threat to the peace, despite the potential of a wide understanding of

---

175 For example, see SC Res 1870 (30 April 2009) which in paragraph 28: '*Requests* the Secretary-General to continue to take the necessary measures to ensure full compliance by UNMIS with the United Nations zero tolerance policy on sexual exploitation and abuse and to keep the Council fully informed, and urges troop contributing countries to take appropriate preventive action including redeployment awareness training, and other action to ensure full accountability in cases of such conduct involving their personnel'.

176 Orford, 'The Politics of Collective Security', 17 *Michigan Journal of International Law* (1995) 373, at 408 to 409.

177 Ibid.

178 Ibid; Confortini, 'Galtung, Violence and Gender', 31(3), *Peace and Change* (2006), 333.

the phrase 'breaches of the peace' under Article 39 to include non-military threats, and despite the linkage of the internally repressive apartheid regime in South Africa with that state's external acts of aggression, women's security concerns remain hidden in a system that universalises elite (white) men's definitions of threats and harms to humans.[179] Godec records the development of the trafficking industry in Kosovo after the 1999 NATO intervention and the role Western militaries and personnel played as both actors profiting from the new industry and as clients creating a need for sexual services. In response to Security Council resolution 1820, which has subsequently been affirmed in Security Council resolution 1888 and 1960,[180] Godec writes:

> Operative paragraph 1, which ambiguously infers that the Council may exercise its Chapter VII power to counter systematic sexual violence, how can the Council ensure that the use of force will not be a catalyst for new forms of sexual violence as seen in Kosovo?[181]

While reform of the Security Council and the collective security regime generally is a project outside of the scope of this book, the underlying claim, that force as a solution complicates and extends threats to women's security, is utilised to further demonstrate the weakness of the use of justified unilateral force in forthcoming chapters. In this section, I argue that the post-millennium narratives emergent in response to changing threats and changing political relationships between states create an extension of rather than a break from past security norms. The three institutional reports, *A More Secure World*,[182] *in Larger Freedom*[183] and *the Summit Outcome Document*,[184] failed to challenge the ingrained sex and gender of international laws on the authorisation of force and measures short of force. I begin by focusing on the work of peacekeeping operations. I argue that the peacekeeping continuum, across peacekeeping, peacebuilding and peace enforcement, relies on military actors in a manner that undermines any potential for change through peacekeeping operations. This point is emphasised through recent Security Council practice where peacekeeping operations have morphed into chapter VII enforcement operations. I then return to the two documents issued by the Secretary-General, *A More Secure World* and *In Larger Freedom*, and assess their recommendations for the future of collective security. To challenge the contemporary UN collective security model it is necessary that the war scholar and the international jurist learn to understand gender like 'the cook knows salt'.[185] Feminist legal scholarship must also work to provide ongoing analysis of the collective security framework from a feminist legal perspective.

179 For an alternative approach see Askin, 'Prosecuting Wartime Rape and Other Gender Related Crimes under International Law: Extraordinary Advances, Enduring Obstacles', 21(2), *Berkeley Journal of International Law* (2003), 288 at 349 where she claims, 'sexual violence, at very least rape and sexual assault, have risen to the level of a *jus cogens* norm'.
180 SC Res 1820 (19 June 2008); SC Res 1888 (30 September 2009); SC Res 1960 (16 December 2010).
181 Above note 146.
182 Above note 71.
183 Above note 70.
184 Above note 69.
185 Goldstein, *War and Gender* (Cambridge: Cambridge University Press, 2001), chapter one.

The UN peacekeeping continuum can be described as the range of activities encompassed by the terms peacekeeping, peacebuilding and peace enforcement. Peacekeeping refers to the monitoring of ceasefires or early intervention before armed conflict breaks out. For example, the deployment of peacekeepers to Lebanon after the 2006 attacks by Israel was framed around the maintenance of a ceasefire agreement.[186] Peacebuilding refers to a longer process of renewal and re-development of institutions and civil infrastructure; for example, as occurred in Timor Leste (after the use of force by UN forces in 1999) under the guises of the UN Transitional Authority.[187] Peace enforcement describes peacekeeping missions that have developed into chapter VII forces, such as occurred in Somalia and Bosnia in the 1990s.[188]

The United Nations records a total of US$69 billion dollars spent and the loss of 2850 lives since the first peacekeeping operation was deployed to the Middle East in 1948.[189] During the Cold War the Security Council authorised a total of 15 peacekeeping operations, 5 that remained in operation beyond 2010.[190] During the 1990s the number of peacekeeping operations instigated increased dramatically so that by 2011, 64 different peacekeeping operations had been mandated across the UN era. By 2011, over 98 000 uniformed soldiers, from 115 different countries and in conjunction with over 5000 civilian international staff members and approximately 14 000 local civilian staff members, as well as over 2000 volunteers, were deployed under the UN flag.[191] These figures, with only 20 per cent of personnel drawn from civil communities, demonstrate how the UN peacekeeping enterprise is predominantly staffed by trained military personnel.

That the Security Council to continues to authorise peacekeeping without recognition of the incipient militarisation, and the relationship of militarisation with negative gender discourse for men and women, is to perpetuate a model of peace premised on (sexed and gendered) force. In response to the *More Secure World Report*, the Secretary-General established a Peacebuilding Commission to oversee the activities of peacekeeping operations and to 'effectively address the challenge of helping countries with the transition from war to lasting peace'.[192] The role of the Peacebuilding Commission includes the provision of a central intergovernmental body to better facilitate the 'immediate post-conflict phase to longer term reconstruction and development'.[193] To achieve this goal, it is vital that the Peacebuiling Commission examines the persistent gender weaknesses of past peacekeeping operations. Peacekeeping and peacebuilding fail women as a solution to security threats as not only are they seen to

---

186 SC Res 1701 (11 August 2006).
187 SC Res 1272 (25 October 1999).
188 Gray above note 61, at 225; Resolution 770 (August 1992); SC Res 836 (June 1995).
189 For up to date figures see: http://www.un.org/en/peacekeeping/resources/statistics/factsheet. shtml (last accessed February 2011).
190 Gray, above note 61, at 204.
191 Above note 189.
192 *In Larger Freedom* above note 70, at paragraph 114.
193 *More Secure World Report*, above note 71: introductory note by Kofi Annan at paragraph 15; also see Report of UN Panel on Peace Operations, available at: http://www.un.org/peace/reports/peace_ operations/ (last accessed February 2011).

downplay women's role in communities, contributing to women's future low status in the 'new' state, but peacekeeping and peacebuilding, as military-based operations, bring increased threats (rather than protection) to women. Such threats include sexual violence, from peacekeepers or from the sex industries that spring up alongside military bases, as well as the threat of sexual and domestic violence from local men. Each aspect of the peacekeeping continuum raises these issues. For example, peacekeeping, as an activity deployed in the 'post-conflict moment' must address the increasing feminist scholarship that questions the militarisation of post-conflict communities,[194] the failure of international institutions to be inclusive of women in decision-making process[195] and the increased levels of violence against women in post-conflict communities.[196] Peacebuilding initiatives in East Timor,[197] in Kosovo,[198] Afghanistan and Iraq[199] demonstrate how women's rights have either been implemented through simple formal equality models[200] or, in the case of Afghanistan and Iraq, been 'traded' for constitution building initiatives that tolerate religious laws and customs that are built on gender constructions that are often harmful to women.[201]

The peacekeeping continuum, therefore, offers an illusionary 'alternative' to force from a feminist perspective. The incipient militarisation of peacekeeping endeavours is of key concern, especially in terms of the associated sexual exploitation and abuse that is increasingly apparent as an element of peacekeeping communities. The shift by the United Nations to record and challenge sexual exploitation and abuse by peacekeepers is undermined by strategies, for example, the production of a Code of Conduct,[202] that depend upon gendered images of women's sexual vulnerability that also negates women's agency. This replicates the lack of agency, and low levels of participation, offered to women in post-conflict communities. In the context of a discussion of authorised force, these narratives suggest the gendered faultlines of Article 42 force – especially with regard to the role of militarisation as dependent on gender for successful functioning and the consequential limited theory of sexual agency – extend into peacekeeping narratives. By 2011, the distinction between

194 Cockburn and Zarkov, *The Postwar Moment* (London: Lawrence and Wishart, 2002).
195 Chinkin, *Peace Agreements as a Means of Promoting Equality and Ensuring Participation of Women*, UN Doc. EGM/PEACE/2003/ BP; Mazurana, Raven-Roberts and Parpart, *Gender, Conflict and Peacekeeping* (London: Rowman and Littlefield, 2005).
196 Above note 194; Durham and Gurd, *Listening to the Silences: Women and War* (The Hague: Kluwer, 2005), chapters 6, 8, 16; Orford, above note 92, at 389, citing Hibaaq Osman, *Somalia: Will Reconstruction Threaten Women's Progress?* Ms. March–April 1993 at 12; Coulter, 'Female Fighters in the Sierra Leone War', 88, *Feminist Review* (2008), 54.
197 Charlesworth and Wood,' Women and Human Rights in the Rebuilding of East Timor', 71 (2), *Nordic Journal of International Law* (2002), 352.
198 Lyth (ed.), *Getting it Right? A Gender Approach to UNMIK Administration in Kosovo* (Johanneshov, Sweden: Kvinna Till Kvinna, 2001).
199 Kandiyoti, 'Between the Hammer and the Anvil', 28, *Third World Quarterly* (2007), 503.
200 See further the discussion of Timor-Leste in chapter four.
201 Above note 199.
202 Secretary-General Report, A Comprehensive Strategy to Eliminate Further Sexual Exploitation and Abuse in Peace Keeping Operations, UN Doc A/59/710, available online at http://www.un.org/Docs/journal/asp/ws.asp?m=a/59/710; Otto, above note 169.

peacekeeping and peace enforcement was blurred in a third of operations where peacekeeping forces were either complemented by or adapted into chapter VII enforcement forces.[203] Recent Security Council practice, then, not only relies on military personnel for peacekeeping purposes the distinction between chapter VII enforcement action and peacekeeping has collapsed in the post- millennium security environment: especially in relation to peacekeeping in Africa. The merging of peacekeeping and peace enforcement was reflected in the Capstone Document[204] and the Peacekeeping 2010 Report[205] both of which saw the merger of peacekeeping and peace enforcement as inevitable.

Beyond peacekeeping, the Secretary-General's post-millennium approach to addressing human security does on its face appear to embrace some of the concerns presented here. Through the creation of the Peacebuilding Commission, it could be hoped that stronger mechanisms for incorporating women's needs into peacekeeping and peacebuilding operations may come into existence. Consequently, peacekeeping operations after the Secretary General's Report have seen gender awareness and dedicated gender offices as integral elements of their sphere of reference.[206] Likewise, the broad understanding of threats contained in the Secretary-General's submissions does include social and economic threats, particularly poverty but also health. These can be read as encompassing threats to women's security within the mainstream of international laws for authorising force.[207] The focus on prevention rather than reaction is also a step forward. In addition, measures short of force, particularly sanctions and mediation, are highlighted as necessary before the authorisation of force occurs.[208]

Yet this chapter has argued that each of these steps forward in the post-millennium security discourse fails to account for the impact of past security norms on women. The Peacebuilding Commission, and the creation of gender units[209] in the most recent operations, is applauded but the emergent work of feminist activists on the failure of gender mainstreaming now needs to be incorporated into the objectives of these bodies.[210] The recognition of poverty and disease as threats to international peace and security is stymied by the nexus with the state required for these to emerge on

---

203 See: SC Res 1912 (26 February 2010) on Timor-Leste; SC Res 1943 (13 October 2010) on Afghanistan; SC Res 1944 (14 October 2010) on Haiti; SC Res 1952 (29 November 2010) on the DRC; SC Res 1961 (17 December 2010) on Liberia; SC Res 1967 (19 January 2011) on the Ivory Coast.

204 Department of Peacekeeping Operations, United Nations peacekeeping Operations: Principles and Guidelines 2008: available online at: http://www.peacekeepingbestpractices.unlb.org/Pbps/Library/Capstone_Doctrine_ENG.pdf (last accessed February 2011).

205 Report of the Secretary-General to the General Assembly on the financing of the United Nations peacekeeping operations UN doc. A/60/696 (24 February 2006).

206 See Charlesworth and Chinkin's discussion of the differences between the Cambodian and Liberia peacekeeping operations, above note 90, at 294–299.

207 Above note 70.

208 Above note 70.

209 See the discussion of the Gender Affairs Unit in East Timor in Charlesworth and Wood, above note 197.

210 See Kouvo, 'The United Nations and Gender Mainstreaming' in Buss and Manji (eds), *International Law: Modern Feminist Approaches* (Oxford: Hart, 2005).

the international agenda. Additionally, the failure of the Secretary-General's Reports to identify specific health threats to women or to address the relationship between poverty and women's lives negates the possibility of human security that is reactive to specific threats to women's security. The focus on prevention in the Secretary-General's Reports is, therefore, undermined by this persistent failure to address women's needs as a different and complex aspect of international security.

When women do emerge in either a *More Secure World* or *In Larger Freedom* it is as mothers, for example, at risk of maternal mortality, or as victims, for example, as susceptible to human-trafficking networks. Women as potential agents integral to the building of processes that challenge international threats are overlooked. Feminist evidence suggests that it is through listening to women and through developing policies aimed at eradicating violence against women that real change within communities is achieved.[211] These conceptual flaws are then played out in peacekeeping operations that fail to accommodate women's health needs, fail to utilise women's potential to act as community leaders and fail to see women's role as actors during and after armed conflict. I have also considered how sanctions, as an alternative to Article 42 force, require analysis from feminist scholars in terms of the limits of the law and violence relationship. This is further evidenced in the *In Larger Freedom's* section entitled 'Protecting Civilians' that identifies women and gender violence within the wider discussion but fails to acknowledge the disproportionate presence of women in civilian communities in times of armed conflict.[212]

Underlying each of these claims is an understanding that military force and armed conflict are influenced by dominant social constructions of gender. Military structures also play a role in the reproduction of gender roles that are based on a hierarchy of relations between men and women. To persist as military narratives the soldier is constructed as the warrior or male actor poised to save feminised communities without this gendered assumption, militaries cease to look like military institutions.[213] When projected on to the law on the use of force, the underlying assumption present in the collective security structure – that force can be authorised and thus be a tool to achieve legal enforcement – is recognised a gendered assumption that prioritises and legitimates male forms of violence as legal.

The chapter concludes with reflection on the disparity between mediation and force in the *More Secure World* Report. While the Report reflects at length on the use of force, it fails to provide a full scale analysis of the role of mediation in the international community. Thus, the Report reiterates the division between chapter VI and VII of the UN Charter that Charlesworth and Chinkin highlight as inimical to positive change for women.[214] While the Secretary-General introduces the Report with approval of

---

211 However, note Recommendation 19 (d) which states 'Greater consultation with and involvement in peace processes of important voices from civil society, especially those of women, who are often neglected during negotiations' This recommendation falls short of demanding women's inclusion in decision-making forums, above note 71, page 80.
212 Above note 70; pages 62–63.
213 Gardam, 'An Alien's Encounter with the Law of Armed Conflict', in Naffine and Owens, *Sexing the Subject of Law*, LBC, 1997.
214 Above note 66, at 6.

the recommendation that 'two of the tools which we must improve are sanctions and mediation', the Report has a dedicated section on sanctions and on the use of force but no section on mediation.[215] The capacity of the Security Council to act under chapter VII and authorise force is given extensive attention in the Report. This suggests that while threats to international peace and security continued to be broadened, the capacity to respond to those threats has not been broadened. The Report provides recommendations on the capacity of states to act in self-defence under Article 51 of the UN Charter and the power of the Security to authorise force under Article 42. These recommendations were then re-assessed by states in September 2005 and formalised in international law at the 2005 World Summit and the subsequent General Assembly Resolution.[216] As such the use of force to 'protect', the use of preventative force and the general enlarged scope of Security Council action (including humanitarian actions, peace enforcement, peacekeeping and peacebuilding) gained re-iteration rather than renewal. For feminist scholarship these developments are important as they entrench authorised force as the preferred means of international arbitration in times of crisis. However, any benefits gained by the use of force are challenged by the chorus of women's voices highlighted in this chapter, which not only identify a different range of threats to human security, but demonstrate force, whether illegal or authorised, as complicit in domestic and sexual violence against women.

My final concern is that in a system where the use of authorised force gains increased probability, justifications for unilateral force are also widened. In the final four chapters, I consider self-defence rights, self-determination as a justification for the use of force, humanitarian interventions as a justification for force and the 'War on Terror' as a justification for the use of force. Implicit in each discussion is an understanding that state justifications function by referencing authorised force. That international law has a collective system for authorising force suggests force may be used proportionately and that the use of force may occur with justice as the goal. This fuels state justifications to use force unilaterally. Had the Secretary-General applied the broad approach used to define human security in the attempt to develop measures to curb threats, the status quo of force may have shifted. Without such a re-focus, the collective security system contained in chapter VII, and reinforced by recent Secretary-General and General Assembly initiatives,[217] at this stage fails to address the association of gender with armed conflict or the role of military activity in the perpetuation of violence against women, particularly sexual violence. The consequence is the denial of the impact of armed conflict on women's lives and the incapacity of the current system to challenge threats to women's security.

---

215 See above note 70, at 50–51 (sanctions) and 53–62 (the use of force); the Report does encourage the use of treaties and intergovernmental bodies in response to specific threats, but does not specifically develop understanding of international mediation as a means to prevent or halt threats.

216 Importantly, the Report's five stage test for the legitimacy of Security Council acts authorising force was left out of the outcomes document; see above note 69, recommendation 56, at page 85.

217 Above notes 69, 70 and 71.

3   Justifying force: self-defence

The domestic analogy between both the regulation of international justifications and interpersonal justifications constructs and limits the international law on the use of force in a sexed and gendered way. This chapter focuses on the international legal right of states to use force in self-defence. The international right to self-defence, preserved in the UN Charter and customary international law, mimics the faultlines of Western domestic self-defence laws. This occurs through the construction of a paradigm case of self-defence that is assumed by legal narratives across domestic and international accounts. As a consequence, I argue that feminist analysis and philosophical accounts on the limits of the interpersonal right offer useful tools to understand the limitations of the international right of states to use force in self-defence.

Under the title of 'Domestic Analogy' I analyse Article 51 of the UN Charter and the application of this right in the UN era. The domestic analogy illustrates a conceptual weakness of the international model. Feminist accounts of the limitations of domestic laws on self-defence are instrumental in demonstrating the flaws of the international model. Akin to its domestic counterpart, the international right to use force in self-defence is circumscribed by the requirements of necessity and proportionality. This is the point where the analogy is most evident and where feminist approaches to international law must work to build an international legal response that is not presupposed on a masculine legal subject. Feminist reconstruction of international law on self-defence, therefore, requires exposure rather than reinforcement of the analogy. As such, strategies are required that construct the scope of international self-defence outside of the sexed interpersonal parameters of self-defence. The conceptual disparity between international and interpersonal self-defence is also present through the inclusion of a right to collective self-defence under Article 51.

In the third section, titled 'Narratives of Self-defence' I analyse how the sexed and gendered contours of international self-defence are masked by contemporary debates on the scope of self-defence under the conditions of the global war against international terrorism. In section three, I argue that the preemptive self-defence claim articulated under the 'War on Terror' or as a justification for the use of force in the global war against international terrorism is an extension of the self-defence analogy, as the preemptive self-defence justification attempts to revive a provocation-type excuse on the international plane.

As such, I make two claims in response to contemporary narratives on the use of force against terrorist actors and in light of the domestic analogy. First, as preemptive force is closer to a provocation-type excuse, rather than a self-defence justification, preemptive force is riddled with analogous conceptual flaws to those identified by domestic feminist legal theories in response to Western domestic provocation laws. This argument leads to a rejection, from a feminist perspective, of the usefulness of preemptive force as a justification for the use of force under international law. Second, through the significant shifting of debate on international self-defence since 2001, preemptive self-defence narratives entrench Article 51 as normatively unproblematic (even when argued to be temporally surpassed by the conditions of the global war against international terrorism). This has the further consequence of embedding the sexed and gendered contours of Article 51 as an international legal narrative that is normal and natural. I argue that feminist approaches to international law on self-defence must engage the normative contours of the right to use force in self-defence to build an understanding of possible re-conceptualisation of this area of law that does not prioritise a socially constructed male understanding of justified violence. Through understanding Article 51 as a narrative with distinct descriptive purchase in Western communities, the heroic and Western male state and the assumption of Western spectator privilege in defining the parameters of the international right to use force are exposed.

I conclude the chapter with the argument that feminist appraisal of international self-defence laws must look beyond narratives on terrorism and preemptive self-defence to expose the sexed constructs entrenched in apparently less controversial readings of Article 51. Analysis of the limitations (necessity and proportionality) of international self-defence is an important site for future feminist scholarship. The chapter closes with a discussion of the merits of the domestic analogy as a discursive tool, considering whether this approach, as used by other commentators, should be amended or rejected.

The domestic analogy

State arguments for justified force attempt to gain legal acceptance for acts that would otherwise be prohibited under Article 2(4). In the absence of Security Council authorisation under Article 42 of the UN Charter, Article 51 allows states to claim self-defence as a justification for the use of force. Article 51 declares the following:

> Nothing in the present Charter shall impair the inherent right of individual or collective self defence if an armed attack occurs against a member of the United Nations, until the Security Council has taken measures necessary to maintain international peace and security. Measures taken by Members in the exercise of this right of self-defence shall be immediately reported to the Security Council and shall not in any way affect the authority and responsibility of the Security Council under the present Charter to take at any time such action as it deems necessary in order to maintain or restore international peace and security.[1]

---

1   UN Charter, Article 51.

Prior to looking at contemporary debates on the range and scope of Article 51, it is important to understand the accepted parameters of the right of states to act in self-defence. Despite recognised tensions between customary international law and Charter based self-defence, there remains a settled 'core' of international self-defence.[2]

The core includes the following: Article 51's role in protecting (and forming understandings of) the sovereignty of states through the armed attack requirement,[3] the function of self-defence as a private right of states,[4] the capacity of Article 51 to be exercised either individually by states or collectively by a group of states, and the settled role of the general international legal principles of proportionality and necessity as parameters on defensive actions.[5] Each of these features has been reiterated by the International Court of Justice (ICJ) and each is generally regarded as an uncontroversial element of Article 51.[6] For example, in the *Nicaragua* Case the Court stated 'the exercise of this right is subject to the State concerned being the victim of an armed attack'[7] so that '[w]here collective self-defence is invoked, it is to be expected that the State for whose benefit this right is used will have declared itself to be a victim of an armed attack'.[8] The Court also found 'general agreement on the nature of acts which can be treated as constituting an armed attack' alongside affirming collective self-defence as an important component of the international right.[9] Later statements from the ICJ, including in the *Oil Platforms* case where the Court re-iterated the necessity that a state be the victim of an actual armed attack,[10] the *Israeli Wall* Opinion where the Court found the building of the wall could not be a form of self-defence due to the absence of an armed attack,[11] and the *Democratic Republic of the Congo v. Uganda*

---

2 Greenwood, 'International Law and the Preemptive Use of Force: Afghanistan, Al-Qaida and Iraq,' 4, San Diego International Law Journal (2003), 7; Gray, International Law and the Use of Force (Oxford: Oxford University Press, 2008, 3rd edition), at 70, 121.

3 See Bothe, 'Terrorism and the Legality of Preemptive Force' 14 EJIL (2003) 227, at 228–233. Note, while it is accepted that 'an armed attack' triggers the right to self-defence, the definition of what constitutes an armed attack has been the subject of controversy, see Military and Paramilitary Activities in and Against Nicaragua, Merits, 1986 ICJ Reports 14, [henceforth Nicaragua case], paragraph 195.

4 However, note some commentators suggest the Security Council does play a role in Article 51 actions, see Gray, above note 2, at 101; also see Nicaragua case, ibid, at paragraph 200.

5 For further descriptions of the 'core' of Article 51 self-defence, see Cassese, International Law (Oxford: Oxford University Press, 2001), at 310; Dinstein, War, Aggression and Self-defence (Cambridge: Cambridge University Press, 2001, 3rd edition), chapter 7; Gray, above note 2, chapter 4; Mgbeoji, Collective Insecurity (*Kelowna, BC*: UBC, 2003), at 83.

6 See Gray, above note 2 at 70 and at 121, stating '[t]he core content of self-defence is universally accepted'; Gardam, 'Proportionality and Force in International Law', 87, AJIL (1993), 391 at 403.

7 Nicaragua Case above note 3, paragraph 191.

8 Ibid, paragraph 195.

9 Ibid; see Mgbeoji's discussion arguing General Assembly Res 3314, the Definition of Aggression settles this, above note 5, at 90.

10 Oil Platforms Case (Case Concerning Oil Platforms (Islamic Republic of Iran v. USA) (2003) ICJ Reports, 161, paragraph 51.

11 Legal Consequences of the Construction of a Wall in the Occupied Palestinian Territory, Advisory Opinion, ICJ 9 July 2004, paragraph 139 [henceforth Israel Wall Opinion].

decision where the Court found states must be the victim of an armed attack imput-able to another state for Article 51 to initiate a private right of states to act defen-sively,[12] reference the primacy of state sovereignty and territory as that which must be under attack. Outside of this core of self-defence, each of these judgements has been the subject of dissension amongst international lawyers and states have made a range of controversial claims, particularly the right to protect nationals abroad,[13] the right to use force on a foreign territory when an invitation from the government exists,[14] and the right to use anticipatory self-defence.[15]

Furthermore, the use of the phrase 'the inherent right' in Article 51 has produced tension over the continuation of customary international law on self-defence during the UN era. The ICJ, in the *Nicaragua* case, indicated that the Charter and customary international law on self-defence function as compatible rather than oppositional.[16] However, this never really resolved the different approaches that, on the one hand, argued for a reading of Article 51 subject to customary international law doctrine, and therefore incorporating a notion of anticipatory self-defence,[17] and, on the other hand, scholars that emphasised the requirement of a literal reading of Article 51[18] and thus perceiving an actual armed attack as a prerequisite to state invocation of Article 51. This debate has developed again in the early twenty-first century with preemptive self-defence adding a potential third category to be accommodated within the self-defence justification. I review this development in section three.

Rather than engaging with this tension between the articulations of customary international law versus Charter formulations of self-defence, I place the settled 'core' of self-defence under scrutiny. This is because an important aspect of the core of Arti-cle 51 is the incorporation of an analogy between interpersonal and international self-defence into the contours of the international right.[19] For example, Rodin explains the role of state sovereignty in international self-defence law as follows:

> The structure of international law suggests a strong analogy between individual self-defence and national-defense: persons are constituted by their existence as organic entities and they have the claim-right against other persons not to destroy their life or interfere in their bodily integrity. States are constituted by their exist-ence as sovereign entities and they have the claim-right against other states not to destroy their political independence or interfere in their territorial integrity.[20]

---

12 Armed Activities on the Territory of the Congo (Democratic Republic of the Congo v. Uganda) ICJ 19 December 2005, paragraph 143 [henceforth DRC v. Uganda].
13 See Gray, above note 2, at 75.
14 Ibid, at 74.
15 Dinstein, above note 5; O'Connell, *The Myth of Preemptive Self-defence,* paper prepared for the American International Law Task Force on Terrorism (2002).
16 Above note 3.
17 For example, see: O'Brien, The Conduct of Just and Limited War (1981), 133.
18 Henkin, How Nations Behave (1979) 141–144; Brownlie, International Law and the Use of Force by States (Oxford: Oxford University Press, 1963), 257–276.
19 Murphy, 'The Doctrine of Preemptive Self-Defense', 50, Villanova Law Review (2005) 699, at 744.
20 Rodin, War and Self-Defense (Oxford: Oxford University Press, 2002), at 110.

The reiteration of the state as the primary victim of the armed attack requirement replicates, in international law, a legal subject that is drawn from national legal structures, particularly Western legal structures. However, feminist legal theories have analysed how common law accounts of self-defence configure a masculine legal subject.[21] Furthermore, the unqualified acceptance of an armed attack,[22] as the primary trigger to initiate a state's right to act under Article 51, replicates the public, one-off and aggressive nature of attacks envisaged in interpersonal relations.[23] This projects a similar vision of masculine-defined violence onto international law. As a result international law construes the state in analogy with the masculine subject of interpersonal self-defence laws, despite the inclusion of collective self-defence in the international model that from the outset indicates the different circumstances and degrees of violence apparent in a simple comparison between international and interpersonal self-defence. This then leads to examination of the articulation of limitations on the scope of international self-defence (necessity and proportionality) and the consequences of this analysis for the persistence of the domestic analogy. I conclude that through the explicit linkage with the legal features of interpersonal self-defence, Article 51 is given a sexed meaning that draws on Western canons of masculinity to define danger, violence and aggression.[24]

Which 'self' defended? Construing the male state

Article 51 is constructed so that the decision to use force is shifted from the collective (represented by the UN Security Council acting under Article 42) to the individual state. In this designation of state capacity to recognise an armed attack and to respond with defensive force, Article 51 embeds a model of sovereignty drawn from interpersonal self-defence rights. For many writers, this point is self-evident.[25] The analogy between the sovereign status of the state and citizen is evidenced and underpinned by the right of legal subjects to act in self-defence, in a somewhat circular relationship. When explaining why self-defence exists, many commentators describe

---

21 Coomaraswamy, Report of the Special Rapporteur on Violence Against Women, its Causes and Consequences, UN Doc. E/CN.4/1996/53 (7 February 1996); Jacobs and Ogle, Self-Defense and Battered Women Who Kill: A New Framework (Santa Barbara, CA: Praeger, 2002); Lyons and McCord, 'Moral Reasoning and the Criminal Law: the Example of Self-defence', 30, American Criminal Review (1992), 97.

22 While contemporary debates argue for the shift to inclusion of 'preemptive self-defence' to include responses to challenge future rather than actual attacks, this leaves the armed attack requirement in tact as the central understanding of Article 51, see below.

23 R v. Lavalee [1990] 1 S.C.R. 852; also see Kim, 'The Rhetoric of Self-defense', 13, Berkeley Journal of Criminal Law (2008), 261.

24 I use the term 'sexed' in preference to 'gender' because self-defence constructs the 'normal' or 'natural' legal subject that, I argue, is the sexed male; see further discussion in chapter one.

25 Glennon, 'The Fog of Law: Self-defence, Incoherence and Article 51', 25, Harvard Journal of Law and Public Policy, 539 (2001–2002), at 557; Dinstein, above note 5, at 160; also see: Dickinson, 'The Analogy between Natural Persons and International Persons in the Law of Nations', 26, Yale Law Journal (1916–1917), 564.

interpersonal self-defence as functioning as a form of 'basic norm' that the international right accrues from.[26] For example, Grotius, who develops international self-defence through the analogy, declares the 'right of defending our persons and property... may nevertheless be applied to public hostilities'.[27] Similarly, in the early twentieth century, the US Secretary of State suggested to the French Ambassador, during the drafting of the Kellogg–Briand Pact, that 'no treaty provision can add to the natural right of self-defence'.[28] The interpersonal right is perceived as explaining the existence of defensive rights accruing to states. Because interpersonal self-defence is regarded as an inherent aspect of personhood, the assumption is that the right of self-defence is replicated in the international system as a right of all legal subjects.[29] This is further supported by the language of Article 51, which refers to self-defence as an 'inherent right'.[30] Some commentators underscore this with reference to the French text of the Charter that describes self-defence as *droit naturel*.[31] Dinstein describes the international right of self-defence as having 'its roots in inter-personal relations' adding it 'has been sanctified in domestic legal systems since time immemorial'.[32] Walzer grounds the analogy in the understanding of the functioning of the international legal system as a whole:

> Our primary perceptions and judgements of aggression are the products of analogical reasoning. When the analogy is made explicit, as it is among lawyers, the world of states takes the shape of a political society the characterisation of which is entirely accessible through such notions as crime and punishment, self-defense, law enforcement, and so on.[33]

Lauterpacht uses the domestic analogy to explain the manner in which self-defence vests in states but is limited by law.[34] Similarly, Kelsen, suggests:

26 On the function of a basic norm in a legal system see, Kelsen, Introduction to the Problems of Legal Theory (Oxford: Oxford University Press, 1934, 2002 Reprint).
27 Grotius, De Jure Ac Pacis (The Law of War and Peace) (translated by Campbell, 1814), chapter 1, XVI available online at http://www.constitution.org/gro/djbp.htm
28 Telegram from Frank B. Kellogg, Secretary of State, to the Ambassador in France (23 April 1928) in Foreign Relations of the US (1928) 34, 36–37.
29 However, international law no longer regards states as the only legal subject: Reparations for Injuries Suffered in the service of the United Nations, Advisory Opinion, ICJ, 11 April 1949, page 174; the extension under international law of a right of self-defence to legal subjects other than states has not been mooted.
30 However, this choice of wording has not been without controversy or alternative interpretations see Gray, above note 2, at 98–99. Due to space restrictions I have not developed a comparative analysis of national self-defence provisions. Such a project may be a valuable tool to exposing the partiality of the contours of international self-defence.
31 Schachter, 'Self-defence and the Rule of Law', 83, AJIL (1989), at 259; see also Nicaragua Case, above note 3, at paragraph 176
32 Dinstein, above note 5, at 160, however see also p.164 where Dinstein acknowledges 'even if the right of self-defence will never be abolished in the relations between flesh-and-blood human beings, there is no guarantee of a similar immobility in international law'.
33 Walzer, Just and Unjust Wars (Basic Books, 2006, 4th edition), at 58.
34 Lauterpacht, The Function of Law in the International Community (1933), 179–180.

[i]mposing obligations on, and granting rights to states by way of international law has the same character as imposing obligations on, and granting rights to, a legal person by way of the state legal system, the state is the legal person. . . .[35]

This approach to self-defence continues to resonate through contemporary documents where some discernable core is perceived as existing prior to contemporary international legal developments. A claim to state rights, including self-defence, is evidence of the sovereignty of a state and vice versa. This is intimately connected to understandings of the ongoing existence of the legal system, so Walzer goes on to claim, 'the rights of member states must be vindicated, for it is only by virtue of those rights that there is a society at all. If they cannot be upheld (at least sometimes), international society collapses into a state of war or is transformed into a universal tyranny'.[36] Similar sentiments, predicting the demise of the UN system regulating the use of force, after flagrant violations of Article 2(4) and Article 51, have been expressed by commentators[37] including, most recently, after the US-led invasion of Iraq in 2003.[38]

Yet in discussing the right of states to act in self-defence most writers fail to consider why a right to act in self-defence exists at either the interpersonal or international level. Furthermore, rare philosophical accounts of (interpersonal) self-defence prove to be complicated, unconvincing and largely abstract.[39] Uniacke, one of the few scholars to offer an extended and convincing philosophical account of self-defence, explains the failure of other philosophical engagements:

> An account of justified homicide in self-defence must elaborate, rather than simply assume, a theory of forfeiture, because important human rights such as the right to life are typically said to be unconditional. The claimed unconditionality of human rights creates an immediate, insurmountable difficulty for a theory of forfeiture in respect of the right to life: an unconditional right cannot, by definition, be forfeited. . . . If I forfeit my right to life when I unjustly threaten someone else's life, then the right to life is not an unconditional human right.[40]

Uniacke provides a comprehensive survey of the attempts of other scholars to pin down the normative reasoning that lies behind self-defence. Uniacke's conclusion is to regard self-defence as a limited right. This avoids the difficulty of the existence of a justification that abrogates the right to life.[41] Under international self-defence laws,

---

35 Kelsen, above note 26, at 110.
36 Walzer, above note 33, at 59.
37 Notably, Franck, 'Who Killed Article 2(4)?' 64, AJIL (1970), 809.
38 Franck, 'What Happens Now? The United Nations After Iraq', 97 (3), AJIL (2003), 607; Glennon, above note 25.
39 For a helpful discussion of the legal and moral ambiguity in interpersonal self-defence, see Kim, above note 23, at 33–44.
40 Uniacke, Permissible Killing (Cambridge: Cambridge University Press, 1994), at 195.
41 Also see: Ashworth, 'Self-Defence and the Right to Life', 34, Criminal Law Review (1975), 282, at 296.

the same conundrum must be faced with respect to Article 2(4), which has been perceived as a *jus cogens* norm.[42] Schachter explains:

> Recognising these rights as exceptions to the general prohibition on force necessarily presupposes that the exercise of the right is limited by law. If this were not the case and each state remained free to decide for itself when and to what extent it may use force, the legal restraint on force would virtually disappear.[43]

The circularity that Uniacke identifies as existing in philosophical understandings of interpersonal self-defence[44] remains in international understandings of the right because the right exists through the acceptance of Article 2(4)'s absolute prohibition on force and the acceptance of justified acts in abrogation of Article 2(4). Uniacke argues, to justify (interpersonal) self-defence and move beyond the circularity of other accounts, it is therefore necessary to 'specify the scope of such rights in terms of what is just and unjust treatment of, and interference with, the particular individuals who possess these rights'.[45] There is no absolute right to self-defence as this would lead to incompatibility with Article 2(4) or, under national laws, lead to a violation of the right to life. Instead philosophical engagement with the normative structure underpinning self-defence laws, as either an international or an interpersonal right vesting in legal subjects, demonstrates how self-defence must always be a limited, or curtailed, right. Consequently, philosophical engagement indicates that the right of a state to act in self-defence is always a qualified right. In this sense the requirements that force be judged under standards of necessity and proportionality maintains the very possibility of self-defence as a justification for use of force in the international sphere. *It is therefore the limits of the right to self-defence and not its analogy with interpersonal self-defence that are required to explain the existence of the right under any legal system.*

However, the pliability of international self-defence – through tests of necessity and proportionality – continue to be explained through references to interpersonal self-defence. Thus one commentator explains:

> . . . international law contains no rigid rules about what amounts to reasonable measures of self-defence. Just as English law has gradually discarded inflexible rules about the degree of force which may be used in self-defence in favour of a principle that the force must be reasonable in the light of the circumstances

---

42 Chinkin, 'A Gendered Perspective to the International Use of Force', 12, *Australian Yearbook of International Law* (1992) 279, at 280.

43 Schachter, above note 31.

44 'if the possession and content of human rights is determined by a prior view about what is and what is not morally permissible, it is then circular to explain the permissibility of particular acts, such as homicide in self-defence, in terms of the non-violation of these rights' above note 40, at 211, referencing 'Self-Defense and Rights' in Thomson, Rights, Restitution and Risk (Harvard: Harvard University Press, 1986), 33.

45 Ibid, at 211.

of each case. Thus, as the scope and extent of a conflict increases, the range of measures which a state may legitimately take in self-defence broadens . . .[46]

This interpretation of English self-defence laws precedes feminist interrogation of the application of the interpersonal right to act in self-defence. In the late twentieth century, however, alongside the rise of feminist theories and activism in Western states, there emerged feminist understandings of the inadequacies of interpersonal self-defence laws in framing female violence as justifiable. Feminist critiques of the sexed nature of interpersonal defences remain pertinent, for example, a US study in 2002 found the following:

Self-defense law has not been especially successful in the defense of battered women who must claim it as a justification for killing their abusers to survive. This legal defense generally fails because the critical elements of the defense are not met – most often, a factual base for finding that the threat requiring lethal force was *imminent* and a factual base for finding the decision to use deadly force was *reasonable* (italics in original).[47]

Similar accounts have been offered in other Western states by feminists, in law reform processes and by the judiciary in some states.[48] In 1990, the Canadian Supreme Court found:

The law of self-defence is designed to ensure that the use of defensive force is really necessary. It justifies the act because the defender reasonably believed that he or she had no alternative but to take the attacker's life. If there is a significant time interval between the original unlawful assault and the accused's response, one tends to suspect that the accused was motivated by revenge rather than self-defence. In the paradigmatic case of a one-time bar room brawl between two men of equal size and strength, this inference makes sense.[49]

The Canadian Supreme Court highlights three assumptions of the bar-room brawl model of self-defence laws. First, the defensive acts are in response to a single act of irrational force. Kim describes the impact of this as setting, 'the parties in dramatic opposition – the violator of peace versus the law abiding citizen, or, more simply, antagonist versus protagonist, villain versus hero'.[50] Second, the act of irrational force occurs in a public space, so that:

46 Greenwood, 'The Relationship between Jus ad Bellum and Jus in Bello', 9, Review of International Studies (1983), 221, at 223.
47 Jacobs and Ogle, Self-Defense and Battered Women Who Kill: A New Framework (Santa Barbara, CA: Praeger, 2002), at 4.
48 See, for example, in the context of the UK, Quick and Wells, 'Getting Tough with Defences', Criminal Law Review (June 2006), 514.
49 R v. Lavalee [1990] 1 S.C.R. 852, page 868.
50 Above note 23, at 8.

. . . countering unjust violence with violence which is just evokes romanticized images of the cowboy or adventurer, defending himself (and perhaps also his honor) against the perils of the lawless frontier.[51]

Third, the parties are assumed to come to the conflict with relatively equal strength. In Western, and particularly common law legal traditions, the consequence of these features has been the development of the scope of self-defence without consideration of the impact of power inequalities associated with social constructions of gender.[52] What is perceived in philosophical, national and international accounts of self-defence as fundamental to the normative integrity and existence of the right – the requirements that self-defence be necessary and proportionate – has been identified by feminist legal theories as relying on interpretations that poise a male subject or actor to benefit.

From this perspective what is important for international versions of self-defence is the acknowledgement that the very features that should be seen to justify the existence of a legal right to self-defence for states, necessity and proportionality, reflect domestic legal standards that have been demonstrated as being subjective in a manner that projects male characteristics on to perceptions of the legal subject. *This is not argued so as to develop a 'female' version of proportionality or necessity: rather to acknowledge the spectrum of experiences we encounter, and are at risk of encountering, as gendered subjects.* The limitations on interpersonal self-defence construct a legal subject that is presumed to be male and presumed to act in stereotypically male ways. This is achieved through a legal narrative that evokes a paradigm case of self-defence that is assumed to be morally just. That a parallel paradigm is transplanted into international relations, where the state is assumed to be at greatest risk from an armed attack from another state, replicates a masculine model of interactions between legal subjects.[53] This allows the rightness (or moral valour) of the right of states to act in self-defence to dictate a violent response that, as is argued in chapter two when conducted as military force not only reflects a sexed legal model but also produces complex gendered consequences and harms. Consequently, if self-defence is developed as an inherent right of states and without adequate attention to the limitations of the right, the understanding of an international legal structure premised on the prohibition on the use of force is placed at risk. The conclusion is largely supported by state practice during the UN era,

51 Ibid.
52 Byrd, 'Till Death Do us Part: A Comparative Approach to Justifying Lethal Self-defence by Battered Women', Duke Journal of Comparative and International Law (1991), 169.
53 However, in political discourse the state is often referenced through a female pronoun, especially when the integrity of the state appears to require defending, see, for example, the discussion of the defence arrangements between the US and Canada, Ignatieff, 'State Failure and Nation Building' 'in Holzgrefe and Keohane, Humanitarian Intervention (Cambridge: Cambridge University Press, 2003) at 313; in the context of a weaker state drawing on the military power of another state the feminised reference for the state protected is not surprising and corresponds with sexed narratives between protectors and protected persons in liberal discourse; for discussion see Kinsella, 'Gendering Grotius', 34 (2), Political Theory (2006).

where spurious attempts by states to justify force as self-defence have generally been regarded as calling international law itself into question.

Each of the features identified in the *Lavelee* case,[54] therefore, retains meaning under the international right of self-defence. This includes the public nature of violence that attracts the attention of the international system (through the armed attack requirement of Article 51), the assumption that deployment of force occurs in a simple attack – counter force binary and that the parties using aggressive and defensive force are of equal size and strength. Domestic feminist legal theories demonstrate how these features are more likely to protect some male violence and determine female violence as unjustifiable. Reflection on the relationships between states demonstrates how these same features represent a limited account of the manner that communities encounter threats or of the way that conflicts emerge between states. Of particular importance is the understanding that responses to the primary threats to women's safety and security are not construed as crossing the threshold that deems international or individual defensive measures justifiable.

As a result the sexed legal subject of international self-defence laws has specific repercussions for women.[55] First, constructions of the state as a masculine actor contribute to the devaluation of characteristics associated with the feminine. The corollary of this is when women act outside dominant projections of gender norms they are often ridiculed, demonised or ignored. This plays a role in women devaluing their own voice, authority and agency regardless of their specifically feminine or masculine traits because the voice of 'reason', 'rationality' and 'authority' is associated with culturally described masculinity (and consequently attributed to male actors) and reinforced by legal structures. Second, the construction of self-defence through a masculinised state gives military behaviour – the use of force – the appearance of being exercised, when defensive, as rational and controlled behaviour. Of particular concern, as was demonstrated in chapter two, are the specific threats military behaviour holds for women and that such threats exist whether a woman is local to a conflict, internally displaced or a refugee, a participant in the military action, or the member of the family of a military actor.[56] Moreover, under international self-defence the dis-analogous inclusion of collective self-defence enhances the narrative of rational force as within the capacity of the international legal subject of the state through a projection of heroics onto the powerful state able to 'save' and 'rescue' a state violated by the aggression of the rogue state. Finally, the international reasonableness requirements further entrench a sexed form of subjectivity into international law while failing (like their national counterparts) to gauge harms to women and violence against women in tests of proportionality or necessity.

---

54 R v. Lavalee [1990] 1 S.C.R. 852, at 868.
55 This shift from a conceptual/analytical account to a descriptive/empirical evaluation is indicative of the feminist assumption of the role of practice in theory and vice versa.
56 Houppert, 'Another KBR Rape Case', *The Nation* (3 April 2008); Amnesty International, *Lives Blown Apart: Crimes against Women in Times of Conflict. Stop Violence Against Women.* Amnesty International Report (London, November 2004).

How to defend? Necessity and proportionality

While functioning as general international legal principles, as well as having discrete meaning in the international humanitarian law of armed conflict,[57] necessity and proportionality are perceived as the parameters that the use of defensive force must occur within to be considered lawful. As has been discussed, above, attempts to explain the existence of self-defence lead to circular arguments unless attention is paid to the limits of the right. Rodin tells us 'the legal and philosophical literature on self-defense has identified three intrinsic limitations to the right. These limitations are necessity, imminence, and proportionality'.[58] Brownlie describes proportionality as 'innate in any genuine concept of' and the 'essence' of self-defence.[59] Gardam describes the joint requirements of necessity and proportionality 'as integral components' of self-defence.[60] These descriptions are reiterated by other writers, who describe the proportionality and necessity requirements through reference to the *Caroline* incident[61] as the *fons et origo*[62] of self-defence and indicative of when 'the modern law of self-defence was born'.[63] For Bowett, the *Caroline* incident is the *locus classicus* of international self-defence rights.[64] Like, philosophical accounts of the interpersonal right, international accounts of self-defence see these limitations on the right as self-evident and integral to the existence of the right. Rodin describes the limitations as 'a deeply intuitive restriction to rights of defense', although he acknowledges the necessity requirement, under the international right, as broader than interpersonal accounts.[65]

Through the domestic analogy enlarged in this project, the contrast between state and scholarly acceptance of the limits on self-defence and the failure of states to develop clear practice in this area is explained by the sexed core of the analogy. To explore this further, I will consider each limitation on international self-defence, that is, necessity and proportionality, in turn. Under the discussion of necessity I will dem-

57 Gardam, Necessity, Proportionality and the Use of Force (Cambridge: Cambridge University Press, 2004), chapters 3 and 4.
58 Rodin, above note 20. Also note, while necessity and proportionality are accepted international legal principles in contexts outside of self-defence, the notion of imminence is often subsumed into the category of necessity. I use the broader expression of reasonableness to embrace all three concepts.
59 Brownlie, International Law and the Use of Force by States (Oxford: Oxford University Press, 1963), at 434 and 279.
60 Gardam, above note 57, at 186.
61 See Jennings, 'The Caroline and McLeod Cases', 32, AJIL (1938), 82; this is a discussion of the 1837 British attack on a civilian vessel to halt the initiation of action by American rebels in support of the Canadian challenge to British rule. The subsequent correspondence between the US Secretary of State, Daniel Webster and his British counterpart, Lord Ashburton, is accepted as defining the parameters of necessity for the purpose of international self-defence laws.
62 Greenwood, 'War, Terrorism and International Law', 56, Current Legal Problems (2003), 505 at 517.
63 Byers, 'Terrorism, the Use of Force and International Law at 11 September', 51, ICLQ (2002), 401 at 406.
64 Bowett, Self-defence in International Law (Manchester: Manchester University Press, 1958), at 58.
65 Above note 20, at 43; and at 111–112 'In domestic law the test of necessity is applied through the period of domestic action. . . . In international law however, the test of necessity is applied only to the commencement of a conflict not throughout the war'.

onstrate how the state is sexed male through the application of the necessity standard that assumes, in analogy with the domestic right, the equal strength of the parties and the public nature of the armed attack. Under the discussion of proportionality, I will consider the attack–counter attack model that ignores other forms of forcible intervention and also overlooks the consequences of military behaviour to non-military actors, thus paralleling the masculine subject of interpersonal self-defence.

Necessity (and Imminence)

Necessity refers to the choice to use force to repel an armed attack and addresses the aim of defensive force, that is, the state must believe there is no other option other than to use defensive force. Schachter explains, 'force should not be considered necessary until peaceful measures have been found wanting or when they clearly would be futile'.[66] Ago suggests the state under attack 'must not, in the particular circumstances, have had any means of halting the attack other than recourse to armed force. In other words, had it been able to achieve the same result by measures not involving the use of armed force, it would have no justification for adopting conduct which contravened the general prohibition against the use of force'.[67] States appear to accept this formulation, underpinning it with references to the *Caroline* test that necessity under self-defence must be 'instant, overwhelming, leaving no choice of means, and no moment of deliberation'[68] and thus incorporating a test of imminence (or immediacy) into self-defence.[69] Immediacy incorporates a temporal element into necessity through focus on the possibility of the necessity of force to prevent further attacks. As necessity (and imminence) adheres to the private aspect of self-defence, which shifts the initial decision to use force from the collective body (the Security Council) on to the state claiming defensive rights, external regulation of the necessity of action taken in self-defence by a state will be difficult.[70]

Franck argues that the 'jury' of states in accepting or rejecting the actions of other states functions as an adequate arbiter on claims of necessity.[71] The reliance on the public jury of states assumes that the original attack takes a form that is public in nature. In the *Nicaragua* case the ICJ found the absence of an armed attack negated the US's claim to be acting in self-defence. While in this case the consequence was a reaffirmation of the territorial integrity of a smaller state, the armed attack requirement

---

66 Schachter, 'The Right of States to Use Armed Force', 82, Michigan Law Review (1984), 1626 at 1635.

67 Addendum to the Eighth Report on State Responsibility, by Roberto Ago, Agenda Item 2, A/CN.4/Ser.A/198/Add.1 (Part 1) II (1) Yearbook of the International Law Commission (1980), 69.

68 Above note 61.

69 On imminence in self-defence, see Nicaragua Case, 14 ICJ Reports 1986, Dissenting Opinion of Judge Schwebel, at 362–367.

70 The necessity requirement, therefore, undermines contemporary debates on preventative, preemptive or anticipatory force that attempt to re-define the parameters of an 'armed attack' under Article 51 (and thus the necessity of defence).

71 Franck, Recourse to Force (Cambridge: Cambridge University Press, 2002), at 107 and 187.

also protects more powerful states from having other types of interventions assessed in the international sphere. For example, France's multiple interventions into its prior African colonies have not always taken the form of an armed attack as they have been justified as policing-type acts or at the consent of the state.[72] This limits the capacity of former colonies, and economically and politically less powerful states, to respond with a self-defence justification as the use of military force does not always conform to the public nature of an armed attack and is frustrated by the less powerful position of the former colony.

Ultimately, this approach lends itself to the influence of powerful states in controlling when and where self-defence is deemed necessary in an analogous manner to interpersonal self-defence assuming a masculine legal actor. While the use of defensive force in Kuwait against Iraq in 1991, and by the United States and its allies in Afghanistan since 2001, have been perceived as consolidated by Security Council resolutions recognising the existence of the right in these circumstances, Security Council recognition of the right to act in self-defence is not deemed an integral component of Article 51.[73] This is despite the ICJ indicating in the *Nicaragua* Case that the reporting of defensive force by a state to the Security Council may enhance the credibility of a state's claim. Rather the identification by powerful states that a violation of its or its allies' territorial integrity has occurred constructs the possibility of rational self-defence under international law. Consequently, the international right incorporates an analogous model of subjectivity to the interpersonal right. Legal subjects, under both legal structures, are deemed equal so that inequalities between the parties are not perceived to impact on the capacity of a state to act in self-defence. Underlying this is an assumption about the legal subject having the capacity to choose to use force in a rational manner. Less powerful states using force will either have to risk applying what appears to be unnecessary force or embark on a course of action that appears irrational because of their lesser military might.

This recalls the critique of interpersonal self-defence, from feminist theorists, that argues the necessity requirement assumes the equal strength of legal subjects who find their life to be under threat. Consequently, the judge in the *Lavalee* case acknowledged interpersonal self-defence offers little justification for defensive action that appears unnecessary because of the disparity in physical strength between partners. In this case, the defendant, Ms Lavalee shot her common law husband after prolonged physical and sexual abuse. Although not under threat at the time when she shot her partner, he had previously threatened to kill her and, immediately before his death, raped her. The Supreme Court of Canada acknowledged that in a situation of self-defence, as envisaged by the Canadian legal system at the time of the trial, Ms Lavalee's acts would be regarded as unnecessary. The mapping of human relationships in interpersonal accounts of self-defence directly affects the construction of the

---

72 See the discussion in Gray, above note 2, at 85.
73 Greenwood, 'New World Order or Old? The Invasion of Kuwait and the Rule of Law', 55, *Modern Law Review* (1992); SC Res 1368, 12 September 2001; Dinstein, 'International law as a Primitive Legal System', 19, *New York University Journal of International Law* (1986–1987), 1 at 12.

proportionality and necessity requirements under international law, favouring those that are perceived by law as physically strong. The public nature of the 'bar-room brawl model' associated with interpersonal self-defence can be seen to pervade the way international lawyers construct the scope of international self-defence, which provides only loose parameters on what is 'necessary' in the international system, assuming the equal position of states before the law and assuming the public nature of interstate aggression. Implicit in this construction of the necessity principle is the requirement that an attack be directed against a state. The consequence is an inadequacy within international self-defence that is analogous to the inadequacies of interpersonal self-defence. That is, rather than illustrating the need to adjust the necessity requirement in parallel to feminist reconstruction of the scope of interpersonal self-defence, a feminist analysis of the international principle of necessity indicates that the underlying analogy between the state and individual as legal subjects with the capacity to self-defend may require severance. Severance would involve a reconsideration of when it is necessary for a state to use force outside of the collective security system, and a reconsideration of what constitutes an armed attack to recognise how inequalities between states allow for different standards to be applied.

Proportionality

Gardam describes the factors to be assessed in reviewing the proportionality of international defensive force and includes consideration of the geographical and destructive scope of a forceful response, the temporal scope of the response, the choice of means and the method of warfare and the effect of force on third parties.[74] Under international law, necessity is judged at the beginning of a defensive action while proportionality is perceived as applying to the duration of the conflict. Proportionality under *jus ad bellum* is distinct from the test of proportionality under *jus in bello*, as the latter refers to the individual acts within a military engagement while the *jus ad bellum* test looks at the proportionality of the defensive action as a whole. Greenwood emphasises the need to understand the contingencies of each conflict as shaping and changing the potential proportionality requirements, in addition to the need to acknowledge that proportionality is not a test of sameness.[75] The resultant model of state-assessed proportionality recognises that '[v]ery different conclusions may be reached as to what is proportionate action depending on how the equation is defined and applied'.[76] In her analysis of the use of force against Serbia in 1999, Chinkin considers indicators of proportionality to be applied when states seek to justify humanitarian interventions and that could reasonably be extended to tests of proportionality under Article 51. Chinkin extends the ambit of possible factors to include

---

74 Gardam, above note 57, at 162 to 179.
75 Greenwood, 'Self-defence and the Conduct of International Armed Conflict', in Dinstein (ed), International Law at a Time of Perplexity (Utrecht, the Netherlands: Nijhoff, 1989), 273.
76 Gardam, above note 57, at 155.

environmental damage, the impact on civilian infrastructure and the cultural and social meaning of force on a community.[77] Chinkin's broad understanding of proportionality has not been accepted in state practice. Instead Greenwood's narrower test permitting considerable leeway to individual states using force in self-defence to self-regulate has general acceptance.

The proportionality equation with respect to international self-defence relies, on the one hand, on an assessment of the trigger and, on the other hand, an application of appropriate (proportionate) consequences. Both of these assessments, however, reinforce the sexed subject of international law as underlying this is a perception of a force–counter force binary that mimics the 'bar-room brawl' of the interpersonal acts.

With regard to assessment of the trigger, two standards operate. Less powerful states, when subject to the interventions of neighbouring states through cross-border incursions or the 'policing' interventions of former colonial powers, cannot rely on Article 51 to establish a right to self-defence due to the absence of a clear armed attack. Yet more powerful states (such as Western and former colonial powers) consistently manipulate this standard to argue defensive force that is in response to less than an armed attack can be proportionate, for example to defend against the actions of terrorist actors. Underlying this is an assumption that a state's legal subjectivity, and thus capacity to exercise self-defence, is defined through the state's military capabilities, or strength. Consequently, powerful states retain the right to exercise the right in a wider range of circumstances.

In relation to the counter force test of the proportionality equation, the gendered impact of military force further undermines contemporary assessments of what constitutes proportionate defensive force. For example, the assessment of overall civilian harm and deaths through the defensive action or the displacement of the civilian population do not form part of the proportionality *jus ad bellum* equation. This is because, to a degree, these are the expected consequences of the use of force. However, women constitute a disproportionate number in civilian and refugee populations during armed conflict making this a gendered harm.

Furthermore, Gardam's work on the segregation of *jus ad bellum* and *jus in bello* indicates how these different standards function to exclude particular types of harms from the discourses of international law. Gardam writes:

> Long term civilian causalities resulting from starvation and disease do not appear to be part of the equation. Neither is the extent to which any forceful action will lead to the displacement of the civilian population and the creation of large numbers of refugees.[78]

Self-defence, like all uses of force, often leads to the displacement of civilian populations. However, this has not been accommodated within discussion of proportionality requirements. As the majority of refugees and displaced persons are

---

77 Chinkin, 'Kosovo: A "Good" or "Bad" War?', 93, AJIL (1999), 841 at 844.
78 Gardam 'Proportionality as a Restraint on the Use of Force,' 20, Australian Yearbook of International Law (1992), 161.

often women and children the failure to adequately weigh population displacement in proportionality equations represents an unacknowledged gendered consequence of force.[79] Currently, states, when assessing the proportionality of the use of force, need not consider potential civilian causalities (although this is an aspect of proportionality under international humanitarian law). As a consequence *jus ad bellum* proportionality imposes few real limits to the acts of a state in a defensive situation, especially in terms of the assessment of civilian deaths or injuries, in terms of the long-term psychological impact of force on a community or the gender disparate harm that occurs as a result of conflict.

The focus on single acts invoking the international right,[80] despite the multitude of interactions between states that lead to the use of force, also matches the isolated bar-room brawl model of interpersonal self-defence. The perception, that attacks must occur in public to cross the threshold of violence to invoke Article 51, and the assumption, that the formal equality of states can provide a level playing field for judging the reasonableness of state action, mimics problematic, gendered aspects of interpersonal self-defence laws as they stand in common law countries.

Beyond the domestic analogy

Beyond recognising the role of a sexed and gendered domestic analogy in self-defence laws, it is useful to reflect on what to do with this knowledge. One strategy would be the development of increased feminist legal analysis of international self-defence that works to sever the analogy and to disrupt the personification of the state as the international legal subject. This would entail a radical re-imagining of the structures and processes of international law and, thus, have to confront the realities of the contemporary international legal regime that, for the most part, functions to maintain the power of global and national stakeholders.[81] This strategy may be limited in terms of political expediency but is appealing as a way of focusing on a horizon where international law is re-envisaged at a structural level through gender-disruptive strategies.[82]

---

79 Amnesty International Report, Lives Blown Apart: Crimes Against Women in Times of Conflict. Stop Violence Against Women Amnesty International London (November 2004), available online at http://web.amnesty.org/library/ (last accessed February 2011).

80 However, note the discussion, below, on contemporary shifts to accept preemptive force in response to numerous small scale attacks or the acquisition of weapons of mass destruction as crossing the threshold of an armed attack, below.

81 Knop also considers the impact of severing the analogy between states and individuals, see: Knop, 'Re/statements: Feminism and Sovereignty in International Law', 3, *Transnational Law and Contemporary Problems* (1993), 239; other studies, for example, Koskenniemi, 'The Fate of Public International Law' 70 *Modern Law Review* (2007), 1 at 28–29, focus on the changing nature of sovereignty and power but do not explicitly address the continued legal perception of the sovereign state as analogous to the individual under Western liberalism.

82 On role of horizons in international feminist legal theories, see Lacey, 'Feminist Theory and the Rights of Women' in Knop, Gender and Human Rights (Oxford: Oxford University Press, 2004), at 46; on gender disruptive strategies, see: Otto, Otto, 'A Sign of "Weakness"? Disrupting Gender Certainties in the Implementation of Security Council Resolution 1325', 13, Michigan Journal of Gender and Law (2006), 113.

The study of self-defence laws presented here indicates how the de-personification of the state is a possibility in our re-imaginings of international law. This would involve acceptance and full examination of the fundamental difference between a state as a legal subject and an individual as a legal subject.[83] Without the depersonalisation of the state, it is difficult to imagine the state without the current projection of sexed and gendered characteristics.

As has been noted, other features of the international right of states to act in self-defence, for example, the possibility of collective self-defence, also limit the persistence of the analogy. Under common law structures, collective self-defence has not received support, at least in circumstances where women have enlisted the support of other family members when defending against long-term abuse from a male partner.[84] This is not necessarily the case outside of common law legal systems. A difference in the structuring of interpersonal justifications, particularly self-defence, across municipal legal systems also militates against the continued reliance on the domestic analogy to explain international self-defence.

An alternative strategy would be to work towards maintaining the analogy but developing reasonableness requirements (i.e. necessity and proportionality) to better reflect women's experiences of conflict. This approach presents a risk of essentialising woman's experiences of conflict but has the advantage of being conceptually and politically convenient. That is, the continued acceptance of the structural ordering of international relations – even in light of acknowledged changes to the role of institutions and states under post-millennium conditions of globalisation – only places some women's experiences in a position where they are able to be articulated within the framework of international law. Additionally, central tensions in feminist writing, including the intellectual trope of essentialism and the victim–agency binary, often influence legal developments that occur within the existing framework of international law. As a consequence specific liberal feminist reform strategies are accommodated by the international legal structure with greater ease than the complex dialogues across feminist strands.[85] However, the political and symbolic expedience of working within the structures of international law, in this case the reasonableness requirements under self-defence laws, should not be undervalued. The re-articulation of the principles of necessity and proportionality in a manner that acknowledges not only the distinction between states and individuals acting defensively but one that is also able to incorporate the specific harms women experience during conflict is a possible process that shifts towards the de-gendering of the application of Article 51.

In mainstream analysis, only a handful of commentators consider the differences between state and individual citizen as legal subjects and the impact on this has the

---

83 However, see Lauterpacht who suggests the analogy between state and individuals lies in the 'fact that states are composed of individual human beings' in Lauterpacht, 'The Grotian Tradition in International Law', 23, BYIL (1946), 26, at 27.

84 For example, see *R v. Keaveney* [2004] EWCA Crim 1091 (Unreported Case) in the UK and *Osland v. The Queen* [1998] HCA 75, in Australia.

85 See Otto, 'Feminist Engagements with International Law through the UN Security Council' 32 Australian Feminist Law Journal (2010).

scope of international self-defence. The difference is often articulated in relation to understandings of the requirement of necessity. Rodin describes this as:

> A significant disanalogy between the application of necessity in international and domestic law. In domestic law the test of necessity is applied throughout the period of defensive action .... In international law, however, the test of necessity is applied only to the commencement of a conflict, not throughout the war.[86]

However, nearly all commentators, while reiterating the importance of necessity and proportionality to international self-defence, also suggest that these features have been inadequately developed, applied or realised under international law.[87] A feminist appraisal of the use of the domestic analogy to underpin international self-defence laws, alongside recognition of the sexed structure of interpersonal self-defence laws, particularly through the articulation of proportionality and necessity, advocates re-imagining the limits on the scope of self-defence in a way that does not depend upon the sexed legal subject of the state.

This approach highlights that the error of the domestic analogy does not rest in the re-configuration of self-defence as a justification for the use of force under international law but instead in the reconfiguration of gendered forms of both aggressive and defensive force under international law. Gardam concludes:

> The potential of necessity and proportionality to restrain unnecessary and excessive force should not be underestimated, particularly during times when the legal regime regulating the situations in which States can resort to force is under strain. The more dubious the arguments validating the use of force in the first place, arguably the more stringent the requirements of necessity and proportionality.... However, to a considerable degree, proportionality remains a rhetorical tool in the hands of States that they rely on either to justify their forceful actions or to condemn those of other States.[88]

Gardam's approach shifts away from the largely subjective nature of necessity and proportionality to suggest that the principles can be useful legal tools if refined and developed to produce the outcomes ostensibly claimed by their presence. Gardam's approach avoids the reiteration of the sexed legal subject as the lynchpin of Article 51 self-defence and avoids the sexed model of self-defence that is currently accepted under international law, through a focus on the role of human rights and humanitarianism as the basis for understanding restraints on force.[89] Gardam's recommendation that proportionality and necessity be developed as real restraints on unilateral and collective force develops a re-imagining of this area of

---

86 Rodin, above note 20, at 111.
87 See Dinstein, above note 5, at 184.
88 Gardam, above note 57, at 187.
89 Gardam, 'Legal Restraints on Security Council Military Enforcement Action', 17, Michigan Journal of International Law (1995–1996), 285.

international law that, if inclusive of understandings of the gendered continuum of violence, may challenge and change the way states use force in the future or, at least challenge, the readiness of states to use Article 51 as a catch-all justification for the use of military force.

Gardam, in line with other feminist approaches,[90] identifies how the broadening of understandings of proportionality and necessity does not lie in attempts to justify force but in understanding and expanding the concepts to fully consider the proportionality of military behaviour in terms of its impact on all citizens within a community. This would include an understanding of the impact of force on the citizens in the community exercising force as well as the impact of force on the community subject to defensive attacks. Increased militarism within states exercising the use of force also has gendered repercussions that lead to specific, although often different, risks for women and men.[91] Ultimately such an approach would lead to the narrowing of the behaviours tolerated under the principles of proportionality and necessity as it involves a re-imagining of what is valued when we speak of the 'state' or state sovereignty so that this encompasses more than military capabilities.

Narratives of self-defence

In addition to understanding the sexed base of international self-defence laws, it is essential to engage in contemporary debates on the changing nature of international self-defence laws. Key debates have emerged in response to the perception of changing global threats, particularly global terrorism and changing forms of weaponry.[92] While in the previous chapters the discussion has been on how the collective security structures have responded to these concerns, in this chapter, I consider how the perceived broadening of the threshold for Chapter VII measures has increasingly led to state practice that uses the concerns of the collective security regime to broaden justifications for unilateral action.

In contrast to my approach above, which argues that the refinement of defensive rights is required to limit the capacity of states to choose to use force outside of the collective security structure, contemporary narratives put forth by some Western states and Western commentators have developed an expansion of defensive rights. Consequently, the Bush doctrine of preemptive self-defence and the Obama administration's practice of using force against international terrorists on the territory of another state relies upon Article 51 functioning as an adequate and universally

---

90 See, for example, Charlesworth, 'International Law: a Discipline of Crisis' 65 Modern Law Review (2002) 377; Chinkin, above note 42; Wright, 'The Horizon of Becoming' 71 Nordic Journal of International Law (2002), 215.

91 Sharoni, 'Homefront as Battlefield' in Mayer (ed) Women and the Israeli Occupation (London: Routledge, 1994) at 10; Turner, et al., 'Acute Military Psychiatric Causalities from the War in Iraq', 186, British Journal of Psychiatry (2005), 476–479.

92 *A More Secure World: Our Shared Responsibility*, Report of the High Level Panel on Threats, Challenges and Change, UN Doc A/59/565 (2 December 2004); Gray, 'A Crisis of Legitimacy for the UN Collective Security System?', 56, *International and Comparative Law Quarterly* (2007), 157.

accepted component of the international security regime. While it may be difficult to imagine a global legal system without the right of states to act in self-defence, this does not mean that we can be complacent in our acceptance of Article 51.

Preemptive self-defence shifts the focus of debates considerably and, rather than engaging the aspects of customary international law that I have discussed in this chapter, preemptive self-defence justifications challenge the armed attack requirement in Article 51, while using the *Caroline* incident[93] as indicative of a factual precedent rather than as a statement of legal principle. That is, prior to the 'War on Terror', now referenced as the global war against international terrorists, the *Caroline* incident emerged in international legal discourse as a statement of a legal principle, that there 'must be a necessity of self-defence, instant, overwhelming, leaving no choice of means and no moment for deliberation'.[94] In the aftermath of the 11 September 2001 terrorist attacks on the United States, the facts of the *Caroline* incident have been used to demonstrate the pedigree of preemptive and anticipatory force. For example, Greenwood considers, first, the range of actor incorporated under the armed attack requirement ('the threat in the *Caroline* case came from a non-state group of the kind most would probably call terrorist today . . .').[95] Greenwood then considers the nature of the armed attack in the *Caroline* incident, which occurred prior to any actual attack taking place, as affirming the right of anticipatory self-defence as a central feature of contemporary self-defence. This approach overlooks the manner in which the absence of an armed attack constituted the centre of the US–UK disagreement in the *Caroline* incident, and that the phrase 'there must be a necessity of self-defence' represented an agreement of the state of *the law* between the American Webster and his UK counterpart although they remained in disagreement of the application of this principle to *the facts*.[96]

Under contemporary approaches to justifying the use of force against terrorist actors, such as that elaborated by Greenwood, the facts of the *Caroline* incident are instrumentalised to indicate a type of self-defence rather than to indicate a legal standard (that self-defence must be necessary and proportionate). Furthermore, the contemporary narrative on preemptive force deploys both Article 51 and the *Caroline* incident as signs to establish its legitimacy. The consequence is a shift away from discussing Article 51 self-defence as a limited right – and articulation of the correct parameters of those limitations – towards the use of Article 51 to justify otherwise unlawful acts.

Article 51 as a sign in the 'War on Terror'

Prior to the advent of the US-led 'War on Terror', scholarly debate and inconsistency in state practice with respect to the self-defence justification indicated an impasse

---

93 See above note 61.
94 Letter from Daniel Webster (24 April 1842), 29 British and Foreign State Papers, 1129, 1138 (1857) quoted in Greenwood, above note 2, at 13; also see, above notes 61, 65 and accompanying text.
95 Greenwood, above note 2, at 17.
96 See, Occelli,' "Sinking" the Caroline', 4, San Diego International Law Journal (2003), 467; also see extracts of the correspondence between Webster and Ashburton in Noyes, Janis and Dickinson, International Law Stories, Foundation (2007), at 275 –278.

existed between actors who regarded Article 51, through inclusion of the term 'an inherent right', as maintaining the right of states to use force in response to an imminent attack and those who focussed on the plain meaning of the drafting of Article 51, that is, that self-defence must be in response to an armed attack.[97] For example, Israel's claim that it was justified in attacking the nuclear reactors in Iraq in 1981, as a form of anticipatory self-defence, was rejected by most states and the vast majority of scholars.[98] Despite this rejection of anticipatory self-defence by the majority of states and scholars during the Cold War and the 1990s, the possibility always remained that the anticipatory defence exception might crystallise into a formal rule of the international system. This position received some support when the ICJ found in the *Nuclear Weapons* Advisory Opinion in 1996 that it could not describe the use of nuclear weapons as unconditionally prohibited. The Court advised that the use of a first strike with nuclear weapons in an extreme case of self-defence, where the very survival of a state was at risk, may not be illegal.[99] Nevertheless, any right to anticipatory force was framed in extremely narrow terms, supporting the earlier position that: 'in a very limited number of situations force might be a reaction proportionate to the danger where there is unequivocal evidence of an intention to launch a devastating attack almost immediately'.[100]

In the era of the global war against international terrorism, the debate on anticipatory self-defence has shifted considerably. That is, an acceptance of anticipatory self-defence has increasingly become apparent in the writing of international legal scholars. Furthermore, anticipatory self-defence can be distinguished from preemptive self-defence and the broader notion of preemptive self-defence has transcended anticipatory self-defence as the locus of contemporary debates. For example, O'Connell's, otherwise useful, account of the failure of the preemptive force argument, finds anticipatory force as an acceptable aspect of international law.[101] What was in the past the exception or the anomaly (anticipatory self-defence) has become the rule. As a consequence, debates and disputes move further away from the linguistic parameters of Article 51 (i.e. the extent that the use of the word 'inherent' incorporates pre-existing customary international law) to argue the merits or demerits of preemptive defence. Unlike anticipatory self-defence, which uses the necessity requirement of self-defence to claim a state need not wait for an actual attack if knowledge of an imminent attack

---

97 Brownlie, 'The Use of Force in Self-defence,' 37, BYIL (1961), 183, at 227, finding 'when there is only circumstantial evidence of an impending attack would be to act in a manner which disregarded the requirement of proportionality'.

98 Schachter, 'The Right of States to Use Armed Force', 82, Michigan Law Review (1984), 1620; Cassese, International Law (Oxford: Oxford University Press, 2001), at 309–310; however, O'Connell describes this as an example of preemptive rather than anticipatory self-defence, above note 15, at 12; see also Franck, above note 71, at 106–107.

99 Legality of the Threat or Use of Nuclear Weapons (Advisory Opinion) ICJ Reports (8 July 1996), 226.

100 Ibid, at 227.

101 O'Connell, above note 15, suggests 'To maintain a legal order that restrains other states and to uphold the rule of law, the United States should continue its conservative commitment to limits on the unilateral use of force, and reject a reckless doctrine of preemptive self-defence' at 21.

exists, preemptive self-defence responds to the possibility of a future attack or attacks without specific evidence to measure necessity or proportionality. The shift from debating anticipatory to preemptive self-defence accedes to Barthes' description of the structure and the role of new narratives. New narratives (in this case preemptive force) do not emerge fully formed and in contradistinction to past narratives. Instead, new narratives, to gain legitimacy, invoke signs from previously accepted narratives to enhance their credibility.[102] The debates for, against, and around preemptive defence deploy Article 51 and the *Caroline* incident as a sign of their continuity with past (accepted) narratives and play an important role in attaching the possibility of preemptive defence to the Charter and to customary international law. When the old narrative is re-asserted as acceptable and uncontroversial, the previously contentious issue (anticipatory force) also appears uncontroversial and scholars and states are pushed to articulate a position on preemptive force. The very act of incorporating preemptive force into the narrative has the function of giving it the appearance of an appropriate topic for legal debate. However, Gray demonstrates the weakness of arguments for preemptive force through the North Korean response to the US identification of that state as a part of the 'Axis of Evil':

> After the USA denounced North Korea as part of the Axis of Evil, North Korea on the basis of reciprocity invoked the right of self-defence. This escalation of rhetoric illustrates vividly the danger of preemptive action and the abandonment of the language of diplomacy. The destabilizing impact of the 'Bush' doctrine and the perverse incentive it offers States to hasten to acquire weapons of mass destruction may be seen. North Korea in withdrawing from the Non-Proliferation Treaty (NPT) regime in January 2003 said that it was entitled to take a preemptive strike against the US because of US threats.[103]

The practice of North Korea illustrates the poverty of assessing the proportionality of the level of a threat that is yet to materialise or be acted upon. Furthermore, the rapid shift in state, scholarly and institutional narratives is alarming and supports the contention that the parameters of Article 51 are far from settled and should not be overlooked or under-theorised by feminist legal scholars.

The second aspect of the preemptive force narrative revolves around the invocation of the *Caroline* incident. Again what was previously controversial[104] is articulated as a settled, clear and satisfactory legal doctrine. The *Caroline* incident has come to be encapsulated in the phrase, 'instant, overwhelming, leaving no choice of means and no moment of deliberation.'[105] Yet, read in the actual correspondence between Daniel Webster and Lord Ashburton,[106] as well as in light of the circumstances of the actual incident, the *Caroline* doctrine appears to be elaborating a higher standard than contemporary

---

102 Barthes, Image-Music-Text (New York: Hill and Wang, 1977, Trans. Heath).
103 Gray, above note 92, at 162 (footnote 24).
104 Kearly, 'Raising the Caroline', 17, Wisconsin International Law Journal, 325, 1999.
105 Above note 61.
106 See Stevens, Border Diplomacy: The Caroline and McLeod Affairs in Anglo–American–Canadian Relations, 1837–1842 (Birmingham, Alabama: Alabama Press, 1989).

international law requires.[107] By demanding imminence within the test of necessity the *Caroline* doctrine necessarily becomes an inadequate guide to the scope of contemporary defensive actions. For example, following the attacks in New York, Washington and Pennsylvania in 2001, the United States chose to *wait* before exercising the right to act in self-defence, while the use of force to defend Kuwait after Iraq aggression commenced five months *after* the initial attacks by Iraq on Kuwait territory. This indicates how the 'immediacy' aspect of the *Caroline* doctrine has been adapted to the realities of contemporary warfare, where the transportation of troops, logistics and weaponry in collective defence is a long term rather than an immediate project.

When preemptive force is included in the narrative, the *Caroline* incident cannot provide any guidance with respect to the articulation of standards of reasonableness, so scholars tend to use the facts of the *Caroline* to support arguments in favour of preemptive self-defence. Occelli's analysis leads her to find that the *Caroline* facts establishes a customary international law permitting states to use force on the territory of a neutral state where a threat of future attacks compels the state to act (i.e. as a form of factual precedent). She incorporates terrorist acts into the range of plausible justifications for preemptive self-defence because they are 'characterised by continuing, but intermittent, acts. When one attack is completed, the threat does not end'.[108] For O'Connell the response of the United States to the Al-Qaeda terrorist network is justified because it can be accommodated in the narrative of anticipatory self-defence, while the (at the time proposed) use of force against Iraq (that occurred in 2003) could not be justified as it would constitute preemptive force. O'Connell argues:

> The Security Council action after September 11 can be cited to support anticipatory self-defense in cases where an armed attack has occurred and convincing evidence exists that more are planned, though not yet underway. By contrast, international law continues to prohibit preemptive self-defense or even anticipatory self-defense, if that is understood to be different from responding to incipient attacks or ongoing campaigns. In other words, a state may not take military action against another state when an attack is only a hypothetical possibility, and not yet in progress – even in the case of weapons of mass destruction.[109]

O'Connell's analysis of anticipatory self-defence is replicated in the writing of Greenwood at the time of the US and UK instigation of force in Iraq in 2003.[110] However, Greenwood tells us he will 'avoid treating such words as though they were terms of art' and thus he favours the term anticipatory action that he describes as 'within the concept of self-defence' in the example of the use of force in Afghanistan in 2001 because 'the threat from Al-Qaeda was imminent'.[111] Attempts to

---

107   Occelli, ' "Sinking" the Caroline', 4, San Diego International Law Journal (2003), 467.
108   Ibid, at 484.
109   Above note 15, at 11.
110   Above note 2.
111   Ibid, at 25, although note Greenwood describes the use of force by the US as 'pre-emptive action' that 'fell within the concept of self-defense because the threat from Al-Qaeda was imminent' (at 25); further Greenwood argued that the use of force in Iraq would be justified through implied authorisation from the Security Council.

describe and justify the use of force in Afghanistan since 2001, whether under the umbrella of anticipatory or preemptive force, appear to embrace the earlier writing of Bowett, who advocated this approach prior to the 'War on Terror' narrative but was, at the time, criticised by other scholars.[112] Central to the new narrative is the use of the *Caroline* incident as indicative of a factual situation similar to the 'War on Terror' rather than as the elaboration of the legal doctrine that international self-defence is circumscribed by some form of reasonableness – that is, proportionality and necessity – test.[113]

In addition to shifting the legal narratives regarding the legacy of the *Caroline* incident, the 'War on Terror' also produces a new narrative regarding state responsibility for terrorist attacks by non-state actors. Previous ICJ pronouncements constructed a relatively high threshold for invoking the responsibility of states for the acts of non-state actors. In the *Nicaragua* case, the Court found responsibility for the acts of non-state actors can be attributed to the state if the state actually participated in or directed the acts;[114] while in the more recent *DRC v. Uganda* case the court emphasised that there must be actual involvement of the state in the attacks.[115] While a lower threshold was established in the ICTY *Tadic* judgement, that focused on effective control,[116] commentators distinguish this for the purposes of establishing individual criminal, rather, than state responsibility.[117] The 'War on Terror' narrative, in contrast, invokes the non-legal standard of states harbouring terrorists. At one level, this exposes the complicity of repressive regimes in creating safe havens for terrorist actors, yet at another level, the standard is meaningless as all states – willing or unwilling – harbour some terrorists. For Western states, however, Security Council resolution 1373 applies, directing states to freeze terrorist assets and impose travel bans. This constructs a split between the manner that international law is applied across the divide of powerful (Western) and weak (third world/ non-Western) states.[118]

Underlying the narrative of the 'War on Terror' violating the territorial integrity and political independence of states harbouring terrorists is an extension of the Article 51 narrative. Prior to the September 11 attacks on the United States, the question of instrumentalising Article 51 against non-state actors was accommodated by the *Nicaragua* standard of widespread and actual control so that the assumption persisted that the armed attack requirement, therefore, must have a clear nexus to the state.[119]

---

112 Bowett, Self-defence in International Law (1958), 112; this position was rejected by Brownlie, International Law and the Use of Force by States (1963), 112; also see Dinstein, above note 5, at 172 (describing incipient armed attacks); for a rejection of Dinstein's claim at this time, see: Cassese, International Law (Oxford: Oxford University Press, 2001), at 308–309; see also Franck, above note 71, at 107–108.

113 See, for example, Greenwood, above note 2.

114 Above note 3, at paragraph 75–125, 215–220.

115 Above note 12, at paragraph 146.

116 Tadić Case, 105 ILR 453.

117 Aust, Handbook of International Law (Cambridge: Cambridge University Press, 2005), at 413.

118 Baxi, 'Operation Enduring Freedom' in Anghie, Chimni, Mickelson and Okafor, The Third World and International Order (London: Kluwer, 2003).

119 See Greenwood, above note 2.

The contemporary narrative allows for a side stepping of state responsibility norms through the reliance on a lower than accepted standard for attributing the acts to the state perceived as harbouring terrorists, while engaging Article 51 to justify the use of force (and thus shield the state using force against terrorists from responsibility for forceful incursions on the territory of another state). This has seen a further extension under the Obama administration in the United States, where Security Council resolution 1373 has been argued to provide implied authorisation for the use of force against terrorist actors on the territory of another state.[120]

To conclude, since the advent of the 'War on Terror' there has been a shift from debating anticipatory to preemptive self-defence. There also appears to be an increased reliance on the *Caroline* incident as a factual precedent rather than as a description of legal doctrine on the correct customary international law principles relevant to self-defence. What was previously contentious (e.g. anticipatory self-defence and self-defence in response to attacks by non-state actors) has become increasingly accepted and perceived as within the 'normal' range of Article 51 self-defence and its incorporation of customary international norms on self-defence, while preemptive force has become the central controversy. A similar shift occurs from the language of *Nicaragua* test of effective control to the articulation of states harbouring terrorists again through the use of Article 51 to supplement the new narratives.

These shifts in Western state practice and scholarship demonstrate how Article 51 is used as a sign available to assist the deployment of new narratives. Franck is quite explicit about this and argues this was the intention of the drafters of the UN Charter using a domestic analogy to underpin this idea.[121] For Koskenniemi, this is a product of the international system, where 'the legal subjects that are bound by the law interpret it, and that's an aspect you can't avoid'.[122] However, Koskenniemi acknowledges the key consequence of the preemptive force argument is not that states can 'auto-interpret' the law,[123] rather a right to deploy preemptive force shifts the limitations of the right away from a measure against an armed attack to the objective underlying the force. 'The reasonable objective is to protect the state. Anything you do to protect the state, you can then use armed force for because anything that threatens the state tends to be equal to a threat or use of force'.[124] In other words, the tests of proportionality and necessity become measured against the objective (the protection of the state) rather than an actual armed attack.

Returning to the domestic analogy, the preemptive force justification appears to be closer to the partial defence of provocation rather than self-defence. Provocation defences, under common law, mitigate a violent response to behaviour that is

---

120 See: Heathcote, 'Feminist Reflections on the 'End' of the War on Terror' 11 Melbourne Journal of International Law (2010), 277.
121 Above note 71, at 4–5, chapters 7 and 10.
122 Koskenniemi, 'Iraq and the "Bush Doctrine" of Preemptive Self-Defence' Crimes of War Project, Expert Analysis (20 August 2002), available at http://www.crimesofwar.org/print/expert/bush-Koskenniemi-print.html (last accessed February 2011).
123 Ibid.
124 Ibid.

persistent and that the legal subject feels unable to control.[125] Brownlie records the appearance of provocation as a justification for the use of force during the 1920s in a number of alliance treaties.[126] Brownlie demonstrates the inadequacy of interstate force justified on provocation grounds, through the test of proportionality:

> The concept was extremely vague and any act or omission by the authorities of a State could be regarded as provocation if it displeased a powerful opponent . . . even if the term were restricted, which it was not, to some military or frontier crossing, it justified full scale assault, a formal war, and had no regard for proportionality.[127]

Arguments in favour of preemptive self-defence,[128] or a definition of anticipatory self-defence that includes the use of force against terrorist threats,[129] use a similar argument justifying the use of force through analysis of a state's subjective assessment of the magnitude of a threat rather than through reasonableness requirements gauged by the nature of an actual attack. Furthermore, the legal structure of interpersonal defences distinguishes between justifications (usually self-defence) and excuses (provocation). The international legal system recognises justifications for the use of force but has no sense of excuses as a defence for the use of force.[130] The implicit provocation analogy in preemptive self-defence arguments demonstrates the limitations of justifications for the use of force against global terrorist actors.

In the following section, I reflect on how these developments extend the sexed and gendered base of international self-defence laws through the production of social and cultural narratives that resonate with images of the Western state as the male hero of the narrative, the Western state as the male spectator implicitly in control of the narrative, and through images of the terrorist as the rogue, male actor. Each of these images of masculinity distinguishes women's lives and actions from the solar plexus of international law, that is, the law on the use of force.

Article 51 as a heroic spectator narrative

Feminist legal theories encourage the perception of law as a narrative. As Thornton states:

---

125 Quick and Wells, above note 48.
126 Brownlie, above note 96, at 199; for example, the Locarno Treaty, 16 October, 1925.
127 Ibid.
128 Greenwood, above note 2; Glennon, above note 25; National Security Strategy of the United States 6 (September 2002), available at: www.whitehouse.gov.nsc.nss/2002/index.html (last accessed May 2009); National Security Strategy of the United States 23 (March 2006), available at www.whitehouse. gov/ncs/nss/2006/nss2006.pdf (last accessed February 2011).
129 O'Connell, above note 15.
130 Note, too, that the Articles on the Responsibility of States for Internationally Wrongful Acts, annexed to GA Res56/83, 12 December 2001, find circumstances precluding the responsibility of states cannot be used as an excuse for a serious breach of international law, see Article 26.

We can no longer be bound by a blind obeisance to legal authority that typified a bygone age. Popular evocations of the disillusionment with law bear this out. Law is a dynamic social and cultural phenomenon, which cannot be explained by reference to itself alone. To escape the vacuous circularity and to persist with the task of revisioning law as an intellectual discipline, it has to be located within a wider frame, which includes the world of popular imagination, with its hope, as well as its cynicism.[131]

Thornton's approach is developed as an international method in the work of Orford, who analyses justifications for humanitarian interventions under a scheme that perceives law as narrative.[132] Orford considers the type of popular (Western) narrative that cloaks ideas about the role and purpose of Article 51 and suggests:

> The fact that the reader is invited to identify with a white, violent, masculine hero limits the capacity of international law to address the ways in which the hero's journey of action and self-validation affects the lives of the human beings caught up in that quest. . . . As a consequence, violence becomes a logical form of self-defence. The self that is being defended . . . is the competitive, irresponsible and brutal self of white, imperial masculinity, reproduced unendingly in the heroic narratives of militarist internationalism.[133]

Orford's approach is to avoid the quest for a truth 'that can correct existing misrepresentations' in exchange for a method that is 'interested in coming to terms with the "truth" that is produced by texts'.[134] In considering law as a narrative with respect to Article 51, it is important to think through the role Article 51 plays in legitimising a specific range of force and a specific range of narratives for Western communities. How these narratives manifest in legal arguments for and against different aspects of self-defence is relevant but attention might also be paid to the role which the media and popular culture in Western states play in diminishing and strengthening certain narratives around interstate self-defence.

The production of a social narrative in Western communities also attends to Gunning's method of world travelling. Gunning argues that, as part of the anti-essentialist project, feminist approaches need to pay attention to the production of knowledge within their own communities.[135] That is, for Western scholars, there must be an examination of the cultural norms that construct the dominant narratives and discourses prevalent in Western communities.[136] Orford's analysis of the range of

---

131 Thornton, *Romancing the Tomes: Popular Culture, Law and Feminism* (London: Routledge, 2002), introduction.

132 Orford, Reading Humanitarian Intervention (Cambridge: Cambridge University Press, 2003).

133 Ibid, at 180.

134 Orford, 'Muscular Humanitarianism', 10 (4), EJIL (1999), 679, at 682.

135 Gunning, 'Arrogant Perceptions, World-travelling and Multicultural Feminism', 23, Columbia Human Rights Law Review (1991), 189.

136 This was vividly illustrated to me in a discussion with a scholar who had conducted a study of sexual violence in Kurdish communities in Northern Iraq. One of the recorded limitations of the project was the inability of the researcher to ask direct questions regarding sexual violence to women in the

narratives produced in Western communities (in response to what is alleged to be humanitarian interventions) argues that Western accounts of international law play a role in producing a heroic narrative with Western states cast as the 'White Knight' of international law. With respect to international self-defence laws, the key feature of the heroic narrative is the collective self-defence entitlement.

As noted earlier, Article 51 specifically refers to the right of self-defence as an individual and collective right of states. While the inclusion of the word collective during the drafting of the Charter was at the behest of Latin American states,[137] and possibly conceived as linking Article 51 with Article 53 (on collective and regional security arrangements), in practice states have taken this to refer to the use of defensive force to assist an allied state, without necessarily any prior collective security agreement existing. In the *Nicaragua* case, the ICJ stipulated a state must have issued a request for assistance for the collective aspect of Article 51 to be invoked by a state.[138] The use of force in the defence of Kuwait, by Western states during the 1991 Gulf War, complied with these requirements and was, therefore, widely accepted as a correct exercise of Article 51 powers.

Rather than facilitating the development of regional security norms, collective self-defence, for Western states, has facilitated an image of the militarily powerful 'saving' the smaller state through the use of its defensive muscle. While at the time of its deployment, Western force in the defence of Kuwait was potentially controversial,[139] it has since become embedded in Western narratives as an appropriate and fair use of force. Questions about Kuwaiti government structures, inclusions and exclusions, particularly with respect to the provision of civil and political rights of women,[140] the Bedoon people[141] and migrant workers in Kuwait,[142] are not inserted into the international narrative of Western heroics and, consequently, these actors are denied the protection of international legal narratives. The male and elitist Kuwaiti government was re-installed as the legitimate government as a consequence of this use of collective force. At the same time Iraq, through its choice to use aggressive force, has since had its internal political structure destroyed. For women in Iraq, there has been a significant retraction of women's rights since the early 1990s, one that Western military activities in the region, including the post-2003 Occupation, and Western-led

communities. It seemed the researcher's own cultural norms and taboos made her acutely aware of the pain and invasion of these questions and she refrained from asking them specific questions as a consequence. She recorded how a male colleague did not experience the same inhibitions as was able to maintain a more clinical approach to the research. Far from a representation of Kurdish gender stereotyping this research indicated the strong Western social norms regarding transgressions and social facilitation which men and women often experience differently.

137 Mgbeoji, above note 5.
138 Nicaragua Case, above note 3.
139 Greenwood, above note 75.
140 Al-Mughui, *Women in Kuwait: the Politics of Gender* (London: Saqi, 2000).
141 The 2000 Human Right Watch Report on Kuwait focuses on the discrimination and lack of legal rights afforded the Bedoon and can be found online at: http://www.hrw.org/reports/2000/kuwait/kuwait-04.htm (last accessed February 2011).
142 Charlesworth, and Chinkin, *The Boundaries of International Law: A Feminist Analysis* (Manchester: Manchester University Press, 2000), at 262.

Article 41 sanctions during the 1990s, have played a role in producing.[143] The heroic discourse of collective self-defence simplifies the consequences of military action and distracts attention from important issues, such as, women's rights within a state, that are a necessary component of state, regional and international security.

It is at this point that the analogy with criminal law or interpersonal self-defence looks uneasy. Collective self-defence has not generally been accepted as an element of the interpersonal right to use force in self-defence. Where women have requested help from a physically stronger party to defend against an aggressive partner, courts have perceived this as negating the imminence of the threat of an attack or the necessity of defence.[144] The existence of collective self-defence under international law, therefore, either alludes to the ineffective base of the analogy or forces us to acknowledge that states cannot be personified. Possibly there is some merit in both claims. Furthermore, it is reasonable to suggest if a state is able to request collective assistance then this should be achieved through the collective security system, either under Chapter VII or VIII of the Charter or for requests for Security Council involvement under Chapter VI. This reading would be in line with the larger themes of the UN Charter.

Focussing on the role of collective self-defence as a narrative that functions to embed Western heroics as a normal element of the international legal structure also compels questions about the capacity of collective force to be achieved within the confines of proportionality. By allowing more players to act as defenders (a privilege not given to the aggressor), collective self-defence anticipates the greater strength of a state's allies. For Western states, superior military might has been achieved through airpower.[145] McInnes describes how the superior airpower of the West, particularly the United States, plays an important role in Western domestic narratives of the fairness of Western-led force, such as that provided as collective self-defence against Iraq during the Gulf War. The fairness, or perceived proportionality, is narrated through the protection offered to Western military actors and by extension Western civilian communities who can remain outside the theatre of war. As a consequence, the narrative of heroic Western states assisting their allies with 'safe' airpower and precision bombing also constructs a spectator relationship between the bulk of Western citizenry and the use of force. That is, Western actors – politicians, legal advisers, NGOs, diplomats, military leaders and media outlets – play a convincing role in framing the contours of the narrative of a conflict without risk to their own lives. As Western citizens, we gain the privilege of watching the production of this narrative without facing the direct threat of force, aggression or conflict in our communities.[146] This

---

143 Al-Ali, and Pratt, What Kind of Liberation? Women and the Occupation in Iraq (Berkeley, CA: California University Press, 2009).

144 Above note 84.

145 McInnes, Spectator-Sport War: the West and Contemporary Conflict (London, 2002), chapter five.

146 McInnes discusses how the events of 11 September 2001 reinforce the spectator narrative, rather than unsettle it, *ibid*, at 3; also see Heathcote, 'Article 51 Self-Defense as a Narrative: Spectators and Heroes in International Law', 12 (1), *Texas Wesleyan Law Review* (2005), 131.

is underscored by policies geared towards minimum casualities for Western military personnel. In this sense, collective self-defence, exercised proportionally, reads as a narrative of empire and imperialism; integral to the construction of empire and imperialism are images of masculinity and femininity that conform to dominant Western gender hierarchies.[147]

When the United States and the United Kingdom, alongside the 'Coalition of the Willing,' embarked on the use of force in Iraq in 2003, this narrative began to look unstable. The perceived proportionality of airpower was exchanged for the brutality of occupation and narratives on the futility, rather than the heroics of force, have emerged in Western dialogues. The disproportionate tally of Iraqi civilian deaths against Western military deaths, the excesses of and abuses by Western soldiers and the shift towards increased political chaos in Iraq, suggests that the Western masculine hero captured in the heroic narrative of 'freeing' Iraq is no longer so easy to script.

What is evident is not the loss of the heroic narrative, or the failure of the spectator's justification for armchair articulation of the normative contours of force, rather the failure of the gendered narrative to produce long-term security for any of the actors involved. As Western citizens, our complicity in the narrative of the collective defence of Kuwait has focussed on military narratives of necessity and proportionality that appease our sense of danger to our own militaries, yet this has been at the cost of recognition of the disproportionate civilian deaths in states where defensive force is exercised and our wilful ignorance of the role enhancing the agency of all actors might play. In Iraq after 2003, where the measure of proportionality must be judged against a perceived threat rather than an actual armed attack, the heroic narrative appears to have unravelled.

Perceiving international laws on self-defence as narratives with cultural and social meanings in our communities exposes our complicity in force, abuse, deaths and silencing. To articulate norms that envisage self-defence as a right of states without a Western, masculine origin is to listen for the voices of those damaged and dislocated by war and armed conflict. For feminist approaches to international law, this involves taking descriptive data of the lives of non-Western women and the political demands of non-Western women and recording these as meaningful and instrumental in the development of future narratives of law on the use of force.

Conclusions

This chapter examines the way an analogy with domestic self-defence laws has been used to explain the existence of a right of states to act in self-defence under international law. While the prospect of an analogy, in itself, may not be a fundamental flaw of the international system, this chapter demonstrates how the analogy is currently an inadequate means to develop international self-defence rights because of the masculine subject invoked by the analogy. This detracts from claims of Article 51 as 'inherent', 'natural' or 'universal'.

---

147 Nesiah, 'Resistance in the Age of Empire', 27, *Third World Quarterly* (2006), 903 at 907.

By looking at philosophical accounts of the rationale behind the right of (individuals) to self-defence, the limitations on the right – articulated in interpersonal and international self-defence as reasonableness requirements – are demonstrated as intrinsic to Article 51. From the perspective of feminist legal theories, the development of reasonableness requirements has reinforced a masculine subject as the primary beneficiary of the self-defence justification. This generally excludes female violence from reliance on the defence in common law systems. Under international law, through the use of replica legal language to limit Article 51 self-defence, the customary international law standards of necessity (imminence) and proportionality embed the sexed legal subject of legal liberalism in international accounts.

To move beyond the reiteration of a sexed legal subject under international law, two alternatives have been considered. First, it is suggested that the analogy – and hence the right to self-defence – could survive the criticisms evidenced through the domestic analogy and the use of feminist theories. This approach acknowledges the entrenched reality of self-defence having political meaning to states (and individuals) and the difficulty (although not impossibility) of conceiving of an international legal subject that is not predicated on the human subject of domestic legal systems. For the feminist legal account to retain meaning, however, future articulations of the limitations on the use of Article 51 self-defence would require review and development. This would involve a refinement of international self-defence, possibly developed through empirical accounts of the impact of military behaviour on civilian communities, to address the discrepancy between civilian understandings of necessity and state projections of necessity. The impact of attacks on the electrical grid and essential services of Iraq in the 1991 Gulf War provide an excellent example of necessity blinkered to long-term civilian suffering.[148] Feminist methods that invoke 'peripheral subjects' and promote 'world travelling' to listen to and understand the needs of those most harmed by conflict would be necessary to challenge current (masculine) paradigms of defensive necessity.[149]

Feminist engagements with proportionality would involve re-examination of the types of harms military action inflicts upon a community and necessitate a reconsideration of the international focus on armed attacks as the key trigger for Article 51. This would require attention to the limited success of military endeavours in 'protecting' or 'defending' communities when viewed through the perspective of civilians, who, in conflict, are predominantly women and children. Chinkin's analysis of the proportionality of the use of force in Serbia to halt atrocities against Kosovo exposes the impact of modern airpower technology on the communities experiencing defensive (or this case humanitarian) force.[150] McInnes suggests that modern weaponry gives the illusion of proportionality through the lessening of risks to Western communities even though they are usually far removed from the use of force, highlighting the role the law on the use of force plays not just in the acceptability of some forms of

148 See the contrasting accounts of Gardam, above note 6, and Greenwood, above note 73, at 174.
149 Kapur, 'The Tragedy of Victimisation Rhetoric: Resurrecting the Native Subject', 15, *Harvard Human Rights Journal* (2002); Gunning, above note 136.
150 Above note 78; also see Gardam, above note 57, at 114–115.

violence but also in the Western expectation that the narrative for Western citizens is experienced as a spectator narrative.[151] Using feminist theory on the role of engaging the 'Other' in international norm-making suggests a need to expose and move beyond our complicity in spectator narratives to fully assess the proportionality of airpower, the use of defensive force and 'smart' weapons as securing the proportionality of defensive force.

The alternative to re-scripting the customary law limitations attached to Article 51 would be for feminist legal approaches to work towards the rejection of the analogy between state and citizen and to, consequently, challenge the viability of a continued right of states to act in self-defence. Contemporary reports, such as, the *More Secure World Report*, also suggest this possibility as the role of the collective security system is seen as preferential to the use of unilateral force by states. This strategy would accommodate the consideration that the armed attack requirement, on the one hand, is too narrow in that it is not inclusive of threats to women's security while, on the other hand, acknowledging the broader claim that any move towards increased forms of justified force ultimately undermine women's security. The rare instances when a 'classical' right of self-defence has been perceived to exist, suggests the absence of the right under international law would only be detrimental in the sense that the increasingly creative arguments for justified self-defence put forward by states would be the main casualty.

The space for a feminist analysis of the key and accepted components of Article 51 has been made increasingly difficult by the contemporary narrative surrounding preemptive self-defence and the right to use force to combat terrorism. This has distracted attention from the framework of self-defence, focussing on the scope of self-defence rather than paradigm Article 51 cases. While few states or commentators have argued for broad recognition of these extensions to justifications for force, one of the consequences of the articulation of the preemptive force justification has been a shifting of debates. As such, the site of controversy has moved so that self-defence in response to an imminent attack is increasingly perceived as acceptable, and within the remit of Article 51 and customary international law on self-defence, while the broader notion of preemptive force has become its controversial edge.[152]

Article 51 functions as a sign in this narrative where its deployment allows the development of new narratives. Furthermore, the sign functions as a sexed sign embedding Article 51 as a natural and self-evident aspect of the international legal regime. The controversies exposed by the domestic analogy, above, become increasingly difficult to expose and challenge as a consequence.

Finally, self-defence further protects Western states by scripting a masculine narrative of heroics on to contemporary accounts of international law. To re-script Western narratives, it is important that the producers of Western jurisprudence consider their role in the production of narratives and the contemporary incapacity of Western

---

151 Above note 147.
152 Reisman and Armstrong, 'The Past and Future of the Claim of Preemptive Self-Defense', 100 (3) AJIL (2006), 525.

actors to hear alternative conceptions of law, of human relations and of the impact of armed conflict. I have argued that feminist legal theories must place critical analysis of the personification of the state through domestic analogies, such as found in self-defence laws, as the starting point for re-imagining international law. In the following chapters, I consider how this approach impacts on further justifications for the use of force, specifically self-determination, humanitarian intervention and the use of force against terrorist actors, using the method to develop strategies for a reconstructive feminist project.

4 Justifying force: self-determination

This chapter analyses the role of military force in the context of self-determination conflicts. I argue that the domestic analogy between states and individuals, when used to explain the regulation of the right to self-determination, illustrates an underlying tension in liberal legal discourse between agents and victims that has been identified by feminist and critical theorists. In the context of self-determination under international law, Berman describes this tension as follows:

> A group seeking self-determination is, by definition, one which feels it has been excluded, albeit unjustly, from the community of legal individuals recognized by international law. Hence the paradox involved in the legal notion of a legal right to self-determination: how can international law recognise a right accruing to an entity which, by its own admittance, lacks international existence?[1]

Feminist legal theories offer substantial dialogue on the paradoxical claim to agency and victim-hood which those outside of legal subjectivity must negotiate to gain a voice and rights under liberalism.[2] This chapter uses feminist knowledge on legal subjectivity to engage international legal accounts of self-determination.[3] The chapter

---

1 Berman, 'Sovereignty in Abeyance: Self-determination and International Law,' 7, *Wisconsin Law Journal* (1988), 52, at 52.
2 Brown, *States of Injury* (Princeton, NJ: Princeton Press, 1995); also see: Heathcote, 'Feminism, Force and the Security Council' SOAS School of Law Legal Studies Research Paper Series, 2010.
3 Naffine, 'Can Women be Legal Persons?' in James and Palmer, *Visible Women* (Oxford: Hart, 2002). My approach to self-determination is foregrounded by prior feminist engagements with self-determination, see: Chinkin, 'A Gendered Perspective to the International Use of Force', 12, *Australian Yearbook of International Law* (1992), 279; Chinkin and Wright, 'The Hunger Trap: Women, Food and Self-determination', 14, *Michigan Journal of International Law* (1993), 262; Gardam, 'A Feminist Analysis of Certain Aspects of International Humanitarian Law', 12, *Australian Yearbook of International Law* (1992); Knop, *Diversity and Self-determination in International Law* (Cambridge: Cambridge University Press, 2002); Knop, 'Re/statements: Feminism and Sovereignty in International Law', 3, *Transnational Law and Contemporary Problems*, (1993), 239; McDonald, 'Self-determination and Kurdish Women', in Mojab, *Women of a Non-state Nation* (Costa Mesa, CA: Mazda, 2001); Pahuja, 'The Postcoloniality of International Law', 46 (2), *Harvard International Law Journal*, 459; Wright, *International Human Rights, Decolonisation and Globalisation: Becoming Human* (London: Routledge, 2001).

consciously shifts from the use of domestic analogy as a tool of analysis to argue for the potential of the domestic analogy to build strategies for change. I argue that international legal scholarship can utilise feminist critiques of liberalism and liberal legal personhood to challenge the victim–agent paradox at the centre of the international legal narrative of self-determination.[4]

To understand international self-determination laws, and the use of force often associated with self-determination struggles,[5] I argue that the three layers of self-determination need to be jointly interrogated.

The first layer is *external* self-determination. This is a reference to the right of peoples to freely assert their status as a state and, if desired, reject foreign forms of domination or state control.[6] In the history of the United Nations, the process of achieving external self-determination has been regarded as a possible justification for the use of force and emerges as a potential right of 'peoples' in the context of decolonisation.[7] The First Additional Protocol to the Geneva Conventions is inclusive of situations 'in which peoples are fighting against colonial domination and alien occupation and against racist regimes in the exercise of their right of self-determination' thus establishing self-determination conflicts as within the definition of international conflict for the purposes of the application of the international humanitarian law of armed conflict.[8] The legal position with respect to *jus ad bellum* is less clear. According to Crawford, the relationship between external self-determination and the use of force can be examined from the perspective of three different potential aggressors: colonial, administering or occupying powers; liberation groups; and third parties. Within these categorisations the use of force by colonial, administering or occupying powers to frustrate the right to self-determination of 'peoples' has not been accepted as a justified form of force.[9] For example, the aggressive techniques used by the pro-Indonesia militia in Timor-Leste

---

4 See, for example, Cornell, *Beyond Accommodation* (London: Routledge, 1991); Frazer and Lacey, *The Politics of Community* (Hassocks, Sussex: Harvester, 1993); MacKinnon, *Towards a Feminist Theory of the State* (Harvard: Harvard University Press, 1989); Matsuda, 'Liberal Jurisprudence and Abstracted Visions of Human Nature', 16, *New Mexico Law Review* (1986); Nussbaum, *Sex and Social Justice* (Oxford: Oxford University Press, 2000).

5 Crawford, *The Creation of States in International Law* (Oxford: Oxford University Press, 2nd edition, 2006), at 135 lists four different situations where the relationship between self-determination and the use of force must be considered (see footnote 9 and accompanying text).

6 In the *Legal Consequences of the Construction of a Wall in the Occupied Palestinian Territory*, Advisory Opinion, ICJ, 9 July 2004, the ICJ found external self-determination to be a right rather than a mere principle of international law; see Cassese, *Self-determination of Peoples* (Cambridge: Cambridge University Press, 1998), chapter 4.

7 GA Resolution 2625 (XXV), 24 October 1970 (*The Declaration on Friendly Relations*), for an extended history see Crawford, above note 5, at 107–147 and Higgins, *Problems and Processes* (Oxford: Oxford University Press, 1994), chapter 7.

8 Protocol Additional to the Geneva Conventions of 12 August 1949 and relating to the Protection of Victims of International Armed Conflicts (Protocol 1), adopted on 8 June 1977.

9 Crawford, above note 5; however, this statement is misleading as although not officially condoning the use of force by colonial and occupying powers this type of force has not been consistently challenged by international law, see Berman, 'In the Wake of Empire', 14, *American University International Law Review* (1998–1999), 1515.

(formerly East Timor) in 1999 were challenged by the international community.[10] In contrast, liberation struggles seeking to challenge oppressive regimes, especially those that have emerged as a consequence of colonisation, may have a right to use force.[11] Crawford argues that this is not an exception to UN Charter Article 2(4) as liberation struggles are ostensibly internal conflicts and thus Article 2(4) applies to states rather than entities seeking the right to be states through self-determination. For Crawford, as a consequence, the situation for non-state entities is 'legally neutral' and 'not strictly regulated by international law.'[12] Finally, third parties who wish to facilitate a claim to self-determination in a foreign state may be able to argue that a justified exception to Article 2(4) exists. Such an argument would rest on identification of state acceptance of various General Assembly resolutions[13] and on the assumption that the use of force in question is not an attempt to control the territory in the long term.[14] The latter category, then, is where self-determination narratives intersect with justifications for the use of force.[15] The construction of self-determination as a justification for the use of force is largely associated with the acquisition of external self-determination. This may include forms of autonomy less than the acquisition of statehood or the exercise of a choice to remain under the governing structures of the foreign state, as well as the formal acquisition of statehood through the control of territory.

This chapter is structured around the contention that the manifestation of self-determination as an external right identifiable through a range of processes (e.g. electoral or institutional) ignores the role of structural and cultural violence that inhibits internal and individual self-determination within communities. The 2010 authorisation of force by the Security Council to monitor the election in the Ivory Coast epitomises this focus on process over substance. The failure of the UN presence to nurture a secure environment in the Ivory Coast, despite the long-term presence of a chapter VII force, illustrates how self-determination (or democracy) is a limited process without attention to the internal factors that create instability within a community.[16] As such, the failure of the UN Security Council chapter VII force to steer the Ivory Coast away from pre- and post-election violence as well as the consequential political impasse demonstrates the persistent gap between the idea and the realisation of democratic states.

---

10 Security Council Resolution 1264 (1999), 15 September 1999.
11 GA Resolution 1514, 14 December 1960 (*Declaration on the Granting of Independence to Colonial Countries and Peoples*); GA Resolution 2625 further suggests the use of force would be justified in situations of apartheid or when control of a territory has been acquired through military occupation.
12 Crawford, above note 5, at 135, 136; however, note the significant shift in international dialogues on the capacity of non-state actors to be recognised as responsible for launching an armed attackable to satisfy the Article 51 threshold under the global war against international terrorist actors. I discuss the consequences of this development in chapter nine.
13 Specifically, GA Resolutions 1514 and 2625; also GA Resolution 2105 (XX), 20 December 1965.
14 Crawford, above note 5, at 139.
15 The distinction between international armed conflict and non-international armed conflict is important with respect to the application of the international humanitarian laws of armed conflict, see Gardam, *Necessity, Proportionality and the Use of Force by States* (Cambridge: Cambridge University Press, 2004), at 122–123, 126.
16 SC Res 1933 (30 June 2010), SC Res 1942 (29 September 2010), SC Res 1967 (19 January 2011).

The second layer, *internal self-determination*, does not have widespread acceptance as a justification for the use of force.[17] In references to internal self-determination throughout this chapter, I am referring to the cultural, economic, social and political development of a community and the capacity of a community to articulate an identity from within its population. Charlesworth and Chinkin refer to internal self-determination as 'the right of a people to develop forms of governance within a state structure'.[18] This form of self-determination is broader than the first layer and is identifiable in the UN Charter as a principle of international law and forms a purpose of the United Nations.[19] Drew argues that this is self-determination as substance, while external self-determination can be described as self-determination as process.[20] For Crawford internal self-determination may be described as an international *principle* but internal self-determination is not an inherent element of the internationally recognised *right* to self-determination.[21] Other scholars, for example Cassese and Higgins, argue that the realisation of internal self-determination rests in minority rights and rights to equality, which function as individual rights and do not accrue to peoples in the manner external self-determination does.[22] To perceive internal self-determination as resolvable through attention to minority rights, and essentially contained within the domestic jurisdiction of states, is to invoke (or avoid) Berman's identification of the conundrum between victim and agency that haunts self-determination. Non-state entities, by not qualifying as a state, may be presumed to be outside the scope of this aspect of the principle of self-determination, except insofar as the state with administrative control of the territory must guarantee the rights of minorities. The failure of the international legal structure to attend to the internal self-determination of non-state entities as more than an issue of minority rights is a product of the association of force with external self-determination and perpetuates the vulnerability of peoples seeking self-determination in the international order.

Within the category of internal self-determination, space exists for developing self-determination rights as a means to uphold the entitlement of peoples to democracy. This extension of the right to self-determination is controversial; as it not only finds internal self-determination to be an international right, rather than a principle, but dictates the form of governance to be determined and argues force could be justified to protect the right.[23] I do not engage directly with this position as it has received little support from states and may be said to be replaced via arguments for humanitarian

---

17 Higgins, above note 7, at 124.
18 Charlesworth and Chinkin, *The Boundaries of International Law* (Manchester: Manchester University Press, 2000), at 153.
19 UN Charter Article 1(2) and Article 55.
20 Drew, 'The East Timor Story: International Law on Trial', 12, *EJIL* (2001), 651.
21 Crawford, above note 5, at 85–102.
22 Note, however, Drew, who argues that self-determination is linked to decolonisation 'has a discernible core content' and confers self-determination as process (external) and self-determination as substance (internal) on beneficiary peoples, see: Drew, above note 20.
23 See Franck, 'The Emerging Right to Democratic Governance', 86, *AJIL* (1996), 46; however, compare Franck's approach to that of Falk in 'The Haiti Intervention: A Dangerous World Order Precedent', 36, *Harvard International Law Journal* (1995), 341.

intervention that re-imagine and refine arguments justifying force to restore or uphold democracy.[24] It should be noted that the argument to 'restore democracy' by force assumes democracy to be a neutral rather than a loaded term.[25] Pre-determined forms of democracy and the use of force to impose democracy run counter to the key sentiments of this book's central contention.[26]

The third layer of self-determination, which is largely overlooked in international discourses,[27] is *individual self-determination*. The right to personal, or individual, self-determination is not an express norm of international law.[28] Individual self-determination is either relegated to the concerns of national legal structures or regarded as the *rationale* for international human rights laws but is not an element of positive or customary international law.[29]

In this chapter, I argue that realising self-determination under international law involves attention to all three layers: external, internal and individual. I perceive the layers as overlapping and dependent rather than distinct. The relationship between external, internal and individual self-determination is demonstrated through women's narratives that connect international law's failure to guarantee individual and internal forms of self-determination to the preoccupation with external self-determination. Consequently, the usefulness of force to achieve external self-determination often occurs at the expense of the attainment of individual and internal self-determination. I use the narratives of women from within self-determination struggles to articulate the limitations of current approaches to self-determination and to demonstrate the necessity of engagement with all three layers under international law.

To illustrate the contention of this chapter, I focus on the three major self-determination conflicts that straddled the transition to the new millennium. I have chosen conflicts that have had specific international engagement in terms of the right to self-determination: all have had ICJ Advisory Opinions, Security Council and General Assembly engagement that acknowledge the existence of a right to self-determination. However, the use of force and the circumstances for the justification in each case have varied; indicating that rules on the relationship between the use of force and self-determination are not clear in practice.[30]

The first case study is the Saharawi in the Western Sahara, where the use of force has not been authorised by the international community, despite institutional

24 See chapter five, also see Franck, *Resort to Force* (Cambridge: Cambridge University Press, 2003) and Tesón, 'Collective Humanitarian Intervention', 17, *Michigan Journal of International Law* (1996), 323; however, Higgins' argues that the capacity to freely choose government is integral to self-determination in a sense which would pre-suppose a democratic system, above note 7, at 120.
25 For discussion on the meaning of democracy as reflective of Western liberalism rather than universal rights; Otto, 'Challenging the "New World Order": International Law, Global Democracy and the Possibilities for Women', 3, *Transnational Law and Contemporary Problems* 371 (1993).
26 Charlesworth, 'Think Pieces: Law after War', 8 (2), *Melbourne Journal of International Law*, 233 (2007).
27 However, see Chinkin (1992); Chinkin and Wright (1993); Gardam (1992), above note 3.
28 Higgins describes self-determination as accruing to peoples rather than individuals thus marking its difference to other human rights, above note 7.
29 Chinkin and Wright, above note 3, at 300–304.
30 Crawford, above note 5, at 147–148.

recognition of the right to (external) self-determination for the Saharawi.[31] The post-2007 shift towards negotiations indicates a stepping away by the Security Council from support for the process of a referendum towards continued respect for Morocco's wishes to dictate the sequence of events. The second case study focuses on the Palestinian people living in the Occupied Palestinian Territories. Aggressive and military acts by the Israeli state have been routinely condemned by the international community, as have the retaliatory tactics employed by the Palestinian community, but no overt international military assistance has been extended to the Palestinian people. The ICJ Advisory Opinion, on the legality of Israel's West Bank Barrier, described the right of self-determination as an accepted norm of international law that exists *erga omnes* and that is applicable to the Occupied Palestinian Territories.[32] The 2006 conflict between Israel and Lebanon, the January 2009 attacks on Gaza by Israel and the escalation of violence across 2010 to include suspected attacks by the Israeli military on humanitarian actors in international waters are in contrast to the ongoing peace talks instigated by high-level Western politicians and perpetuate a gap between substance and process relevant to the discussion here. The third case study considers the granting of external self-determination to the people of Timor-Leste, via the UN-supervised popular consultation in 1999, followed by the provision of an UN-authorised military force and a transitional administration. In each case study, I draw on women's narratives to demonstrate the failures of current international approaches through a descriptive analysis. This forms section two of this chapter.

In addition to arguing for the practical interdependence of the layers of self-determination, I use feminist legal theories to highlight conceptual weaknesses that emerge in self-determination justifications for the use of force. I argue that the conceptual limitations of the international legal system are analogous to national models of subjectivity that have proven to be ineffective guarantees of women's rights. I highlight a domestic analogy that can be made between women's pursuit of full self-determination as individuals within national legal structures and the challenge of non-states subject status before international law. This forms section three of the chapter.

This chapter demonstrates how tying the external right to self-determination to the potentiality of force undermines the capacity of communities to achieve internal self-determination and individuals a guarantee of personal self-determination within those communities. Feminist scholarship, through analysis of the layers of self-determination and through understanding of the limitations of constructions of the legal subject under liberalism, engages this knowledge to provide dialogues for shifting forward, away from force, and towards 'respect for the principles of equal rights and self-determination of peoples' as demanded by the UN Charter.[33] This approach

---

31 Chinkin contrasts this to the history of Timor-Leste where the Security Council authorised the use of force without explicitly acknowledging self-determination as the justification for the use of force, see Chinkin, 'Western Sahara and the UN Second Decade of Decolonisation', in Arts and Leite (eds), *International law and the Question of Western Sahara* (IPJET, 2007), at 335.

32 *Legal Consequences of the Construction of a Wall in the Occupied Palestinian Territory*, Advisory Opinion, ICJ (9 July 2004), paragraph 88, 155/ 156.

33 UN Charter Article 1(2) and 55.

resonates with the work of feminist theorist McRobbie whose writing critiques the liberal states 'hijacking' of feminism from the late 1990s and the consequence of this for feminist projects in the West. I pick up on this aspect in the final chapter of the book when I return to the conundrum of feminist knowledge both influencing and yet constrained by the international legal structure.[34]

Narratives of self-determination

In this section, I consider three case studies where self-determination struggles have gained attention under international law. In particular, each case has drawn statements from the International Court of Justice (ICJ) finding that a right to self-determination exists.[35] In discussing each case study, I provide a narrative on the three layers of self-determination, as exposed by women's and feminist perspectives.

Feminist legal engagements with the limitations of sovereignty under Western liberal legalism are central to my approach. Thus, while it is usual to 'read' unrealised self-determination as a failure of process (as contemporaneously in Western Sahara and Palestine, and during Indonesian occupation in Timor-Leste) I find the failure of the self-determination process is indicative of normative weaknesses in mainstream accounts of international law; where 'peoples' are afforded only limited legal subjectivity in a manner that significantly detracts from the viability of self-determination as right of peoples. The potential of force justified by third parties in response to repressive regimes that are seen to stall the self-determination of peoples is challenged as, first, frustrating internal and individual self-determination and, second, providing an ineffectual enforcement mandate in the process of self-determination.

Consequently, international feminist jurisprudence that re-imagines international sovereignty offers pathways to re-imagining the right of peoples to self-determination.[36] In section three, I connect this approach to feminist legal theories, which find Western liberal accounts of personhood within national legal structures to be equally confined. The nexus between liberalism's failure to grant women full personhood under national laws and international law's limitation on the entities qualifying for full international legal personality is then exposed. To move beyond the limitations of international legal personhood underpinned by the version of sovereignty international self-determination depends upon, engagement with feminist legal theories must occur at both a practical and normative level. At a practical level, international law must engage women as citizens whose involvement and individual self-determination is crucial to achieving successful internal and external self-determination of a community. By elevating women's voices within Western Sahara, Palestine and

---

34 McRobbie, *The Aftermath of Feminism: Gender, Culture and Social Change* (London: Sage, 2008).

35 See: *Legal Consequences for States of the Continued Presence of South Africa in Namibia*, Advisory Opinion, ICJ Reports (21 June 1971), 16; *Western Sahara* Advisory Opinion, ICJ Reports (16 October 1975), 12 at 72–73 and *Case Concerning East Timor (Portugal v. Australia)* (ICJ Reports, 1995) paragraph 29.

36 See, for example, Knop, above note 3; also see TWAIL approaches, for example, Okafor, *Redefining Legitimate Statehood: International Law and State Fragmentation in Africa* (Utrecht, the Netherlands: Nijhoff, 2000).

Timor-Leste I begin this process. In the concluding part of this chapter, I explore how, at the normative level, mainstream international law must also recognise the sexed model of legal subjectivity propounded as universal and, through engagement with non-Western communities and with feminist strategies for individual self-deter-mination, begin the process of re-imagining sovereignty.[37] I argue that the use of force to secure the right to self-determination is a counter-productive model owing to the emphasis on territory and external self-determination at the expense of the internal and individual self-determination of peoples.

Western Sahara

At the conclusion of Spanish colonial control of Western Sahara, the emergence of a self-governing Saharawi territory was superseded by an agreement between the Span-ish and the Western Saharan neighbouring states of Morocco and Mauritania.[38] In 1975, as the Spanish government withdrew, the Moroccan and Mauritania govern-ments asserted their right to control the territory. Consequently, a large proportion of the Western Saharan community fled as refugees into Algeria.[39] While Mauritania withdrew its claim to Western Sahara in 1979, Morocco continues to challenge the right of the Saharawi to self-determination or control of Western Saharan territory. Initially the Saharawi (through the Polisario Front)[40] challenged Moroccan control of the territory through force. However, a UN-brokered ceasefire was agreed to in 1991. At the time, this was perceived as a precursor to a referendum in which the Saharawi could indicate their desires for the future of the territory.[41] This would be in line with the accepted international legal position with regard to the self-determination of peo-ples, established through General Assembly Resolution 1514.[42] Currently, Morocco controls the majority of the Western Saharan territory, and the division between Moroccan controlled territory and non-Moroccan territory is established by the Berm – a wall or barrier constructed by the Moroccan military in 1981.[43] East of the Berm is inhospitable desert, considered dangerous through the presence of landmines. While the Polisario claim control of the region east of the Berm, this region is also subject to a UN observer mission and creates a 'buffer' zone between the refugee camps in southern Algeria and the Moroccan controlled areas west of the Berm.

---

37 For example, Nesiah writes of 'space' and 'places' in international law transcending the physical to play an important role in linguistic categories and, thus, exclusions, see: Nesiah, 'Placing International Law: White Spaces on a Map', 16, *Leiden Journal of International Law* (2003), 1.

38 Shelley, *Endgame in the Western Sahara* (London: Zed, 2004) introduction; for a description of the his-tory of the Western Sahara, see in Arts and Leite (eds), *International law and the Question of Western Sahara* (IPJET, 2007), chapters one and two.

39 Franck, 'The Stealing of the Sahara', 70, *AJIL* (1976), 694.

40 Omar, 'The Position of the Frente Polisario', in Arts and Leite (eds), above note 31.

41 SC Res 690 (29 April 1991).

42 Declaration on the Granting of Independence to Colonial Countries and Peoples, 14 December 1960, Article 4; General Assembly Resolution 3314 (The Definition of Aggression), 14 December 1974, Article 7.

43 Shelley, above note 38, at 192.

After the Spanish withdrawal from the territory in 1975, the ICJ found, in an Advisory Opinion addressing the legal status of the Western Sahara at the time of colonisation, that there were some legal ties between the Sultan of Morocco and some of the communities living in Western Sahara. However, the ICJ went on to find that:

> ... the materials and information presented to it [the Court] do not establish any ties of territorial sovereignty ... as might affect the application of resolution 1514 (XV) in the decolonisation of Western Sahara and, in particular, of the principle of self-determination through the free and genuine expression of the will of the people of the territory.[44]

Thus, the Court denied any ongoing claim by Morocco to the territory of the Western Sahara. In the thirty years since this ICJ Opinion, the UN General Assembly and Security Council have consistently described self-determination as 'an optimum political solution' while affirming the 'inalienable right of all peoples to self-determination and independence' in the countless resolutions written in reference to Western Sahara.[45] Throughout this period, the state of Morocco has occupied the territory of Western Sahara.

Contemporary documents issued by the various UN institutions,[46] particularly the reports of the Secretary-General to the Security Council, focus on the development of negotiations between Moroccan and Polisario officials. In 2007, the Secretary-General reported, '[t]he parties did, indeed, express their views and even interacted with one another, but they did so by rejecting the views of the other party, and there was hardly any exchange that could be in earnest characterised as negotiations'.[47] The role of the UN in facilitating political processes towards a possible referendum did little to resolve the stalemate between Morocco and Saharawi.[48] The shift by the Security Council, since 2007, to a focus on negotiations between the two parties, and a distinct rejection of any coerced solution has left what Chinkin describes as a 'light institutional footprint'.[49] By 2010, the Security Council was supporting informal talks prior to a fifth round of negotiations with procedures for a referendum seemingly permanently suspended.

In contrast to international legal instruments that combine a reiteration of rights with little action, the Western Saharan people in exile, the Saharawi, have developed their own coherent political and social processes. These could be described as processes that facilitate internal self-determination as they have resulted in a constitution built on self-proclaimed democratic ideals, a democratically elected government

---

44 *Western Sahara*, Advisory Opinion, above note 35, paragraph 162.
45 See GA Res 690 (1991) and GA Res. 61/125 (2007); SC Res 1495 (31 July 2003), SC Res 1675 (28 April 2006), SC Res 1783 (31 October 2007) and SC Res 1920 (30 April 2010).
46 See SC Res 1754 (30 April 2007).
47 UN Doc. S/2007/619, Report of the Secretary-General to the Security Council on the situation concerning the Western Sahara, 19 October 2007.
48 See SC Res 1813 (30 April 2008).
49 Above note 31, at 334.

and robust social institutions, which provide health and education services, amongst other social institutions, to the Saharawi living in the Tindouf camps in Algeria.[50] The Saharawi Arab Democratic Republic (SADR) has been recognised by 45 states and is a member of the African Union (which Morocco is not). The SADR has created a constitution and model of government derived from the Western liberal model.[51] However, because Western liberal governments have proved reluctant to recognise the SADR government, or state, the features of liberalism have been developed and applied by the Saharawi themselves, rather than imposed.[52] This point is underscored by the narratives representing the participation and achievements of Saharawi women within their community, as well the commitment of the Saharawi to peaceful transition and the respect for human rights within their community.[53]

Article 30 of the SADR constitution states: 'the State will aim to defend the political, economic, and social rights of Saharawi women and will guarantee their participation in the improvement of society and in the development of the country'.[54] As such, through the legal recognition that the SADR constitution grants Saharawi women, the process of building a government in exile appears to have facilitated Saharawi women's empowerment and appears to have been built on women's participation.[55] The forms of the words in the SADR constitution are, perhaps, provocative in their 'guarantee' of participation and their 'aim to defend' women's rights, as they offer rights of individual self-determination and internal self-determination in a form that women in the West are yet to realise. Evidence from the camps suggests that these constitutional provisions have been matched with substantive equality between women and men in the Saharawi community.[56]

In 1979, the National Union of Saharawi Women (UNMS – Union Nacional de Mujeres Saharaui) was formed, and continues to function, with its 57 members elected for five-year terms and with representatives attending world conferences, such as the parallel NGO conference to the UN Women's Conference in Beijing 1995. In 1975, at the end of Spanish rule, only ten per cent of Saharawi women were literate yet in the camps today all men and women are taught to read and write and illiteracy is close

---

50 Shelley records the artistic and creative endeavours of the Saharawi, as well as the capacity for dissent within the community, Shelley, above note 38; also see Chinkin (1992), above note 3; Charlesworth and Chinkin, above note 18, at 264.

51 Shelley, above note 38.

52 This can be contrasted with the experiences in Timor-Leste where institutional structures were imposed by Indonesia and, after the use of force by the international community in 1999, the UN: Scheiner, 'Self-determination Requires More than Political Independence' in Arts and Leite (eds), above note 31.

53 Above note 31, at 349.

54 http://www.arso.org/03-const.99.htm (last accessed February 2011).

55 This empowerment is within their community, the exile has had a negative effect on the international voice of women with the exception of representation in feminist texts, such as Charlesworth and Chinkin, above note 18; Saharawi women's voices and activism remains suppressed by men's voices which dominate the texts available. Moroccan voices are given expression in international legal narratives, as states remain the primary legal subjects under international law.

56 Above note 38, at 172–173, 176.

to being eradicated.[57] The UNMS has also set up and run schools, childcare, hospital and medical centres as well as museums, nursing schools and language centres (for learning Spanish as a second language).[58]

Data from SADR highlights the role that women have played in shaping a robust internal social structure for the Saharawi. Yet, this has little, if any, weight in influencing international legal narratives. This demonstrates one of the key flaws of external self-determination. That is, the right to self-determination locates the holder of the right as peoples. Yet there is some irony in 'peoples' being unable to gain an international voice until the international community shifts to acknowledge the 'people' as a state.[59] While such a process is reliant on external events (foreign state recognition, voter lists, UN approved/monitored elections), the 'people' remain muted in international legal dialogues.[60] In the process of claiming statehood, communities, like the Saharawi, are expected to mimic foreign forms of governance. Admirably, the Saharawi have demonstrated substantial success in this process, yet without territory, the articulation of their identity is silenced by Moroccan military occupation and territorial control. This contrast between external and internal stages of self-determination for the Saharawi highlights the territorial base of international understandings of sovereignty, as Moroccan control of Western Saharan territory maintains the status quo. This is connected to the limitations of building a legal system with force at the apex of coercion and that defines political stability through the control of territory. That is, force cannot be used to protect or develop the creative, psychological aspect of 'community' or 'people' yet without creative development within a community the emergence of stable government is unlikely to be successful.[61]

When international law does move towards defining self-determination, the legal process focuses only on 'external' determination – that is, the holding of a referendum and the recognition of the referendum result by the international community and the processes of negotiation and co-operation between states.[62] This can be contrasted with the violent exclusion, as well as the social and economic consequences, caused by Morocco's building and maintenance of the Berm as a military structure. Although the Saharawi have developed strong internal governance structures, the provision of adequate nutrition and health in the Algerian camps is limited and contributes to the structural inequalities and harm experienced by the Saharawi.

57 Ibid.
58 Ibid.; also see: UNIFEM, *Gender Profile of the Conflict in Western Sahara*, available online at: http://www. arso.org/westernsahara_UNIFEM.pdf (last accessed November 2010)
59 Berman, above note 1.
60 However, in 2005 the ICJ did allow submissions from Palestinian representatives before issuing their Advisory Opinion on the *Legal Consequences of the Construction of a Wall in the Occupied Palestinian Territory*, ICJ, 9 July 2004. The UN General Assembly permits a range of non-member states observer status, including Palestine. In contrast, the Security Council has yet to expand its mandate to allow non-state groups to address it directly. However, regional organisations have some rights, and consequent obligations, under international law.
61 See McDonald's discussion of the failure of the Kurdish community to build a stable social fabric in Northern Iraq during the 1990s, above note 3.
62 Drew, above note 20, at 663.

When an occupying state frustrates processes associated with the attainment of self-determination through 'domestic violence'[63] and is allowed to do so unhindered, the international legal narrative becomes a replica of the gendered liberal construction of individual personhood: where formal equality rights are acknowledged and substantive inequality is ignored. This is a model of citizenship that feminists have persistently challenged as sexed. This is the model, as we will see below, achieved through the use of force that ultimately led to the formation of the independent state of Timor-Leste. Regrettably this coercive action has failed to eradicate group violence in Timor-Leste, as it denies the layers of oppression that may exist within a society, as well as the propensity for oppressed communities to perpetuate violence through the subjugation of minorities within the group.[64]

The characterisation of aggression under international law is an important aspect of this international legal narrative. Under the narrative of international law, the Berm strengthens Morocco's control of the territory. The physical impact of the Berm structure is to deny the Saharawi people fundamental rights: the right to self-determination, as well as the right to shelter and basic resources as the Berm physically and legally restricts the Saharawi from claiming the territory of Western Sahara. To survive, the Saharawi people in the Tindouf refugee camps are consequently dependent on humanitarian aid from external sources. The Saharawi are also dependent on the continued Algerian acceptance of the camps on Algerian territory. This can be aligned with Chinkin and Charlesworth's understanding of the right of individuals to self-determination, which they describe as unsatisfactory for women when:

A woman may be technically free to work in the paid, public workforce, but if a man is given the right to prevent his wife from participating in public, political or cultural activities outside the home this freedom is meaningless.[65]

Under the international legal narrative, the Saharawi are technically free to exercise the right to self-determination. Morocco is able to exploit the structural weaknesses of the international legal system through the violent existence of a physical division and occupation of the territory, thereby gaining a foothold in determining the future of the region. By refusing localised knowledge and narratives – for example, the strong internal self-determination of the Saharawi – within its sources of understanding, international law remains focussed on the public sphere. One consequence of this structural limitation is a resistance to alternative understandings of international relationships.[66] Crucial to this narrative is the location of force as a means to resolve

---

63 See chapter five on humanitarian intervention.
64 See, for example, oppression of Roma people in Kosovo after the 1999 NATO intervention as well as the negative effects of the intervention for women: Rodgers, 'Bosnia and Kosovo: Interpreting the Gender Dimensions of International Intervention' in McInnes and Wheeler (eds), *Dimensions of Western Military Intervention* (London: Cass, 2002); European Roma Rights Centre, 'Justice for Kosovo', 4, *Roma Rights* (2005).
65 Charlesworth and Chinkin, above note 18, at 162.
66 For example, the alternative structure of the African Charter on Human rights is often acknowledged as 'different' rather than an 'alternative'; Banda, *Women, Law and Human Rights: An African Perspective* (Oxford: Hart, 2005) at 44.

disputes in place of sophisticated reflection on the capacity of the international system to secure positive ends without the use of force. When force is politically unfeasible, as in the Western Sahara, the international system is devoid of answers to fundamental questions, such as how to secure a right to self-determination that is meaningful for the communities claiming the right. This is not to promote, or justify, the use of force in retaliation to Morocco's political stalling and control of the Western Sahara territory. Instead, the Western Sahara example demonstrates the limitations of force as a model of enforcement.

Palestine

> ... in a context where every man is a soldier, every woman becomes an occupied territory .... [67]

This section highlights the narratives Israeli and Palestinian women bring to international law. My conclusion is that, despite the diversity and challenges represented in these narratives, a resonant and recurring theme is voiced by Israeli and Palestinian women: all the women whose voices are represented draw attention to the nexus between the public and private violence in their lives.[68] From this, I argue that the recognised right to external self-determination, as affirmed by the ICJ in its Advisory Opinion in the *Legal Consequences of the Construction of a Wall in the Occupied Palestinian Territories*,[69] is meaningless not only because it lacks resources geared towards the facilitation of internal self-determination but also because a large proportion of the community lacks the capacity to choose the model of individual self-determination that constructs their lives and participation in that community. Although the Court was given the opportunity in its Opinion to discuss the inadequacy of security achieved through military and forceful means, there is a notable absence of references to the violence – of either the construction of the 'Wall' or of the occupation of Palestinian territory – and an absence of recognition of the complicity of third states in perpetuating the status quo in the region.[70] Additionally, the role of Israeli and Palestinian women in shaping alternative narratives for the region and in bringing oppositional factions together was undermined by an Opinion that reiterated legal rights but declined to offer guidance on the means to achieving those rights.

For example, the Court considers the appropriateness of the term 'wall' to describe the barrier built by Israel and concludes:

---

67 Sharoni, 'Homefront as Battlefield' in Mayer (ed), *Women and the Israeli Occupation* (London: Routledge, 1994) at 10.
68 Sharoni, 'Middle East Politics Through Feminist Lens', 18 *Alternatives* (1993) 5; Mayer, ibid.; Abdo and Lentin (eds), *Women and the Politics of Military Confrontation* (Oxford: Berghahn, 2002); El-Sarraj, 'Screaming in Silence' in Waller and Rycenga, *Frontline Feminisms* (London: Routledge, 2001); Mayer, 'From Zero to Hero' in Mayer, *Gender Ironies of Nationalism* (London: Routledge, 2000).
69 Above note 35.
70 Ibid.

The "wall" in question is a complex construction, so that that term cannot be understood in a limited physical sense. However, other terms used, either by Israel ("fence") or by the Secretary-General ("barrier") are no more accurate if understood in a physical sense. In this Opinion, the Court has therefore chosen to use the terminology employed by the General Assembly.[71]

Recalling the prior discussion of the Moroccan built Berm in Western Sahara and drawing on Nesiah's analysis of space and place under international law,[72] the terminology employed – and a discussion of its merits – represents linguistic violence where the meaning and relevance of the 'wall' to those partitioned by its presence are effectively silenced by the nature of legal debates. The technical detail offered by the ICJ in paragraphs 81 through 84 of the Opinion, on the exact location and materials forming the 'wall', are segmented from the discussion of the impact and meaning of the act of physical segregation that the 'wall' produces. This enables the legal narrative to segregate social and economic knowledge from the legal/technical discussion and give the appearance that the two are unrelated. Furthermore, the submission of written and oral statements to the Court by state and organisations of states can be contrasted with the process of listening developed by the Women's International War Crimes Tribunal, which used testimony from survivors to develop the format of legal narrative.[73] Unlike the testimonies of female survivors of sexual violence during conflict, the testimonies of women living under occupation have not found a repository in international law.[74] By elevating the voices of Israeli and Palestinian women alongside legal narratives on self-determination, the inadequacy of current legal narratives can be exposed.

In contrast to externally driven legal narratives, internal narratives are better evidenced through the texts and dialogues of inhabitants of the Israel and the Occupied Palestinian Territories. The complex combination of historical, political and global factors in the region makes it clear that many alternative narratives could be used to represent the realities of life in Israel and the Occupied Palestinian Territories. My goal is to present one stream of narratives, so I analyse the narratives that emerge from Israeli and Palestinian women working for peace in the region.[75] I argue that these narratives are important and transformative dialogues with the potential to re-direct the future for Israelis and Palestinians. The transformative potential lies in the implicit

---

71 Ibid. paragraph 67.

72 Above note 37.

73 Chinkin, 'Women's International Tribunal on Japanese Military Sexual Slavery', 95, *AJIL* (2001), 326.

74 For an optimistic account of international institutional responses to sexual violence in conflict, see Bergoffen, 'Toward a Politic of the Vulnerable Body', 18 (1), *Hypatia* (2003), 116.

75 The purpose of using these narratives is to identify flaws in international narratives rather than offer 'one true representation' of women in Israel or Palestine. Furthermore, it is not my intention to suggest women's narratives are predisposed to see peace rather than force as a means to solving community dilemmas; rather I have consciously sought non-violent, peace-seeking narratives to demonstrate an alternative to mainstream accounts.

recognition of, first, the interdependence of the layers of self-determination and, second, the rejection of public violence as a means of securing self-determination. The visibility of women's narratives in Israel and the Occupied Palestinian Territories remains limited and outside of international legal narratives. This is because the narratives emerging from women and feminist peace activists tend to attach to our understandings of internal self-determination, which lack international legal enforcement. The narratives emerge outside the dominant, and public, narratives of militarisation in both the Israeli and Palestinian communities so they are doubly gendered as 'female'. As women's narratives they are obscured by the failure of equal representation in political and military institutions, structures which are built around predominantly male and masculine narratives and histories of articulation.[76] Furthermore, as narratives that focus on the re-organisation of private space as a means to develop the political, the women's narratives I introduce here are generally conceived as feminised and outside of public notice because of their content.[77] The narratives may also have trouble becoming visible because they seek to circumvent the role of the state as the centre of the international legal process by connecting private violence to public violence.

The discussion in this section builds on the prior representation of the Western Sahara narratives. Here the continuum of external–internal self-determination is extended to understand individual self-determination as having relevance to international legal narratives. The history of the Occupied Palestinian Territories weaves through the history of the United Nations, as an ever-present 'crisis' region that has thus far been unable to harness the enforcement mechanisms of the Charter to secure peace or stability for either Israeli or Palestinian citizens. Sharoni has written extensively on the role of militarised violence in shaping the private and public experiences of Israeli men and women describing Israeli women as 'occupied territories'. Sharoni's work illustrates the consequences of occupation for the occupier and challenges the Israeli identification of security with occupation.[78] Sharoni also highlights how the distancing of women from international and national decision-making forums undermines the confidence that women have 'in the legitimacy of their own judgement'.[79]

Sharoni's work is complementary to the analysis of Palestinian women who also challenge the role of militarised masculinity in the construction of group identity.[80]

---

76 While women are required to serve in the Israeli armed forces, the list of exemptions from national service is broader for women, the length of commitment is shorter and women are not expected to take combat positions. Reportage on women's experiences in the Israeli army is difficult to obtain; however for a history of women's roles in the Israeli Defence Force, see: van Creveld, 'Armed But Not Dangerous' 7 *War in History* (2000) 82. Also see: Sasson-Levy, 'Feminism and Military Gender Practises: Israeli Women Soldiers in 'Masculine' Roles' 73 *Sociological Inquiry* (2003) 440 finding: 'although these women soldiers individually transgress gender boundaries, they internalise the military's masculine ideology and values and learn to identify with the patriarchal order of the army and the State'.

77 On public and private ordering in international law, see: Chinkin, 'A Critique of the Public and Private Dimension', 10 (2), *EJIL* (1999), 387.

78 Sharoni, above note 67.

79 Ibid. at 6.

80 Mayer, above note 67; Abdo and Lentin, above note 68.

For example, Mayer describes the increasingly complex layers of narrative emergent from Israeli and Palestinian women:

> On the one hand, the Occupation has provided an area of resistance within which many Israeli Jewish women have found their political voice; while the imperative of resisting the Occupation has renewed forces of cultural, national and religious fundamentalism which have pressured Palestinian women to return to traditional roles. Yet, on the other hand, examinations of Jewish and Palestinian women's lives ... also show that the prolonged occupation and its reinforcement of Israeli militarism have in many ways enhanced Jewish women's marginalization and changed Israeli society for the worse – while they have, at the same time, empowered the Palestinian women who have adjusted to new roles.[81]

Mayer's identification of the multiple narratives that are able to exist to define the same events, as well as her understanding of the further intersections of group difference, for example class, may appear paradoxical. The paradox of the vectors of difference shaping simultaneous narratives receives considerable feminist attention elsewhere and informs my approach to self-determination rights.[82] By elaborating multiple and potentially paradoxical or oppositional narratives I hope to avoid what Talukdar refers to as 'the complicity of makers and viewers in promoting a discourse that maintains the status quo' acknowledging 'even when disadvantaged groups are conferred a resistant voice, in practice, this may work as reversal'.[83] So, while the internal dialogues of self-determination expressed by Israeli and Palestinian women demonstrate a multitude of positions and concerns, not always expressed through gender perspectives or feminist perspectives, what is constant is the distance women have from expressing views in a manner that will impact on the mainstream security discourses that inform their lives.[84] The security discourses, emergent from either the militarised Israeli state or the Palestinian leadership continue to equate security with public acts of violence. In contrast, both Israeli and Palestinian feminist scholarships equate public violence/aggression with the escalating private violence in their communities.[85]

The absence, then, is not in the women's narratives or perspectives; rather it is in the mainstream or dominant legal and political accounts that suppress women's understandings of violence and self-determination. This is not to suggest all Israeli and Palestinian women are anti-violence or anti-military or that all men instinctively perceive public violence as justifiable while women have a deeper intuitive understanding of the consequences of violence.[86] In Israel and Palestine, where there is a historical

---

81 Mayer, Ibid. at 2.
82 Mohanty, Russo and Torres (eds), *Third World Women and the Politics of Feminism* (Indiana, 1991); Braidotti, 'The Migrant, the Exile and the Nomad', 15, *Women's Studies International Forum* (1992) 7.
83 Talukdar, 'You Have a Voice Now, Resistance Is Futile!' in Waller and Rycenga, above note 67.
84 Hannan Ashrawi is a notable and welcome exception; see Ashrawi, *This Side of Peace: A Personal Account* (New York: Touchstone, 1996).
85 I am wary of the suggestion that there is an essential association between women and peace, for a discussion on this point, see: Lentin, 'Existential States of Exile', in Abdo and Lentin, above note 68, at 297.
86 See further, Sjoberg and Gentry, *Mothers, Monsters, Whores: Women's Violence in Global Politics* (London: Zed, 2007).

and contemporary absence of the use of force under the Security Council chapter VII powers, both communities continue to argue that the force they apply is justifiable.[87] This is a modelling of the international legal narrative rather than a rejection of it. This chapter argues that alternative narratives exist to those that place the use of force at the apex of international relations and these narratives have relevance to international law.

For feminist activists and theorists, a key alternative narrative centres on exposing the role that public violence plays in perpetuating and justifying private violence within a community. Sharoni presents a disturbing view of militarised violence in Israel, which extends to the manner in which women and men relate to each other.[88] In an evocative example, Sharoni retells the story of an Israeli soldier charged with the point-blank shooting of a Palestinian woman, Amal Muhammad Hasin.[89] Although charged under Israeli military law the soldier was released on appeal. Two years later this soldier shot and killed his 19-year-old Israeli girlfriend, Einav Rogel, who Sharoni describes as having unconditionally supported the soldier during his military trial. Sharoni concludes:

> Einav Rogel lived and died in a society that draws clear distinctions between 'us' and 'them', and usually doesn't even record the names of Palestinians who are shot. At the same time, she did not realize that, like many other Israeli women and most Palestinians (both women and men) in the West Bank and the Gaza Strip, she belonged to a high risk population since she lived in the line of fire of an Israeli man who had learned to use his gun to deal with crises and difficult situations.[90]

For Sharoni, women in Israel remain unable to reach full individual self-determination while violence defines their lives. The same must be said of Israeli men. For Lentin, the consequence of living as the militarised oppressor must be examined by Israeli men and women.[91] That is, the consequences for their own community, particularly in the construction of Israeli gender relations, which have become infused with narratives of force and difference.[92]

El-Sarraj describes a similar linkage between public and private violence in the lives of Palestinian women, concluding, 'Palestinian women . . . are faced with two burdens: the violent environment and a seemingly eternal victimization by their own authoritarian and patriarchal society. They are victims of all kinds of violence: political, social, domestic'.[93] El-Sarraj draws on the case study of a 20-year-old Palestinian, Samiha, who had married at the age of 16:

---

87 See Written Statement of the Government of the State of Israel, to the International Court of Justice 30 January 2004.
88 Sharoni, above note 67.
89 Ibid.
90 Ibid. at 121–22.
91 Lentin, above note 85, at 314.
92 Sharoni, above note 67.
93 El-Sarraj, 'Screaming in Silence', in Waller and Rycenga, above note 68, at 19–20.

It was an arranged marriage like most marriages. I moved to join his family in their home. One week later I was in despair. He used to beat me with plastic pipes . . . My husband was imprisoned before we got married. Everything he experienced in prison he used against me.[94]

The self-evidence of the chain of violence from public to private in the lives of these women fails to reverberate in international legal narratives.

The image of private space in the Occupied Palestinian Territories is further complicated by the direct attacks the Israel state has made against the homes of Palestinian citizens, either through Israeli settlements or through the direct destruction of Palestinian homes and towns. For example, the building of the Wall required the removal of Palestinian homes in the path of the barrier. The encirclement of the Palestinian territory by the Wall has, moreover, created an economic, health and education prison, isolating Palestinian communities from basic services. El-Sarraj contrasts Palestinian refugees' memories of home: 'my father keeps this key with other documents of family properties, still dreaming of the day he will return' with the reality of those who have been able to remain in Palestinian homes:

The stagnant political process and the aggressive Israeli response have both contributed to the re-emergence of feelings of frustration and of calls for radical violent tactics. This is particularly the case in the Gaza Strip, which in many ways fits the model of a prison . . . In this environment, everyone is affected by the overwhelming stress, which is bound to reactivate various forms of violence. According to a study of adult Palestinians, 64 per cent of the participants had been subjected to humiliation, harassment and beating. The resulting anxiety is transmitted to children . . .[95]

In contrast to El-Sarraj's perspective from within the Occupied Palestinian Territories, Espanioly writes from the perspective of a Palestinian woman living in Israel. Espanioly identifies a different narrative for women in her community from those of Israeli-Jewish women and from Palestinian women living in the Occupied Territories.[96] Yet, the narrative continues to be constructed around the nexus between public and private violence. Espanioly explores the lives of Palestinian women caught between the modern, Western lifestyle embraced by the Israeli state, and the traditional role women are expected to maintain to emphasise their Palestinian identity under Israeli rule.[97] The positive impact of this has been the emergence of political consciousness and political activism in Palestinian women living in Israel. This has impacted on the provision of health and education services to the Palestinian community in Israel, as Palestinian women in Israel have, through political activism, organised around these rights.[98] Yet, at the same time, Palestinian women living in

94 Ibid. at 22.
95 Ibid. at 19.
96 Espanioly, 'Palestinian Women in Israel', in Mayer, above note 67, at 106.
97 Ibid. at 116–117.
98 Ibid. at 112, 118.

Israel must negotiate the continual threat of being targeted by the repressive and violent policies of the state of Israel, which is also their home. Like Sharoni's understanding of the close relationship between public and private violence, Espanioly's work leads towards the conclusion that the provision of military 'security' in the state of Israel has important consequences for the capacity of individuals to pursue personal security. The complex interaction of nationalism, militarism and security is underscored by daily, intimate threats to women's livelihoods.[99]

An additional group of narratives emerges from Palestinian women living in the Gaza Strip and the West Bank, and addresses the role of liberation struggles in providing a positive conduit for women's social and political determination.[100] Mayer suggests that the major conflict for these women is between social determination and national determination.[101] Likewise, Dajani writes:

Palestinian women are becoming acutely aware of their vulnerability. They realise that national liberation is not necessarily synonymous with social liberation. They want their political activism . . . to be translated into real social gains and democratization throughout the whole of Palestinian society, so that they do not find themselves, as women, relegated to a permanently subordinate position after national liberation.[102]

The Western failure to understanding the limited success of social movements, in their own histories, to produce sex equality alongside other social goals provides clear parallels.[103]

To draw this discussion back to the use of force to promote self-determination, it may be concluded that the self-determination of women in Israel and the Occupied Palestine Territories is a complex issue with multiple narrative sites and extended and differing narratives within each site. Providing a legal answer, which offers an opportunity for the individual self-determination of women in the Occupied Territories as well as within Israel itself, would be dependent on providing political agency to women and men equally.[104] It would also be grounded in programmes for the eradication of private violence, particularly violence enacted by men against women. To hear women's voices from Israel and the Occupied Palestinian Territories is to identify the nexus between individual and collective self-determination as each articulates the role military security strategies play in limiting their personal safety and visibility.

99 Mayer (ed.), *Gender Ironies of Nationalism* (London: Routledge, 2000).
100 Mayer, 'From Zero to Hero', in Ibid., at 283.
101 Ibid.
102 Dajani, 'Between National and Social Liberation', in Mayer, above note 98, at 34; see also Chinkin (1992) above note 3.
103 Morgan, *Sisterhood is Powerful* (Vintage, 1970), introduction.
104 While a delegation of Israeli and Palestinian women with leadership roles met at the UN in New York in September 2006, that this was a gender segregated event suggests women are not accepted as mainstream 'statesmen', see: http://www.unifem.org/news_events/story_detail.php?StoryID=512 (last accessed February 2011).

In a final narrative from Israel and the Occupied Palestinian Territories, Emmet demonstrates the continuum of public and private violence in relation to the chorus of Israeli and Palestinian women who form the Women in Black movement, who:

> ... lift the veil of democratic rhetoric that proclaims citizens' equality in the state and reveal the ongoing and heated Israeli debate on the nature of citizenship. In forging gendered peace vigils, the Women in Black address several issues. They question whether all citizens (Israeli Jews and Israeli Palestinians, women and men) are equal. The vigils also test the right of citizens to dissent from a national consensus in a society that places high value on the collective.[105]

Reforming Palestinian self-determination struggles in terms of the individual self-determination of women in the region has multiple answers to the counter-position that advocates the use of force either to achieve or defeat self-determination. This elevates the worth of individuals before nations, and it ties the violence Israeli women suffer at the hands of militarisation within the Israel state to the self-determination of Palestinian women and, additionally, makes individuals responsible for their actions rather than subsuming them in the politics of the state. The ICJ Advisory Opinion on the building of the Wall by the Israeli state consistently affirms the right of self-determination for the Palestinians while denying the violence of the Israel social, political and military choices through a focus on an external, limited understanding of self-determination.[106] This is reinforced in other ICJ opinions and judgements, Security Council Resolutions and the practice of states, and it may be said, in international legal structures generally.[107] This status quo is further maintained and demonstrated through Israel's reservations to the CEDAW that demonstrate a lack of commitment to the protection of women's rights in Israel.[108]

By choosing to see the solution to the Israel–Palestinian conflict in the dialogues and conversations of women in the conflict, I have grounded the self-determination of those women in their future actions. International law cannot tell Palestinian women or Israeli women what to say or to do to achieve their freedom, nor can the international legal system promise such a process through the provision of force. The role of the international legal structures in securing self-determination needs to be grounded in the eradication of violence against women, built on programmes towards women's literacy and education and fulfilled through women's health services. These rights are only gendered in the sense that they are identifying a gender imbalance that can be redressed with the purpose of developing the self-determination of women and men.

105 Emmett, *Our Sisters' Promised Land: Women, Politics and Israel-Palestinian Co-existence* (Michigan, 1996) at 22.
106 Above note 35, paragraphs 122, 155 and 159.
107 GA Res 1541; see also *Case Concerning the Frontier Dispute (Burkina Faso v Mali)*, ICJ Reports (22 December 1986) 554 at paragraphs 25/6; also, above note 31.
108 Reservations to CEDAW by Israel affect the application of Article 7(b) (on the appointment of women as judges to religious courts), Article 16 (the reservation exempts religious laws on personal status in Israel from CEDAW) and Article 29(2) (on the possibility of non-observance being referred to the International Court of Justice).

No collective voice in Israel or the Occupied Palestinian Territories will make sense until individuals are granted the opportunities to work together to create a meaningful collective for all citizens. To emerge as a collective under the international, individual self-determination must be acknowledged as a pre-requisite and a right.

Timor-Leste

In contrast to the struggles of the Saharawi and the Palestinians, the legal narrative regarding Timor-Leste's external identity suggests that self-determination has been secured by the use of Security Council authorised force.[109] In 1999, after the Indonesian militia embarked on a programme of violent repression against the East Timorese people, the UN Security Council authorised the use of force by the UN International Force in East Timor (INTERFET). INTERFET's mandate was to use all means necessary to halt the pro-Indonesia violence, to provide security in the region and to facilitate the implementation of popular consultation for the East Timorese, in accordance with the expressed desire of the population in the 1999 popular consultation.[110] INTERFET was later joined by the UN Transitional Administration in East Timor (UNTAET).[111] In 2002, the UN-administered territory known as East Timor formally gained its independence and is now the independent state of the Democratic Republic of Timor-Leste.[112]

From the international legal narrative a process of external self-determination culminating in statehood and control of territory is evident. As a legal narrative, this appears to be the last act in a process begun during the UN era of decolonisation.[113] Timor-Leste was a Portuguese colony for 300 years until withdrawal by the Portuguese and invasion by Indonesia in 1975. Viewed from this angle, the legal narrative begins in colonisation and concludes with full citizenship in the international community. However, the legal narrative omits many important aspects of the process of self-determination. This includes more than 20 years of repressive Indonesia practices in the territory and the complicity of third states in Indonesian's aggressive determination of the lives of the Timor-Leste (at the time named East Timor) people during 1975 to 1999.[114] For example, the ICJ in the *Case Concerning East Timor (Portugal v. Australia)* explicitly refrained from commenting on the Indonesian occupation, implicitly reinforcing the status quo of Indonesian control and the benefits derived by third-party states.[115] For Nevins, the international legal narratives, 'barely mention the pre-ballot period' offering only silence 'on the matter of external support for Indonesia's crimes in Timor-Leste, especially that of the world's most powerful

109 Nevins, '(Mis)representing East Timor's Past', 4 (1), *Journal of Human Rights* (2002), 523, at 525–526.
110 SC Res 1264 (15 September 1999), acting under UN Chapter VII.
111 SC Res 1272 (25 October 1999).
112 SC Res 1414 (23 May 2002).
113 See Chinkin, 'East Timor: A Failure of Decolonisation', 20, *Australian Yearbook of International Law* (2000) 1.
114 Nevins, above note 109, at 525.
115 *Case Concerning East Timor* (Portugal v Australia) [1995] ICJ Reports 90.

countries'.[116] The level of violence against the Timorese from the Indonesian military during the popular consultation and the ineptitude evidenced by the UN decision that permitted Indonesia to provide security during the popular consultation is also sidelined in the formal legal narrative.[117]

Chinkin presents the sequence of events in Timor-Leste as 'A Play in Five Acts', while Drew describes the 'story' of Timor-Leste, which hides under the 'Hollywood ending' of 'the triumph of right (self-determination) over might (the Indonesian Army)'.[118] Orford uses a personal narrative of the period from August 1999 until the arrival of UNTAET to explore her own feelings of ambiguity over the use of force to justify the 1999 intervention.[119] Nevins refers to the misrepresentation of Timor-Leste's past.[120] As such, each of these authors highlights the narrative element of law either explicitly, as Orford does, or implicitly through the reference to the 'story', the theatre or misrepresentation of Timor-Leste's history. The general dissatisfaction critical accounts cast on to the international legal narrative of the self-determination of Timor-Leste are echoed in the words of the former President of Timor-Leste, Xanana Gusmao, who, in his 2001 New Year's address, criticised the role of international narratives in the shaping of the future of Timor-Leste.[121]

In researching the shift in Timor-Leste after independence in 2002, a plethora of narratives can be placed alongside the legal narrative recorded above. My personal priority in this work was the recording of women's narratives, be they from international feminist scholars or women in Timor-Leste. My intention was to evidence the links between individual, social and international self-determination, in line with the rest of this chapter. Unfortunately, although I found multiple narratives that I might insert here there is an absence of representation of the voices of Timor-Leste women,[122] the authors tend to be Western feminists or international humanitarian or NGO workers.[123] For example, Charlesworth and Wood's analysis of the impact of the Gender Affairs Unit in Dili is built on consultation with women's groups in the region and they conclude, 'it was unclear whether gender mainstreaming was aimed at UNTAET international workers, or East Timorese women, or Timor-Leste people in general. This led to misunderstandings about the practical and ethical basis of sex

---

116 Nevins, above note 109, at 527; also see: Cotton, *East Timor, Australia and Regional Order* (London: Routledge, 2004).

117 Above note 52, at 137.

118 Chinkin, above note 112; Drew, above note 19; for an alternative narrative see: Philpott, 'East Timor's Double Life: Smells Like Westaphalia Spirit' 27(1), *Third World Quarterly* (2006) which praises 'the resilience and political maturity of the people of East Timor' at 159. Note both authors refer to 'East Timor' rather than 'Timor-Leste' as this was correct at the time the articles were produced, I have used the name 'Timor-Leste' unless referring to specific UN documents that use the name 'East Timor'.

119 Orford, *Reading Humanitarian Intervention* (Cambridge: Cambridge University Press, 2003) 1–37.

120 Above note 109.

121 Quoted in Charlesworth and Wood, 'Women and Human Rights in the Rebuilding of East Timor', 71, *Nordic Journal of International Law* (2002) 325, at 335.

122 Niner, 'Martyrs, Heroes and Warrors', in Kingsbury and Leach (eds), *East Timor: Beyond Independence* (Monash, 2007).

123 See, for example, Cristalis, and Wood, *Bitter Dawn: East Timor A People's Story* (London: Zed, 2002).

equality rhetoric in the UNTAET mission'.[124] Charlesworth and Wood move on to discuss the difficulties of merging institutional and Western feminist approaches, as is found in the United Nations under the gender mainstreaming mantra, into a community with its own feminist structures and women's organisations.

While Charlesworth and Wood's approach utilises the narratives of the women of Timor-Leste, it is directed at international legal audiences and ultimately represents a Western feminist understanding of events in Timor-Leste. The resonance of their findings illustrates the limitations of international law rather than the self-determination of the people of Timor-Leste.[125] In contrast to Charlesworth's and Wood's study, Cristalis and Scott's book, *Independent Women: the Story of Women's Activism in East Timor*, endeavours to 'dispel the myth that women working for women's advancement in East Timor are agents of a foreign or Western agenda'.[126] The authors trace the role of women in the resistance and independence movement in Timor-Leste. Although they build on their experiences of living in Timor-Leste and their consequential intimacy with events and people in Timor-Leste, the authors are not themselves from Timor-Leste.

So in an attempt to add the narrative of the women of Timor-Leste, I looked to courtroom narratives, which through the East Timor Judicial System Monitoring Programme (JSMP) are available online.[127] Courtroom narratives add insight into the relationship of the women of Timor-Leste to legal structures implemented after self-determination. The JSMP has compiled two key reports on gender justice in Timor-Leste. The first Report, *Statistics on Cases of Violence Against Women in Timor-Leste*, released in February 2005, records, of the 361 reports collected by police, less than three per cent of cases involving violence against women were resolved in court.[128] In the second Report, the eight cases where violence against women was prosecuted were analysed by the JSMP.[129] The Report commends the prosecutions that occurred, suggesting that previously, 'there had never been any decisions handed down in cases of violence against women'.[130] However, the leniency of sentences and the insensitivity of judicial personnel to gender issues were of high concern to the authors of the Report, as was the lack of application of 'international standards'.[131] These internal legal narratives may allow us to make certain inferences about the development of Timor-Leste, post-independence. Yet I would suggest that they have greater relevance in illustrating the limitations of international, and Western narratives, around gender-based violence.[132]

---

124 Above note 121, at 344.
125 Also see, Charlesworth, 'Not Waving, Drowning', 18, *Harvard Human Rights Journal* (2005) 1.
126 Above note 123.
127 See: http://www.jsmp.minihub.org/ (last accessed February 2011).
128 Judicial System Monitoring Programme, *Statistics on Cases of Violence Against Women in Timor-Leste*, Dili, Timor-Leste (February 2005).
129 Judicial System Monitoring Programme, *Analysis of Decisions in Cases Involving Women and Children Victims: June 2006 – March 2005*, Dili, Timor-Leste (April 2005); also see Judicial System Monitoring Programme, *VSS's Activity Report on Legal Aid for Victims of Gender Based Violence*, Dili, Timor-Leste (April–Nov 2009).
130 Ibid., at 250.
131 Above note 129.
132 Gunning, 'Arrogant Perceptions, World Travelling and Multicultural Feminism', in Wing (ed.), *Critical Race Feminism* (New York: New York University Press, 1997), at 352.

With respect to Timor-Leste, the Reports demonstrate a commitment to change grounded in bringing women's experience into the realm of the criminal justice system. This commitment is also prevalent in the Commission for Reception, Truth and Reconciliation Report,[133] and the Criminal Process and Criminal Law Codes.[134] Yet, the interrogation of Timor-Leste's judicial processes demonstrates the role the enforcement and practice of law, now built on a liberal model of formal equality, plays in impairing women's capacity to secure justice for violent crime directed towards them. To suggest, as the Reports do, that the lack of prosecutions for violence against women is a feature of the Timor-Leste social structure is to misunderstand the role of liberalism in gender-based injustices. Thus, rather than offering a narrative on the internal social fabric of Timor-Leste, the Reports should direct us towards the international narrative of which the experience in Dili is indicative. That is, under Western models of liberalism law is a key barrier to the recognition of gender-based crimes and the prosecution of domestic or sexual violence.[135]

By suggesting that the 'root causes of domestic violence' lie in the 'culture, tradition and religion' of Timor-Leste, the Reports deny the role law, either that imposed by the Indonesian occupation or transplanted after the UN transitional administration, plays in scripting the possibilities for tackling gender-based crime.[136] As a result, my response to the narratives of women's rights and gender justice in Timor-Leste is apprehensive. While there is a tendency in the Reports of the JSMP to blame the local culture and traditions for the prevalence of gender-based violence,[137] there is an implicit denial of the role played by international law, in both the use of force to resolve the 1999 'crisis' and through the implementation of Western liberalism, in the global non-prosecution of gender-based violence.[138] For example, to be living in the United Kingdom and to be shocked by a rate of under three per cent judicial resolution of gender-based crimes in Timor-Leste is to ignore the comparable statistics for the judicial resolution of sexual offences in the United Kingdom, which, at the time of writing, are at six per cent of reported cases.[139] Similarly UK government statistics highlight that, on average, two women die from violence perpetrated by partners or ex-partners every week in England and Wales.[140] Studies of sex trafficking, sexual

---

133 For the text of the Report (titled *Chega!*) see: www.cavr-timorleste.org (last accessed February 2011).

134 Judicial System Monitoring Programme, *Overview of Timor-Leste Justice Sector*, Dili, Timor-Leste (January 2006).

135 Vlachova and Bison (eds), *Women in an Insecure World*, Geneva Centre for the Democratic Control of Armed Force, 2005, Part I; although note too Niner describes gender-based violence as 'possibly the greatest issue facing the justice system in East Timor' above note 122, at 125.

136 Above note 128, at 23; above note 129, at 4 and 9.

137 Judicial System Monitoring Programme, *The Law of Gender-Based Violence in Timor-Leste*, Dili, Timor-Leste (April–November 2005), at 14 and 26.

138 I place crisis in inverted commas as this understanding of events denies the lengthy and violent occupation of East Timor by Indonesia; Nevins, above note 109; Charlesworth , 'International Law: A Discipline of Crisis', 65 (3), *Modern Law Review* (2002), 377.

139 Her Majesty's Inspectorate of Constabulary, *Without Consent*, Central Office of Information (UK) (January 2007).

140 See Povey, *Crime in England and Wales 2002/3: Home Office Statistical Bulletin No. 02/05* (London: Home Office, 2004).

exploitation and abuse perpetrated by UN staff also present an alarming adjunct to the national strategies to prosecute sexual violence in Timor-Leste.[141]

With respect to the internal, or substantive, self-determination of the people of Timor-Leste my own narrative remains equally apprehensive. My conclusions lead me to question the absences apparent in the international narratives rather than proffering an 'authentic' account of the Timor-Leste journey to self-determination. The continued political and communal unrest after the creation of the new state of Timor-Leste adds further discomfort to my acceptance of the international legal narrative that suggests that the use of force in Timor-Leste was successfully justified on the grounds of self-determination. The absence in international law begins in the denial of international and powerful state complicity in the violence perpetrated by the Indonesian government over the period of occupation and is traced through the post-1999 endeavours to nurture a social structure compliant with international legal norms, even when those norms, especially criminal law structures available to prosecute domestic and gender based violence, remain ineffectual in the West. I am troubled by the quickness to find the source of weak gender prosecution in 'culture, tradition and religion' rather than in an international legal structure dependent on a division between public and private that frustrates the termination of domestic violence and is dependent on understandings of rape and sexual violence premised on masculine definitions of consent. Furthermore, the persistent violence in Timor-Leste raises questions around the impact of the use of force as an international lever to resolve a 'crisis'.

My conclusion with respect to the narratives of internal self-determination of Timor-Leste is to emphasise the depth that Pahuja's focus on the 'postcoloniality of international law' grants to our perspective.[142] The internal narratives defining international understandings of Timor-Leste play off 'culture, tradition and religion' against the legitimacy and rationality of the liberal democracy, defining our self understanding and projecting the Western state/subject as definitive of the universal. Feminist theory suggests international law will remain stymied by this self-ignorance unless the voices and choices of the most marginalised are perceived as equal. The women of the new state of Timor-Leste may, therefore, teach Western scholars much about the limitations of the right to self-determination and provide a site for challenging the dominance of patriarchal, imperialist devised versions of the international. Or, they may not. What is certain is that without their participation we will never know.

Consequently, while Knop is correct in asserting self-determination rights as a place where international law must confront diversity and the Other,[143] a general neglect of the process of 'internal' self-determination leads to the perpetuation of sexed forms of the state and all its gendered repercussions. I have focussed on the Western Saharan conflict, although currently endorsed under international legal narratives as under a ceasefire, as a territory where the use of force by Morocco has not heralded adequate

---

141 Spurling, 'Peacekeepers; Timor; and the Need to Address the Warrior Ethic', Conference Paper, *Sexual Abuse and Exploitation of Women in Violent Conflict, Netherlands Defense Academy*, Amsterdam, 19 June 2007.

142 Above note 3.

143 Knop, above note 3.

international condemnation. The building of the Berm and the placing of landmines along it can be described as acts of aggression.[144] By contrasting Timor-Leste with the Western Saharan struggle – the post-referendum aggression by Indonesian military forces with the continued stalling by Morocco to facilitate self-determination in the Western Sahara – different understandings of violence and aggression are evidenced. Additionally, the building of the Wall by Israel and its violent impact on both the daily lives of Palestinians as well as their public rights, especially that of self-determination, should be addressed in light of the Moroccan built wall in the Western Sahara that has equally stalled implementation of the right of self-determination. However, international legal narratives continue to hide behind externally driven understandings of self-determination and a consequential neglect of social and individual self-determination.

Since 2000, and the Security Council's first resolution on women, peace and security, the Council has increasingly included references to the challenges presented by sexual violence in armed conflict and to the Council's own strategies to combat sexual exploitation and abuse by UN personnel. Security Council resolutions on the three conflicts examined here have been no exception, for example, resolution 1920 on Western Sahara[145] and resolutions 1934 and 1937 on the Middle East[146] all include paragraphs referencing the UN's zero-tolerance policy on sexual exploitation and abuse perpetrated by UN personnel. Security Council resolution 1912 on Timor-Leste[147] includes, in Operative Paragraph 15, recognition of the need to fully take into account 'gender considerations . . . especially to protect them [women and girls] from gender-based violence'. None of these resolutions, however, acknowledge Security Council resolution 1325 where the Security Council '[e]xpresses its willingness to ensure that Security Council missions take into account gender considerations and the rights of women, including *through consultation with local and international women's groups*' (emphasis added)[148] or the approach of Security Council resolution 1889 which urges action 'to improve women's participation during all stages of peace processes, particularly in conflict resolution, post-conflict planning and peacebuilding, including by enhancing their engagement in political and economic decision-making'.[149] As such, each of these conflicts indicates how women's rights have been confined by narratives on sexual violence in armed conflict at the expense of local women's participation and knowledge as a tool for international legal change.

Self-determination dialogues also indicate the role of women's rights, and feminist articulation of those rights, can play in articulating new narratives for international law. Self-determination rights show how women's rights activism and feminist insight engage both the practical aspect of international norms, for example, the demand for

---

144 See GA Res 3314, the Definition of Aggression, Article 2 (a); see discussion in Clark, 'Western Sahara and the United Nations Norms on Self-determination and Aggression', in Arts and Leite (eds), above note 31, at 55.
145 SC Res 1920 (30 April 2010).
146 SC Res 1934 (30 June 2010) and SC Res 1937 (30 August 2010).
147 SC Res 1912 (26 February 2010).
148 SC Res 1325 (31 October 2000).
149 SC Res 1889 (5 October 2009), Operative paragraph 1.

participation of all members of a community in self-determination processes and substance, and engage the normative aspect of international norms, demonstrating the weakness of norms that are committed to a form of formal equality and recognition (external self-determination) without understanding substantive equality (internal and individual self-determination). Through challenging gender-based discrimination, particularly violence against women, but also ensuring women's free political participation and female sexual autonomy, lasting and effective social norms that will lead societies away from conflict and towards social or internal self-determination are the result.

The domestic analogy

In this, the final part of the chapter, I argue that legal regulation of women's self-determination and autonomy parallels international understandings of autonomy and the self-as-state. I argue that improving women's participation, freedom and autonomy strengthens communities and consequently builds states that are able to shift away from narratives that justify violence. At a conceptual level, I contend that the regulation of states under international law provides parallels with the regulation of individuals within the liberal state. There are factual, political, social and structural differences between states and individuals yet the legal regulation of each is markedly similar. I explore these similarities and the consequences for women and non-states in this section of the chapter. While in other chapters I have argued that there may be some merit in dissolving the analogy, this chapter reflects on how the solutions offered by feminist theories to the self-determination of women as individuals may offer strategies that may be of relevance to peoples seeking self-determination under international law. The additional claim I make is that this has descriptive and conceptual purchase for international law on self-determination, as not only is there an analogy in regulation but the facilitation of women's individual self-determination increases the internal coherence of a community.

Victims and Agents

Berman's identification of the paradox of self-determination, that 'a right accru[es] to an entity which, by its own admittance, lack international existence' provides a crucial lever for understanding the conceptual relevance of feminist scholarship to the right to self-determination.[150] Feminist jurisprudence builds its projects on the empirically recognised oppressions and violence that women encounter in their lifetimes. Yet to speak, and to challenge these oppressions, women must first take for themselves a measure of power or control and present themselves as full legal subjects. This creates, for feminist theory, the same paradox that Berman sees in self-determination, the paradox between agency and victimhood. However, unlike scholarship on the right to self-determination, feminist jurisprudence seeks both to live with and move beyond the internal paradox presented by the dual victim–agent status.[151] The complex

---

150 Above note 1.
151 See, for example, MacKinnon, *Are Women Human?* (Harvard: University Press, 2006).

international legal issues raised by the paradox of victim–agency in the expression of a right to self-determination might listen to and speak with feminist scholarship to gain increased understanding of this paradox.[152]

In both stages of legal regulation, the severance of the layers of self-determination has curtailed the achievement of self-determination for those who find their experience is not perceived to replicate the 'normal' citizen.[153] As such, feminist discourse on the curbing of individual autonomy for women through the benchmark of formal neutrality under liberalism has relevance for international understandings of self-determination. As attention to the narratives of women in Israel and Occupied Palestinian Territories demonstrates, without individual guarantees of freedom from violence, communities will be unrepresentative of all members' experiences. To challenge the preference for a formal equality model under liberalism, feminist reform strategies directed at creating substantive equality for women could be utilised to build strategies for the substantive equality of peoples.[154] Such feminist strategies include the re-imagining of the public and private spheres,[155] discursive challenges to liberal constructions of binaries that distance certain narratives from legal understandings, and the interrogation of both sexed and gendered categories within legal discourse. Feminist revisions also include philosophical projects that aim to re-imagine the liberal subject without the sexed and gendered limitations that circumscribe an individual's freedom from hunger, violence and illiteracy.[156] States or peoples, like individuals, need freedom from hunger, violence and illiteracy to allow their communities the space to create a meaningful identity.[157]

The right to self-determination under international law rests on unspoken assumptions about the definition of a state under international law as a neutral and acceptable aspect of international legal personality. Feminist legal theories challenge both the construction of the state and the primacy of the state itself under international law.[158] Understanding self-determination as challenging legal subjectivity – of states, of individuals and of peoples – is thus a crucial aspect of feminist reconstructions.

Wright considers the role of state agency in international political relations as further limited by the manifest inequalities between states that are suppressed by the Westphalian system. As a consequence, according to Wright, inequalities in power between states lead to a lack of belief in their agency as international legal subjects.[159] Likewise, Reisman and Armstrong have recorded the 'mimetic' role of US allies in parroting US foreign policy for combating global terrorism during the Bush

---

152 Talukdar, above note 83, at 73.
153 Naffine, 'The Body Bag', in Naffine and Owens, *Sexing the Subject of Laws* (London: LBC, 1997).
154 For example, Nussbaum, *Sex and Social Justice*, Oxford (1999) or Jackson, *Regulating Reproduction: Law, Technology and Autonomy* (Oxford: Hart, 2001) at 3–8.
155 Lacey, *Unspeakable Subjects* (Hart, 1998), chapter three; Thornton (ed.), *Public and Private: Feminist Legal Debates* (Oxford: Oxford University Press, 1995).
156 See: Fineman, 'The Vulnerable Subject: Anchoring Equality in the Human Condition', 20, *Yale Journal of Law and Feminism* (2008), 8.
157 Chinkin and Wright, above note 3.
158 Knop, above note 3; Charlesworth and Chinkin, above note 18, chapter five.
159 Wright, 'The Horizon of Becoming', 71, *Nordic Journal of International Law* (2002) 215.

administration,[160] and Otto has written that the failure of international law in securing democracy within states must be connected to the failure of the United Nations to build democracy between states within the organisation's participation procedures for states.[161] These reflections on the gap between the promise of sovereign equality and the reality of state power replicate, in international law, a status quo and liberalism that feminist theories identify as silencing women and deflecting female energies away from a belief in their own agency in the public sphere. Self-determination rights, from this perspective, extend well beyond the shift to self-government for previous colonial territories. The recent General Assembly Declaration on Indigenous Rights,[162] which considers self-determination a right of indigenous communities, as well as regional instruments such as the Banjul Charter,[163] may indicate that self-determination in the decolonisation process has been a first but not last stage of an emergent norm. To move effectively and productively on from the confined model born in the decolonisation era, there needs to be a shift away from force at the outer boundaries of the enforcement of the right. In this sense, self-determination may represent an important site for feminist re-imagining of states and communities, 'post-identity'.[164]

Participation

If the status of the State in international law rests on its respect for the right to participation in democratic governance, then it is open to women to insist, drawing on arguments developed in feminist critiques of domestic law, that the right be interpreted in ways that truly afford women equal representation in government.[165]

Self-determination struggles, the site where the subaltern seeks expression and thus inclusion in the international, on the one hand may be argued to be a site where women are doubly excluded.[166] At the same time, using self-determination as a site to re-imagine the self – within international and national legal structures – is a valid and relevant place for feminist conversations. By definition, those conversations are inclusive of women from within communities seeking self-determination and inclusive of women within communities seemingly 'determined'.[167]

The participation of women in international processes is recognised across feminist literature and increasingly in UN documentation.[168] Security Council Resolution

---

160 Reisman and Armstrong, 'The Past and Future of the Claim of Preemptive Self-Defense', 100 (3), *AJIL* (2006) 525.
161 Otto, above note 25.
162 GA Res 61/295, 2 October 2007, Article 3 states 'Indigenous peoples have the right to self-determination. By virtue of that right they freely determine their political status and freely pursue their economic, social and cultural development'.
163 African Charter on Human and Peoples Rights, 1981, 2 ILM 58 (1982).
164 Above note 156.
165 Knop, above note 3, at 298.
166 McDonald, above note 3, at 7.
167 Kandiyoti, 'Between the Hammer and the Anvil', 28, *Third World Quarterly* (2007) 503.
168 Charlesworth and Chinkin, above note 18.

1325 falls short of identifying women's participation as necessary for increased gender equality in international responses to conflict and peacebuilding. The Resolution requires 'the particular needs of women and girls' to be taken into account at the various stages of peacebuilding and conflict resolution but does not demand women's participation as necessary to achieve an understanding of the needs of women and girls. Similarly the production of gender disaggregated statistics under gender mainstreaming also falls short of demanding the participation of women in the United Nations and its activities.[169] For example, the equal participation of women and, in some cases, positive discrimination to ensure more than 50 per cent female representation requires more than the insertion of women alongside men at decision-making tables. This is a demand for attention to social and economic rights for women that gives them the opportunity to (self-)determine futures, which will prepare them to participate in the international sphere and with full capacity to articulate their experiences and needs. Anything short of this will lead to a continuation of elite Western women as the key female participants in the international arena.

In this sense, Wright's work as the Northern Director of the Akitsiraq Law School in Nunavut, Alaska stands as a groundbreaking initiative. Wright's action and choices reconstruct dialogues of power and otherness to work towards the empowerment of a local community and its individual members through the provision of education equal to the educational demands many in the developed world see as an inviolable right and choice.[170] Consequently:

> training indigenous lawyers, especially women, means that international law is no longer impermeable to the power of those traditionally seen as on the margins (and in the Arctic, literally on the margins!) of world events. Canada's presence in the Arctic depends on Inuit cooperation . . . . Nunavut itself is a creation of Inuit, Canadian and international law structuring sovereignty and self-determination in the Arctic. The creation of the Akitsiraq Law School shows that the structure of sovereignty and rights must be about *Inuit* agendas, and that these agendas must be responsive to the demands of women and their needs.[171]

The process of securing slow, long-term internal self-determination for the Inuit community can be contrasted with the use of force to secure autonomy for the Kurdish people in northern Iraq, now Kurdistan, in the 1990s. McDonald documents the failure of this process to be inclusive of women's social and economic rights or women's civil and political rights, particularly in terms of political representation and participation. McDonald, writing in 2001, argues the consequence was, that:

169 Spurling, 'Peacekeepers; Timor; and the Need to Address the Warrior Ethic' Confrence Paper, *Sexual Abuse and Exploitation of Women in Violent Conflict, Netherlands Defense Academy*, Amsterdam, 19 June 2007 suggests equal representation of women in military and peacekeeping organisations is an important aspect of increasing women's participation.

170 Chinkin, Charelsworth and Wright, 'Feminist Approaches to International Law: Reflections from Another Century', in Buss and Manji, *International Law: Modern Feminist Approaches* (Oxford: Hart, 2005), at 36.

171 Ibid. at 43; the authors note the Akitsiraq Law School has a predominance of women students which has lead to the incorporation of strategies to 'support the needs of female students with childcare and other 'women's' responsibilities' (at 42).

[t]he male leaders of the PKK, the Kurdish Democratic Party, the Patriotic Union of Kurdistan, and other parties, claim to speak on behalf of the Kurdish people. Men have defined the goals and have negotiated with the states . . . . This perpetuation of the patriarchal power base has serious implications for the well-being of the Kurdish population, a great proportion being the women and children who suffer the consequences of these struggles.[172]

The post-2003 situation in Iraq, where further Western force contributed to extensive violence and insecurity within Iraqi communities, has led the claims of the Kurdish population in Northern Iraq to move down the international political and legal agenda. While national trials in Iraq prosecuted previous Iraqi government officials for crimes against the Kurdish population, the shifting of international attention to the rights and actions of Western military forces in Iraq left little space for considering the discrimination encountered by Kurdish women or Kurdish communities more generally.[173] In fact, members of the PKK appear to have been 're-classified' as terrorist following attacks along the Turkish border.[174] The line between 'liberation fighters' and 'terrorists' that non-state actors must navigate under international law in a post-September 11 political environment adds a further dimension to the victim–agent paradox.[175] After the 2003 invasion and subsequent occupation of Iraq, the lack of agency experienced by Kurdish women in the autonomous Kurdish region in the 1990s has been replicated across Iraqi institutional and government structures that have not pursued women's rights as a priority in the re-building of Iraq.[176]

The participation of women in international forums and decision-making processes must begin with greater attention to women's social and economic participation in the community and access to education and employment. A corresponding element of this may be the development of social programmes that regard child rearing and the management of domestic space as positive choices for men or women and as sites of economic relevance to the state. Of course, this level of social reform can only be achieved through ongoing and slow social programmes, which have long-term goals of handing over power and knowledge rather than the imposition of foreign or Western social structures. To return to the example of the Kurdish autonomous region secured in Northern Iraq through force in the 1990s, it is clear that the use of force and preoccupation with external forms of self-determination is also a slow process without guarantees of success.

I place women's participation at the centre of legal reforms to enhance the self-determination of peoples because of the flow on intergenerational impact this has on a community, as evidenced by the social infrastructure of the Saharawi camps in Algeria. The experience of Afghan women under Taliban rule, where the education

---

172 McDonald, above note 3, at 148.
173 Ibid.
174 Dymond, *US and Turkey to Hit PKK*, BBC News (2 October 2007).
175 Chinkin, above note 31, at 339.
176 Al-Ali, and Pratt, *What Kind of Liberation? Women and the Occupation in Iraq* (Berkeley, CA: California University Press, 2009).

of girls was forced into private dwellings and performed in secret, is a similar example of women investing in 'social capital' despite the lack of external state/international support.[177] To conclude, it must be acknowledged that this is not a project that is perceived as applicable to 'others' or that hoists Western communities as a pinnacle of achievement for women's rights and participation but one which prioritises women's rights and the elimination of violence against women in all states for self-determination to be a meaningful term.

Conclusions

In providing a framework for re-scripting the international legal narrative on self-determination, I have argued for the importance of the following three ideas. First, the layers of self-determination, identified at the beginning of the chapter, need to be regarded as concurrent, overlapping and equally important categories to the facilitation of self-determination. Second, the positioning of force as a possible enforcement measure indicates the processes attached to the international right to self-determination need to be challenged and re-considered. Third, the narratives of those marginalised in current self-determination narratives must be elevated so that participation is democratic. These projects involve a shift from seeing self-determination as 'closed', or close to closure as decolonisation narratives become redundant, towards reframing self-determination as entering the international with ongoing significance to all states.[178] There is a need to see the securing of individual self-determination – freedom from hunger, freedom from violence and freedom from illiteracy – as the cornerstone of future global, legal narratives that move beyond the promises of formal liberalism.

To conclude, there is a sentiment that runs through this chapter and all those proceeding, which focuses on the agency of those under whose name force is justified. I recently found a similar sentiment in a children's picture book, written by Nobel Prize winner Toni Morrison. The picture book tells the story of three children who are forced to live in a large box; each child speaks in turn to the adults around them who seem not to listen. The children say:

> *I know you are smart and I know that you think*
> *You are doing what is best for me*
> *But if freedom is handled just your way*
> *Then it's not my freedom or free.*[179]

Feminist legal methods and the vast feminist scholarship on the different meanings of freedom and autonomy highlight the gendered constructions of the self that is

---

177 Rostami-Povey, *Afghan Women* (London: Zed, 2007).

178 Higgins goes some way towards this formulation, above note 7, but ultimately ties self-determination rights to decolonisation so as to maintain the efficiency of territory in defining the international legal subject.

179 Toni Morrison (with Slade Morrison), *The Big Box* (Children's Picture Book) (New York: Hyperion Books, 1999).

permitted to self-determine under international law.[180] Not surprisingly, the recipients of the use of force deployed on self-determination grounds find their communities stuck in a perpetuation of violence rather than a shift away from violence. The three self-determination conflicts given increased attention over the millennium, Timor-Leste, Palestine and the Western Sahara, remain trapped in modes of violence and law that offer little space for self-definition as communities or for individuals within those communities. Each community demonstrates a troubling lack of agency and voice in the period in which they remain in the 'grey space' between 'peoples' and 'states'. Notably, the Saharawi have attempted to avoid the perpetuation of violence and shifted towards the creative process of building internal self-determination. This is despite the failure of the international legal process to adequately support these internal self-determination gains.

It has been shown in this chapter that force by third parties justified on the grounds of assisting the self-determination of peoples is a gendered narrative dependent on Western legal structures. By moving outside the debates on the illegality or legitimacy of force, justified on self-determination grounds, and interrogating these legal debates through the lens of feminist theory, the potential for reframing self-determination is envisaged. Rather than dictating an answer or solution, this approach opens dialogues to those outside traditional power structures in the UN and the international structure. In addition to the practical evidence of the relationship between individual, internal and external self-determination, the regulative analogy between women's autonomy in liberal legal systems, which has been consistently undermined by the lack of legal structures guaranteeing women's self-expression and definition, can be mirrored with the way international law has demanded non-states emulate (Western) states to gain recognition under international law. A feminist project centres on those marginalised by liberal legal structures as a means of challenging the abuse of communities, or individuals, perceived to lack power. This has the potential to avoid the imposition of ill-fitting international legal norms so as to offer the people who seek self-determination the skills to define their own freedom.

These conclusions are of importance to Western feminism and Western legal scholars. It is necessary to consider the limitations on the self-determination of many within our own communities rather than deploy universals to non-Western communities. Furthermore, non-Western communities offer important leads to understanding the limitations within liberal conceptions of the legal subject.[181] Even in an era where 'decolonisation' struggles seem historical; these debates are of importance to feminist scholarship: important as a site where feminist analysis would suggest that some form of international enforcement and protection of the right to self-determination may be necessary. Yet feminist scholarship demands we ask how to secure these rights without force. I have argued that women's narratives require inclusion and have demonstrated the shortcomings of self-determination without women's full citizenship

---

180 Also see: Third World Approaches, for example, Anghie, 'Finding the Peripheries: Sovereignty and Colonialism in Nineteenth Century International Law', 40, *Harvard International Law Journal* (1999), 1.
181 Mutua, 'Savages, Victims, and Saviours: The Metaphor of Human Rights', 42, *Harvard International Law Journal* (2001) 201.

and participation. I have also argued that mainstream international scholarship could utilise the extensive feminist critique of liberalism and liberal legal personhood to challenge the victim–agent paradox at the centre of the international legal narrative of self-determination. Without increased feminist engagements with self-determination and without mainstream engagements with feminist findings, debating justification for the use of force on self-determination grounds will remain irresolvable, as will the violence in those communities struggling to achieve external, internal or individual self-determination for their people.

5 Justifying force: humanitarian intervention

In analysing justifications for the use of force, in this book I have argued that state claims for the legality of the use of force rely significantly upon a domestic analogy with the legal construction of interpersonal justifications for violence, particularly as they exist in Western legal structures. In this chapter, I argue that the use of humanitarian arguments to justify the use of force on the territory of another state, as was debated extensively after the NATO use of force in Serbia in 1999, also benefits from the use of a domestic analogy geared towards exposing the sexed and gendered contours of international law. I contend that the regulation of the domestic space of states under international law parallels the regulation of domestic space (or the private sphere) associated within the home under Western domestic legal structures. I particularly focus the analogy on the legal regulation (and non-regulation) of intimate partner violence,[1] including the contemporary turn to mandatory interventions into domestic partner violence.

Humanitarian intervention can be defined as:

> The threat or use of force across state borders by a state (or group of states) aimed at preventing or ending widespread and grave violations of fundamental human rights of individuals other than its own citizens, without the permission of the state within whose territory force is applied.[2]

Unlike self-defence, humanitarian interventions respond to violence internal to a foreign state. There is no armed attack requirement or identification of a threat to the

---

1 The World Health Organisation defines domestic violence, or intimate partner violence, as 'any behaviour within an intimate relationship that causes physical, psychological or sexual harm to those in the relationship', Krug et al, *World Report on Violence and Health* (Geneva: WHO, 2002); also see the World Health Organisation typology of violence (available in Krug's Report, ibid.), which situates violence between intimates in the wider context of family violence and highlights the similarities with collective violence, including political violence. In this chapter, I use the terms 'domestic violence', 'domestic family violence' and 'intimate partner violence' interchangeably but recognise, outside the context of this study, there is value in providing definitional distinctions.
2 Holzgrefe and Keohane, *Humanitarian Intervention: Ethical, Legal and Political Dilemmas* (Cambridge: Cambridge University Press, 2003) at p. 1; there is currently no accepted legal definition of humanitarian intervention.

nationals of the state using force.[3] Neither will there have been an invitation from the government of the state where the violence is manifest.[4] Therefore, states wishing to use force justified as humanitarian interventions must look outside the Charter law on the use of force to articulate the justification. Customary international law on the use of force, international human rights laws and the need to protect individuals from wide scale human rights abuses are used to explain the use of force justified as humanitarian interventions.

In 2000, the Canadian government commissioned a group of independent experts to address the issue of humanitarian intervention, resulting in the Responsibility to Protect Report that left open the possibility of unilateral interventions while acknowledging Security Council authorised interventions as an accepted component of international law. In the 2005 Summit Outcome Resolution, the General Assembly found humanitarian interventions fell within the range of chapter VII authorised force yet remained silent on the issue of unilateral state interventions.[5] These institutional developments cohere with state and institutional practice during the 1990s. The Security Council endorsed the ECOWAS intervention in Liberia (albeit retrospectively)[6] and the US-led intervention in Somalia in 1992,[7] while unilateral state interventions were not accepted without qualification or criticism from the international community (e.g., the use of force by NATO against Serbia in 1999).[8] After the 1999 NATO force ceased its bombing of Serbia, the Security Council identified the situation as constituting a threat to international peace and security and authorised a 50,000 strong military force, KFOR, to supervise the withdrawal of Serbian military, police and paramilitary forces from the Kosovo Province using 'all means necessary'.[9] In 2009, the General Assembly held debates on the Responsibility to Protect doctrine without any resolution while in the same year, US President Obama, when collecting his Nobel Peace Prize, articulated a position indicating that '[t]here will be times when nations – acting individually or in concert – will find the use of force not only necessary but morally justified' and 'that force can be justified on humanitarian grounds'.[10] While the Security Council continued to authorise force on humanitarian

3 See chapter three on self-defence for further discussion.

4 On the invitation by a government to use force, see: Gray, *International Law and the Use of Force* (Oxford: Oxford University Press, 2004, 2nd edition), chapter 3.

5 UN Doc A/Res/ 60/1 2005 World Summit Outcome (24 October 2005) paragraph 139; Evans, Sahnoun, et al, *The Responsibility to Protect*, Report of the International Commission on Intervention and State Sovereignty (International Development Research Centre, 2001)

6 Mgbeoji, *Collective Insecurity* (Vancouver, BC: UBC Press, 2003).

7 Gray, above note 4, at pp. 222–224; also see Hipold, 'Humanitarian Intervention: Is There a Need for a Legal Reappraisal?', 12(3), *EJIL*, 437, at 446 identifying interventions in Rwanda (SC Res 929, 1994) and Haiti (SC Res 940 1994) as additional examples of Security Council authorized humanitarian interventions.

8 See, for example, Jokic (ed.), *Lessons of Kosovo: The Dangers of Humanitarian Intervention* (Broadview, 2002); also see the discussion in Gray, above note 4, at 260–262, 267–270; O'Connell, 'The UN, NATO, and International Law after Kosovo', 22, *Human Rights Quarterly* (2000), 57.

9 SC Res 1244 (10 June 1999).

10 See: http://nobelprize.org/nobel_prizes/peace/laureates/2009/obama-lecture_en.html (accessed February 2011).

grounds after the NATO intervention in Kosovo in 1999, unilateral interventions, as a practice, have remained a possibility rather than a reality.

In this chapter, these debates and developments provide the backdrop for considering the limitations of humanitarian intervention as a justification for the use of force. Mainstream approaches, especially the literature that emerged after the use of force to protect the Kosovo people by NATO in 1999 are analysed however primarily I argue for an alternative account of humanitarian interventions.[11] The chapter is directed at unilateral state interventions justified on humanitarian grounds rather than authorised interventions; however, the wider implications of this chapter apply to state and Security Council interventions justified on humanitarian grounds. Although the Security Council is not required to justify the authorisation of force it can be assumed that the rationale for authorising a humanitarian intervention would follow many of the contours presented here regarding unauthorised interventions.[12]

To develop the domestic analogy apparent in humanitarian intervention narratives I focus, therefore, on constructions of public and private violence and how these are replicated across national and international legal discourse. Feminist theory makes the link between private (individual) acts of violence and public (state) violence.[13] Not only are the consequences of private and public violence connected, legal regulation of one reinforces the gendered image of the types of violence tolerated within our communities in both public and private spaces.[14]

I also analyse two further binaries apparent in the discourse on humanitarian intervention. The first is the implicit distinction made, by law, between protectors and protected subjects in the process of granting legal subjects agency. Under humanitarian intervention narratives, although developed in the name of a community or group with only limited representation under international law, agency remains fixated on the acts of states. Within international law it is states that must articulate justifications for humanitarian intervention, or reject them, in a manner that distances the act of force from the group the force is proposed to protect. I argue that this genders the international narrative on humanitarian intervention, similar to the way Mills has described mandatory interventions into domestic partner violence as robbing women

---

11 For mainstream accounts, see: 49(4), *International and Comparative Law Quarterly* (2000) [various authors]; Cassese, '*Ex iniuria ius oritur.* Are We Moving Towards a International Legitimation of Forcible Countermeasures in the International Community?', 10, *EJIL* (1999), 23; Chesterman, *Just War or Just Peace* (oxford: Oxford University Press, 2001); Franck, *Recourse to Force* (Cambridge: Cambridge University Press, 2003); Gray, above note 4; Holzgrefe and Keohane above. note 3; Kritsiotis 'Appraising the Policy Objections to Humanitarian Intervention', 19, *Michigan Journal of International Law* (1993), 1010; Lillich, *Humanitarian Intervention and the United Nations* (University Press of Virginia, 1973); O'Connell, above note 8; Simma, 'NATO, the UN and the Use of Force: Legal Aspects', 10, *EJIL* (1999), 1.

12 For a thorough discussion, see Mgbeoji, above note 6, chapter 3.

13 Charlesworth, Chinkin, and Wright, 'Feminist Approaches to International Law', 85, *AJIL* (1991), 613; Moser, 'The Gendered Continuum of Violence and Conflict' in Moser and Clark (eds), *Victims, Perpetrators, Actors?* (London: Zed, 2001), at 30; Kelly, 'Wars Against Women' in Jacobs, Jacobson and Marchbank, *States of Conflict* (London: Zed, 2000), at 45.

14 See Buss 'Austrelitz and International Law: A Feminist Reading at the Boundaries', in Buss and Manji, *International Law: Modern Feminist Approaches* (Oxford: Hart, 2005), at 94–100, on critiques of public and private space in international law.

of legal agency. Those that 'save' and 'protect' are cast as legal actors (who have access to the public sphere) while those who are saved and protected are given limited legal agency (and are associated with the private or domestic sphere).

The additional binary, prevalent in humanitarian intervention narratives, and relevant to the discussion in this chapter is the tension between legal positivism and natural law accounts.[15] Arguments that focus on legal positivism are pitched against natural law approaches in a manner that again refracts attention away from the survivors of humanitarian crises to the reiteration of a central tension in Western political philosophies. I argue that feminist legal theories represent a useful means to step beyond the natural law–legal positivism dilemma and towards building strategies for preventing and challenging domestic state violence.[16] I argue that the debate on whether states can or should act forcefully in response to humanitarian crises in other states is cast as a dialogue between morality and legality that significantly distances dominant international legal accounts from the needs articulated by the survivors of intrastate violence. This bolsters the international legal subjectivity of states wishing to intervene and perpetuates the denial of public space for non-state actors on the international plane, as those enduring violence as well as survivors of violence must wait until a recognised legal subject articulates the justification for an intervention.

Therefore, by exposing the persistent debates between public and private spheres, construction of protecting and protected subjects and the legal positivism/natural law binary, I critique the way in which a perpetuation of the status quo of force continues under the humanitarian intervention justification. To move away from the seemingly perpetual exchange between morality and legality, public and private, protector and protected, I propose the use of the domestic analogy as a tool for re-conceptualisation of approaches to humanitarian intervention.

To build this argument, the domestic analogy between the regulation of domestic state violence (i.e., the 'humanitarian' crisis that leads to an intervention) and the regulation of domestic violence within the home is analysed.[17] I explore the potential, and the limits, of such an approach in this chapter. Drawing on the work of Mills, which describes interventions into domestic family violence as 'doing harm to women'; I consider how humanitarian interventions into domestic state violence embed similar gendered narratives of public and private space and of sexed agency.[18] The purpose of the chapter is not to provide a comprehensive solution to the complicated dilemmas humanitarian crises pose for international law, instead I use Mills' model of survivor-centred agency to re-imagine the terrain of intervention justifications. As such, the chapter expands feminist dialogue on humanitarian interventions through

---

15 For an account of the tension between natural law and legal positivism in international humanitarian interventions, see: Koskenniemi, 'The Lady Doth Protest Too Much', 65, *Modern Law Review* (2002), 159.

16 See Frazer and Lacey, *The Politics of Community* (Brighton: Harvester, 1993).

17 For a definition of domestic violence, see above note 1; also chapter one.

18 Mills, 'Killing Her Softly', 113(2), *Harvard Law Review* (1999) 550; also see Mills, *Insult to Injury: Rethinking our Responses to Intimate Abuse* (Princeton, NJ: Princeton, 2003). Mills argues that mandatory intervention strategies ultimately harm women through replicating the patriarchal power relations that make women vulnerable to domestic violence in the first place.

recognition of the analysis feminist legal theories have already developed to understand legal narratives of protector and protected; public and private; and morality and legality.

The structure of the chapter is as follows. In section two, I give a brief history of the role force has played in the regulation of domestic state violence by international legal organs and evidenced through state practice. I argue that this mirrors the regulation of domestic violence in the home under Western national legal structures. I then contrast my use of a domestic analogy to the work of Franck, which compares humanitarian interventions with the common law defence of necessity. This is contextualised through a discussion of other mainstream explanations of unilateral state humanitarian interventions.[19] In section three, I argue that the analogy with domestic violence in the home provides a focus on emergent strategies for halting domestic family violence. As such, I consider the possibility of transposing feminist solutions to interpersonal violence onto intra-state violence.

Feminist solutions can be compared with the narrow focus of current Western accounts of the legitimacy of humanitarian interventions and, despite the difficulties of transposition, feminist investigations of humanitarian interventions through a domestic analogy with domestic violence in the home offer real avenues for change in international law. Consequently, feminist dialogue on the role of identity and diversity within critical projects aids understanding of the meaning of international legal narratives on humanitarian interventions. I argue against the use of force justified as humanitarian intervention but acknowledge that without structural changes to the international legal system that refocus on private violence as relevant to the international and that see the survivors of violence as the key to challenging future violence the interventionist model will continue to appear humane.[20]

Regulating intra-state violence

The history of the United Nations has seen a rejection of the right of states to intervene in the domestic affairs of another state to halt human rights abuses or widespread humanitarian crises, unless an invitation has been issued by the state requiring assistance or the Security Council has authorised the intervention.[21] When states have intervened to (ostensibly) halt humanitarian crises the action has often been justified by the states in question as a form of self-defence. For example, India's intervention in Bangladesh in 1971 has been described as an instance of humanitarian intervention.[22] India claimed, however, that the use of force was justified as the influx

---

19 See Franck, *Recourse to Force* (Cambridge: Cambridge University Press, 2002); Tesón, *Humanitarian Intervention: an Inquiry into Law and Morality* (1997); Greenwood, 'Humanitarian Intervention: the Case of Kosovo', *Finnish Yearbook of International Law* (2000) 141; also see above note 10.

20 While tremendous inroads have been made with respect to prosecuting internal state violence through the development of international criminal law, this is distinct from enforcement and preventative strategies.

21 See UK Foreign Policy Document No.148 57 *BYIL* (1986) 614.

22 Chesterman notes, however, that the intervention did have political and economic payoffs for India, see Chesterman, *Just War or Just Peace* (2001), at 75; see also Hipold, above note 7, at 444.

of refugees into Indian territory constituted a form of 'civil aggression'.[23] When Tanzania intervened in Uganda in 1978, and Vietnam intervened in Kampuchea (now Cambodia) in 1978, both states used Article 51 and the right to self-defence as the platform for their justification. This was despite the force arising in response to widespread internal violence and gross human rights abuses in Uganda and Kampuchea rather than an armed attack on the territory of Tanzania or Vietnam.[24] The failure of these states to consider humanitarian goals as adequate to justify their actions before the international community suggests the collective rejection of humanitarian interventions as a justification for the use of force during this period.[25]

In addition to state practice, the UN Charter and the Definition of Aggression indicate an absence of institutional support for the use of force justified in the absence of an armed attack or Security Council authorisation.[26] This is further endorsed by the International Court of Justice that considered the use of force to protect the human rights of the citizens of a foreign state in the *Nicaragua Case* and found: '[w]hile the USA might form its own appraisal of the situation as to the respect for human rights in Nicaragua, the use of force could not be the appropriate method to monitor or ensure respect'.[27] The Court's approach reiterates its earlier conclusions in the *Corfu Channel Case*, when it found humanitarian justifications for the use of force 'would be reserved for most powerful states' and create the potential for serious abuses of international law.[28]

In the 2005 Summit Outcome Resolution humanitarian interventions authorised by the Security Council were acknowledged as an appropriate use of the collective security structure.[29] Member states resolved on the words:

[W]e are prepared to take collective action, in a timely and decisive manner, through the Security Council, in accordance with the UN Charter, including

23 GAOR (XXVI) 2003rd Plenary Meeting, 7 December 1971, at 15, paragraph 165; the term 'civil aggression' is used by Franck, above note 19, at 141.
24 On Bangladesh, see 1971 UNYB 144; on Uganda see 1979 UNYB 262; on Cambodia see 1979 UNYB 271. In the case of the Tanzanian intervention into Uganda, prior acts of aggression had been instigated by the Amin government in Uganda against Tanzanian territory see S/13141, Letter dated 5 March 1979 from the Representative of Angola to the Secretary-General. These attacks, however, were not of such consequence to justify the scale of intervention embarked upon by the Tanzanian government. In the case of the Vietnamese intervention, despite the gross violence conducted by the Khmer Rouge regime, the use of force failed to gain even the semblance of acceptance offered to Tanzania and India, with states keen to reiterate the centrality of Article 2(4) in the Charter era in response to Vietnam's actions. For further discussion, see Franck, above note 19, chapter 9.
25 However, that states obviously saw humanitarian crises in neighbouring states as requiring force suggests to other commentators that the right to use force on humanitarian grounds has some precedent in the life of the UN, see Franck, ibid. at 172.
26 The Charter only justifies the use of force in self-defence (article 51); the Definition of Aggression fails to explicitly endorse humanitarian interventions as exceptions to the prohibition on force, GA Res 3314 (14 December 1974); also see GA Res 2625 (24 October 1970).
27 *Case Concerning Military and Paramilitary Activities in and against Nicaragua*, ICJ Reports (1986) paragraph 202 and 268 [hereafter *Nicaragua Case*].
28 *Corfu Channel Case*, ICJ Reports 4 (1949), at 34.
29 GA Resolution A/Res/60/1 2005 World Summit Outcome.

Chapter VII, on a case by case basis and in cooperation with the relevant regional organisations as appropriate, should peaceful means be inadequate and national authorities are manifestly failing to protect their populations from genocide, war crimes, ethnic cleansing and crimes against humanity.[30]

The Summit Outcome document does not, however, endorse the unilateral use of force on humanitarian grounds or develop a framework to guide states considering the use of force on humanitarian grounds.[31] Moreover, this reiterates the documented and customary approach to humanitarian interventions in the UN era.[32] Additionally, the General Assembly endorsement of authorised humanitarian interventions by the Security Council invokes a high threshold. That is, the Security Council should only authorise interventions in instances of genocide, war crimes, ethnic cleansing or crimes against humanity.

In the next section of the chapter, I consider how this legal narrative of humanitarian intervention – especially the lack of legal weight for unilateral state force – mirrors the regulation of domestic family violence. Tensions exist, under international and national laws, with respect to the regulation of what is termed 'domestic' violence. Rather than seeing this as an argument justifying future interventions, I use the analogy to argue that a conceptual flaw exists in discussions of humanitarian interventions into, either, domestic state violence or domestic partner violence.

The domestic analogy

During the early twentieth century in Western states, particularly in common law states, such as the United States, the United Kingdom, Australia and Canada, domestic family violence was considered beyond the remit of legal enforcement.[33] Thus, *the regulation of domestic state violence and domestic family violence are both sites where the early*

---

30 Ibid. at paragraph 139.
31 See, in contrast, the Report of the Secretary-General's High Level Panel on Threats, Challenges and Change, *A More Secure World: Our Shared Responsibility* (2 December 2004), UN Doc A/59/565 (henceforth *A More Secure World*), which pre-dates this document and which proposes (in paragraph 207) five basic criteria of legitimacy for the Security Council to address when considering whether to authorise or endorse the use of military force and adds, in paragraph 209: 'we would also believe it would be valuable if individual member states, whether or not they are members of the Security Council subscribe to them'. This appears to envisage the possibility of justified humanitarian interventions without Security Council authorisation. The removal of the criteria for legitimacy and the reference to unilateral state action in response to humanitarian crises suggests the NATO intervention has not led to a change in the law. For discussion, see: Bellamy, 'Whither the Responsibility to Protect? Humanitarian Intervention and the 2005 World Summit', 20 (2), *Ethics and International Affairs* (2006), 143.
32 Gray, above note 4, at 49; Koskenniemi, above note 15, at 163; also see Schachter, 'The Right of States to Use Armed Force', 82, *Michigan Law Review* (1984), 1620 at 1629; for extended discussion see Lillich, above note 11; for an alternative approach see Franck, above note 19, at 138–139.
33 The failure to include an analysis of domestic family violence beyond these states represents a limitation of the thesis drawn from time and space considerations. However, the selection of these states also reflects the methodological concern with the impact of Western liberalism on Western accounts of international law and the development of international law more generally.

*twentieth century legal structure denies responsibility and fails to offer the victims of either site of vio-
lence any real source of redress or protection against perpetrators.*[34] Under national liberal legal
structures the domestic space of the home was generally regarded as outside of legal
regulation. Violence enacted by a family member against other family members in the
home, in addition to being (and remaining) largely gendered as male violence against
female family members, was seen as a legitimate exercise of patriarchal power.[35] In the
same period, the domestic interior of the state was regarded as outside of the purview
of international law. Violence enacted by the state, or its agents, against its citizens
was not regarded as within the domain of international law.[36] The categorisation of
violence, at both sites, by the relevant legal structures, as *domestic* and *private* constructs
the analogy between domestic family violence and domestic state violence.

By tracing the shift across the twentieth century in the regulation of domestic violence – in the home and within the state – the analogy develops and culminates in a
shift to interventions at the close of the twentieth century. At an international level
the shift is slow but apparent from as early as the 1948 Universal Declaration of
Human Rights, although the concept of minority rights emerged prior to the creation
of the UN.[37] In national legal structures the shift, at least for Western states, towards
recognition of the impact and illegality of domestic violence in the home, was trig-
gered by the women's movement that emerged as a visible political voice in the West
during the late 1960s, although some activism pre-dates this period.[38]

The idea that the home is private and outside of legal regulation has kept family
violence outside of law's gaze in Western liberal states until relatively recently. International law extended the separation of public and private into its construction of
legal relationships, casting the state in the guise of the male citizen who emerges in
public separate to his/its private relationships. This is sexed because a seemingly 'natural' aspect of legal regulation under liberalism, the separation of the public and private spheres, reflects Western men's constructions of law and political relationships.
This dichotomy has extensive pedigree in international law. This is a point made by
early international legal thinkers, such as Grotius who: 'defined the power of the head
of households as essentially similar to the power of the state.'[39] This characterisation
of the state as a public international entity, with a separate domestic legal system

---

34 However, note, when the legal category of the 'state was not satisfied intervention seemed possible,
    just as when the legal category of 'family' was not satisfied interventions could occur without issue, i.e.
    through colonial histories (under international law) and through social service interventions such as
    those that created the 'stolen generation' in Australia (under national laws).

35 Power Cobbes, 'Wife Torture in England', 32, *Contemporary Review* (1878), 55; Mahoney, 'Legal Images
    of Battered Women', 90, *Michigan Law Review* (1991) 1; Pizzey, *Scream Quietly or the Neighbours Will Hear
    You* (London: Penguin, 1974).

36 For example, Oppenheim, *International Law* [Vol 1 Peace] (IDC: 1981) at 171–172.

37 See Steiner and Alston, *International Human Rights in Context* (Oxford: Oxford University Press, 2004,
    2nd edition) Part A.

38 Morgan, *Sisterhood is Powerful* (Random House, 1970); Pateman, *The Sexual Contract* (Cambridge: Cam-
    bridge University Press, 1988).

39 Kinsella, 'Gendering Grotius', 34 (2), *Political Theory* (2006), 161, citing Grotius, Book II chapter V,
    para XII, 240.

outside of the main interests of international law, has largely persisted in the UN era, underscored by Article 2(7) of the Charter.[40] Moreover, Article 2(4) of the UN Charter expressly controls the public acts of states while ignoring the 'domestic', internal or private violence within a state. The image of the state as a benevolent provider to citizens draws upon a stereotype of the paternalistic, male state that mimics the family as a site of gendered oppression. While the creation of the distinction is sexed, the application and interpretation of this knowledge in the development of international law can be described as gendered. The transposition of the state as the legal subject, akin to the citizen in Western states, is not, on this reading, a benign re-appropriation of a legal device but a reflection of the sexed and gendered history of liberalism.

The analogy between the regulation of domestic state and domestic family violence continues in the legal developments across the twentieth century. The human rights movement in international law grew after the Nuremberg trials and further with the creation of the International Bill of Rights, as well as in response to the shifts in civil society that recognised the franchise rights held in international relations and the move to influence state action through lobbying.[41] Throughout the UN era, NGOs have led the human rights movement in terms of practice, strategy and identification of need, as well as often instigating responses to humanitarian emergencies.[42] While the work of NGOs in the field may not be without criticism, the shift towards the greater protection of human rights under international law can be described as emerging from grassroots movements and with origins in civil society rather than at the impetus of states. This input has increasingly led to state awareness of the impact domestic unrest in foreign states has on regional and global stability.[43] Similarly, the advent of greater recognition of the harm domestic family violence holds for the larger community has been led by non-government organisations, particularly women's groups and feminist advocates.[44] Both, international legal regulation of domestic state violence and Western national legal regulation of domestic family violence, can then be said to follow the best practices and lead of civil society rather than be driven by government policy.[45] By the end of the twentieth century, international law and

40 Article 2(7) states: 'Nothing contained in the present Charter shall authorize the United Nations to intervene in matters which are essentially within the domestic jurisdiction of any state or shall require the Members to submit such matters to settlement under the present Charter; but this principle shall not prejudice the application of enforcement measures under chapter VII'; see Steiner and Alston, above note 37, at 188 for a discussion of the changing emphasis states have placed on Article 2(7).

41 Higgins, *Problems and Processes* (Oxford: Oxford University Press, 1995), chapter 6.

42 Chandler, 'The Road to Military Humanitarianism: How the Human Rights NGOs Shaped a New Humanitarian Agenda', 23 (3), *Human Rights Quarterly* (2001) 678; Leyton, 'Touched by Fire: Doctors without Borders in a Third World Crisis', in Lawrence and Karim (eds), *On Violence: A Reader* (Duke, 2007).

43 For example, in relation to the apartheid government in South Africa, see SC Res 392 (1976), 577 (1985).

44 Gordon, *Heroes in their Own Lives* (Illinois, 2002) from page 289.

45 The 2003 CEDAW Thematic Shadow Report on Violence Against Women in the UK states, 'Government attention to the significant issue of domestic violence has been comparatively slow to develop . . . In spite of new policy initiatives, the shift to a more integrated approach within criminal justice remains weak, with few domestic violence courts, low conviction rates, vulnerable witness status by

national laws (in Western states) have witnessed the evolution of legal processes for dealing with 'domestic' violence as a consequence of the emergent social narratives on humanitarianism and on domestic family violence. In national legal structures this is yet to lead to any Western state developing a comprehensive legal strategy that eradicates, or even effectively prosecutes, domestic family violence.[46] At an international level a similar story of regulation has occurred: mechanisms exist to challenge and to halt domestic state violence but enforcement issues remain unresolved.[47]

The real value of identifying an analogy in the legal regulation of domestic violence emerges, however, when intervention narratives are appraised. The shift towards interventionism into domestic state violence in the 1990s (by the Security Council and by states or groups of states acting without authorisation) is paralleled in Western domestic legal systems where there has been a significant shift towards mandatory interventions into domestic family violence.[48] In both cases, this shift is, in part, in response to past criticisms of state omissions to act voiced by non-government actors: human rights lobbyists (in the case of domestic state violence) or feminist advocates (in the case of domestic family violence).[49] This is where, I argue, the analogy merits further interrogation by international scholars and from states advocating the use of force to secure humanitarian objectives. Humanitarian interventions continue to be supported by a range of human rights actors;[50] in contrast, interventions into domestic family violence have received fragmented support from feminist theorists. Feminist scholarship that challenges intervention strategies for domestic family violence is of particular relevance and offers insight into interventions on the international plane.

While some feminist advocates promote the use of mandatory interventions to halt domestic family violence there is now additional, and increasingly persuasive, feminist analysis that argues interventions into domestic family violence leads to increased violence and threats to women who are the victims of domestic violence.[51] It is this range

application only and few advocacy and support schemes . . . there are good examples of local initiatives [yet] it is difficult for these good practice initiatives to continue without guaranteed funding. It also means the lessons learned from these projects cannot be more widely delivered' Humphreys, Kelly and Sen, *Violence Against Women: A CEDAW Thematic Shadow Report* (Womankind, March 2004) at 10; in the international arena see: Chandler, above note 42; also see: Kennedy, 'The International Human Rights Movement: Part of the Problem', *Harvard Human Rights Journal* (2001) 101.

46 Valchová and Biason (eds), *Women in an Insecure World* (DCAF, 2005), chapter four; Krug, above note 1.

47 Brilmeyer, 'What's the Matter with Selective Intervention?', 37, *Arizona Law Review* 955, (1995); the Human Rights Council being the most recent international body created to ensure human rights compliance from states, created by GA Res 60/251, 3 April 2006.

48 Known as 'zero tolerance' in Canada, 'pro-arrest' policies in the UK and also referred to as 'no-drop' policies.

49 Choudhry and Herring, 'Righting Domestic Violence', 20 (1), *International Journal of Law, Policy and the Family* (2006), 95; Ellison, 'Prosecuting Domestic Violence without Victim Participation', 65, *Modern Law Review* (2002) 834.

50 Chandler, above note 42; Cain, Postlewait and Thomson, *Emergency Sex* (Ebury, 2006). Note, however, critical responses to humanitarian interventions tend to use descriptive rather than conceptual evidence to substantiate their claims. This chapter considers conceptual limitations of intervention models.

51 Smith, 'It's My Decision, Isn't It? A Research Note on Battered Women's Perception of Mandatory Intervention Laws', 6 (12), *Violence Against Women* (2000), 1384.

of scholarship that explains why humanitarian interventions fail to offer an adequate justification for the use of force. This is because there is an analogy that can be made in the continued feminising of the victims of the violence. Intervention dialogues justifying the use of forceful measures, to halt either domestic state or domestic family violence, revolve around rescue narratives that ignore the autonomy of the victim. Hence, under intervention narratives the victim of the violence needs to be perceived as powerless and without agency. I pick up this theme in Part Three of the chapter. Before reaching this discussion, I will contrast my approach, first, with the use of an (alternative) analogy with the Western legal defence of necessity and, second, other theoretical justifications for humanitarian interventions.

The necessity analogy

My use of an analogy between the regulation of domestic family and domestic state violence is in contrast to the approaches of other writers.[52] For example, Franck suggests there is an analogy between the criminal defence of necessity and the framing of justifications for international humanitarian intervention:

> Legal systems worldwide accept the need for some such way out of the legal conundrum in which good law, strictly enforced, conduces to a result which opens an excessive chasm between law and common moral sense. There may be differences between national systems as to whether necessity excuses a crime or merely mitigates its consequences, but all recognize the obligation of law to make available one or the other way to resolve – or at least manage – the conundrum.[53]

To explain the relevance of the necessity defence in the context of understanding humanitarian interventions, Franck draws on two separate nineteenth century common law cases.[54] Furthermore, Franck suggests moral norms play a distinctive and important role in shaping the contours of legal norms. While this book challenges the failure of legal norms to adequately account for other normative structures, a law and morality dualism fails to shift law from its hierarchical self-appointment over social and cultural accounts, and fails to recognise the entwined relationship, influence and overlap of legal, moral, social, cultural, political and economic norms.[55]

---

52 None of the key commentators makes a link between the regulation of domestic family violence and domestic state violence, however, see Chinkin, 'The State that Acts Alone: Bully, Good Samaritan or Iconoclast?', 11, *EJIL*, 2000. Chinkin uses a narrative of interpersonal violence taken from Western Christian ideologies (the Good Samaritan) and compares this with justifications for the use of violence to halt human rights abuses in Kosovo in 1999; also see Charlesworth and Chinkin's analysis in *The Boundaries of International Law* (Manchester: Manchester University Press, 2000), at 268.

53 Franck, 'Interpretation and Change in the Law of Humanitarian Intervention' in Holzgrefe and Keohane (eds), above note 3, at 214.

54 *Regina v. Dudley* 14 QBD 273 (1884) and *US v. Holmes*, 26 Fed. Cas, 1 Wall Jr. 1 (1842); Franck develops a similar argument, above note 19.

55 Davies, "Feminism and the Flat Law Theory" 16 *Feminist Legal Studies* (2008)281.

For Franck, the relationship between law and morality is conclusive of law's source and authority in a manner that appears to be derivative of the work of prominent US liberal theorist Dworkin.[56] Consequently, Franck's approach leads him to assert, '[t]he law's self-interest, therefore, demands that a way be found to bridge any gap between its own institutional commitment to consistent application of formal rules and the public sense that order should not be achieved at too high a cost in widely shared values'.[57] By suggesting that law must uphold a series of moral norms, in addition to, and perhaps occasionally at the expense of formal application of the rules, Franck allows for an analogy between international and domestic law and between the international justification of humanitarian intervention and the criminal defence of necessity, writing, '[i]nternational law, like domestic law, also has begun gingerly to develop ways to bridge the gap between what is requisite in strict legality and what is generally regarded as just and moral'.[58] The analogy pivots on the recognition that necessity defences neither fully exculpate the actors nor render the law 'nugatory'.[59] Necessity, and by extension humanitarian interventions, are consequently constructed as defences that allow illegal acts to occur should extenuating or mitigating factors exist to reduce liability for the use of force.[60]

Franck further extends the analogy with domestic legal structures to the use of trial by jury to assess culpability in common law states, suggesting, '[t]he UN system, too, facilitates a sort of trial by jury and pleas in mitigation. This ensures due attention to the appropriate situational variables and brings into play the contextual, textual – not absolute or simple – standards.'[61] While this may sound reasonable at a theoretical level, the legal norm that Franck is advocating as 'contextual and textual' is Article 2(4), the prohibition on the use of force. While some international legal standards may invite this type of analysis it is unlikely that many states will agree that Article 2(4) permits such subjective readings and application. As discussed in chapter one, Article 2(4) plays a role as a sign of the legitimacy of the international legal order. Franck himself has lamented the disastrous consequence of the shift away from a position that projects Article 2(4) as absolute.[62]

Leaving aside the loose reliance on reasonably old accounts of the concept of necessity and the convenient avoidance of the ILC articles on state responsibility and necessity as a circumstance precluding wrongfulness,[63] Franck's analogy fails to

---

56 See Dworkin, 'Hard Cases', 88, *Harvard Law Review* (1975) 1057.

57 Franck, above note 19, at 178.

58 Ibid. at 180.

59 Ibid. at 179.

60 Note, too, the different approach of the ILC on necessity in the Articles on the Responsibility of States for Internationally Wrongful Acts, discussed in Crawford, *The International Law Commission's Articles on State Responsibility: Introduction, Text and Commentaries* (Cambridge: Cambridge University Press, 2002), at 178.

61 In Holzgrefe and Keohane, above note 3, at 227.

62 Franck, 'Who Killed Article 2(4)?' 64 (4), *AJIL* (1970, 809.

63 See Simester and Sullivan, *Criminal Law: Theory and Doctrine* (Cambridge: Cambridge University Press, 2007), from 713; under one of the key cases referred to by Franck, above note 19 (*Dudley and Stephens* (1884), 14 QBD 273) the rule stated is that the necessity defence is not available as a defence to murder; however also see the judgement of Lord Justice Brook in the recent UK case: *Re A (children)* [2000], 4 All ER 961.

offer an adequate legal justification for humanitarian interventions as it is dependent on a broader moral justification drawn from human rights laws. As the multitude of responses from states and from scholars to the NATO intervention in Serbia in 1999 suggest, a shared global ethic is far from realised in contemporary human rights laws[64] and even further from realisation, is an understanding of what global ethics or an international morality might equate to in terms of enforcement practices.

Furthermore, a feminist reading of Franck's analogy would challenge his reliance on Western jurisprudence and debates. Franck's insistence on seeing humanitarian interventions as a straddling of natural law (morality) and positive law (legality) approaches is drawn from a Western jurisprudential history that is steeped in imperialistic and sexist accounts.[65] My use of an analogy, while also dependent on Western legal structures, differs because it uses these structures to understand the limitations of the international legal model rather than re-asserting irresolvable debates on the role of morality in the construction of legal norms.[66] Franck's account is simplistic in its assumption that a distinction between, 'what is lawful and what is right' can be evidenced through the examination of state claims and actions. The use of force, with the serious consequences it entails for states – those using force and those attacked – demands a stronger critical engagement than the suggestion that after the event international institutions will condone or mitigate behaviour akin to a common law defence of necessity.[67]

The focus on these jurisprudential questions by Franck revolves around a Western history of positive and natural law debates allowing liberal arguments drawn from common law jurisprudence to seep into debates over the nature and expression of international law. Consequently, liberal perceptions of the legal subject and the domain of law's narrative, particularly the excision of legal from social norms, are able to neatly sever expressions of justifications for humanitarian interventions from the consequence of the use of force. The preoccupation with possible moral criteria that underpin humanitarian justifications for the use of force neatly re-directs concern from the social, cultural, environmental and health implications associated with the use of force.[68]

64 See for example: Mutua, *Human Rights: A Political and Cultural Critique* (Pennsylvania, 2002).
65 See: Barnett, *Sourcebook of Feminist Jurisprudence* (London: Cavendish, 1997), Part III.
66 Green, 'Positivism and the Inseparability of Law and Morals', *Hart-Fuller Conference* (New York: New York University School of Law, February 2008).
67 However, Franck does state, 'For state's seeking to invoke the law's margin of flexibility, there are hard tests, requiring sophisticated pleading backed by relevant and highly probative evidence, for example, the US could not adduce before the General Assembly to support its claim to be rescuing its citizens from lethal danger in Grenada'. My criticism rests on the retrospective aspect of Franck's account which suggests it is reasonable for the international system to supply a judgment on justifiability of the use of force after its use. I would suggest, in line with feminist legal methodologies, rather than developing humanitarian interventions as a potential exception to the prohibition on force, strengthening the ICC capacity to prosecute the crime of aggression would act as a greater deterrent to the use of force, and consequently build the future of Article 2(4) rather than detract from its impact.
68 Chinkin, 'The Legality of NATO's Action in the Former Yugoslavia (FRY) under International Law', 49(4), *International and Comparative Law Quarterly* (2000) from 910.

Other justifications for humanitarian interventions

Beyond Franck's account, three approaches for arguing for justified humanitarian interventions in the international legal order seemed to emerge after the 1999 NATO intervention. All engage foremost with Western jurisprudence. Despite the range of approaches each ultimately invokes a model of law that accommodates exceptions, excuses and mitigated behaviour for forceful behaviour akin to the common law concept of necessity. A fourth approach would be to consider no right of humanitarian intervention to exist under the UN Charter and/or customary international law. This approach is not considered in this section of the chapter as I am interested in the range of arguments developed to justify humanitarian intervention rather than those that oppose this type of intervention.[69] I have labelled the three dominant approaches to justifying humanitarian interventions: the exceptional–legitimacy approach, the human rights trump and the textual flexibility approach.[70] I provide an introduction to each approach, and identify works that utilise each approach in this part of the chapter to support my argument that justifications for humanitarian intervention are unable to shift outside of a liberalist paradigm, at either a jurisprudential level (that is, through debates over the tensions between natural law and legal positivism) or at an enforcement level (through hinging on narratives of protection over agency).

Exceptional – legitimacy approach

The first approach emphasises the illegality of interventions, reiterating the role of the principle of non-intervention and the centrality of sovereignty rights in the international legal system.[71] Moral and ethical arguments are then drawn on to establish humanitarian intervention as legitimate under exceptional circumstances. The UK government presented this type of reasoning during NATO's intervention to assist the Kosovo people in 1999 and developed criteria to assess the legitimacy of humanitarian intervention claims.[72]

To establish the legitimacy of force that is otherwise illegal, a normative claim about the justness of exceptional interventions is invoked. The interventions against Serbia and Iraq (enforcing the no-fly zones in the 1990s) then become evidence of

---

69 See ibid.; O'Connell, above note 8, p 88–89; Chinkin, 'Kosovo: Good or Bad War?', 93 (4), *AJIL* (1999); also see Gray, above note 4, at 31–49.

70 My description of the three approaches is similar to that of Stromseth, 'Rethinking Humanitarian Intervention' in Holzgefe and Keohane, above note 3; commentators and states often draw on a combination of the three approaches in application to particular events. For example, the International Commission on Intervention and State Sovereignty (henceforth ICISS), uses a mixture of approaches one and three; using textual flexibility to avoid the need to condemn NATO in Kosovo while affirming sovereignty rights of states and the doctrine of non-intervention when developing criteria for future 'exceptional' cases.

71 Cassese, *International Law* (Oxford: Oxford University Press, 2001) at 98 (on non-intervention) and 86 (on the sovereign equality of states).

72 'United Kingdom Guidelines on Humanitarian Intervention' Speech by Mr. Robin Cook, Secretary of State for Foreign and Commonwealth Affairs, 19 July 2000, reproduced in 71, *British Yearbook of International Law* (2000) 646.

state practice.[73] Advocates of this approach argue legal standards cannot account for all possible eventualities and in extreme and unusual circumstances states must resort to making decisions on ethical or moral grounds. In this sense, this first approach is similar to Franck's appropriation of the law of necessity.

This first approach leaves intact the distinction between public and private violence and the public/private division in international law. Without challenging any of the current law on the use of force, construing humanitarian intervention under claims of exceptional legitimacy protects the construction of Article 2(4) as a prohibition on international violence without jurisdiction in the realm of intra-state violence. Consequently, this approach to humanitarian intervention protects a status quo that feminist scholarship contends stems from a gendered understanding of violence and gendered strategies for halting violence. That is, the exceptional-legitimacy approach perpetuates the supposed distance between private and public harms. The act of using force to halt humanitarian crises is given quasi-legal status, while the initial violence retains a domestic and private label under international law. The exceptional–legitimacy approach is immediately too narrow and too broad. The approach is too narrow in terms of the assessment of the forms of internal state violence that attract the coercive practices of the international community. For example, all forms of violence against women are left unregulated by this approach, despite uniform global statistics.[74] Yet, an exceptional–legitimacy approach is too broad as it places the task of assessing the legitimacy of the use of force with individual states in the first instance rather than in the collective security structure.

This approach also adds to the legal semantics on the use of force, a further stratum of less confrontational wording for military endeavours. The use of humanitarian intervention as a metaphor for military interventions is itself a cloak on the use of force. For scholars advocating this approach, to suggest interventions can be described as legitimate rather than legal, adds to the existing binaries of international law the hierarchy of illegitimate and legitimate acts of states. The convenience of this parlance for powerful states mimics the traditional development of justifications in Western criminal codes that have provided sliding scales of legality for violence and force from the perspective of men. The reality is interventions, such as the NATO intervention against Serbia, use strategic military technology, for example, aerial bombing, that has long term consequences for the communities and environment targeted.[75] This is military violence that is no more or less exceptional than wars fought in self-defence. The idea of 'legitimately' deployed force to protect at-risk communities imagines a dichotomy of protector and protected to construct the justificatory narrative. Not only is the use of force seemingly justified because its goal is to protect others, the force has the appearance of fairness because it involves technology geared

73 Franck, above note 19, at 152–155; this argument ignores the parallel claim that implied authorisation existed for both of these interventions; see Greenwood, above note 19.
74 Mackinnon, *Are Women Human?* (Harvard, 2006), at 262.
75 McInnes, 'Fatal Attraction? Air Power and the West', in McInnes and Wheeler, *Dimensions of Western Military Intervention* (Cass, 2002).

to protect the interveners. This extends the narratives evidenced in the discussion of Article 51 self-defence rather than disrupting them.[76]

The human rights trump

The second approach seeks to establish the legality (as opposed to the exceptional legitimacy in the first approach) of interventions. This approach draws on human rights standards, suggesting human rights 'trump' sovereignty rights through finding '[n]on-interventionism is a doctrine of the past . . . Rescuing others will always be onerous, but if we deny our moral duty and legal right to do so, we deny not only the centrality of justice in political affairs, but also the common humanity that binds us all'.[77] This approach is developed in the work of Tesón and invokes human rights as peremptory norms in the international system.

The human rights approach circumvents the sovereignty rights of states by emphasising human rights as *jus cogens* under international law, that is, no derogation is permitted.[78] From the point of view of feminist theory some aspects of Tesón's argument sound like the expression of feminist concerns, for example, the challenge to sovereignty and the challenge to the primacy of the state as the international legal subject.[79] However, using the rhetoric of feminists, and other critical thinkers, in this manner disregards the particular concerns that lead to the formation of human rights law in the first place. The 'human rights trump sovereignty' approach disregards much of the discourse that would ultimately see humanitarian intervention, and the forceful military endeavours it co-opts in the pursuit of securing human rights, as detrimental to the long term protection and promotion of human rights agendas.[80]

The ICISS Responsibility to Protect Report suggests human rights will always 'trump' sovereignty rights, as 'it loads the dice in favour of intervention before the

---

76 Apart from the UK, this was not the type of argument most NATO states relied on to justify their actions in Kosovo. Other NATO states, such as France and the US drew on more than just these 'excusable breach type arguments' and incorporated arguments of implied authority through Security Council resolutions and the evolution of human rights law to justify the use of force in Kosovo; see Stromseth, above note 70.

77 Tesón, 'The Liberal Case for Intervention', in Holzgrefe and Keohane, above note 3, at 128–129.

78 For an approach similar to Tesón's, see: Nardin, 'The Moral Basis of Humanitarian Intervention', 16(1), *Ethics and International Affairs* (Springer, 2002).

79 Tesón does acknowledge the impact of feminist theory on rights discourse in, *The Philosophy of International Law: Human Rights Approach* (1998), at 163 and 177. His approach builds on a Kantian conception of rights which draws on natural law perspectives and does not challenge the limited definition of individuals in Kantian theory which is ultimately in conflict with much feminist theory; see Fraser and Lacey, *The Politics of Community* (Harvester-Wheatsheaf, 1993); contrast Tesón's approach to sovereignty to the approach of Knop, 'Re/statements: Feminism and Sovereignty in International Law', 3, *Transnational Law and Contemporary Problems* (1993) 239.

80 On human rights as trumps: see Thakur, 'Intervention, Sovereignty and the Responsibility to Protect', 33 (3), *Security Dialogue* 2002; on human rights as 'part of the problem' see: Kennedy, above note 45; Chandler above note 42; Orford, 'Muscular Humanitarianism: Reading the Narratives of the New Interventionism', 10 (4), *EJIL* (1999) 679; Petersen, 'Whose Rights? A Critique of the 'Givens' in Human Rights Discourse', 15, *Alternatives* (1999), 303.

argument has even begun'.[81] For the ICISS, the preferred legal course is to change the focus from intervention talk, which Thakur suggests focuses on the rights, claims and prerogatives of the states intervening and re-harness concern on the 'intended, putative beneficiaries of a given action'.[82] Whether the ICISS formulation of a Responsibility to Protect achieves this goal of refocussing concern on the communities suffering, rather than the states offering to rescue, is challenged by Chandler as a thinly veiled return to imperialist discourse.[83] This echoes the ICJ's reluctance to see interventions as little more than permission for strong states to use force.[84] The language of the Responsibility to Protect Report seems to add to the semantic 'game' distancing the action (responsibility) from the military consequences. Despite this, the language of the Responsibility to Protect Report continues to gain support.[85] However, regional adaptations of the Responsibility to Protect model suggest one of its strengths as a potential legal approach is the malleability to regional conditions the model implicitly contains. Recognition of the variety of conflict and the temporal and regional differentiations tends to be overlooked in 'human rights trumps' arguments.[86]

Finally, the human rights approach, and the ICISS Responsibility to Protect Report, invokes the troubling dichotomy between protectors and the protected to enhance the justification for humanitarian interventions. Feminist analysis of the role of this binary in the sexing of international humanitarian law may be applied to the *jus ad bellum* arguments to evidence this as a retrograde step.[87] This second approach, while superficially appealing, especially to those that have peacefully fought for the improved enforcement and compliance with human rights standards in the state-centred international system, under scrutiny demonstrates how posing an equation between sovereignty and human rights ultimately denies the complexity and contingency of human rights.[88]

Implied authorisation

The third approach argues that past interventions were not contraventions of international law as there was implied Security Council authorisation in each instance. This

---

81 Thakur, Ibid. at 328; Evans, Sahnoun, et al, *The Responsibility to Protect*, Report of the International Commission on Intervention and State Sovereignty (International Development Research Centre, 2001) paragraph 2.28; Stahn, Responsibility to Protect: Political Rhetoric or Emerging Legal Norm?', 101, *AJIL* (2007) 99.

82 Thakur, Ibid.

83 Chandler, 'The Responsibility to Protect: Imposing the 'Liberal Peace' ?' 11, *International Peacekeeping* (2004) 59.

84 *Corfu Channel Case*, ICJ Reports 4 (1949), at 34; *Nicaragua Case*, above note 27, paragraph 202 and 268.

85 For example, see the *Pact on Security, Stability and Development in the Great Lakes Region* (December 2006), Protocol on Non-Aggression and Mutual Defence in the Great Lakes Region.

86 See further discussion of Mgbeoji, above note 7, at 31.

87 Kinsella, above note 39, at 164.

88 On the contingency of human rights see: Orford, *Reading Humanitarian Intervention* (Cambridge: Cambridge University Press, 2003) chapter 6.

approach draws on the resolutions of the Security Council before and after NATO's 1999 use of force against Serbia, to find implied authorisation by the Security Council. This approach mimics the statements of France and the USA justifying NATO's 1999 action and is also similar to the manner in which the United Kingdom, United States and France justified the patrolling of the no-fly zone in Iraq during the 1990s.[89] This framing of the right to humanitarian intervention leaves the international legal system unchallenged. It suggests nothing extraordinary needs to be read into these particular instances of humanitarian intervention as they comply with Security Council resolutions and the Charter. The interventions of India, Tanzania and Vietnam during the Cold War are presented as evidence under this approach that states have practiced interventions even when they have not argued for them, while the interventions in Serbia and Iraq are offered as evidence of the growing acceptance by the global community that when necessary a humanitarian intervention is excused.[90] The interventions in Liberia and Somalia, retrospectively authorised by the Security Council, are added to the list of past interventions that evidence the shifting acceptance by the international community of humanitarian goals as a justification for force, even when state have not always been forthright about their underlying humanitarian justification.[91]

Exponents of this approach, including the majority of NATO states, re-affirm the Charter system and the centrality of states' interests in the international order. Consequently, the inherent inequalities of the system, which includes those between states and those between citizens, are also affirmed, echoing the warning of the ICJ in the Corfu Channel case.[92] This approach to humanitarian intervention asserts the applicability of international law while creating a space for the neglect of international law by those with the power to use force and legal argument in their best interest. As with the first approach, key concerns of feminist jurisprudence, such as the use of a gendered hierarchy of binary relationships under law, and the specifically gendered division of public and private spheres, remain unchallenged and out of view. As with the second approach, an encroaching return to natural law themes emerges in this final approach as it relies on calls to 'ethics', 'morality' and 'fairness' that avoid complex reflection on the implications of interventions for citizens in both the intervened and intervening state. The notion of states acting as the jury on the legitimacy of an intervention's necessity closes off feminist concerns about the nature of public space in international law and the role of the state in perpetuating gender violence.

In conclusion, all three approaches invoke extra-legal notions of 'legitimacy', 'morality' or 'fairness' that remain open-ended and unsatisfactory guides for for-

---

89 This is the position of France with respect to the Kosovo intervention, see Stromseth above note 70, at 235; Simma, 'NATO, the UN and the Use of Force', 10(1), *European Journal of International Law* (1999) 12; Stromseth suggests the US stressed the extraordinary situation, the resolutions and the threat to international peace and security (including through the refugee crisis) at 236; on the no fly zone in Iraq to protect the Kurdish population, see Gray, above 4, at 3–38 and 'UK Materials on International Law', 63, *BYIL* (1992) 824.

90 See Franck, above note 19.

91 On Liberia, see Mgbeoji, above note 7. On Somalia, see the discussion in Gray, above note 4, at 222.

92 Above note 28.

mulating a right to humanitarian intervention. Koskenniemi describes this as a shift from 'formalism to ethics' that is apparent after NATO used force in Serbia in 1999, because it 'enlists political energies to support causes dictated by the hegemonic powers and is unresponsive to the violence and injustice that sustains the global everyday'.[93] Consequently, the criteria for testing the legality, or legitimacy, of interventions is distanced from engagements with global deficiencies with respect to gender equality, distanced from reflection on the role of gender stereotypes in the formation of rights and distanced from the impact of gender in the construction and consequences of force. The focus of all three approaches is heavily weighted towards identifying the rights of intervening states rather than identifying the rights and needs of the people within the states that will experience the consequences of the intervention and, as discussed above, even the Responsibility to Protect Report fails to fundamentally shift the imbalance between states and communities. All three approaches and the Responsibility to Protect Report maintain a dialogue that divides the public from the private in international law, segregating the social and cultural effects of interventions from the legal repercussions for states wishing to use force. The term 'humanitarian intervention' further clouds debates by denying the military implications – for both states using force and the states targeted by the use of force – of interventions, a process that is continued in the ICISS recommendation that humanitarian interventions be discussed as a 'Responsibility to Protect' – terminology that carries further gendered and imperialist connotations rather than one that escapes them.[94] In response to these criticisms, in the remaining section of this chapter, I offer an alternative construction of debates on humanitarian intervention via the domestic analogy between the regulation of domestic state violence and domestic family violence.

The domestic analogy as a strategy for reform

Mills constructs a survivor-centred model for challenging domestic family violence that is useful as a critical tool to re-evaluate and challenge the limitations of military interventions into humanitarian crises within a state.[95] The consequence of using Mills' approach would be a shift away from the justification for the use of force on humanitarian grounds towards empowerment of the survivors of violence. This is important to create a shift away from legal dichotomies that invoke a gendered distinction between the protectors and the protected within a state.

In this section, I will use non-legal narratives from Kosovo during the 1990s to illustrate how the path towards intervention by NATO in 1999 was neither inevitable nor desirable for the Serbian and Albanian populations of the Former Yugoslavian Province of Kosovo. In the decade prior to the NATO intervention, narratives from the non-violent opposition to Serbian repression and on the role of international economic institutional interventions in the region challenge the image of a 'crisis' moment

93 Koskenniemi, above note 15, at 160.
94 See further: Bond and Sherret, *A Sight for Sore Eyes: Bringing Gender Vision to the Responsibility to Protect Framework* (Instraw, 2005); Bellamy, above note 31.
95 Mills (1999) above note 18.

as represented by NATO states in 1999.[96] Through juxtaposition of the alternative narratives from Kosovan peace movements with the legal narrative – that pivots around force and urgency – the limitations of contemporary Western approaches are demonstrated. International humanitarian discourses fail communities because important sites of knowledge – social, cultural, economic, historical and power relations – are excised from the discourse.[97] The dichotomous thinking that informs Western legal approaches is imperialist and gendered and 'tends to lead to unduly polarised debates in which middle positions are marginalised as merely compromises and as unprincipled. A dichotomised distinction implies not only that the two concepts in question are used to mark out phenomena which are analytically distinct, but also that they refer to opposites'.[98] The key dichotomies apparent in humanitarian intervention narratives (public–private, legality–morality and protector–protected) limit international legal debates in precisely this manner. Furthermore, the analogy between interventions into domestic state violence and mandatory interventions into domestic family violence is able to expose the role the gendered dichotomies play in legal narratives of intervention. By engaging this analogy, I argue that the types of dialogues require movement beyond the straitjacket of a natural law–positivist dichotomy or the protector–protected binary, as well as engaging the public and private, requires focus on the binaries occurring on a continuum rather than as mutually exclusive.

Transposing national models onto the international

In 2004 the UK government, under the Domestic Violence, Crimes and Victims Act, made common assault an arrestable offence. This provision was developed to ensure police compliance with the policy of mandatory criminal justice interventions into domestic family violence.[99] Similar laws have emerged in other Western states since the late 1990s, particularly those with common law genealogies.[100] The broad impact of these policies is compulsory intervention and prosecution once domestic family violence is brought to the attention of the police. The advent of this development was in response to feminist research that had previously criticised the poor enforcement and policing of domestic family violence.[101] After the introduction of mandatory interventions into spousal violence a further strand of empirical and analytical

---

96 Orford, 'Locating the International', 38, *Harvard International Law Journal* (1999); Charlesworth, 'A Discipline of Crisis', 65 (3), *Modern Law Review* (2002)377.
97 Koskenniemi, above note 15.
98 Frazer and Lacey, *The Politics of Community* (Harvester, 1983), at 168.
99 Domestic Violence, Crime and Victims Act 2004 UK; Hester and Westmarland, *Domestic Violence: Effective Interventions and Approaches*, Home Office Research Study 290 (Development and Statistics Directorate, Feb 2005).
100 In Canada there have been 'mandatory charging directives' in some Provinces since the early 1980s and zero tolerance policies for police forces were introduced in the early 1990s, for discussion see: Ursel, 'The Possibilities of Criminal Justice Intervention in Domestic Violence: A Canadian Case Study', 8 (3), *Current Issues Criminal Justice* (1997) 263; in the US more than 20 states have mandatory intervention laws, as well as 'no-drop' policies, see: Mills, above note 18.
101 Choudhry and Herring, about note 49.

feminist research has emerged that describes mandatory interventions as a negative consequence for many women who experience domestic family violence. Feminist criticisms of mandatory interventions into domestic family violence are not uniform;[102] however, feminist accounts that are critical of criminal justice interventions provide a useful conceptual analogy that can be applied to the regulation of domestic state violence.

Mills presents a compelling analysis of the limitations of interventions into domestic family violence. In her article 'Killing Her Softly', Mills gives an empirical account of the effects of mandatory interventions into domestic family violence and concludes the interventions ultimately 'do violence to battered women'.[103] Mills begins by acknowledging the role of feminist scholarship and activism in the emergence of mandatory intervention policies. Mills also acknowledges feminist arguments in favour of interventions, including enforcement failures and racial bias in the prior application of domestic violence laws. This parallels the international debate where the failure of the international community to respond to the internal violence in Rwanda drew criticisms over the selectivity of interventions reflecting the imperial history and racial bias of the structures of international law.[104] Mills goes on to identify mandatory interventions as perpetuating rather than halting violence against women. Mills contends that intervention policies rob women of control over the consequences of the reporting of domestic family violence and consequently dislocates women from the arrest and enforcement process.[105] The process of mandatory interventions, therefore, replicates the patriarchal power relations that can be said to have been a key factor in the prevalence of domestic family violence in the first place. Mills work is supported by analysis of data from Manitoba, in Canada, where intervention policies appear to have been successfully developed by the provincial criminal justice system in an environment conducive to *radical structural reform* of criminal justice practice.[106]

My analogy identifies the continued feminisation of the victims of domestic violence under international laws as akin to these (Western) national legal processes. International law casts domestic state violence as primarily outside of its gaze and, when international laws do recognise domestic state violence, the identification of the violence as private/internal/domestic is as important, perhaps more important, than the recognition of the violence itself.[107] This allows intervention strategies to revolve around rescue narratives that ignore the autonomy of the victims. Shifting

---

102 For example, Durham, 'The Domestic Violence Dilemma: How Our Ineffective and Varied Responses Reflect Our Conflicted Views of the Problem', 71, *California Law Revie* (1998); Davis, *Domestic Violence: Facts and Fallacies* (Westport, CT: Greenwood, 1998); Currie, 'Battered Women and the State: From the Failure of Theory a Theory of Failure', 1 (2), *Journal of Human Justice* (1993); Snider, 'The Potential of the Criminal Justice System to Promote Feminist Concerns', 10, *Studies in Law, Politics and Society* (1990).
103 Mills, above note 18, at 550.
104 Mgbeoji, above note 7.
105 Ibid.
106 Ursel, above note 100.
107 This is because internal state practices continue to be considered as outside of the 'everyday' concerns of international law.

what was previously private into the public domain, through legal regulation, fails to challenge the sexed version of law ground in the liberal insistence on a gendered division between public and private.

Otto describes a similar process in the institutional responses to women's human rights activism.[108] Legal developments utilise a distinction between the protected (feminised, female) object and the legal subject/actor who gains the capacity to protect (and thus act) within the scope of the law. Consequently, the application of any new legal practice is at the mercy of the gendered and sexed structure that legal practices are imagined to function within. Public violence (what has been characterised in the UN era as the use of force) remains the benchmark for understanding the aggression and violence of states. Conversely, private violence is reinforced as outside of international law under humanitarian interventions when the interventions are grounded in recognition of their exceptionality and unusualness. Furthermore, intervention justifications illustrate the persistent division between public and private through their preoccupation with the legality/legitimacy of the intervening force rather than the prevention of the domestic state violence.

Kinsella identifies how 'sex is a prior materiality upon which gender acts'.[109] The shift to justifications for humanitarian interventions in the late twentieth century and at the advent of the new millennium that preserve a distinction between public and private violence is an excellent example of this process. Humanitarian interventions reify the sexed binary rather than offering a positive re-interpretation of the relationship between public and private spheres under law. The dependence on the public/private distinction in humanitarian intervention justifications makes narratives around the necessity to protect, and the consequential dichotomy between the protectors and the protected, seem natural rather than constructed through law and gendered. This replicates, on the international level, what Mills describes as occurring when mandatory interventions are conducted into domestic family violence. Mills also argues that: 'policies that support victims of battering must respect their emotional, cultural and financial challenges and must not reinforce the emotional oppression, initiated by violent actors, that the state currently perpetuates'.[110]

Survivor-centred models

While Mills' work is not alone in documenting the disconnection between feminist strategies and the consequences of mandatory interventions, her strategies for challenging domestic family violence without mandatory interventions form a conceptual model that can be re-developed to challenge humanitarian interventions under international law. Mills strategies focus on 'survivor centred' responses and are premised on a respectful, sometimes slow, but gentle, attitude towards empowering the

---

108 Otto, 'Disconcerting "Masculinities": Reinventing the Gendered Subject(s) of International Human Rights Law', in Buss and Manji, *International Law: Modern Feminist Approaches* (Oxford: Hart, 2005), at 124.
109 Kinsella, above note 39, at 165.
110 Above note 18, at 557.

survivors of domestic family violence. Crucially, Mills' approach acknowledges there is a relationship of importance between the abuser and the survivor of domestic family violence. Mills acknowledges that her approach may prolong the oppression and violence initially, but suggests her approach will ultimately lead towards both survivor and abuser as willing participants in the process of halting domestic family violence. Mills concludes:

> Engaging survivors in the political struggle against domestic violence must begin with facilitating personal empowerment in the intimate sphere. Coercive tactics serve only to disengage these women and alienate them from the larger feminist power base that has become so strongly identified with these approaches.[111]

Transposing this idea onto domestic state violence would be difficult yet not impossible. The three key features of Mills' model, the use of law to empower individuals (rather than protect), the recognition of the relationship between the survivor and the abuser and the reliance on survivor articulated goals for change, can be applied and analysed in terms of international justifications for humanitarian interventions.

Using law to develop agency

Feminist legal theories have developed sophisticated dialogues on the role of individual agency and autonomy under law and the capacity of liberal legal structures to guarantee these aspects of legal personhood to women.[112] Mills draws on this range of feminist theory to demonstrate how intervention strategies rob survivors of domestic family violence of agency, by deeming them ineffective or unreliable agents in the process of securing a conviction. By recognising the agency of survivors of violence, Mills changes the legal response from one concerned with negative freedom to one concerned with an approach centred on securing positive rights and freedom for survivors. That is, rather than a regulative (legal) response that functions to justify enforcement action, Mills advocates laws that function to empower the potential and actual victims of violence. A key element of empowering the victims of violence is the focus on measures to eradicate women's poverty and the provision of comprehensive health services and rights.[113] A comprehensive Australian analysis of approaches to domestic violence concluded current criminal justice approaches are flawed through their preoccupation with violence after it occurs rather than seeking to challenge future violence prior to its manifestation.[114] Mills' study, similarly, shows that mandatory interventions can lead to the perpetuation of violence as the survivor is disempowered when her capacity to challenge the violence is re-appropriated by

---

111 Ibid. at 569.
112 See further chapter four on self-determination.
113 Krug, above note 1.
114 Carrinton and Phillips, *Domestic Violence in Australia – an Overview of the Issues* (7 August 2003), Parliamentary Library of Australia, available online at: www.aph.hov.au/library/intguide/SP/Dom_violence.htm (last accessed February 2011).

the state in the guise of police enforcement. Not only does this invoke the protec-tor–protected myth, the approach permits the revocation of female legal subjectivity, deeming women unreliable agents in the criminal justice process.

Research demonstrates that female financial dependence as well as broader social relations (including legal norms) that perpetuate images of male aggression as accept-able forms of interpersonal interaction are causal factors in the continued existence of domestic violence.[115] A particularly poignant research project in the United States found that the provision of housing to the survivors of domestic family violence was the single most effective mechanism for halting future abuse.[116] Mills' work on chal-lenging domestic family violence through survivor centred strategies with specific attention to the agency and full legal subjectivity of survivors has resonance with contemporary feminist approaches to international law. For example, Otto in her analysis of the conundrum of women's human rights advocacy is critical of feminist strategy that 'repeats the gendered subjectivities of the hierarchies that are responsible for producing the gendered violations in the first place'.[117] Otto places the gendered hierarchy between protector and protected classes of persons as both a product of and an assumption of human rights discourse. While this analysis is directed at the sex/gender of the specific rights bearers in human rights laws, the same sex/gender binary emerges, generally, in international law on the use of force and, specifically, in the discourse on humanitarian interventions. Feminist legal theories work to shift beyond the mere recognition of sex/gender confines to develop strategies 'that are disruptive of gender hierarchies'.[118] For Otto, the strategy with respect to human rights laws is to 'consciously reject constructions of gender as hierarchy and fully embrace the insight that knowledges about sex/gender are socially constructed and therefore open to infinite possibilities beyond the relentless dualisms that have been naturalised by so many laws and practices'.[119]

Mills' approach asks that the turn to law be centred on empowering the survivor of violence rather than offering 'protection', 'rescue' or 'saving'. In the international arena, a similar approach to combating violence against women is emergent. So the recent WHO Report on the gender responsiveness of the Millennium Summit Out-comes finds combating violence against women through policy integral to all of the Outcomes, rather than pertaining to specific 'women's' provisions, and through pol-icy centred on the re-imagining of legal provisions as tools for the creation of positive rights rather than negative rights.[120] Rees, similarly, argues for the development of special provisions for the promotion and development of women's social and eco-

---

115 Ibid.
116 Hunter, 'Law's (Masculine) Violence', 17(1), *Law and Critique* (2006), 27; also see: Sokoloff (ed.), *Domestic Violence at the Margins: Readings on Race, Class, Gender and Culture* (Piscataway, NJ: Rutgers Uni-versity Press, 2005); with respect to the role of economic interventions and international humanitarian crises, see: Orford, 'Locating the International: Military and Monetary Interventions after the Cold War', 38, *Harvard International Law Journal* (1997), 443.
117 Otto, above note 108.
118 Ibid.
119 Ibid.
120 Above note 1.

nomic rights in post-conflict communities. Rees indicates that this is necessary to facilitate communities that can develop strong human rights mechanisms rather than submitting communities to the paternalism latent in the mantra of the protection of rights imposed externally.[121]

A similar range of criticisms have been made by some international scholars in response to humanitarian interventions.[122] For example, Orford directly links the flaws of 'saving' others to the gendered narratives of international law and concludes:

> The subject of the intervention narrative, the muscular hero, is portrayed as the character able to act in the world, and to imagine, create and bring about new worlds in his own image. . . . Missing is any sense of the agency of the peoples of the states where the intervention is to be conducted.[123]

Feminist theory as a process of listening to personal expressions of political conundrums centres on practices of empowerment developed through real engagement with those suffering under the status quo. Therefore, not only does Mills work on mandatory interventions into domestic family violence offer a conceptual understanding of the limitations of interventions, feminist legal theory offers theoretical and practical reflections on how to make empowerment, agency and autonomy exist for all people.

Important studies and voices from Kosovo highlight the failure of the provision of such positive rights in 1999 prior to the Western intervention.[124] While NATO states argued for the legality or legitimacy of a Western intervention there was little discussion around offering the people of the Kosovo Province agency or a platform for exercising choices. Instead it was deemed appropriate by foreign states that foreign states and international organisations find the best way to 'achieve the liberal peace' in Kosovo.[125] The strong non-violent movement in Kosovo, which had involved a decade-long struggle against repressive Serbian forces, was effectively silenced by international debates that emerged in Western states. Furthermore, harmful cultural constructions of gender within the Kosovan community were hidden by a process that was not interested in securing the plethora of narratives that emerged from the community. Rodgers writes of the 'extremely patriarchal construction of gender relations amongst Kosovo Albanians'.[126] Likewise, further repressive practices against minority groups in the Province, particularly against the Roma people who live in the Kosovo Province, were not acknowledged in the process of challenging Serbian repression.

121 Rees, 'A Comprehensive Presentation on Consequences of SEA in Violent Conflict', Conference Presentation, NLDA Symposia, *Sexual Exploitation and Abuse of Women in Violent Conflict*, 17–19 June 2007.
122 Chandler, above note 42; Mgbeoji, above note 7; Chinkin, above note 52.
123 Orford, above note 88, at 170.
124 For example, the failure of the international community to see the 1990 Declaration of Independence by Kosovo leaders as a response to Serbian violations in the Province.
125 Chandler, above note 83.
126 Rodgers, 'Gender Dimensions of International Interventions' in McInnes and Wheeler, *Dimensions of Western military Interventions* (London: Cass, 2002), at 184.

One of the consequences of this has been continued violence against Roma communities in Kosovo after the NATO intervention.[127] While the NATO intervention and the subsequent UN Transitional Administration have ultimately led to the creation of a new Kosovan state, this has not lead to the cessation of group violence.[128]

Like the discussion in the previous chapter, it becomes apparent that the use of force as a mechanism of international regulation is inadequate to create lasting solutions for all citizens within a community. The participation of women and minorities is crucial in the articulation of the demands a community makes of the international network of states.[129] In discussions of humanitarian interventions, however, it becomes apparent that this articulation of the role of law in emphasising the rights and participation of some subjects over others, applies not just at an individual level but also between communities of peoples. To speak, or write, of using law to develop agency is to reconfigure expectations of the appropriate agents. This knowledge, taken from understandings of individual/intimate violence and its regulation, when projected onto the international law on the use of force develop across the continuum of legal subjects (from individual to state) and across the continuum of acts (private/community/state violence). One of the resounding findings of this book is that international laws on the use of force do merit from exposure of the conceptual contingencies between the regulation of private violence from the individual to the international. The strategies elaborated for re-imagining the regulation of international violence manifests in the private – the empowerment of individuals – and in the public realm – the re-imagining of state structures/participation and subjectivity. Feminist legal theories open up understandings of the laws on the use of force and anticipate increased dialogues that challenge the terrain and its participants.

Understanding the relationship between perpetrators and survivors

Returning to Mills' work on challenging domestic family violence, the second feature focuses on acknowledging that the relationship between survivor and abuser is of central importance in formulating strategies to halt domestic/family violence. This is magnified in the domestic state violence scenario where, by definition, both perpetrators and survivors of violence will continue to share territory and resources.

Ursel's data on the impact of intervention strategies in Manitoba, Canada is illustrative of this point. Ursel is largely in favour of interventions into domestic family

---

127   'Justice for Kosovo' Special edition Nos 3 and 4, *Roma Rights* (2005), published by the European Roma Rights Centre.

128   Also see: Amnesty International, *Document – Serbia (Kosovo): The Challenge to Fix a failed UN Justice Mission* (January 2008) available at: www.amnesty.org/en/library/info/EURO70/001/2008 (last accessed February 2011); on the current and potential future status of the Republic of Kosovo, see: 'Agora: Kosovo', 8, *Chinese Journal of International Law* (2009), 2 [Various Authors].

129   Chinkin, 'The International Law Framework with Respect to International Peace and Security' in Glasius and Kaldor, *Advances in International Relations and Global Politics* (London: Routledge, 2006); Charlesworth and Chinkin, 'Building Women into Peace: The International Legal Framework', 27, *Third World Quarterly* (2006) 937; Zeigler and Gunderson, The Gendered Dimensions to Conflict's Aftermath', 20 (2), *Ethics and International Affairs* (2006) 171.

violence; however, her work differs from that of other pro-intervention feminists as she acknowledges, 'we must change our definition of success within the justice system from short term outcome (conviction) to a longer term process (redressing an imbalance of power)'.[130] Ursel demonstrates how the 'successes' of the Manitoba mandatory intervention model incorporates a multi-agency shift away from the 'rigid hierarchical 'justice' system' towards a flexible model able to 'respond to social as well as legal imperatives'.[131] The Manitoba approach to domestic violence interventions included strategies to change prosecutor, crown and judicial expectations of an intervention in order to 'abandon the all or nothing expectation . . . survival and recovery are rarely a one-off proposition'.[132]

The law on the use of force, and specifically humanitarian intervention narratives, invoke an image of force as a short term, useful solution to halt violence. Recognition of the ongoing relationship between survivors and perpetrators – and the further recognition that some actors will fall into both categories – changes the expectation of force and the possibility of its usefulness in assisting communities. Returning to Gunning's model of world travelling we can invoke her three methods, seeing oneself in context, seeing oneself as the other sees and seeing the other in her context, as a guide.[133]

By combining Mills' and Gunning's methods, a different picture of the Kosovo community in the 1990s can be narrated. Firstly, seeing oneself in context would require Western recognition of the involvement of international economic institutions in the Balkans during the decades preceding the break up of the Former Yugoslavian Republic. This approach would acknowledge the complicity of Western states in the decision-making structures of international economic institutions and the role this plays in the capacity of developing states to determine their internal practices.[134] Seeing oneself as the other sees you, Gunning's second challenge, would involve engaging the people of Kosovo, as well as engaging Serbia as the 'Other' of international dialogues on the intervention in 1999. In this sense, Serbian associations with the Kosovan territory and the presence of Serbian communities within the Province need to be regarded as having relevance, at least to Serbian people. Engaging with this knowledge would require acknowledgement that 'ethics' and 'morality' are not one-dimensional categories. Finally, seeing the other in her context would ask us to understand Kosovan and Serbian communities as similar to us and as different to us, in the sense that this is a condition of humanness.[135] This approach – which draws on a range of feminist methods as a means to listen to the plethora of narratives appropriate to any legal 'crisis' – challenges us to reconstruct our relationship with law, especially understandings of legal subjectivity. At the base of this project is an

---

130 Ursel, above note 100, at 273.
131 Ibid. at 273.
132 Ibid. at 273.
133 Gunning, 'Arrogant Perceptions, World-travelling and Multicultural Feminism', 23, *Columbia Human Rights Law Review* (1991), see discussion in chapter one.
134 Orford, above note, 96.
135 See the discussion of natality in chapter six.

acceptance of the historical and ongoing relationship between survivors and perpetrators of violence. In the context of the Kosovo intervention, both the non-violent resistance movement prior to the NATO intervention and the inter-community violence after the intervention become elements of the law and violence relationship that require international attention as a consequence.

Setting internal driven goals

> The debates reveal that 'Kosovo' is not only about what happened 'out there'. . . . but also, and importantly, about what took place 'in here', the audience. . . . Kosovo has come to be a debate about ourselves, about what we hold as normal and what exceptional, and through that fact, about what sort of law we practise.[136]

Mills advocates, for domestic family violence, the need for internally rather than externally set goals to change abusive relationships. To suggest otherwise, that the police or any other external agency might set an agenda that challenges the domestic violence relationship, replicates the destructive gendered paradigm the woman experiencing abuse is trapped in. Police and other external agencies perpetuate the notion that women require a masculine protector to escape violence, rather than promoting a version of events where the survivor's agency is paramount. We can see how the same narrative is played out in the case of domestic state violence, where the community under threat is denied the opportunity to respond or articulate what they need in order to challenge the continued threat of violence. Koskenniemi's description, above, of the NATO action in Serbia presents a telling narrative of the incapacity of the Western legal mind to let foreign communities formulate and express their desires for autonomy, or even freedom from violence, in their own voice. A look at the Security Council resolutions in response to the Serbian violence in the Kosovo Province demonstrates a similar shift away from the expressed desires of the Kosovar Albanians. In resolution 1160, one of the Council's earliest comments on Serbian violence in the Province of Kosovo, the Council acknowledges the 'clear commitment of senior representatives of the Kosovar Albanian community to non-violence'.[137] This recognition is left out of subsequent resolutions and state justifications for the use of force.[138]

To deny the applicability of Mills' survivor centred model to gross humanitarian crises within states is a denial of human agency, equality and identity for the survivors of human rights abuses. It should be noted that precisely this manner of change often occurs away from the centre of international law's gaze, as non-violent social movements demand tremendous resources and commitment over an extended period of time. The slow resolution of the territorial dispute and aggression in the Cameroon with Nigeria is an example of this type of progress.[139] This is intertwined with the

---

136   Koskenniemi, above note 15, at 162.
137   SC Res 1160, 31ˢᵗ March 1998.
138   See, for example, SC Res 1199, 23 September 1998; SC Res 1203, 24 October 1998; SC Res 1239, 14 May 1999; SC Res 1244, 10 June 1999.
139   Gray, above note 4, chapter one.

requirement that the processes to stem state violence are premised on respect for and listening to the survivors, rather than to intervene and make decisions on the survivor's behalf. To connect Mills' survivor centred model to a practical example, where a supposed justified humanitarian intervention might have taken a different (less violent) form, we need only to return to Kosovo in the decade prior to NATO's intervention.

Challenging humanitarian interventions/identity and diversity in feminist theories

> They worry about what kind of fashion statement they make as they dress for a demonstration calling for the re-opening to ethnic Albanians of the schools and universities. Shots of handkerchiefs being dipped in vinegar ('Tear Gas' explains a bopping computer graphic), alternate with shots of shoes and slacks being tried on, reflected in full length mirrors. The video mischievously mirrors 'us' as it presents 'them'. The West's projections of the exotic and the unknown onto these hip Europeans becomes a joke that we all share.[140]

NATO states' use of force in 1999 presented a dialogue, assisted by Western media representations, of a desperate situation where Kosovar Albanians risked immediate danger from the discriminatory, violent practices of the Serbian government. Both Western media and Western legal accounts leave out of this narrative the role of Kosovar Albanians in shaping a resistance to Serbian repression for ten years prior to the NATO intervention.[141] This was a largely non-violent resistance movement that focussed on the establishment of a parallel government, health system and education system to counter Serbian discrimination against ethnic Albanians in the Kosovo Province. Waller writes:

> The elected president of the ethnic Albanian population, Ibrahim Rogova, successfully orchestrated a non-violent response to Milosevic's repression. Fearing that any or all versions of militarization would indeed make Kosova another Bosnia (a position that proved utterly accurate), Rogova and others evolved the strategy of creating a parallel government, parallel schools and parallel clinics, though all these institutions had to operate essentially without funding.
>   Unfortunately the nation-states of the militarized and militaristic West failed to support Rogova, either symbolically or materially, an omission that opened the way for the formation of the armed KLA....[142]

The lack of Western (non-violent) intervention to support the non-violent challenge to the Serbian repression and discrimination in Kosovo, in the ten years of oppression

140 Waller, 'Not Your Usual Agit-Prop', 3(1), *International Feminist Journal of Politics* (2001), 119, at 121.
141 Ibid.
142 Waller, above note 140, at 120; Waller uses the spelling 'Kosova' which matches the ethnic Albanian spelling; Rugova was elected President of the Kosovo Assembly in March 2002. Rogova passed away on 21 January 21 2006.

against the ethnic Albanians, reads uncomfortably with the legal narratives regarding the necessity of the intervention in 1999. While the Western world looked elsewhere during the 1990s Rogova's non-violent challenge to Serbian repression was doomed to failure. The commitment of the Kosovo people to their own form of 'internal self-determination' in response to the overtly racist practices of the Serbian government was a narrative that had limited articulation in Western communities. The multiple answers to why such a failure to listen occurred must offer little solace to the Kosovo community now. These answers resonate with our limited Western understanding of law's capacity to accommodate diversity. This is a theme that emerges consistently in feminist jurisprudence. For example, Orford writes of the failure of elite Western men to recognise either their own particularity or the capacity of the particularity of the 'Other' to inform their practices.[143]

Imposed democracy homogenises communities and obscures the complex diversity across all groups of humans and within any group identification. This is not to say Western states and Western jurisprudence have nothing to offer the non-Western state. It is to add that as Westerners we must meet and engage with the Other – inside and outside of our communities – to better understand our own limitations and to gain insight into alternative methods of achieving democracy. Recognition of the diversity within, and around us, grants us the capacity to learn and to listen outside of the predetermined narratives of statehood and militarism under international law. This includes recognition by Western feminist theories of the potential for third world feminist methodologies and scholarship to add to and to challenge the production of Western feminist texts.

To conclude, the main argument of this chapter lies in the evidencing of an analytical claim. That is, there is a correlative legal form across international and Western legal systems in the regulation of domestic violence. This has a continued negative impact on women's lives and the victims of state violence within in the territory of the state. I have not focussed on the further negative, disproportionate and harmful reality of military and state force on women's lives. This is well documented elsewhere, including in earlier chapters of this book. Instead I have focussed on current theoretical engagements with domestic family violence. This has paralleled developments in international law around the containment of domestic state violence. By exposing this analogy in regulation, the base of international law, particularly the distinction between public and private acts of states, is exposed as incorporating a sexed model.

The evidence of the chapter further serves to illustrate why past feminist reforms on the nature and content of international law have been inhibited in application, often remain unenforceable and offer little challenge to pervasive and dominant gender norms, which continue to function to place women, globally, in danger of violence justified as private. Feminist engagements with law must not just explore the outward reach of legal norms in the construction of wider gendered and social dialogues. This chapter demonstrates the internal reach that is required by feminist legal theories to expose the very central, seemingly impenetrable, sexed construction of the foundations of law. Feminist legal theory suggests, in evidencing the sexed nature of

---

143 Orford, 'The Politics of Collective Security', 17, *Michigan Journal of International Law* (1996), 376.

the distinction between public and private that there is a need to disrupt this sexed coupling, rather than increased regulation of the private sphere or the shifting of acts and their meaning from the private into the public domain.[144]

I have used Mills survivor-centred approach to halting domestic family violence, as a potential guide to reconsidering the regulation of the domestic sphere of the state under international law. Mills centres on the survivor as the legal subject rather than the public actor (of the state or the foreign state seeking to intervene) and she perceives the relationship between the abuser and the survivor as crucial, instead of focussing on the relationship between the abuser and the larger legal structure. Finally, Mills suggests private knowledge can lead public action, rather than vice versa, when she suggests internally driven responses must be prioritised over external assessments of needs. To re-develop such a framework under the guise of international law would not be simple nor would it be expedient or without cost. The continued international presence in Kosovo, now under EU leadership,[145] heads into its second decade while the destruction of public infrastructure and killing of civilians during the bombing of Belgrade in 1999, although no longer occurring, has lasting repercussions for the people of Serbia.[146] Similarly, the consequences of NATO's intervention continue to impact on the lives of citizens in NATO states. Military interventions are complex, lengthy and expensive. What I have sought to suggest, in this chapter, is they are not the only type of response the international community has at its disposal.

144 Kinsella suggests a similar project with respect to the nature of the protector/protected binary in international humanitarian law, above note 39.

145 The current mission is titled EULEX, European Union Rule of Law Mission Kosovo; see: http://www.eulex-kosovo.eu/en/front/ (last accessed February 2011).

146 See Amnesty International, *'Collateral Damage' of Unlawful Killings? Violations of the Laws of War by NATO during the Operation Allied Force* (2000); Human Rights Watch, *Civilian Deaths in the NATO Air Campaign* (2000).

6 Justifying force in the era of global terrorism

This future man . . . seems to be possessed by a rebellion against human existence as it has been given, a free gift from nowhere (secularly speaking), which he
wishes to exchange as it were for something he made himself.[1]

As I write this final chapter, I realise that the toddlers of the book's preface have
grown and now engage with constructions of gender through a larger web of connec-
tions than those encountered when they were at pre-school. I am being nudged off
the computer to allow for time on a MMORPG: a massively multiplayer online role-
playing game. For my children, there is attraction to MMORPGs that involve a level
of violence or military-type behaviour. The strong and diverse gender narratives they
have encountered at home are continually measured against a world where Action
Man is for boys and Barbie is for girls. In a cyber-era, this appears to have morphed
into categories of online gaming that are often disturbingly pre-feminist.

In the case of Offspring Number One these online preferences have also produced
a real world fascination with armies. As I researched the material for this chapter, I
was shocked to discover that his online proficiency may indeed make him a candi-
date for future military units; already a reality in the United States where weapon dis-
pensary is increasingly dislocated geographically from the battlefield. Fortunately, my
children are yet to discover the online game America's Army, that is free to download,
now in its third incarnation and designed to 'provide players with the most authentic
military experience available'.[2] This 'authentic' military experience contains male-only
roles because the US army does not allow women to take on combat roles. However,
the online game does not, of course, include the real world experience of being unable
to continue to participate should grave injuries or death in combat occur.

This chapter reflects on similar developments in the international law on the use
of force: first the use of unmanned drones which allow 'online players' onto real battlefields and second, the question of women's participation in the military and within
the state. As such, this final chapter of the book considers the state of the law on the
use of force after the first decade of the new millennium. Since the year 2000, two significant developments have emerged that have the potential to dramatically re-shape

---

1 Arendt, *The Human Condition* (Chicago: Chicago Press, 1998: Original Edition 1958).
2 See: http://www.americasarmy.com/aa/ (last accessed February 2011).

the manner in which we understand the law on the use of force in the twenty-first century: the shift to the use of new types of weaponry, particularly the use of unmanned drones by the United States, and the inclusion of texts engaging women, peace and security in the collective security agenda.

The use of unmanned drones, on the one hand, is an issue pertinent to the international humanitarian law of armed conflict, yet on the other hand, issues of *jus in bello* and *jus ad bellum* are raised by the use of unmanned drones.[3] This chapter considers how this technology develops or hinders the arguments made across this book. Significantly, and despite the changing nature of state sovereignty in the UN era, the role of the state in the law on the use of force remains relatively retrograde, employing both traditional international legal categories of state consent as a barrier to the development of sophisticated legal rules and using a version of legal subjectivity informed by Western patriarchal legal structures. This claim remains pertinent to a study of the use of unmanned drones in the early twenty-first century. This is the focus of section two of this chapter, where a discussion of Arendt's model of natality leads to an analysis of weaponised unmanned drones. This is then followed by application of the domestic analogy to analyse the weaknesses inherent in the excuses for the use of force articulated under the global war against terrorists.[4]

Section three of this chapter reviews the significant shift in Security Council dialogues across the first decade of the twenty-first century particularly the production of five resolutions on women, peace and security. Two of these resolutions prioritise women's participation and this has had some impact on women's participation in UN peacekeeping and UN peacebuilding missions while also addressing, within the text of the resolutions, the need for increased gender parity in local, national, regional and international governing structures. The other three resolutions, as was discussed in chapter two, focus on combating sexual violence in armed conflict. The discussion of these resolutions in this chapter analyses the need for a feminist politics that addresses questions of participation that are larger than the current quota driven assessments within the Security Council's initiatives on women, peace and security. The chapter

---

3 O'Connell, *International Law and the Use of Drones*, speech given to the International Law Discussion group at Chatham House, 21 October 2000. A summary of the meeting is available, here: http://www.chathamhouse.org.uk/files/17754_il211010drones.pdf (last accessed February 2011). Also see: O'Connell, 'The Choice of Law Against Terrorism' 4 *Journal of National Security Law and Policy* (2010) 343; O'Connell, *Lawful Use of Combat Drones*, Testimony to the Congress of the United States, House of Representatives, Subcommittee on National Security and Foreign Affairs, 28 April 2010, available online at: http://www.fas.org/irp/congress/2010_hr/042810oconnell.pdf (last accessed February 2011).

4 After the change of administration in the US in 2009, the Obama government initially announced the end of the 'War on Terror' (see Oliver Burkeman 'Obama Administration says Goodbye to 'War on Terror'' *The Guardian* UK, Wednesday 25 March, 2009) however the use of force by the US against terrorist actors abroad has continued under the name of 'Overseas Contingency Operation' and, after the arrest of Umar Farouk Abdulmutallab on 25 December 2009, the Obama administration increasingly referred to the global action against international terrorism and by March 2010 acknowledged 'the United States is waging a global campaign against al-Qaida and its terrorist affiliates' in the 2010 US National Security Strategy (2010) page ii, available at: http://www.whitehouse.gov/sites/default/files/rss_viewer/national_security_strategy.pdf (accessed February 2011).

then concludes with an analysis of Arendt's model of natality as a starting point for future engagements with law on the use of force before providing a summary of chapter-level and general conclusions and recommendations of the book. As the quote from Arendt, above indicates, the starting point is to value our humanity over our capacity to destroy.

Weaponised unmanned drones and the global war against terrorism

Arendt's political model of natality can be developed as a feminist framework to build new narratives on force. However, as a non-legal narrative the radical potential of Arendt's insightful work is difficult to shape into a legal narrative that can be accommodated in the contemporary international legal structure.[5] This demonstrates the limitation of the law as narrative technique that is at once 'inside' (as it engages with and is inside the existing mainstream of international law) and 'outside' (as it posits solutions that engage discourses and narratives outside of law's disciplinary boundaries).

Arendt's writing provides a myriad of descriptions and insights into political arrangements, modern conditions and violence. Analysis of the full range of Arendt's claims is beyond the scope of this book.[6] However, it is Arendt's description of natality that has lain at the base of the conclusions of this study. While the book has used feminist thinking and particularly feminist legal methods, it has not been projected as the essential account of feminist thinking on the international law on the use of force, rather the approach of this book is that of a glass prism, where shifting perspective casts new light, angles and reflections over existing material. This approach can also be aligned with Arendt's model of natality. Arendt sees, at the centre of natality, the plurality of humans so that '[p]lurality is the condition of human action because we are all the same, that is, human, in such a way that nobody else is ever the same as anyone who ever lived, lives, or will live'.[7] Human action, for Arendt, consequently requires this condition of human existence: plurality. With this thought in my mind I have avoided a direct answer to the (perhaps implicit yet) central question underlying this book: When, if ever, would feminisms justify the use of military force? This book, while informed by feminist studies on the destructive nature of militarism for women's security and an appreciation of women's peace building and peaceful resistance, leaves the answer to the possibility of feminist friendly force to the feminisms of the future. That is, the development of this discussion lies in a politics of natality where action is conceived in the plurality of human individuality and the intrinsic capacity for new ideas that Arendt defines as that which makes us human.

Arendt's politics of natality also emphasises a separation between natality and destruction. Other writers have described militarism and the use of force, or the

---

5 See: Arendt, *On Violence* (New York: Harcourt, 1970), above note 1.
6 An excellent analysis is provided in: Owens, *Between War and Politics* (Oxford: Oxford University Press, 2007).
7 Above note 1, at 8.

infliction of pain through weaponry, as a gendered politics through the substitution of the capacity to bring forth new life (or ideas) with a capacity to create new means of destruction.[8] The development of unmanned drones as a weapon in the global war against terrorists by the United States in the first decade of the new millennium seems to epitomise this creation–destruction confusion. Arendt also studies the human proclivity to make real the science fiction of earlier generations, so that:

It would be as though our brain, which constitutes the physical, material condition of our thoughts, were unable to follow what we do, so that from now on we would indeed need artificial machines to do our thinking and speaking. If it should turn out to be true that knowledge (in the modern sense of know-how) and thought have parted company for good, then we would indeed become the helpless slaves, not so much of our machines as of our know-how, thoughtless creature at the mercy of every gadget which is technically possible, no matter how murderous it is.[9]

Arendt's politics of natality, that starts with the centrality of human difference as that which makes us the same, is a pertinent starting point for thinking through the consequences of living in an era of know-how that sends machines to kill, and thus turns individuals into targets on a computer screen. Targets not dissimilar to the ones children and young people are encouraged to seek out as entertainment. Targets that all look the same and targets that are removed from the political space of action in Arendt's terms. This is removal from the political space of action because the drone is not an encounter between two humans; rather the humans are bracketed from each other by two machines. Individuals targeted by individuals controlling weaponised unmanned drones are being denied their humanity if there is no space to speak or think in response to a machine. There is only the know-how of technology.

In this sense, the extension of battlefields and the retraction of the political space through the use of weaponised unmanned drones is an important issue for feminist activism and scholarship. The creation of a potential space for (some) women to speak within the debates of the UN Security Council has, ironically, emerged in the same period when the use of force has gained the capacity to exclude others from status as humans in such a profound and morally challenging manner. To have even a limited form of participation in the public space of the Security Council is a form of complicity and responsibility for the events that the public space defines as action. The development, then, of increased feminist conversations, ideas and demands in the political space is vital when that space is also used to tolerate the destruction of the humanity of others. While the Security Council has not endorsed the use of weaponised unmanned

---

8 Cohn, 'Sex and Death in the Rational World of Defense Intellectuals', 12 (4), *Signs* (1987), 687; Theweleit, 'The Bomb's Womb and the Genders of War', in Woolacott, and Cooke (eds), *Gendering War Talk*, (Princeton, 1993), 283; also see: Heathcote, 'Feminist Reflections on the 'End' of the War on Terror' 11 *Melbourne Journal of International Law* (2010).
9 Above note 1, at 3.

drones, there has been no recognition or discussion of the use of drones in the Council; leaving their use unregulated within the collective security structure.

Some authors have concluded that, '[t]he use of drones in armed conflict is as lawful as any other battlefield delivery system'.[10] That is, the principles of international humanitarian law of armed conflict apply to weaponised unmanned drones in the same manner as they would to any weapon delivery system and the *jus ad bellum*, or international law on the use of force, remains a separate legal issue to the battlefield choice to use drones. These arguments side-step the value of weaponised unmanned drones to the United States: that is, the extension of the battlefield achieved through their deployment, something that the United States argues is a special characteristic of the global war against terror. As such, while the use of weaponised unmanned drones may not be intrinsically illegal under the international humanitarian law of armed conflict, their contemporary deployment does engage with *jus ad bellum*. The special characteristics of the global war on terror, that the United States continues to articulate in its justification for specific weaponised unmanned drone deployments, poses questions on the changing nature of the international law on the use of force.

The United States has argued that when a state has not given consent to the use of unmanned drones in its territory to police terrorist actors, the failure of that state to halt terrorist activity overrides the territorial integrity of that state.[11] The argument finds a potential threat from global terrorist actors constructs a right of self-defence to stop the terrorist threat from materialising. International law on self-defence, as discussed in chapter three, is governed by the general principles of necessity, proportionality and immediacy. Under the principle of necessity, it must be established that non-forcible measures were not available to procure the same outcome. Under the principle of proportionality, the use of force must not exceed that which is required to defend against the initial armed attack and under the immediacy requirement the response must be a reaction to the initial armed attack and not a form of revenge, retaliation or ineffective due to a time gap between the defensive measures and the initial armed attack. Although the use of weaponised unmanned drones may therefore legitimately and legally be used by a state in an exercise of self-defence, the current deployment of drones by the United States ignores the absence of an armed attack to define the parameters of their use. Consequently, the current use of weaponised unmanned drones by the United States relies either on the 9/11 attacks as the initial attack that the defence is in response to or relies on the United States developing either an anticipatory or preemptive self-defence argument to justify its current use of unmanned drones.

The 9/11 attacks on the United States instigated the use of force by the United States and its allies in Afghanistan, an exercise of collective self-defence that was accepted by nearly all states. However, this right to self-defence either terminated in 2002 when the Karzai government was installed and the United States has then

---

10   O'Connell, 'The International Law of Drones' 14 (36) *ASIL Insights*, 12 November 2010.
11   See, O'Connell, 'The Choice of Law Against Terrorism' 4 *Journal of National Security Law and Policy* (2010), 343.

remained at the request of the Karzai government[12] or the claim to be acting in self-defence remains but is increasingly weakened by the time length of hostilities.[13] In either case the armed conflict is contained by the territory it occurs within, a point emphasised by the ICJ in the *DRC v. Uganda* decision.[14]

The use of weaponised drones in states other than Afghanistan as a use of force in the global war against terrorist actors must therefore fall within arguments for anticipatory or preemptive self-defence. Under arguments for anticipatory self-defence the central argument rests on the knowledge that an attack is about to happen, or imminent, justifying the use of force in self-defence. Under arguments for preemptive self-defence the defensive behaviour of a state is justified as in response to an ongoing, low level threat that is yet to materialise into an actual, planned attack. The range of attacks the United States has deployed through its weaponised drones technology, away from battlefields, can be classified as preemptive self-defence as the individuals targeted are not themselves combatants within a regular armed conflict and nor is there evidence of an actual or imminent attack in most cases. As such, while authors such as Schmitt are correct in stating that weaponised unmanned drones are not in violation of either *jus in bello* or *jus ad bellum* rules, the contemporary deployment of unmanned drones by the United States must be either justified under the law on the use of force collectively (in the sense that all the strikes are action within an ongoing conflict and thus engaging international humanitarian law requirements) or individually (so that each strike is justified under the law on the use of force).

Behind explanations for the use of force against terrorist actors on the territory of another state there is a repetition of narratives demanding a response to low-level but persistent threats, such as that posed by transnational terrorists. In chapter three, I have argued that the flaw in this argument made by the United States is demonstrated through a domestic analogy with the provocation defence to homicide. As a common law defence to homicide, mitigating murder to manslaughter, the provocation excuse no longer exists in England and it has been abolished or amended in other common law jurisdictions in response to feminist criticisms of the gendered application of the defence.[15] In England, the provocation defence has been

---

12 O'Connell, *International Law and the Use of Drones*, speech given to the International Law Discussion group at Chatham House, 21 October 2000. A summary of the meeting is available, here: http://www.chathamhouse.org.uk/files/17754_il211010drones.pdf (last accessed February 2011).

13 Gray, *International Law and the Use of Force* (Oxford: Oxford University Press, 2008) at 207.

14 *Armed Activities on the Territory of the Congo* (Democratic Republic of the Congo v. Uganda) (ICJ, 19 December 2005).

15 Leader-Elliott, 'Passion and Insurrection in the Law of Sexual Provocation' in Ngaire Naffine and Rosemary Owens, *Sexing the Subject of Law* (London: LBC, 1997); Quick and Celia Wells, 'Getting Tough with Defences'(June, 2006) *Criminal Law Review* 514, 523; Susan Edwards, 'Abolishing Provocation and Reframing Self-defence' (2004) *Criminal Law Review* 181, at 182; also see: Volpp, ' "(Mis)identifying Culture": Asian Women and the 'Cultural Defence' (1994) 17 *Harvard Women's Law Journal* 57; Victoria Scraps Provocation Murder defence' *The Age* (4 October 2005); de Pasquale, 'Provocation and the Homosexual Advance Defence: the deployment of Culture as a Defence Strategy' (2002) 26 *Melbourne University Law Review*110; Golder, 'The Homosexual Advance Defence and the Law/Body Nexus'(2004) 11, *Murdoch University Electronic Journal of Law*, available at: http://www.murdoch.edu.au/elaw/indices/issue/v11n1.html (last accessed February 2011).

abolished[16] and replaced with the new partial defence to homicide of loss of self-control. Under the English Coroners and Justice Act 2009, a defendant seeking to argue that they lost control must be able to identify a 'qualifying trigger'.[17] This may be a fear of serious violence,[18] circumstances of an extremely grave character [19]or a justifiable sense of being wronged.[20] The analogy with the international excuses made by the United States is the fear of serious of violence – which is the central platform that the use of force against terrorist actors has been articulated from. However, under the new partial defence of loss of self-control the absence of actual violence provoking a response from the defendant ultimately limits the legal shield offered by the excuse. This is recognition of the subjective nature of perceptions of provocation as well as of the loss of self-control. For a state to argue for a similar legal form to excuse the use of force against individuals on the territory of another state illustrates, on the one hand, the poverty of the domestic analogy, despite its persistence in international legal forms, as well as the weakness of preemptive force arguments.

Under international law on the use of force there is no distinction between justifications and excuses. Yet the distinction between justifications and excuses is central to common law defences. Justification for an act erases the illegal nature of the act because it was, in the circumstances, justified. In contrast, an act that is excused (e.g., under provocation or loss of self control defence pleas) remains an illegal act. It is the consequences of the illegal act under an excuse that are mitigated due to the intervening factor (the excuse). International law on the use of force incorporates the legal category of justifications (or to be specific the single justification of self-defence) but does not acknowledge a separate category of excused behaviour.

In the arguments produced in the era of the global war against terrorists the United States has resorted to the language of excuses. This has an important strategic value for the United States as the claim is made that the United States is excused the application of law on the use of force due to the special condition of the global war against terrorist actors. The United States argues that the licence it has to use force against terrorist actors is not available to other states. Furthermore the notion of a provocative trigger under the English statutory defence of loss of self-control indicates the problem with developing this category of legal claim in relation to the deployment of force. The idea that a state might have 'loss of control' after a qualifying trigger mitigates the development of an analogous defence.

Beyond the legal irregularities of the preemptive force argument,[21] the consequential social narrative that focuses on a fear of future provocative or future violent behaviour to justify increased infringements of civil liberties by the state can be highlighted as analogous to the internalised social discourse many women experience

---

16 Coroners and Justice Act 2009(UK) c. 25, s 56.
17 Coroners and Justice Act s 54.
18 Ibid. S 55 (3).
19 Ibid. S 55 (4).
20 Ibid. S 55 (5).
21 See further Gray, above note 13, from 209.

in response to male violence. Feminist writing that emerged in the weeks after the 11 September attacks in the United States, emphasised this connection between the internalisation of the fear of male violence by women and the internalisation of fears of the 'Other' in the guise of the Muslim terrorist within Western communities. For example, Morgan records, on 19 September 2001, the necessity to:

> talk about the need to understand that we must expose the mystique of violence, separate it from how we conceive of excitement, eroticism, and "manhood"; the need to comprehend that violence differs in degree but is related in kind, that it thrives along a spectrum, as do its effects – from the battered child and raped women who live in fear to a entire population living in fear . . . .[22]

The analogy between the global war against terrorists and provocation defences, then, also lies in the strong social narratives of fear that are used by states to explain the curbing of civil liberties. For women, provocation narratives are co-opted into women's self blame for men's violence. This results in the refusal by many women to walk at night, or to move in public spaces unaccompanied, through the fear of rape or attack from an unknown male assailant. This is despite intimate relationships forming the key global threat to women.[23] In the West, after the instigation of the global war against terrorism a similar fear was enacted culturally against the unpredictable Muslim terrorist. This narrative, similar to discourse on the threats to women's safety, misallocates the source of the fear as external, the 'Other', represented by an irrational Muslim terrorist while denying the role Western imperialist strategies contribute to poverty and violence in foreign states and also downplaying the threat of terrorism to Muslim communities outside of the West.[24] This discourse collapses complex religious and nationalist identities with racial and ethnic identities. This is more than a social or cultural narrative as laws have been implemented to detain individuals who fit the profile of the Western conceived image of the terrorist; although these infringements of civil liberties can be potentially expanded to be applied against any citizen they are explained as a necessary sacrifice of liberal freedoms for the goal of greater security.[25]

The impact of the global war against terrorists *for Western citizens* becomes the narrative warning of the threat of future violence rather than any actual violence. This justifies those of us in Western communities averting our attention from other violence and is used to explain governments in Western communities curtailing civil

22 Morgan, 'Reactions: Whose Terrorism?' in Hawthorne and Winter, *September 11, 2001: Feminist Perspectives* (North Melbourne, Vic: Spinifex, 2002), at 25; also see, MacKinnon, *Are Women Human? And Other International Dialogues* (Harvard, 2006), chapter 25.

23 See Kelly, 'Wars Against Women: Sexual Violence, Sexual Politics and the Militarised State,' in Jacobs, Jacobson and Marchbank (eds), *States of Conflict: Gender, Violence and Resistance* (London: Zed, 2000).

24 Above note 51, at 24, stating 'Need I say that there were not nationwide attacks on white Christian males after Timothy McVeigh was apprehended after the Oklahoma City bombing'.

25 See, Harcourt, 'Muslim Profiles Post 9/11' in Goold and Lazarus (eds), *Security and Human Rights* (Oxford: Hart, 2007).

liberties. As New Yorker, Morgan wrote in the weeks after the September 11 attacks: 'the world's sympathy moves me deeply. Yet I hear echoes dying into the silence: the world averting its attention from Rwanda's screams'.[26] Through the narrative of the global war against terrorism, which traverses social and cultural discourses in an attempt to produce a coherent legal discourse, the two-way impact of force continues to resound in Western communities. Both the states where force is deployed and the states arguing for their right to use force are changed by the narrative. The narrative of force also reinforces gendered identities and a gendered division of labour that militaries function within. Women's roles, in relation to military actors, are encapsulated by female stereotypes of women requiring protection, women as wives and mothers and women as providers of sexual and domestic services.

The domestic analogy between provocation defences and the Western cultural discourse on the global war against terrorism further serves to demonstrate some key methodological aspects of the book. The sexing and gendering of laws, exposed by the domestic analogy, connects with the understanding of law's function as a social and cultural narrative. The US discourse on the global war against terrorism, in an effort to build a legal narrative, uses social and cultural narratives linking international and national legal structures.

This chapter also examines some of the limitations of the two methods embraced throughout this book, specifically the level of generality required by the law as narrative technique and the failure of either the alternative or the mainstream narrative to permit subversive accounts. Although the law as narrative technique has been a crucial aspect of the project it is a limited technique in that by admitting the subjectivity of law and legal discourse the fluidity of any text is exposed rather than disguised. Therefore, although an increasingly accepted legal narrative regarding preemptive force, implied authorisation and a responsibility to prevent is apparent in mainstream international discourse on force, an exclusive focus on these narratives ignores the feminist and critical voices that have challenged the narrative of an international law as it has been defined by hegemonic states both, before and after 9/11. It is to these alternative narratives that I now turn.

Women's participation, identities, agency

> Scheherazade breaks the cycle of violence by choosing to embrace different terms of engagement. She fashions her universe not through physical force, as does the king, but through imagination and reflection.[27]

After the acts of 11 September 2001, and the instigation of the United States' global war against terrorism, feminist scholarship emerged in support (occasionally),[28] in opposition and in analysis of this Western narrative.[29] In this section, I concentrate

---

26 Above note 51, at 25.
27 Nafizi, *Reading Lolita in Tehran: A Memoir in Books* (London: Fourth Estate, 2003), at 19.
28 Elshtain, *Just War Against Terror* (New York: Basic Books, 2003).
29 Hawkesworth and Alexander, *War on Terror: Feminist Perspectives* (Chicago: University of Chicago Press, 2008); Hawthorne and Winter, *September 11: Feminist Perspectives* (North Melbourne, Vic: Spinifex, 2002).

on feminist legal responses to the global war against terrorism and post-September 11 narratives. In examining feminist responses to the global war against terrorism, I indicate the wider possibilities – and limitations – of adapting feminist approaches to international law and to understanding the international law on the use of force. My purpose is to reflect on how contemporary anti-terrorism narratives have significantly disrupted any larger feminist study of the law on the use of force. I argue that international legal developments that acknowledged the relevance of feminist approaches and women's participation appear to have been either sidelined by the global war against terrorism narrative or developed around the production of restrictive categories of female victim-status.

Alongside the limited narrative of terrorist actors as rogue male actors functioning outside the boundaries of the state are images of women's sexual vulnerability and need for protection that miscasts the threat to women's sexual autonomy as also outside the state. The production of a restrictive female sexuality, vulnerable to attack from rogue male actors is a reiteration of sexed and gendered discourse prevalent in security discourse prior to the global war against terrorism. Consequently, initiatives, such as Security Council resolution 1960 on women, peace and security[30] with its focus on female sexual vulnerability during armed conflict do not challenge the underlying legal structure that is inimical to women's security. Underlying this restraint is the feminist methodological limitation related to the construction of a feminist ethics. While feminist analysis of sex and gender is sophisticated and multifaceted, bringing this knowledge to law collapses categories and reinforces gendered distinctions feminist legal theorists have worked towards dismantling.

What is notable about institutional responses to women's issues after 11 September 2001, is the entrenched association of women with peace alongside elaboration of women as a category of protected (usually sexualised) subjects.[31] The anti-terrorism narrative, which revolves around the dynamic of the rogue terrorist versus the just male warrior, also functions as a gendered discourse.[32] To complete the narrative of the threat of the violent male actor increasingly represented within Western states as the Muslim terrorist, the emergence of an increased number of images of the female mother/child/victim requiring protection is not unexpected. Post-9/11 institutional developments use gendered representations of women's sexual vulnerability and consistently suppress the agency of women, in a retrograde manner.[33] Placed alongside the gendered image of the Muslim terrorist, it is not surprising that the narrative of male violence expounded under the global war against terrorism is contemporaneous to projects that centre on women's sexual vulnerability

---

30 SC Res 1960 (16 December 2010).
31 Charlesworth, 'Are Women Peaceful?' *Annual Lecture* (Centre LGS, 15 May 2008); Otto, 'Dissonance Between Survival and Consent', *Second Annual Shimizu Lecture in International Law* (London: London School of Economics, 7 March 2007); Otto, 'Disconcerting "Masculinities" in Buss and Manji, *International Law: Modern Feminist Approaches* (Oxford: Hart, 2005).
32 Morgan, above note 22.
33 Otto, above note 31.

rather than female empowerment or agency.[34] Facilitating the increased sexualised representation of women under international law, is a general neglect of women's participation and agency. In chapter three, I argued that fundamental questions regarding the development of Article 51 become difficult to ask because preemptive force shifts self-defence jurisprudence away from the Charter model. A further consequence of the discourse on the global war against terrorism is the averting of attention from women's rights and women's participation at the international level. However, the global war against terrorism has not diverted Security Council attention and international legal narratives away from the issue of women, peace and security. Instead a specific component of the pre-9/11 women, peace and security discourse has been persistently addressed under post-1325 initiatives: that of women's vulnerability to sexual violence during armed conflict. This has been achieved through resolutions 1820, 1888 and 1960 – all of which centre on sexual violence during armed conflict.[35]

While strategies that challenge sexual violence during armed conflict are required, as a strategy in isolation from other feminist strategies they appear to lose their value as feminist reforms. These three resolutions refer to sexual violence in a manner that disregards significant aspects of feminist knowledge. First, the use, throughout these resolutions, of the conjoined term 'women and children' is disturbing in the image projected of women as requiring special protective laws in the same manner as laws to protect children. This approach is regressive in its view of women and significantly dismantles many years of feminist and women's rights activism under the mandate of women's rights as human rights.[36]

The sexual violence resolutions also render the word gender in a non-technical manner, and it is often used as a synonym for 'women'. This disregards the distinction between sex and gender.[37] This also denies recognition of men as gendered humans. In the regulation of sexual violence this approach also disregards the role of gendered constructions as sustaining ideologies within militaries that shape acts of sexual violence perpetrated by military actors as well as denying recognition to men who are victims of sexual violence during armed conflict.

Consequently, the focus on sexual violence in these resolutions significantly underplays the potential of resolution 1325's approach[38] for women as participants in legal and political processes and decision making bodies. Although the participation aspect of resolution 1325 was supplemented by resolution 1889, the consistent reiteration and expansion of the sexual violence agenda in the three other Security Council resolutions seems to link women's participation to women's status as victims in conflict

34 Ibid.
35 SC Res 1325 (30 October 2000); SC Res 1820 (18 June 2008); SC Res 1888 (30 September 2009); SC Res 1820 (5 October 2009); SC Res 1960 (16 December 2010).
36 See, for example: Cook (ed.), *Human Rights of Women: National and International Perspectives* (University of Pennsylvania Press, 1994).
37 See the discussion in chapter one.
38 Also see SC Res 1889 (5 October 2009).

as well as entrenching a racialised global class system within the women, peace and security agenda. As such, elite and Western women gain the privilege of participation and women in armed conflicts are marked as victims rather than as participants. The Secretary General reported in September 2008 that 2 per cent of UN military personnel were women.[39] At one level this demonstrates the inadequacy of Security Council initiatives, such as resolution 1325 constructed under chapter VI of the UN Charter as a soft, or non-binding, resolution, and therefore, without compulsory norms for the active participation of women. As a consequence there is little incentive for states to make changes to the profile of military communities. Feminist approaches to international law, however, demand a more sophisticated analysis than this. The reliance by the United Nations on statistical articulation of gender parity indicates a fundamental failure to perceive feminist awareness as requiring more than adding women to existing security strategies. Furthermore, the dependence on militaries as the key strategy to challenge insecurity indicates a larger failure to see the structure of militaries as complicit in the production of women's insecurity.

The alternative image of women, present in international security literature and institutional acts, assumes the success of feminist and women's movements proscribing women's formal equality as a marker of democracy. In this sense the juxtaposed images of the Western woman, the free citizen/actor in a liberal democratic state, beside the non-Western woman, vulnerable to the sexual violence, exploitation and abuse that is prevalent in conflict zones, ignore the agency of the latter and the sexed and gendered notion of freedom available to the former. Current institutional moves, such as Security Council resolution 1960, parallel the global war against terrorism articulation of the non-Western rogue male actor with the vulnerable non-Western female victim. The only acceptable Western feminist narrative, in this context, is the narrative of Western women 'saving' non-Western women through the institutions of international law.

Subversive feminist accounts in response to the global war against terrorism, alongside other critical and/or subversive approaches, become difficult to articulate when the dominant Western narrative on preeruptive force appears to function to reject international legal norms. Underlying this is the acknowledged limitation of approaching law as a narrative. Not only are there multiple alternative narratives, but law, as a discipline, effectively screens out radical alternative narratives precisely because of their status as narratives. Western feminist approaches in the era of the global war against terrorism have been unable to significantly contribute to the debate because of the fundamental lack of feminist approaches to international law that question when, if ever, force would or could be justified. This is consistent with the overall conclusion of the book that feminist approaches enlarge our understanding of the law on the use of force and the consequences of this knowledge are relevant for the development of feminist legal theories and for international legal approaches generally. In this chapter, I have extended this contention to recognise the possibilities of a feminist re-imagining of the base of international law through a politics of natality, and I have also highlighted the

---

39 Report of the Secretary-General on women and peace and security, 25 September 2008, S/2008/622 paragraph 51.

importance of seeing force as having effects on the communities where force is directed and where force is instigated from. A politics of natality, through its embracing of pluralism as a political project, leads feminist legal approaches to sustained engagement on force that listens to those who force is used against, those whose name force is deployed under as well as the agents who retain the capacity to use force.

From the 'War on Terror' to a politics of natality

Separate from the sexual vulnerability focussed agenda pursued by feminist activists through the Security Council, alternative feminist responses to the legal narratives embedded in the global war against terrorism narrative have been difficult to articulate in a cultural environment that originated from the Bush position of, 'you are either with us or against us'.[40] As such, feminist responses to the global war against terrorism often reiterated a legal status quo or developed the production of non-legal narratives. For example, Gardam provided a response that applied a formal legal reading to diminish the viability of the rhetoric that emerged from the United States, and its allies, after the September 11 attacks.[41] In contrast, Charlesworth and Chinkin used social and cultural knowledge to challenge the narrative of the global war against terrorism, as did Buchanan and Johnson who offered a subversive non-legal account that engaged narrativity, law, film theory and gender theory to engage the West(ern) preoccupation with violence and law's foundation.[42] Buss also used a narrative approach to engage the multiple narratives amongst international legal scholarship after 9/11 that seemed limited to a dichotomy between US unilateralism and the cosmopolitan ethic of the international legal order.[43] The consequence is reduced debate on the legal questions produced in the era of the global war against terrorism to one that represents the only 'other' space for discourse as a dichotomy between texts re-imagining international law (constructed by those developing the global war against terrorism narrative) and texts asserting the relevance of the status quo of international law.[44] The assertion of a mainstream return to the key values of the Charter, or international law, leaves little space for feminist approaches to international law that are premised on the possibility of re-imagining international law's core.

For Orford, drawing on the work of Charlesworth, the fake crisis of a dilemma posed between the global war against terrorism and the perceived canons of

---

40 Bush, *Address to the Joint Session of Congress and the American People* (20 September 2001), available online at http://www.whitehouse.gov/news/releases/2001/09/20010920-8.html (last accessed February 2011); also see discussion in Butler, *Precarious Life* (Verso, 2006), at 2.
41 Gardam, 'International Law and the Terrorist Attacks on the USA' in Hawthorne and Winter (eds), *September 11, 2001: Feminist Perspectives* (North Melbourne, Vic: Spinifex, 2002).
42 Buchanan and Johnson, 'The 'Unforgiven' Sources of International Law' in Buss and Manji, *International Law: Modern Feminist Approaches* (Oxford: Hart, 2005); Charlesworth and Chinkin, 'Sex, Gender and September 11th', 96(3), *AJIL* (2002).
43 Buss, 'Keeping Its Promise: Use of Force and the New Man of International Law', in Bartholomew, *Empire's Law* (London: Pluto, 2006).
44 [Various Authors], 'Agora: Future Implications of the Iraq Conflict', 97, *AJIL* (2003), 553–642.
45 Orford, 'The Destiny of International Law', 17, *Leiden Journal of International Law* (2003) 441.

international law acts as a 'founding' moment that ultimately reasserts the legitimacy and potential of international law.[45] Described in this way, the global war against terrorism is demonstrated as a crucial initiatory moment or foundational discourse, a re-affirming of the discipline of international law. We should not be surprised, in this sense, to find feminists, women, critical theorists, writers from the global south, postcolonial theorists and third world approaches excluded from the dialogue.[46] The Western discourse that responded to the 9/11 attacks, and mobilised a forceful solution, becomes, then, not *the* founding moment but *one* founding moment amongst many in a discipline that asserts its legitimacy and authority through crisis.[47] In a text written prior to the global war against terrorism, but with increased relevance since, Rajagopal writes:

> This is nothing but a retelling of that old problem in international law: how to establish order in a world of sovereign states. But at a deeper level, this is a problem faced by law in general: on the one hand, law needs to constitute itself as the 'other' of violence to be legitimate, on the other hand, the law needs to use violence instrumentally to preserve power. The contradictions created by this paradox become part of the constant crisis of international law.[48]

The need for crisis and the role of the crisis moment, as a foundational narrative, illustrate a methodological abyss in feminist approaches to international law. As a theory that posits an alternative vision, indeed the possibility of a re-structured international legal order responsive to feminist knowledge, feminist theory has been able to partake in the unearthing and exposure of the discursive violence associated with foundational narratives in law. What feminist legal theories have failed to do is indicate whether a re-imagined feminist international order must also assert a foundational narrative and whether that narrative is implicitly violent.[49] Law and violence jurisprudence, for example in the work of Cover, argues that founding law is to enact violence. If feminist politics is a quest for a new founding moment, can the violence be in the act of severance from past narratives or must feminist theory take the further step and use force? To articulate the range of feminist positions on when, if ever, force may be justified, I have argued, the relationship between law, violence and gender requires increased engagement and argued for a politics of natality as a method of engagement that is premised on pluralism.

The plural voices of feminist approaches to international law must engage directly, first, with the question of why muster a critique and challenge to the international legal edifice only to find a deep rooted structural bias that potentially negates any future project. The use of the law as narrative technique throughout the book has been, in part, a choice made to illustrate the view that current international legal

---

46 For a TWAIL analysis of the global war against terrorism, see: 43, *Osgoode Hall Law Journal* (2005).
47 Charlesworth , 'International Law: A Discipline of Crisis', 65 (3), *Modern Law Review* (2002), 377.
48 Rajagopal, 'International Law and the Development Encounter', *ASIL Proceedings* (1999) 16, at 22.
49 See, however, Orford, *Reading Humanitarian Interventions* (Cambridge: Cambridge University Press, 2003), chapter six.

arrangements need not be the only international legal arrangement. Furthermore, drawing on the work of Otto, I have argued that feminist approaches must function as projects 'inside' and 'outside' the mainstream of international law to provide long term, productive engagement and solutions.[50]

Additionally, feminist approaches must respond to the claim that perhaps it is law itself that is the 'gentle civiliser'. Throughout the book I have provided evidence that this claim can only be made by blinding ourselves to the realities of armed conflict for women living in conflict regions and to the impact of force on those of us living in our own communities. Furthermore, I have argued, law that seeks to restrain armed conflict through controlled force rests on a fundamental error about the possibility of military violence being controlled, rational or useful for the creation of women's security.

Enlarging the prohibition on force and extending participation

I have endeavoured to show that, beyond the global war against terrorism, the Charter-based norms on the law on the use of force, as well as the customary international law perceptions of justified force, require sustained feminist engagement. This chapter has analysed the US-led global war against terrorism, as well as feminist discourse in response to the global war against terrorism. This final part enlarges the argument that feminist legal theories must look at laws beyond the global war against terrorism discourse to re-examine the law on the use of force generally.

The first two claims discussed here, the demand for an increase in women's participation in security mechanisms and the need for an elaboration and development of the prohibition on the use of force, are directed at feminist strategies that function 'within' the mainstream of international law. Both of these recommendations, however, must be read within the context of the arguments for a politics of natality, discussed above. In this, any reform strategies are of limited value in a system that is structurally sexed and gendered. By drawing conclusions that pertain to the development of laws as they currently exist alongside conclusions that challenge the edifice of international law generally, I utilise Lacey's critique/utopia/reform model and Otto's recognition of the inside/outside status of feminist legal theories.[51]

The book as a whole makes an argument for the increased participation of women in international security mechanisms. This has not been articulated as a quota-type strategy. While the empirical, or substantive, aspect of the participation claim lies in the recognition of the relative absence of women in international and national decision making structures to address this absence the incorporation of women's narratives from outside of the mainstream of international law to explain, analyse and challenge the international law on the use of force is necessary. The methodological aspect of participation claims is to replace demands for gender equality, in terms of women's representation, with a sophisticated and long term commitment approach

---

50   Otto, 'A Sign of "Weakness"? Disrupting Gender Certainties in the Implementation of Security Council Resolution 1325', 13, *Michigan Journal of Gender and Law* (2006), 113.

51   Lacey, 'Feminist Legal Theory and the Rights of Women', in Knop (ed.), *Gender and Human Rights* (Oxford: Oxford University Press, 2004); Otto, Ibid.

to enhancing women's participation in international and state structures. This would involve seeking out women's understanding of their own and society's needs, as well as understanding the role of women on the 'peripheries' in challenging social, cultural and legal norms.[52] Strategies that encourage women to value themselves, their opinions and their capabilities, be they through education or through empowering women and through the challenging of gendered violence that is tolerated because it is directed against them as women, are the kinds of strategies that are incredibly important to enlarging women's participation in institutional and state structures. Contemporary access to power for women who represent elite groups within our communities also needs to be identified as indicative of the intersectional nature of gender discrimination. To seek women's full participation in legal processes is, therefore, to embark on a (slow) re-working of legal structures and normative categories.

Therefore, pursuit of women's participation shifts beyond quotas towards recognition of the failure of current legal arrangements to be inclusive of women at the foundation. Underlying this conclusion then, is recognition that the 'foundations' of international law are not settled or permanent. The foundations of international law are gendered and socially constructed. Furthermore, my claim is, not that women's experiences and knowledge are innately different to men's, but rather that women's experiences and knowledge are informed, globally, by social and cultural norms that result in women having different priorities and needs from those of men. Reflecting the cultural diversity of women's experiences and knowledge, as well as the socially constructed spheres of reference understood as female, demands a re-working of fundamental legal categories and processes built on women's participation that is different to proportional representation. Throughout this book, I have reflected on the possibilities and limitations of the feminist utopia of active inclusion of women in the making of the world. This is a foundational claim so, for example, in chapter four on self-determination, the foundations of a right to self-determination under international law are challenged by focussing attention on women's narratives drawn from communities seeking self-determination.

Beyond the move to incorporate a conceptual shift in understanding how and when women could and should participate in international decision-making, the preoccupation of states and scholars with the articulation of justifications, rather than the prohibition on the use of force, is a status quo that contributes to, rather than diminishes, the level of conflict globally. The placement of Article 2(4) as the epitome of state agreement on the nature of prohibited force was a significant, world changing legal development in 1945. The failure of states to extend and develop the prohibition need not dictate that this may never be possible. The knowledge produced in this book indicates that, rather than perceiving Article 2(4) as the pinnacle of human creativity in the outlawing of violence, time would be well spent on elaboration and development of what it means to have a prohibition on the use of force, its limits, its regulation and its co-option into a gendered understanding of law and violence. This coheres with a politics of natality that acknowledges the capacity for new ideas (birth) as the essential characteristic of the human condition.

---

52 Kapur, *Erotic Justice: Law and the New Politics of Postcolonialism* (London: Routlegde, 2005), chapter 4.

Other attempts to expand the contours of the Article 2(4) prohibition, such as the Definition of Aggression and the Declaration of Friendly Relations, are marked as historical attempts that add little in the contemporary setting and, at the time of their articulation, were circumscribed by political realities. The endorsement of the Definition of Aggression[53] within the Crime of Aggression by the State Parties to the Rome Statute for the International Criminal Court during 2010 does illustrate the difficulties of any attempt to build state consensus rather than any intrinsic appeal of the General Assembly's Definition of Aggression. At the same time, the agreement by the State Parties to the Rome Statute in Kampala in 2010 and the slow shift towards establishing individual criminal responsibility for the crime of aggression does demonstrate the possibilities that law offers.[54] International criminal law is reactive; in this sense, it cannot stop the use of force although it may, in the future, punish those who instigate force. As such, perhaps it is also time to initiate refinement and development of the prohibition on the use of force.

Although contemporary institutional reports, such as the *More Secure World Report* and *In Larger Freedom*, have addressed the law on the use of force, this has been to enlarge and develop justifications rather than to strengthen the prohibition. In contrast, the Non-Aggression and Mutual Security Protocol annexed to the Great Lakes Peace and Security Pact,[55] while not without fault, contains three separate articles to articulate what it means to prohibit the use of force on the African continent post-millennium. In the Protocol on Non-aggression and Mutual Defence, states agree to the following:

1. The Member States undertake to maintain peace and security in accordance with the Protocol on Non-aggression and Mutual Defence in the Great Lakes Region, and in particular:

    (a) to renounce the threat or the use of force as policies means or instrument aimed at settling disagreements or disputes or to achieve national objectives in the Great Lakes Region;

    (b) to abstain from sending or supporting armed opposition forces or armed groups or insurgents onto the territory of other Member States, or from tolerating the presence on their territories of armed groups or insurgents engaged in armed conflicts or involved in acts of violence or subversion against the Government of another State;

    (c) to cooperate at all levels with a view to disarming and dismantling existing armed rebel groups and to promote the joint and participatory management of state and human security on their common borders;

    (d) if any Member State fails to comply with the provisions of this Article, an extraordinary Summit shall be convened to consider appropriate action.[56]

While the Pact does face implementation difficulties, it stems from the cooperation and consultation of heads of states, governments and communities in the region

---

53 GA Res 3314 (14 December 1974).
54 See: http://www.iccnow.org/?mod=aggression (last accessed February 2010).
55 *Pact on Security, Stability and Development in the Great Lakes Region* (December 2006), Protocol on Non-Aggression and Mutual Defence in the Great Lakes Region.
56 Protocol on Non-Aggression and Mutual Defence in the Great Lakes Region, Chapter II, Article 5.

and is supplemented by a further Protocol extending meanings and expectations for states. As a regional document, the Great Lakes Protocol on Non-aggression and Mutual Defence may be inappropriate for direct transplantation into the international collective security structure and it does not explicitly address women's security but it does illustrate the potential and capabilities of states choosing to work to eradicate rather than justify conflict.

My recommendation, to develop the legal finesse of Article 2(4), is in contrast to the increasing emphasis placed on justifications and is voiced in the context of further recommendations regarding women's participation and agency. To develop the legal finesse of Article 2(4) would require recognition of the inadequacy of the prohibition because it has been consistently read as accommodating justifications for violence that use Western patriarchal justifications to underpin their normativity. Development of the prohibition would therefore require strategies that seek to disassociate construc-tions of the nation state under international law from understandings of the Western sexed legal subject. Consequently, what begins as a strategy 'within' the contemporary contours of international law also requires a larger feminist project of re-imagining the basic premises that shape international normativity. Underlying this claim is an expectation that a renewed focus on the prohibition encourages peacebuilding initia-tives and preventative strategies.

Conclusions and beginnings

In addition to these specific recommendations on women's participation and the development of the prohibition on the use of force, this book presents the follow-ing general observations and conclusions. Primarily, justified violence within legal discourse has been constructed through gendered understandings of legal subjectiv-ity. Underlying this knowledge are embedded assumptions, at least in Western legal liberalism, regarding the nature and capabilities of the (sexed) legal subject. Conse-quently, feminist legal theories that challenge the sexed and gendered representations of justified violence within national legal structures provide a useful starting place for a domestic analogy. This is an analogy in terms of the regulation of violence and helps expose how persistent dilemmas will remain unresolved without attention to the gender of justified violence under law. This conclusion is of relevance to feminist approaches to international law and to mainstream scholars. Furthermore, mainstream international legal actors can learn from feminist debates on essentialism, especially techniques I have used throughout the book, such as, engaging peripheral subjects,[57] embracing the potential for multicultural conversations and world travelling,[58] and law as narrative.[59] This knowledge addresses the limitations of Western discourse

57 Kapur, above note 52.
58 Bradiotti, above note 11; Gunning, 'Arrogant Perceptions, World-travelling and Multicultural Femi-nism', 23, *Columbia Human Rights Law Review* (1991) 189.
59 See Davies, Feminism and the Flat Law Theory' Conference Paper at the Centre LGS Conference, *Up Against the Nation States of Feminist Legal Theory* (June/July 2006) available online at: http://www.kent.ac.uk/clgs/documents/nsfltPlenary_MDavies_Flat%20Law_5july06.doc (last accessed February 2011).

(including within this project) and the necessity of perceiving law as a narrative with multiple interpretations and meanings. This allows for attention to the necessary generality of any narrative and the attendant problems of traversing the particular and the universal in legal accounts. My approach to these limitations has been to reiterate the need for the Western subject/author/perspective to be analysed in terms of her own subjectivity. Throughout the book, I have begun a feminist dialogue on how, as Westerners, our culture impacts on constructions of the international law on the use of force and how sex and gender are embedded in Western cultural and legal accounts.

Feminist strategies for change also acknowledge the unpredictability and the limitations of solely legal reform. In this sense, the search for articulations of political theories that re-imagine the relationship between the state and its subjects or, under international law, the state as the legal subject is necessary. I have used Arendt's model of natality as a potential site for this type of work. Other post-liberal articulations of legal subjectivity, such as contemporary work on the vulnerable subject, might also offer relevant contours to re-imagining international legal subjectivity.[60] However, these remain extensions and refinements of the project discussed across this book, so with respect to the law on the use of force, the claim is that a return to the prohibition, rather than increased articulations of justifications, would signal a return to the reduction and limiting of force that coalesces with feminist expectations of international security.

To conclude, the book provides a feminist analysis of the international law on the use of force across six chapters. Chapter one provided an introduction to feminist approaches to international law and how they were developed as a methodology in the book, as well as an introduction to the international law on the use of force. In chapter two, I considered the power of the Security Council to authorise the use of force under chapter VII of the UN Charter. An important aspect of chapter two was the role recent institutional reports play in reiterating a form of security played out in the Council's history, rather than the articulation of a new understanding of the role of the Security Council in the new millennium. Through analysis of the Security Council's use of Articles 39 and 41, as well as consideration of the impact of the use of authorised force under Article 42 on the sexual agency of women, I argued that the move to enlarge the concept of security in documents, such as, *In Larger Freedom* and the *More Secure World Report*, in reality encapsulates a gendered vision of security that had been expounded throughout the history of the United Nations. Furthermore, the expanded rationale for Security Council action – especially with respect to humanitarian motives – functions to enlarge unilateral state justifications for the use of force through the implicit suggestion that force is a rational and useful response to complex emergencies and situations. A feminist analysis of the international security regime focuses on restraining military activity under the collective security banner because of the detrimental impact of authorised force on women's long term security.

---

60 For example, Fineman, 'The Vulnerable Subject: Anchoring Equality in the Human Condition', 20, *Yale Journal of Law and Feminism* (2008) 8.

In chapter three, I focussed on the role of Article 51. I argued that the regulation of the international self-defence justification is analogous with the regulation of the inter-personal self-defence justification, especially as it has been articulated in common law states. The troubling use of the analogy to explain the existence of the international right of states to use force in self-defence was contrasted with philosophical explanations for the existence of legal conceptions of self-defence. Philosophical engagement tended to focus on the limitations on the right as the key to explaining the very existence of a right to self-defence. Consequently, the site where domestic feminisms have interrogated interpersonal self-defence, the requirements of necessity and proportionality, was discussed as transposing a sexed subject that contributed to the gendered consequences of self-defence. I also considered the role of the preemptive self-defence justification as shifting attention away from the formulation of Article 51, yet contributing to the assertion of Article 51 as an unsexed and unproblematic aspect of international law.

Chapter four presented a study of self-determination as a justification for the use of force. This chapter considered three key post-millennium narratives on self-determination, and their relationship with the use of justified force, through the discourse of feminist activists and feminist academics associated with self-determining communities. Each case study built on my contention that self-determination must be explored at three levels – as individual, internal and external self-determination. By incorporating women's narratives on self-determination the role of force to secure international identity for a community is identified as a process that fails to develop or guarantee individual and/ or internal self-determination. In this sense, the chapter demonstrates how feminist legal theories provide useful understandings of conceptualisations of agency that have analogous relevance to conceptions of agency for non-state entities.

Chapter five considered humanitarian intervention as a form of justified force. I developed an analogy between the regulation of domestic partner violence and the regulation of domestic state violence across the twentieth century. Both sites of regulation culminated in a shift towards intervention narratives at the close of the twentieth century. Through the engagement with feminist critiques on the perpetuation of victim status, constructed through mandatory intervention narratives into domestic violence, I argued that international humanitarian intervention narratives risk a similar construction of protected/protector or victims/actors in international law. This helps to demonstrate the futility of the use of force justified through humanitarian goals. Furthermore, I suggested feminist strategies to challenge domestic partner violence have conceptual relevance to international approaches to domestic state violence.

Finally, in this chapter I have considered the global war against terrorism as a narrative akin to Western cultural narratives on provocation that have been used to curtail women's movement in public space. The analysis of provocation narratives fuses the domestic analogy and the law as narrative technique to highlight the continued sex and gender of post-9/11 developments in the laws on the use of force. I have also used this discussion to indicate the limitations of the feminist tools used across the book. Of particular concern, with regard to the use of a narrative approach to explain law, is the consequential level of generality and the invocation of stereotypes to expose the weaknesses of legal narratives. This may play a role in disguising discrepancies in narratives and the capacity for subversive narratives to be articulated alongside, and sometimes within, dominant narratives. A further limitation of the law as narrative approach is the risk of contributing to stereotypes of masculinity and femininity rather than challenging essentialism. I have sought to disrupt this consequence of gender narratives, but I acknowledge that the very articulation of the words, gender, sex, woman, man, women, men, female, male, femininity and masculinity plays a role in enshrining sexed difference in discourse. However, this is also a representation of the gendered reality that we live within and that laws must be enacted amongst. I have also considered the next step for feminist approaches to international law with respect to the international law on the use of force, recognising the necessity of further dialogue on what it means to re-imagine international laws and law's foundation.

The use of the domestic analogy as a method has confined the approach of the book: as it is consequently tied to Western constructions of law, ignoring analogies between international legal forms and non-Western legal structures, as well as those outside of the common law model. This has implications for feminist approaches to international law and for international legal discourse. For feminist legal theories, the historical association of feminist approaches to international law with the tools of Western feminist legal theories requires greater attention. While it may be that feminist approaches to international law will need to develop their own range of tools to engage a sustained discussion with international law there are some problems with this approach because international law itself is so heavily co-opted into a projection of Western legal methods and regulatory practices on to conceptions of the international. For mainstream scholars, the questions Murphy asks of feminist legal scholars working within the discipline of international law,[61] about choices in the construction of methodologies, needs to be focused on the construction of the international legal subject, so that the personification of the state as the international legal subject, and the composite sexing of that subject, is interrogated and critiqued. The purpose of the domestic analogy in this project has not been to endorse the analogy; rather it has been to open the topic for critical engagement and to argue that feminist legal theories offer useful tools for developing hypotheses. It may be that answers, however, extend beyond the remit of feminist legal theories as other vectors of difference beyond sex and gender (certainly race, culture, ethnicity and sexuality) increase our understanding of the limited range of voices and perspectives that shape, and have shaped, international law.

This book has enlarged upon the idea that the law on the use of force is constructed within the larger international legal project that is sexed and gendered. The book begins a dialogue, a conversation, a narrative and a jurisprudence that co-opts the international law on the use of force into the construction of sex and gender. This book also begins a dialogue, a conversation, a narrative and a jurisprudence that co-opts Western constructions of sex and gender into the international law on the

---

61 Murphy, 'Feminism Here and Feminism There', in Doris Buss and Ambreena Manji, *International Law: Modern Feminist Approaches* (Oxford: Hart, 2005).

use of force. Unravelling answers to the questions raised by such a book will involve looking behind the global war against terrorism, preemptive force, implied authorisation, humanitarian intervention and even self-determination, to the law on the use of force under the Charter provisions and the perpetuation of justifications for the use of force under customary international law. Unravelling, of course, threatens our sense of stability gained by these 'signs' of the international legal structure. However, unravelling also indicates we might re-construct the international to better entwine the narratives of humanity, rather than that of man.

Bibliography*

Abdo N., and Lentin, R. (eds). *Women and the Politics of Military Confrontation* (Oxford: Berghahn, 2002)

Abrahms, K., 'Feminist Lawyering and Legal Method', 16, *Law and Social Inquiry* (1991), 373

'Agora: Future Implications of the Iraq Conflict', 97(3), *American Journal of International Law* (2003), [Various Authors]

Al-Ali, N., and Pratt, N., *What Kind of Liberation? Women and the Occupation in Iraq* (Berkeley, CA: University of California, 2009)

Al-Mughui, H., *Women in Kuwait: the Politics of Gender* (London: Saqi Books, 2000)

Al-Radi, N., *Baghdad Diaries: A Woman's Chronicle of War and Exile* (London: Vintage, 2003)

Amis, M., *The Second Plane* (London: Jonathon Cape, 2008)

Anghie, A., 'Time Present and Time Past', 32, *New York University Journal of International Law and Politics* (2000), 243

Anghie, A., 'Finding the Peripheries: Sovereignty and Colonialism in Nineteenth Century International Law', 40, *Harvard International Law Journal* (1999), 1

Anghie A., and Chimni, B.S., 'Third World Approaches to International Law and Individual Responsibility in Internal Conflicts', 2, *Chinese Journal of International Law* (2003) 73

Anghie, A., Chimni, B., Mickelson, K., and Okafor, O. (eds), *The Third World and the International Order* (the Hague: Nijhoff: 2003)

An-Na'im, A. (ed), *Human Rights in Cross Cultural Perspectives: A Quest for Consensus* (Philadelphia, PA: University of Pennsylvania Press, 1995)

An-Na'im, A., and Deng, F. (eds), *Human Rights in Africa: Cross Cultural Dialogues* (Washington, DC: Brookings Institution Press, 1990)

Arendt, H., *The Human Condition* (Chicago, IL: Chicago University Press, 1998, 2nd Edition)

Arts, and Leite (eds), *International Law and the Question of Western Sahara* (Leiden, the Netherlands: IPJET, 2007)

Ashworth, A., 'Self-Defence and the Right to Life', 34, *Criminal Law Review* (1975), 282

Ashworth, A., and Mitchell, B. (eds), *Rethinking English Homicide Law* (Oxford: Oxford University Press, 2000)

Askin, K., 'Holding Leaders Accountable in the International Criminal Court (ICC) for Gender Crimes Committed in Darfur,' 1, *Genocide Studies and Prevention* (2006), 13

Askin, K., 'Prosecuting Wartime Rape and Other Gender Related Crimes under International Law: Extraordinary Advances, Enduring Obstacles', 21(2), *Berkeley Journal of International Law* (2003), 288

---

* All internet resources last accessed May 2009

Austin, J., *The Province of Jurisprudence Determined and the Uses of the Study of Jurisprudence* (London: Weidenfeld and Nicholson, 1955 edition, originally published 1832/1863)

Bahdi, 'Iraq, Sanctions and Security: A Critique', 9, *Duke Journal of Gender Law and Policy* (2002), 237

Banda, F., *Women, Law and Human Rights: An African Perspective* (Oxford: Hart, 2005)

Barnett, H., *Sourcebook of Feminist Jurisprudence* (London: Cavendish, 1997)

Bartlett, K., 'Cracking Foundations as Feminist Method', 8(1), *American University Journal of Gender, Social Policy and the Law* (2000), 31

Becker, T., *Terrorism and the State: Rethinking the Rules of State Responsibility* (Oxford: Hart, 2006)

Bellamy, A.J., 'Whither the Responsibility to Protect? Humanitarian Intervention and the 2005 World Summit', 20(2), *Ethics and International Affairs* (2006), 143

Berger, Leah, *Conflict Prevention, Gender and Early Warning: A Work in Progress*, available online at http://www.carleton.ca/~dcarment/index.html

Bergoffen, D., 'Toward a Politic of the Vulnerable Body', 18(1), *Hypatia* (2003), 116

Berman, N., 'In the Wake of Empire', 14, *American University International Law Review* (1998–1999), 1515

Berman, N., 'Sovereignty in Abeyance: Self-determination and International Law', 7, *Wisconsin Law Journal* (1988), 51

Bibbings, L., and Nicolson, D., *Feminist Perspectives on Criminal Law* (London: Cavendish, 2000)

Billson, J., and Fluehr-Lobban, C., *Female-Well Being: Toward a Global Theory of Social Change* (London: Zed, 2005)

Boisson de Chazournes, Laurence, and Sands, Phillip (eds), *International Law, the International Court of Justice and Nuclear Weapons* (Cambridge: Cambridge University Press, 1999)

Bond, J., and Sherret, L., *A Sight for Sore Eyes: Bringing Gender Vision to the Responsibility to Protect Framework*, IWRP (New York: Instraw, 2005)

Bothe, M., 'Terrorism and the Legality of Pre-emptive Force', 14, *EJIL* (2003), 227

Bowett, D., *Self-defence in International Law* (Manchester: Manchester University Press, 1958)

Boyle, A., and Chinkin, C., *The Making of International Law* (Oxford: Oxford University Press, 2007)

Bradnock, R., *Kashmir: Paths to Peace*, Chatham House Report (Brussels: Royal Institute of International Affairs, 2010)

Braidotti, R., 'The Exile, the Nomad and the Migrant', 15, *Women's Studies International Forum* (1992), 7

Breines, I., Connell D.W., and Eide, I., *Male Roles, Masculinities and Violence* (Paris: UNESCO Publishing, 2000)

Brilmeyer, L., 'What's the Matter with Selective Intervention?', 37, *Arizona Law Review* (1995), 955

Brown, W., *States of Injury: Power and Freedom in Late Modernity* (Princeton, NJ: Princeton University Press, 1995)

Brownlie, I., *International Law and the Use of Force by States* (Oxford: Clarendon, 1963, reprinted 1991)

Buck, L., Gallant, N., and Nossal, K.R., 'Sanctions as a Gendered Instrument of Statecraft: The Case of Iraq', 24, *Review of International Studies* (1998), 69

Bunch, C., 'A Feminist Human Rights Lens of Human Security,' 16(1), *Peace Review: a Journal of Social Justice* (2004), 29

Bunch, C., 'Women's Rights as Human Rights: Toward a Re-vision of Human Rights', 12, *Human Rights Quarterly* (1990), 486

Bunch, C., *Passionate Politics 1968 – 1986 Essays, Feminist Theory in Action* (New York: St. Martin's Press, 1987)

Burton, R., *The 1001 Nights* (London: Panther Books, 1960)

Buss, D., 'The Curious Visibility of Wartime Rape: Gender and Ethnicity in International Criminal Law'', 25, *Windsor Journal of Access to Justice* (2007), 3

Buss, D., 'Keeping Its Promise: Use of Force and the New Man of International Law', in Bartholomew, A. (ed), *Empire's Law: The American Imperial Project and the 'War to Remake the World'* (London: Pluto, 2006)

Buss, D., 'Racing Populations, Sexing Environments: The Challenge of Feminist Politics in International Law', 20(4), *The Journal of The Society of Public Teachers in Law* (2001), 463

Buss D., and Manji A. (eds), *International Law: Modern Feminist Approaches* (Oxford: Hart, 2005)

Butler, J., *Frames of War: When is Life Grievable?* (London: Verso, 2009)

Butler, J., *Precarious Life: The Powers of Mourning and Violence* (London: Verso, 2006)

Butler, J., *Bodies that Matter: On the Discursive Limits of 'Sex'* (New York: Routledge, 1993)

Butler, J., 'Performative Acts and Gender Constitution', in Case (ed), *Performing Feminism* (John Hopkins, 1990)

Byers, M., 'Terrorism, the Use of Force and International Law after 11 September', 51, *International and Comparative Law Quarterly* (2002), 401

Byrd, S., 'Till Death Do us Part: A Comparative Approach to Justifying Lethal Self-defence by Battered Women', *Duke Journal of Comparative and International Law* (1991), 169

Cain, K., Postlewait, H., and Thomson, A., *Emergency Sex and Other Desperate Measure: A True Story from Hell on Earths* (London: Ebury, 2006)

Cameron, 'UN Targeted Sanctions, Legal Safeguards and the European Convention on Human Rights', 72, *Nordic Journal of International Law* (2003), 159

Caprioli, M., 'Gendered Conflict', 37, *Journal of Peace Research* (2000), 1

Cass, D., 'Rethinking Self-determination: A Critical Analysis of Current International Law Theories', 18, *Syracuse Journal of international Law and Commerce* (1992), 21

Cassese, A., *International Law* (Oxford: Oxford University Press, 2001)

Cassese, A., 'Terrorism is Also Disrupting Some Crucial Legal Categories of International Law', 12(5), *European Journal of International Law* (2001), 993

Cassese, A., '*Ex iniuria ius oritur*: Are We Moving Towards a International Legitimation of Forcible Countermeasures in the International Community?', 10, *EJIL* (1999), 23

Cassese, A., *Self-determination of Peoples* (Cambridge, 1998, 2nd edition)

Cassese, A., *International Law in a Divided World* (Oxford: Clarendon, 1986)

Cassese, A., *The Current Legal Regulation of the Use of Force* (Oxford: Oxford University Press, 1986)

Cassese, A. (ed), *United Nations Peace-Keepin: Legal Essays* (the Netherlands: Sijthoff and Noordhoff, 1978)

Chan, W., 'A Feminist Critique of Self-Defense and Provocation in Battered Women's Cases in England and Wales', 6(1), *Women and Criminal Justice* (1994)

Chandler, D., 'The Road to Military Humanitarianism: How the Human Rights NGOs Shaped a New Humanitarian Agenda', 23(3), *Human Rights Quarterly* (2001) 678

Charlesworth, H., 'Think Pieces: Law after War', 8(2), *Melbourne Journal of International Law* (2007), 233

Charlesworth, H., 'Saddam Hussein: My Part in His Downfall', 23, *Wisconsin International Law Journal* (2005), 127

Charlesworth, H., 'Not Waving, Drowning', 18, *Harvard Human Rights Journal* (2005), 1

Charlesworth , H., 'International Law: A Discipline of Crisis', 65(3), *Modern Law Review* (2002), 377

Charlesworth, H., 'The Hidden Gender of International Law', 16, *Temple International and Comparative Law Journal* (2002), 93

Charlesworth, H., and Chinkin, C., 'Building Women into Peace: The International Legal Framework', 27, *Third World Quarterly* (2006), 937

Charlesworth, H., and Chinkin, C., 'Sex, Gender and September 11th', 96(3), *AJIL* (2002), 600

Charlesworth, H., and Chinkin, C., *The Boundaries of International Law: A Feminist Analysis* (Manchester: Manchester University Press, 2000)

Charlesworth, H., and Chinkin, C., 'The Gender of Jus Cogens', 15, *Human Rights Quarterly* (1993), 63

Charlesworth, H., Chinkin, C.,and Wright, S., 'Feminist Approaches to International Law', 85, *AJIL* (1991), 613

Charlesworth, H., and Coicaud, J. (eds), *Faultlines of Legitimacy* (Cambridge: Cambridge University Press, 2010).

Charlesworth, H., and Wood, M., 'Women and Human Rights in the Rebuilding of East Timor', 71, *Nordic Journal of International Law* (2002), 325

Chesterman, S., *Just War or Just Peace? Humanitarian Intervention and International Law* (Oxford: Oxford University Press, 2001)

Chimni, B.S., 'A Just World Under Law: A View From the South' *ASIL Proceedings of the 100th Annual Meeting* (2006), 17

Chinkin, C., 'The Legality of NATO's Action in the Former Yugoslavia (FRY) under International Law', 49(4), *International and Comparative Law Quarterly* (2000), 910

Chinkin, C., 'East Timor: A Failure of Decolonisation', 20, *Australian Yearbook of International Law* (2000), 1

Chinkin, C., 'The State that Acts Alone: Bully, Good Samaritan or Iconoclast?' 11, *EJIL* (2000), 39

Chinkin, C., "Kosovo: A 'Good' or 'Bad' War?", 93, *AJIL* (1999), 841

Chinkin, C., 'A Critique of the Public/Private Dimension', 10(2), *EJIL* (1999), 387

Chinkin, C., 'Rape and Sexual Abuse of Women in International Law', 5, *EJIL* (1994), 326

Chinkin, C., 'A Gendered Perspective to the International Use of Force', 12, *Australian Yearbook of International Law* (1992), 279

Chinkin, C., and Wright, S., 'The Hunger Trap: Women, Food and Self-determination', 14, *Michigan Journal of International Law* (1993), 262

Choudhry, S., and Herring, J., 'Righting Domestic Violence', 20(1), *international Journal of Law, Policy and the Family* (2006), 95

Cockburn, C., 'Feminist Antimilitarism', in *Women's Teach-In: Antimilitarism, Fundamentalisms/Secularism and Civil Liberties and Anti-Terrorism Legislation after September 11th 2001*, Occasional Paper 14 (Women Living Under Muslim Laws, November 2003)

Cockburn, C., and Zarkov, D. (eds), *The Postwar Moment: Militaries, Masculinities and International Peacekeeping* (London: Lawrence and Wishart, 2002)

Cohn, C., 'Sex and Death in the Rational World of Defense Intellectuals' in Wyer (ed), *Women, Science and Technology: A Reader* (London: Routledge, 2001)

Cohn, C., and Ruddick, S., 'A Feminist Ethical Perspective on Weapons of Mass Destruction' in Lee, S., and Hashmi, S., *Ethics and Weapons of Mass Destruction* (Cambridge: Cambridge University Press, 2004)

Confortini, C.C., 'Galtung, Violence and Gender,' 31(3), *Peace and Change* (2006), 336

Cook, Rebecca (ed), *Human Rights of Women: National and International Perspectives* (Pennsylvania: University of Pennsylvania Press 1994)

Cooke, Miriam and Woollacott, Angela, *Gendering War Talk* (Princeton, NJ: Princeton University Press, 1993)

Copelon, R., 'Gender Crimes as War Crimes: Integrating Crimes against Women into International Criminal Law', 46, *McGill Law Journal* (2000), 217

Cornell, D., *The Imaginary Domain* (London: Routledge, 1995)

Cornell, D., 'Gender Hierarchy, Equality and the Possibility of Democracy', in *Transformations: Recollective Imagination and Sexual Difference* (London: Routledge, 1993)

Cornell, D., *Beyond Accommodation* (London: Routledge 1991)

Cotton, J., *East Timor, Australia and Regional Order: Intervention and its Aftermath in South East Asia* (London: Routledge, 2004)

Coulter, C., 'Female Fighters in the Sierra Leone War', 88, *Feminist Review* (2008), 54

Cover, R., 'Violence and the Word', 95(8), *Yale Law Journal* (1986), 1901

Craven, M., 'Humanitarianism and the Quest for Smarter Sanctions', 13(1), *EJIL* (2002), 43

Cristalis, I., *Bitter Dawn: East Timor A People's Story* (London: Zed, 2002)

Crawford, J., *The Creation of States in International Law* (Oxford: Oxford University Press, 2nd edition, 2006)

Crawford, J., *The International Law Commission's Articles on State Responsibility: Introduction, Text and Commentaries* (Cambridge: Cambridge University Press, 2002).

Currie, D., 'Battered Women and the State: From the Failure of Theory a Theory of Failure', 1(2), *Journal of Human Justice* (1993), 77

D'Amico, F., 'Review of Joshua Goldstein, War and Gender', *H-Minerva*, H-Net Reviews, September 2003 available online at http://www.h-net.org/reviews/

D'Amico, F., and Weinstein, L., *Gender Camouflage* (New York: New York University Press, 1999)

Davies, M., 'Taking the Inside Out' in Naffine and Owens, *Sexing the Subject of Law* (Sydney: Law Book Company, 1997)

Davis, R., *Domestic Violence: Facts and Fallacies* (Greenwood, 1998)

Derrida, J., 'Force of Law', 11, *Cardozo Law Review* (1990), 1687

Detter, I., *The Law of War* (Cambridge: Cambridge University Press, 2000)

De Vattel, E., *The Law of Nations*, available online at: http://www.constitution.org/vattel/vattel.htm

Dickinson, E.D., 'The Analogy between Natural Persons and International Persons in the Law of Nations', 26, *Yale Law Journal* (1916–1917), 564

Dinstein, Y., *War, Aggression and Self-defence* (Cambridge: Cambridge University Press, 2001, 3rd edition)

Dinstein, Y.(ed), *International law at a Time of Perplexity* (the Hague: Nijhoff, 1989)

Dinstein, Y., 'International law as a Primitive Legal System', 19, *New York University Journal of International* (1986–1987), 1

Dobash, R., and Dobash, R. (eds), *Rethinking Violence Against Women* (London: Sage, 1998)

Doezema, J.,'Loose or Lost Women?' 18(1), *Gender Issues* (2000), 23

Drakopoulou, M., 'The Ethic of Care, Female Subjectivity and Feminist Legal Scholarship', 8, *Feminist Legal Studies* (2000), 199

Drew, C., 'The East Timor Story: International Law on Trial', 12, *EJIL* (2002) 651

Du Bois, E., Dunlop, M., Gilligan, C., MacKinnon, C., and Menkel-Meadow, C., 'Feminist Discourse, Moral Values and the Law – A Conversation', 34, *Buffalo Law Review* (1985)

Durham, H., 'International Humanitarian Law and the Gods of War: The Story of Athens versus Ares,' 8(2), *Melbourne Journal of International Law* (2007)

Durham, H., 'The Domestic Violence Dilemma: How Our Ineffective and Varied Responses Reflect Our Conflicted Views of the Problem,' 71, *California Law Review* (1998)

Durham, H., and Gurd, T., *Listening to the Silences: Women and War* (The Hague: Kluwer, 2005)

Elshtain, J.B., *Just War Against Terror: the Burden of American Power in a Violent World* (New York: Basic Books, 2003)

Ellison, L., 'Prosecuting Domestic Violence without Victim Participation', 65, *Modern Law Review* (2002), 83

Emmett, A., *Our Sisters' Promised Land: Women, Politics and Israel-Palestinian Co-existence* (Michigan: Michigan University Press, 1996)

Engle, K., '"Calling in the Troops" The Uneasy Relationship among Women's Rights, Human Rights and Humanitarian Intervention', 20, *Harvard Human Rights Journal* (2007), 189

Engle, K., 'Feminism and its (Dis)Contents: Criminalizing Wartime Rape in Bosnia and Herzegovina,' 99 (4) *AJIL* (2005)

Enloe, C., *Maneuvers: the International Politics of Militarising Women's Lives* (Berkeley, CA, University of California Press, 2000)

Enloe, C., *The Morning After: Sexual Politics at the End of the Cold War* (Berkeley, CA: University of California Press, 1993)

Enloe, C., *Bananas, Beaches and Bases: Making Feminist Sense of International Politics* (Berkeley, CA: University of California Press, 1989)

European Roma Rights Centre, 'Justice for Kosovo', 4, *Roma Rights* (2005)

Evans, M., *International Law* (Oxford: Oxford University Press, 2006)

Falk, R., 'The Haiti Intervention: A Dangerous World Order Precedent', 36, *Harvard International Law Journal* (1995), 341

Ferencz, B., 'Getting Aggressive About Preventing Aggression', 61, *Brown Journal of World Affairs* (New York: Springer, April 1999), online access at: http://www.benferencz.org/index.php?id=4&article=79

Fineman, M., 'The Vulnerable Subject: Anchoring Equality in the Human Condition', 20, *Yale Journal of Law and Feminism* (2008), 8

Flax, J.,'Postmodernism and Gender Relations in Feminist Theory', 12, *Signs: Journal of Women in Cultural and Society* (1987), 621

Franck, T., 'What Happens Now? The United Nations after Iraq', 97 (3), *AJIL* (2003), 607

Franck, T., *Recourse to Force* (Cambridge: Cambridge University Press, 2002)

Franck, T., 'Terrorism and the Rights of Self-Defense', 95, *American Journal of International Law* (2001) 839

Franck, T., 'The Emerging Right to Democratic Governance', 86, *AJIL* (1996), 46

Franck, T., 'The Stealing of the Sahara', 70, *AJIL* (1976), 694

Franck, T., 'Who Killed Article 2(4)?', 64 (4), *AJIL* (1970), 809

Frazer, E., and Lacey, N., *The Politics of Community: A Feminist Critique of the Liberal Communitarian Critique* (London: Harvester Wheatsheaf, 1993)

Gardam, A., 'War, Law, Terror, Nothing New for Women' 32 *Australian Feminist Law Journal* (2010) 61

Gardam, A., 'Role for Proportionality in the War on Terror', 74, *Nordic Journal of International Law* (2005), 3

Gardam, J., *Necessity, Proportionality and the Use of Force by States* (Cambridge: Cambridge University Press, 2004)

Gardam, J., 'An Alien's Encounter with the Law of Armed Conflict', in Naffine and Owens, *Sexing the Subject of Law* (Sydney: Law Book Company, 1997)

Gardam, J.,'Women and the Law of Armed Conflict: Why the Silence?', 46(1), *International Comparative Law Quarterly* (1997)

Gardam, J., 'Legal Restraints on Military Enforcement Action', 17, *Michigan Journal of International Law* (1996), 285

Gardam, J., 'Proportionality and Force in International Law', 87, *AJIL* (1993), 391

Gardam, J., 'Non-combatant Immunity and the Gulf Conflict', 33, *Vanderbilt Journal of International Law* (1992), 813

Gardam J., 'Proportionality as a Restraint on the Use of Force', 20, *Australian Yearbook of International Law* (1992), 161

Gardam, J., and Charlesworth, H., 'Protection of Women in Armed Conflict', 22, *Human Rights Quarterly* (2000), 148

Gardam, J., and Jarvis, M., *Women, Armed Conflict and International Law* (The Hague: Kluwer Law International, 2001)

Glennon, M., 'How International Rules Die', 93, *Georgetown Law Journal* (2005), 939

Glennon, M., 'The Fog of Law: Self-defence, Inherence and Incoherence in Article 51 of the UN Charter', 25, *Harvard Journal of Law and Public Policy* (2002), 539

Godec, S., 'Between Rhetoric and Reality: Exploring the Impact of Military Humanitarianism on Post-conflict Sexual Violence' No. 877 *International Review of the Red Cross*, 31st March 2010

Goldstein, J., *War and Gender: How Gender Shapes the War System and Vice Versa* (Cambridge: Cambridge University Press, 2001)

Gordon, L., *Heroes in their Own Lives* (Chicago, IL: University of Illinois Press, 2002)

Gowlland-Debbas, V. (ed), *United Nations Sanctions and International Law* (The Hague: Kluwer Law International, 2001)

Graham, S., *Cities under Siege: the New Military Urbanism* (London: Verso, 2010)

Grant, R., and Newland, K. (eds), *Gender and International Relations* (Indiana: Indiana University Press, 1991)

Gray, C., *International Law and the Use of Force* (Cambridge: Cambridge University Press, 2008, 3rd edition)

Gray, C., 'A Crisis of Legitimacy for the UN Collective Security System?', 56, *ICLQ* (2007), 157

Gray, C., *International Law and the Use of Force* (Cambridge: Cambridge University Press, 2004, 2nd edition)

Gray, C., 'From Unity to Polarization: International Law and the Use of Force Against Iraq,' 13, *EJIL* (2002), 1

Greenwood, C., *Essays on War in International Law* (London: Cameron and May, 2006)

Greenwood, C., 'International Law and the Pre-emptive Use of Force: Afghanistan, Al-Qaida and Iraq', 4, *San Diego International Law Journal* (2003) 7

Greenwood, C., 'War, Terrorism and International Law', 56, *Current Legal Problems* (2003)

Greenwood, C., 'International Law and the NATO Intervention in Kosovo', 49 (4), *International and Comparative Law Quarterly* (2000)

Greenwood, C., 'New World Order or Old? The Invasion of Kuwait and the Rule of Law', 55, *Modern Law Review* (1992)

Greenwood, C., 'The Relationship between *Jus ad Bellum* and *Jus in Bello*', 9, *Review of International Studies* (1983), 221

Grieg, D., 'Reciprocity, Proportionality and the Law of Treaties', 36, *International and Comparative Law Quarterly* (1987) 283

Gross, L., 'The International Court of Justice and the United Nations', 120, *Recueil Des Cours* (1967), 314

Gross, O., and Ní Aoláin, F., *Law in Times of Crisis: Emergency Powers in Theory and Practice* (Cambridge: Cambridge University Press, 2006)

Grotius, H., *De Jure Ac Pacis (The Law of War and Peace)*, translated by Campbell, 1814, available online at http://www.constitution.org/gro/djbp.htm

Gunning, I., 'Arrogant Perceptions, World-travelling and Multicultural Feminism', 23, *Columbia Human Rights Law Review* (1991), 189

Haffajee, R.L.,'Prosecuting Crimes of Rape and Sexual Violence at the ICTR', 29, *Harvard Journal of Law and Gender* (2003), 201

Halley, J., 'Rape at Rome: Feminist Interventions in the Criminalization of Sex-Related Violence in Positive International Criminal Law', 30 *Michigan Journal of International Law* (2008), 1

Halliday, F., 'Hidden From International Relations: Women and the International Arena', 17, *Millennium* (1988), 419

Harris, A., 'Race and Essentialism in Feminist Legal Theories', 42, *Stanford Law Review* (1990), 581

Hawthorne, S., and Winter, B., *September 11, 2001: Feminist Perspectives* (London: Spinifex, 2002)

Heathcote, G., 'Feminist Reflections on the 'End' of the War on Terror' 11 *Melbourne Journal of International Law* (2010) 277

Heathcote, G., 'Force, Feminism and the Security Council' SOAS School of Law Research Paper No. 06-2010, July 2010, available online at http://papers.ssrn.com/sol3/papers.cfm?abstract_id=1636887

Heathcote, G., 'Feminist Reflections on the Use of Force', *Proceedings of the 100th Annual Meeting of the American Society of International Law* (2006)

Heathcote, G., 'Article 51 Self-defence as a Narrative: Spectators and Heroes in International Law', 12 (1), *Texas Wesleyan Law* Review (Fall, 2005)

Henkin, L., 'International Law: Politics, Values and Functions,' 216, *Collected Courses of the Hague Academy of International Law* 13 (IV) (1989)

Heyman R.E., and Neidig, P.H., 'A Comparison of Spousal Aggression Prevalence Rates in US Army and Civilian Representative Samples,' 67 (2), *Journal of Consulting and Clinical Psychology* (1999), 239

Higgins, R., *Problems and Processes: International Law and How We Use It* (Oxford: Oxford University Press, 1994)

Hipold,P., 'Humanitarian Intervention: Is There a Need for a Legal Reappraisal?', 12(3), *EJIL*, 437

Holzgrefe, J.L., and Keohane, R.O., *Humanitarian Intervention: Ethical, Legal and Political Dilemmas* (Cambridge: Cambridge University Press, 2003)

Houppert, K., 'Another Rape KBR Rape Case', *The Nation* (April 3rd 2008)

Humphreys, K., and Sen, P., *Violence Against Women: A CEDAW Thematic Shadow Report* (Bristol: Womankind, March 2004)

Hunter, R., 'Law's (Masculine) Violence', 17 (1), *Law and Critique* (2006), 27

Jackson, E., *Regulating Reproduction: Law, Technology and Autonomy* (Oxford: Hart, 2001)

Jacobs, S., and Ogle, R., *Self-Defense and Battered Women Who Kill: A New Framework* (New York: Praeger, 2002)

Jacobs, S., Jacobson R., and Marchbank J., *States of Conflict: Gender, Violence and Resistance* (London: Zed, 2000)

James, S., and Palmer, S., *Visible Women: Essays on Feminist Legal Theory and Political Philosophy* (Oxford: Hart, 2002)

Jantzen, G., *Foundations of Violence* (London: Routledge, 2004)

Jennings, R., 'The Caroline and McCleod Cases', 32, *American Journal of International Law* (1938), 82

Jennings, R., and Watts, A. (eds), *Oppenheim's International Law Vol 1 Peace* (Essex: Longman, ninth edition, 1992)

Jennings, R., and Watts, A. (eds), *Oppenheim's International Law Vol 2 War* (Essex: Longman, ninth edition, 1992)

Jessup, P., *A Modern Law of Nations* (London: Macmillan, 1948)

Jokic, A. (ed), *Lessons of Kosovo: The Dangers of Humanitarian Intervention* (Calgary: Broadview Press, 2002)

Kaplan, E. Ann, *Looking for the Other: Feminism, Film and the Imperial Gaze* (New York: Routledge, 1997)

Kapur, R., *Erotic Justice: Law and the New Politics of Postcolonialism* (New York: Routlegde, 2005)

Kapur, R., 'The Tragedy of Victimisation Rhetoric: Resurrecting the Native Subject', 15, *Harvard Human Rights Journal* (2002)

Kandiyoti, D., 'Between the Hammer and the Anvil: Post-conflict Reconstruction, Islam and Women's Rights', 28, *Third World Quarterly* (2007) 503

Kearly, T., 'Raising the Caroline,' 17, *Wisconsin International Law Journal* (1999) 325

Kelsen, H., *Law of the United Nations: A Critical Analysis of its Fundamental Problems* (New York: Prager, 1950)

Kelsen, H., *Principles of International Law* (New York: Rinehart and Company, 1952)

Kelsen, H., *Introduction to the Problems of Legal Theory* (Oxford: Oxford University Press, 1934, 2002 Reprint)

Kennedy, D., *Of War and Law* (Princeton, 2006); Smith, *The Utility of Force* (London: Penguin, 2006)

Kennedy, D., *The Dark Side of Virtue* (Princeton, NJ: Princeton University Press, 2004)

Kim, J., 'The Rhetoric of Self-defense', 13, *Berkeley Journal of Criminal Law*, (2008) 261, available online at: http://papers.ssrn.com/sol3/papers.cfm?abstract_id=1288142

Kingsbury, D., and Leach, M. (eds) *East Timor: Beyond Independence* (Victoria: Monash Publishing, 2007)

Kinsella, H., 'Gendering Grotius', 34 (2) *Political Theory* (2006), 161

Knop, K. (ed), *Gender and Human Rights* (Oxford: Oxford University Press, 2004)

Knop, K., *Diversity and Self-Determination in International Law* (Cambridge: Cambridge University Press, 2002)

Knop, K., 'Re/statements: Feminism and Sovereignty in International Law', 3, *Transnational Law and Contemporary Problems* (1993) 239

Koskenniemi, M., *From Apology to Utopia* (Cambridge: Cambridge University Press, 2005, re-issued)

Koskenniemi, M., 'Iraq and the "Bush Doctrine" of Pre-emptive Self-Defence' Crimes of War Project, Expert Analysis (August 20th, 2002), available at http://www.crimesofwar.org/print/expert/bush-Koskenniemi-print.html

Koskenniemi, M., '"The Lady Doth Protest' Kosovo and the Turn to Ethics in International Law', 65, *Modern Law Review* (2002), 159

Koskenniemi, M., 'The Place of Law in Collective Security', 17, *Michigan Journal of International Law* (1996) 255

Koskennienmi, M., 'Book Review of Dallmeyer, *Reconceiving Reality: Women and International Law*', 89, *AJIL* (1995) 227

Koskenniemi, M., 'The Politics of International Law', 1, *EJIL* (1990), 4

Krieger, 'A Credibility Gap: The Behrami and Saramati Decision of the ECHR', 13, *Journal of International Peacekeeping* (2009), 159

Kritsiotis, D., 'Appraising the Policy Objections to Humanitarian Intervention', 19, *Michigan Journal of International Law* (1993), 1010

Krug (ed), *World Report on Violence and Health* (Geneva: World Health Organisation, 2002)

Lacey, N., 'Philosophy, Politics, Morality and History', Paper Presented at *Hart-Fuller Conference*, NYU Law School available online at: www.law.ntu.edu/conferences/hart-fuller/docs/NicolaLacey/paper.doc

Lacey, N., *Unspeakable Subjects: Feminist Essays in Legal and Social Theory* (Oxford: Hart, 1997)

Lauterpacht, H., *Private Law Sources and Analogies of International Law* (The Law Book Exchange, 2002, Reprint of 1927 edition)

Lauterpacht, H., 'The Grotian Tradition in International Law', 23, *BYIL* (1946) 26

Lauterpacht, H., *The Function of Law in the International Community* (Oxford: Clarendon, 1933)

Lawrence, B., and Karim, A., (eds) *On Violence: A Reader* (Durham: Duke University Press, 2007)

Leader-Elliot, I., 'Battered But Not Beaten: Women Who Kill in Self-Defence', 15, *Sydney Law Review*, 1993), 403

Lillich, R., *Humanitarian Intervention and the United Nations* (Virginia: University Press of Virginia, 1973)

Lindsay, E., 'Lysistrata, Women and War', 12, *Texas Wesleyan Law Review* (2005), 345

Lorentzen, L.,A., and Turpin, J., *The Women and War Reader* (New York: New York University Press, 1998)

Lowe, V., Roberts, A., Walsh, J., and Zaum, D. (eds), *The United Nations Security Council and War: the Evolution of Thought and Practice since 1945* (Oxford: Oxford University Press, 2008)

Lyons, S., and McCord, D., 'Moral Reasoning and the Criminal Law: the Example of Self-defence,' 30, *American Criminal Review* (1992), 97

Lyth, A., (ed), *Getting it Right? A Gender Approach to UNMIK Administration in Kosovo* (Kvinna Till Kvinna, 2001)

MacKinnon, C., *Are Women Human? And Other International Dialogues* (Cambridge: Harvard University Press, 2006)

MacKinnon, C., *Women's Lives under Men's Laws* (Cambridge: Harvard University Press, 2005)

MacKinnon, C., *Towards a Feminist Theory of the State* (Cambridge: Harvard University Press, 1989)

MacKinnon, C., *Feminism Unmodified* (Cambridge: Harvard University Press, 1987)

Mahoney, K., 'Legal Images of Battered Women', 90, *Michigan Law Review* (1991), 1

Marcus, D., 'Famine Crimes in International Law', 97, *AJIL* (2003) 245

Matsuda, M., 'Liberal Jurisprudence and Abstracted Visions of Human Nature', 16, *New Mexico Law Review* (1986)

Mayer, T. (ed), *Gender Ironies of Nationalism* (London: Routledge, 2000)

Mayer, T. (ed), *Women and the Israeli Occupation* (London; Routledge, 1994)

Mazurana, D., Raven-Roberts, A., and Parpart, J.L., *Gender, Conflict and Peacekeeping* (London: Rowman and Littlefield, 2005)

McColgan, A., 'In Defence of Battered Women who Kill', 13, *Oxford Journal of Legal Studies* (1983) 508

McDonald, A., 'Self-determination and Kurdish Women' in Mojab, *Women of a Non-state Nation* (Mazda, 2001)

McDougal, M.S., and Feliciano, F.P., *Law and Minimum World Public Order: The Legal Regulation of International Coercion* (New Haven: Yale University Press, 1961)

McInnes, C., *Spectator-Sport War: the West and Contemporary Conflict* (London: Lynne Rienner Publishers, 2002)

McInnes, C., and Wheeler, N. (eds), *Dimensions of Western Military Intervention* (London: Frank Cass Publishing, 2002)

McKay, S., and Mazurana, D., *Where Are the Girls?* (International Centre for Human Rights and Democratic Development, 2004).

McRobbie, A., *The Aftermath of Feminism: Gender, Culture and Social Change* (London: Sage, 2008)

Meron, T., 'Rape as a Crime under International Humanitarian Law', 87, *AJIL* (1993), 424

Mgbeoji, *Collective Insecurity* (University of British Columbia Press, 2004)

Mills, L., *Insult to Injury: Rethinking our Responses to Intimate Abuse* (Princeton, NJ: Princeton University Press, 2003)

Mills, L., 'Killing Her Softly', 113, *Harvard Law Review* (1999), 550

Minow, M., 'Words and the Door to the Land of Change', 43, *Vanderbilt Law Review* (1665), 199

Minow, M., Ryan M., and Sarat, A., *Narrative, Violence and the Law* (Ann Arbour, MI: Michigan University Press (1995).

Mohanty, C., *Feminism Without Borders: Decolonizing Theory, Practicing Solidarity* (New Haven: Duke University Press, 2003)

Mohanty, C., Russo, A., and Torres, L., *Third World Women and the Politics of Feminism* (Indiana: University of Indiana Press, 1991)

Moon, K., *Sex Among Allies: Military Prostitution in US–Korea Relations* (New York: Columbia University Press, 1997)

Morgan, R., *The Demon Lover: The Roots of Terrorism* (New York: Piatkus Publishing, 2nd edition, 2001)

Morrissey, B., *When Women Kill: Questions of Agency and Subjectivity* (London: Routledge, 2003)

Morrison T. (with Slade Morrison), *The Big Box* (Children's Picture Book, New York: Hyperion Books, 1999)

Moser, C., and Clark, F., *Victims, Perpetrators or Actors? Gender, Armed Conflict and Political Violence* (London: Zed Books, 2001)

Mullerson, R., *Ordering Anarchy: International Law and International Society* (New York: Springer 2000)

Mutua, M., *Human Rights: A Political and Cultural Critique* (Pennsylvania: Pennsylvania University Press, 2002)

Mutua, M., 'Savages, Victims and Saviors: the Metaphor of Human Rights', 42, *Harvard International Law Journal* (2001), 201

Naffine, N., *Law and the Sexes*, (Sydney: Allen and Unwin, 1990)

Naffine, N., and Owens, R., *Sexing the Subject of Law* (Sydney: The Law Book Company, 1997)

Nafizi, A., *Reading Lolita in Tehran: A Memoir in Books* (London: Fourth Estate, 2003)

Narayan, U., *Dislocating Cultures: Identities, Traditions and Third World Feminism* (London: Routledge, 1997)

Neff, S., *War and the Law of Nations: A General History* (Cambridge: Cambridge University Press, 2005)

Nesiah, V., 'Placing International Law: White Spaces on a Map', 16, *Leiden Journal of International Law* (2003), 1

Nevins, J., '(Mis)representing East Timor's Past', 4 (1), *Journal of Human Rights* (2002), 523

Nnaemeka, O. (ed) *Sisterhood: Feminisms and Power from Africa to the Diaspora* (New Jersey: Africa World Press, 1998)

Nowrojee, B., ' "Your Justice is Too Slow" : Will the ICTR fail Rwanda's Rape Victims', in Pankhurst (ed), *Gendered Peace* (London: Routledge, 2007)

Noyes, J., Janis, L., and Dickinson, M., *International Law Stories* (Foundation Press, 2007)

Nussbaum, M., *Sex and Social Justice* (Oxford: Oxford University Press, 2000)

Occelli, M.B., ' "Sinking" the Caroline', 4, *San Diego International Law Journal* (2003), 467

O'Connell, M.E., 'The Choice of Law Against Terrorism' 4 *Journal of National Security Law and Policy* (2010) 343

O'Connell, M.E., 'The International Law of Drones' 14 (36) *ASIL Insights*, November 12th, 2010

O'Connell, M.E., *Proportionality and Sustainable Peace in the Middle East*, Policy Brief No. 12 (Joan B. Kroc Institute for International Peace Studies, August 2006) available online at http://kroc.nd.edu/polbrief/documents/polbrief12.pdf

O'Connell, M.E., 'The Counter –Reformation of the Security Council', 2, *Journal of International Law and Relations* (2005), 107

O'Connell, M.E., *International Law and the Use of Force* (Federation, 2005)

O'Connell, M.E., 'Customary International Law on the Use of Force: The UN Charter, Practice and Opinio Juris', Workshop Presentation at the University of Macerata, *International Customary Law on the Use of Force: a Methodological Approach* (11–12 June 2004) available online at www.addix.it/internatzionale/relazoni/connell.pdf

O'Connell, M.E., *The Myth of Pre-emptive Self-defence*, paper prepared for the American International Law Task Force on Terrorism (2002)

O'Connell, M.E., 'Debating the Law of Sanctions', 13 *EJIL* (2002), 63

O'Connell, M.E., 'The UN, NATO, and International Law after Kosovo', 22, *Human Rights Quarterly* (2000), 57

O'Donovan, K., 'Defences for Battered Women Who Kill', 18, *Journal of Law and Society* (1991), 219

Ogata, S., and Sen, A., *Human Security Now* (Report of the Independent Commission on Human Security, 2003)

Okafor, C., *Redefining Legitimate Statehood: International Law and State Fragmentation in Africa* (The Hague: Martinus Nijhoff, 2000)

Olsen, F., 'Feminism and Critical Legal Theory: An American Perspective', 18, *International Journal of the Sociology of Law* (1990), 191

Oppenheim, L., *International Law: A Treatise* (Leiden: IDC, 1981) available online at: http://gallica.bnf.fr/ark:/12148/bpt6k93562g

Orford, A. (ed), *International Law and It's Others* (Cambridge: Cambridge University Press, 2007)

Orford, A., 'The Destiny of International Law', 17(3), *Leiden Journal of International Law* (2003), 441

Orford, A., *Reading Humanitarian Interventions* (Cambridge: Cambridge University Press, 2003)

Orford, A., 'Muscular Humanitarianism: Reading the Narratives of the New Interventionism', 10 (4), *EJIL* (1999), 679

Orford, A., 'Locating the International: Military and Monetary Interventions after the Cold War', 38, *Harvard International Law Journal* (1997), 443

Orford, A., 'The Politics of Collective Security', 17, *Michigan Journal of International Law* (1996), 373

Otto, D., 'Feminist Engagements with International Law through the UN Security Council' 32 *Australian Feminist Law Journal* (2010)

Otto, D., 'A Sign of "Weakness"? Disrupting Gender Certainties in the Implementation of Security Council Resolution 1325', 13, *Michigan Journal of Gender and Law* (2006), 113

Otto, D., 'International Peace Activism: The Contributions made by Women', 82, *Reform: A Journal of National and International Law Reform* (2003) 30

Otto, D., 'Integrating Questions of Gender into Discussion of 'the Use of Force' in the International Law Curriculum', 6(2), *Legal Education Review* (1995), 219

Otto, D., 'Challenging the "New World Order": International Law, Global Democracy and the Possibilities for Women', 3, *Transnational Law and Contemporary Problems* (1993), 371

Owens, P., *Between War and Politics: International Relations and the Thought of Hannah Arendt* (Oxford 2007)

Pahuja, 'The Postcoloniality of International Law', 46 (2), *Harvard International Law Journal* (2005), 459

Palmer, S., and James, S. (eds), *Visible Women Essays on Feminist Legal Theory and Political Philosophy* (Oxford: Hart, 2002)

Pateman,C., *The Sexual Contract* (Oxford: Basil Blackwell, 1988)

Peters, C. (ed) *Collateral Damage 'The New World Order' at Home and Abroad* (Cambridge, MA: Southend Press, 1992)

Petersen, V.S., 'Whose Rights? A Critique of the 'Givens' in Human Rights Discourse', 15, *Alternatives* (1999), 303

Philpott, S., 'East Timor's Double Life: Smells Like Westaphalia Spirit', 27(1), *Third World Quarterly* (2006)

Pizzey, E., *Scream Quietly or the Neighbours Will Hear You* (London: Penguin, 1974)

Pomerance, M., 'The ICJ's Advisory Jurisdiction and the Crumbling Wall Between the Political and the Judicial' in, Agora: Wall in Occupied Palestine, 99, *AJIL* (2005), 26

Power Cobbes, F., 'Wife Torture in England', 32, *Contemporary Review* (1878), 55

Preston, R.C., and Ahrens, R.Z., 'United Nations Convention Documents in Light of Feminist Theory,' 8 *Michigan Journal of Gender and Law* (2001–2002), 1

Quick, O., and Wells, C., 'Getting Tough with Defences', *Criminal Law Review* (2006), 514

Rajagopal, B., 'International Law and the Development Encounter: Violence and Resistance at the Margins', *ASIL Proceedings* (1999), 16

Ratner, S., and Slaughter, M. (eds), *Symposium on Method in International Law*, 93, *AJIL* (1999), 291

Reisman, M., 'Assessing the Lawfulness of Nonmilitary Enforcement: the Case of Economic Sanctions', 89, *AJIL* (1996), 37

Reisman, M., 'Criteria for the Lawful Use of Force in International Law', 10, *Yale Journal of International Law* (1985), 279–85

Reisman, M., and Armstrong, A.,'The Past and Future of the Claim of Preemptive Self-Defense', 100(3) *AJIL* (2006), 525

Riley, D., *'Am I That Name?': Feminism and the Category of Women in History* (London: Macmillan, 1988)

Rodin, D., *War and Self-Defense* (Oxford: Oxford University Press, 2002)

Rosand, E., 'The Security Council Efforts to Monitor the Implementation of Al-Qaeda/ Taliban Sanctions', 98(4), *AJIL* (2004), 745

Rostami-Povey, E., *Afghan Women* (London: Zed, 2007)

Roth, L., *Provocation and Self-defence in Intimate Partner and Homophobic Homicides*, Briefing Paper No.03/2007 (Parliament of New South Wales, 2007)

Ruddick, S., *Maternal Thinking: Towards a Politics of Peace* (New York: Beacon, 1995)

Rycenga, J., and Waller, M., *Frontline Feminisms: Women, War and Resistance* (London: Routledge, 2001)

Sadurska, R., 'Threats of Force', 82, *AJIL* (1988), 239

Salecl, R., *The Spoils of Freedom: Psychoanalysis and Feminism after the Fall of Socialism* (London: Routledge 1994)

Sarat, A., *Law, Violence and the Possibility of Justice* (Princeton, NJ: Princeton University Press 2001)

Sassóli, M., and Bouvier, S., *How Does Law Protect in War? Vol II Cases and Documents* (Geneva: International Committee of the Red Cross, 2006, 2nd Edition)

Satkauskas, R., 'Soviet Genocide Trials in the Baltic States: the Relevance of International Law', 7, *Yearbook of International Humanitarian Law* (2004), 388

Savell, K., 'The Mother of the Legal Person' in Palmer and James (eds), *Visible Women* (Oxford: Hart, 2002)

Schachter, O., *International Law in Theory and Practice* (The Hague: Martinus Nihoff, 1991)

Schachter, O., 'Self-defence and the Rule of Law', 83, *AJIL* (1989), 259

Schachter, O., 'The Right of States to Use Armed Force', 82, *Michigan Law Review* (1984), 1626

Schneider, E, *Battered Women and Feminist Lawmaking* (Yale University Press, 2002)

Schmeidl, S., *Gender and Conflict Early Warning: A Framework for Action* (International Alert, June 2002).

Schomburg, W., and Peterson, I., 'Genuine Consent to Sexual Violence Under International Criminal Law', 101, *AJIL* (2007), 121

Seal, K., Bertenthal, D., Miner, C.R., Sen, S., and Marmar, C., 'Bringing the War Back Home', 167, *Archives of Internal Medicine* (March 12 2007), 476

Shams, I. (ed.), *Iraq: its History, People and Politics.* (Amherst : New York 2003).

Shelley, T., *Endgame in the Western Sahara* (London: Zed, 2004)

Simester, A.P., and Sullivan, G.R., *Criminal Law: Theory and Doctrine* (Cambridge: Cambridge University Press, 2007)

Simma, B. (ed.), *Charter of the United Nations: A Commentary* (Oxford: Oxford University Press, 2002, 2nd edition)

Simma, B., 'NATO, the UN and the Use of Force', 10(1), *European Journal of International Law* (1999), 12

Simpson, G., 'The Death of Baba Mousa', 8, *Melbourne International Law Journal* (2007) 340

Simpson, G., 'Dueling Agendas: International Law and International Relations (again)', 1, *Journal of International Law and International Relations* (2005) 62

Simpson, G., 'The War in Iraq and International Law', 6, *Melbourne Journal of International Law* (2005) 167

Simpson, G., *Great Powers and Outlaw States* (Cambridge: Cambridge University Press, 2004)

Simpson, G., 'Two Liberalisms', 12, *EJIL* (2001), 537

Sjoberg, L., and Gentry, C.E., *Mothers, Monsters, Whores: Women's Violence in Global Politics* (London: Zed, 2007)

Slaughter M., and Feinstein, L., 'A Duty to Prevent', *Foreign Affairs* (Jan./Feb. 2004)

Smith, A., 'It's My Decision, Isn't It? A Research Note on Battered Women's Perception of Mandatory Intervention Laws', 6 (12), *Violence Against Women* (2000), 1384

Snider, E., 'The Potential of the Criminal Justice System to Promote Feminist Concerns', 10, *Studies in Law, Politics and Society* (1990)

Sokoloff, N. (ed.), *Domestic Violence at the Margins: Readings on Race, Class, Gender and Culture* (New Jersey: Rutgers University Press, 2005)

Spivak, G., 'The Subaltern Speaks'in Nelson, C., and Grossburg, L. (eds), *Marxism and the Interpretation of Culture* (University of Illinois Press, 1988)

Stahn, C., Responsibility to Protect: Political Rhetoric or Emerging Legal Norm?', 101, *AJIL* (2007), 99

Stahn, '"Jus in bello, Jus ad bellum – Jus post Bellum"?: Rethinking the Conception of the Law of Armed Force', 17 *European Journal of International Law* (2006), 921

Stark, B., 'What We Talk about When we Talk about War', 32, *Stanford Journal of International Law* (1996), 91

Steiner, H., Alston, P., and Goodman, R., *International Human Rights in Context: Law, Politics, Morals* (Oxford: Oxford University Press, 2007, 3rd edition)

Stevens, K.R., *Border Diplomacy: The Caroline and Mc Leod Affairs in Anglo-American-Aandian Relations, 1837–1842* (University of Alabama Press, 1989)

Stiglmayer, A. (ed) *Mass Rape: The War Against Women in Bosnia-Herzegovina* (Nebraska: University of Nebraska, 1994, English Ed)

Sturchler, N., *The Threat of Force in International Law* (Cambridge: Cambridge University Press, 2007)

Sturdevant, S.P., and Stolzfus, B. (eds), *Let the Good Times Role: Prostitution and the US Military in Asia* (New York: The New Press, 1992)

Szazs, P.C., 'The Security Council Starts Legislating', 96 (4), *AJIL* (2002), 901

Taft, W.H., and Buchwald, T.F., 'Preemption, Iraq, and International Law', 97, *AJIL* (2003), 557

Talon, S., 'The Security Council as World Legislature', 99(1), *American Journal of International Law* (2005), 175.

Tamale, S., *When Hens Begin to Crow: Gender and Parliamentary Politics in Uganda* (Boulder: Westview Press, 1999)

Tesón, F., *Humanitarian Intervention: an Inquiry into Law and Morality* (New York: Transnational Publishing, 1997, 2nd Revised Edition)

Tesón, F., 'Collective Humanitarian Intervention', 17, *Michigan Journal of International Law* (1996), 323

Thomson, M., *Rights, Restitution and Risk* (Cambridge: Harvard University Press, 1986)

Thornton, M., *Romancing the Tomes: Popular Culture, Law and Feminism* (London: Routledge, 2002)

Thornton, M. (ed), *Public and Private: Feminist Legal Debates* (Oxford: Oxford University Press, 1995)

Tickner, A.J., *Gender in International Relations: Feminist Perspectives on Achieving Global Security* (New York: Columbia University Press, 1992)

Uniacke, S., *Permissible Killing* (Cambridge: Cambridge University Press, 1994)

Ursel, E.J., 'The Possibilities of Criminal Justice Intervention in Domestic Violence: A Canadian Case Study', 8 (3), *Current Issues Criminal Justice* (1997), 263

Valchová, M., and Biason, L., (eds), *Women in an Insecure World* (Geneva Centre for the Democratic Control of Armed Force, 2005)

Walker, L., *The Battered Woman Syndrome* (New York: Springer, 1984)

Waller, M., 'Not Your Usual Agit-Prop', 3(1), *International Feminist Journal of Politics* (2001), 119

Walzer, M., *Just or Unjust Wars: A Moral Argument with Historical Illustrations* (New York: Basic Books, 1992, 92nd edition)

Welchman, L., and Hossain, S., *Honor: Crimes, Paradigms and Violence Against Women* (London, Zed, 2006).

Weil, S., and Bespaloff, R. (trans. Mary McCarthy), *War and the Iliad* (New York: New York Review Books Classics, 2005, first published 1945)

Weisbord, N., 'Prosecuting Aggression', 49, *Harvard International Law Journal* (2008) 162

West, R., 'Jurisprudence and Gender', 55, *University of Chicago Law Review* (1988)

Wilde, R., 'The Skewed Responsibility of the Failed State Concept', 9, *ILSA Journal of International and Comparative Law* (2002), 425

Williams, P., 'On Being the Object of Property', 14, *Signs* (1988) 5

Wing, A.K., *Critical Race Feminism: A Reader* (New York: New York University Press, 1997)

Wright, S., 'The Horizon of Becoming: Culture, Gender and History after September 11', 71, *Nordic Journal of International Law* (2002), 215

Wright, S., *International Human Rights, Decolonisation and Globalisation: Becoming Human* (London: Routledge, 2001)

Wood, E.J., 'Variation in Sexual Violence During Armed Conflict', 34 (3), *Politics and Society* (2006), 307

Woolf, V., *Three Guineas* (London: Oxford World Classics, 1992, first published 1938)

Zeigler, S., and Gunderson, G., 'The Gendered Dimensions to Conflict's Aftermath' 20 (2) *Ethics and International Affairs* (2006), 171

Zimmerman (ed), *International Criminal Law and the Current Development of Public International Law* (Duncker and Humblot: 2002), 125

UN documents (arranged by date)

Report of the Secretary-General to the Security Council, 25th September 2008, S/2008/622

Special Working Group on the Crime of Aggression, *Report of the Sixth Session*, 30th November – 14 December 2007, ICC-ASP/6/SWGCA/INF.1

UN Doc. S/2007/619, *Report of the Secretary-General to the Security Council on the Situation Concerning the Western Sahara*, 19th October 2007

Her Majesty's Inspectorate of Constabulary, *Without Consent* (Central Office of Information, UK, January 2007)

Secretary-General In-depth Study of All Forms of Violence against Women, 9th October, 2006, A/61/122/Add.1

Report of the Secretary-General on Darfur, 19 May 2006, UN Doc S/2006/306

Report of the Secretary-General's Special Advisor on Sexual Exploitation and Abuse by UN Peacekeeping Personnel, UN doc: A/59/710, 4th April 2005

Hester, M., and Westmarland, N., *Domestic Violence: Effective Interventions and Approaches* (Home Office Research Study 290, Development and Statistics Directorate, Feb 2005)

Report of the Secretary-General, *In Larger Freedom: Towards Development, Security and Human Rights for All*, 2nd March 2005, A/59/2005

Report of the Secretary-General's High Level Panel on Threats, Challenges and Change, *A More Secure World: Our Shared Responsibility*, 2nd December 2004, UN Doc A/59/565

UNMIK, *Combating Human Trafficking in Kosovo, Strategy and Commitment* (May 2004) available online at: http://www.unmikonline.org/misc/UNMIK_Whit_paper_on_trafficking.pdf

Evans, G., Sahnoun, M., Côté-Harper, G., Hamilton, L., Ignatieff, M., Lukin, V. et al., *The Responsibility to Protect*, Report of the International Commission on Intervention and State Sovereignty (International Development Research Centre, Canada, December 2001)

UN Conventional Against Transnational Organised Crime, GA Doc. 55/25, 15th November 2000 (*entered into force 29th September 2003*)

Report of the Preparatory Commission for the International Criminal Court, Part II Proposals for a Provision on the Crime of Aggression, UN document PCNICC/2002/2/Add.2 (24th July 2002).

International Commission on Intervention and State Sovereignty, *The Responsibility to Protect*, International Development Research Centre, December 2001

Bossuyt, M., *Adverse Consequences of Economic Sanctions and the Enjoyment of Human Rights*, UN ECOSOC, E/CN.42/200/33 (2000).

Optional Protocol to Convention on the Elimination of All Forms of Discrimination Against Women, GA Res 54/4, annex, 54 UN GAOR Supp (No 49) at 5, UN Doc A/54/49 (Vol 1) (2000) in force from December 2000

UNICEF, *The Iraq Child and Maternal Mortality Survey Report 1999* (CF/DOC/PR/1999/29); Secretary-General Report to the Security Council on the meeting of humanitarian needs through the Oil for Food Program, UN Doc. S/2000/208, 10th March 2000

Report of the Second Panel Established Pursant to the Note by the Security Council of 30 January 1990 (S/1999/100), Concerning the Current Humanitarian Situation in Iraq', s/1999/346, annex (30 March 1999)

Prosecutor v. Furunzida, No. IT-9S -17/I-T (December 10th 1998)

ECOSOC Agreed Conclusions on Gender Mainstreaming 1997/2, chapter 1, paragraph A

Fourth World Conference on Women, Declaration and Platform for Action, Beijing, UN Doc A/Conf. 177/20, 1995

UN Fourth World Conference on Women, *Beijing Platform for Action*, September 1995

Declaration on the Elimination of Violence Against Women, GA Res 48/103, 20 December 1993

UN World Conference on Human Rights, Vienna Declaration and Programme of Action, 25 June 1993, UN Doc A/Conf. 157/23, 1993

An Agenda for Peace, Preventive Diplomacy, Peacemaking and Peace-keeping, Report of the Secretary – General pursuant to the Statement adopted by the Summit Meeting of the Security Council on 31 January 1992, 17 June 1992, UN Doc. A/47/277; *Supplement to an Agenda for Peace*, 1 January 1995, UN Doc. A/50/60 – S/1995/1

Addendum to the Eighth Report on State Responsibility, by Roberto Ago, Agenda Item 2, A/CN.4/ Ser.A/198/Add.1 (Part 1) 1980, II (1) *Yearbook of the International Law Commission* 69

Convention on All Forms of Discrimination Against Women, 1979

Definition of Aggression, UN GA Res 3314 (XXIX) UNGAOR 29th Sess. Supp No31 (1974).

GA Resolution 2625 (The Declaration of Friendly Relations, 24th October 1970)

Declaration on the Granting of Independence to Colonial Countries and Peoples, 14th December 1960

International cases

Armed Activities on the Territory of the Congo (Democratic Republic of the Congo v. Uganda), ICJ Reports (19th Dec, 2005).

Legal Consequences of the Construction of a Wall in the Occupied Palestinian Territory, Advisory Opinion, ICJ Reports (9th July, 2004), 136.

Case Concerning Oil Platforms (Islamic Republic of Iran v USA) ICJ Reports (6th November 2003), 161.

Case Concerning the Land and Maritime Boundary between Cameroon and Nigeria, ICJ Reports (10th October 2002), 303.

Legality of the Threat or Use of Nuclear Weapons (Advisory Opinion) ICJ Reports (8th July, 1996) 226

Case Concerning East Timor (Portugal v. Australia), ICJ Reports, 1995

Case Concerning Military and Paramilitary Activities in and against Nicaragua (Nicaragua v USA), ICJ Reports (27th June 1986).

Case Concerning the Frontier Dispute (Burkina Faso v Mali), ICJ Reports (22nd December, 1986) 554

Western Sahara, Advisory Opinion, ICJ Reports (16th October 1975), 12.

Legal Consequences for States of the Continued Presence of South Africa in Namibia, Advisory Opinion, ICJ Reports (21st June 1971), 16

Corfu Channel Case, ICJ Reports (9th April, 1949), 4.

UK cases

Al-Skeini and Others v. Secretary of State [2007] HL 26

Attorney General for Jersey v. Holley (Jersey) [2005] UKPC 23 (15 June 2005)

R v. Keaveney [2004] EWCA Crim 1091 (Unreported Case)

R v. Ahluwalia [1992] 4 All E R 889

Regina v. Dudley 14 QBD 273 (1884)

Cases (non-UK)

Osland v. The Queen [1998] HCA 75 in Australia

Kadic v. Karadzic 70 F.3d 232, 64USLW 2231, United States Court of Appeal, Second Circuit (October 11th 1995).

R v. Lavalee [1990] 1 S.C.R.

US v. Holmes 26 Fed. Cas, 1 Wall Jr. 1 (1842)

Reports/speeches/conference papers (arranged by date)*

National Security Strategy of the United Kingdom (October 2010) available online at: http:// www.cabinetoffice.gov.uk/sites/default/files/resources/national-security-strategy.pdf

National Security Strategy of the United States (March 2010) available at: http://www. whitehouse.gov/sites/default/files/rss_viewer/national_security_strategy.pdf

O'Connell, M.E., *Lawful Use of Combat Drones*, Testimony to the Congress of the United States, House of Representatives, Subcommittee on National Security and Foreign Affairs, April 28th 2010, available online at: http://www.fas.org/irp/congress/2010_hr/042810oconnell.pdf

Charlesworth, H., Sahgal, G., and Lockett, K., *Gender, Human Rights and International Law*, Centre LGS Conversation 2009, transcript and sound recording available at: http://www.kent. ac.uk/clgs/news-and-events/Conversations/Conversations.htm

Heathcote, G., 'From Security Council Resolution 1325 to 1820' Dept of Politics, Bristol University, Department of Politics, *Channelling Our Knowledge ESRC Seminar on 'Understanding Gendered Agency in Violent Conflict'*, 14/ 15th November 2008

Henry, M., and Higate, P., 'Problematising Gender and Security in Peace Missions' paper Presented at the Annual Meeting of the ISA, *49th Annual Conference Bridging Multiple Divides*, San Francisco (March 26th 2008)

Charlesworth, C., 'Are Women Peaceful? Reflections on the Role of Women in Peacebuilding' *Annual Lecture*, AHRC Research Centre for Law, Gender and Sexuality (15th May 2008)

Case, M.A., 'Gender Performance Requirements of the US Military' Paper Presented at Netherlands Defence Academy Conference, *Sexual Abuse and Exploitation of Women in Violent Conflict* (19th June 2007)

Otto, D., 'Dissonance Between Survival and Consent', *Second Annual Shimizu Lecture in International Law*, London School of Economics (7th March 2007)

Law Commission (UK), *Murder, Manslaughter and Infanticide: Project 6th of the Ninth Progamme of Law Reform*, Law Commission Report No. 340 (28th November 2006)

Bellinger, J., *Legal Issues in the 'War on Terror'*, Public Lecture, International Humanitarian Law Project, London School of Economics (31st October 2006) transcript available at http:// www.lse.ac.uk/collections/LSEPublicLecturesAndEvents/pdf/20061031_JohnBellinger. pdf

Franck, T., 'The Laws of Force and the Turn to Evidence' *American Society of International Law Annual Meeting*, Conference Paper (Thursday 28th March 2006).

National Security Strategy of the United States 23 (March 2006) available at www.whitehouse. gov/ncs/nss/2006/nss2066.pdf

Judicial System Monitoring Programme, *Overview of Timor Leste Justice Sector*, Dili, Timor Leste (January 2006).

Davies, M., 'Feminism and the Flat Law Theory' Conference Paper at the Centre LGS Conference, *Up Against the Nation States of Feminist Legal Theory* (June/ July 2006) available online at http://www.kent.ac.uk/clgs/documents/nsfltPlenary_MDavies_Flat%20Law_5july06. doc

---

* All internet resources last accessed February 2011

Judicial System Monitoring Programme, *Analysis of Decisions in Cases Involving Women and Children Victims: June 2004 – March 2005*, Dili, Timor Leste, April 2005

Judicial System Monitoring Programme, *Statistics on Cases of Violence Against Women in Timor Leste*, Dili, Timor Leste, February 2005

Amnesty International Report, *Lives Blown Apart: Crimes Against Women in Times of Conflict. Stop Violence Against Women* Amnesty International London (November 2004). Available online at http://web.amnesty.org/library/

O'Connell, M.E., 'Customary International Law on the Use of Force: The UN Charter, Practice and Opinio Juris', Workshop Presentation at the University of Macerata, *International Customary Law on the Use of Force: A Methodological Approach* (11–12 June 2004) available online at www.addix.it/internatzionale/relazoni/connell.pdf

Chinkin, C., *Peace Agreements as a Means of Promoting Equality and Ensuring Participation of Women*, UN Doc. EGM/PEACE/2003/ BP

Carrington, K., and Phillips, J., *Domestic Violence in Australia – an Overview of the Issues* (7th August 2003), Parliamentary Library of Australia, available online at www.aph.hov.au/library/intguide/SP/Dom_violence.htm

Ackerman, D., *International Law and the Preemptive Use of Force Against Iraq*, CRS Report for Congress, Order Code RS21314 (April 11th 2003), available online at www.au.af.mil/au/awc/awcgate/crs/rs21324.pdf

Ackerman, D., *International Law and the Preemptive Use of Force Against Iraq*, CRS Report for Congress, Order Code RS21314 (April 11th 2003), available online at www.au.af.mil/au/awc/awcgate/crs/rs21324.pdf

US Secretary of State, Colin Powell, Address to UN Security Council (February 5th 2003) available online at: http://www.whitehouse.gov/news/releases/2003/02/20030205-1.html

Bush, L., *Radio Address by Mrs. Bush*, 20th (November 2001), available online at http://www.whitehouse.gov/news/releases/2001/11/20011117.html

National Security Strategy of the United States 6 (September 2002), available at www.whitehouse.gov.nsc.nss/2002/index.html

Lyth, A., (ed), *Getting it Right? A Gender Approach to UNMIK Administration in Kosovo* (Kvinna Till Kvinna, 2001)

Bush, L., *Address to the Joint Session of Congress and the American People* (20th September 2001), available online at http://www.whitehouse.gov/news/releases/2001/09/20010920-8.html

Amnesty International, *'Collateral Damage' or Unlawful Killings? Violations of the Laws of War by NATO during the Operation Allied Force*, AI Index: EUR 70/018/2000 (6th June 2000)

Human Rights Watch, *Civilian Deaths in the NATO Air Campaign* (2000)

Durrant, J.E., *A Generation without Smacking: the Impact of Sweden's Ban on Physical Punishment* (Save the Children (UK), 2000)

Amnesty International, *Women in Afghanistan: the Violations Continue* (ASA 11/05/1997), 1997 available online at http://web.amnesty.org/library/

Amnesty International, *Women in Afghanistan: A Human Rights Catastrophe* (ASA 11/03/95), May 1995 available online at http://web.amnesty.org/library/

Amnesty International, *Bosnia-Herzegovina, Rape and Sexual Abuse by Armed Forces* (January 1993)

Human Rights Watch, *Punishing the Victim: Rape and Mistreatment of Asian Maids in Kuwait*, Human Rights Watch Report (New York: New York University Press, 1992)

Index

9 780415 492874